Y0-BRV-426

U. M. HODGES LEARNING CENTER
WHARTON COUNTY JUNIOR COLLEGE
WHARTON, TEXAS 77488

# PROFITS
# FROM
# COUNTRY
# PROPERTY

**McGraw-Hill
Book Company**

New York
St. Louis
San Francisco
Auckland
Bogotá
Hamburg
Johannesburg
London
Madrid
Mexico
Montreal
New Delhi
Panama
Paris
São Paulo
Singapore
Sydney
Tokyo
Toronto

# PROFITS FROM COUNTRY PROPERTY

## HOW TO SELECT, BUY, MAINTAIN, AND IMPROVE COUNTRY PROPERTY

### James H. Koch
Publisher
COUNTRY PROPERTY NEWS

63191

J. M. HODGES LEARNING CENTER
WHARTON COUNTY JUNIOR COLLEGE
WHARTON, TEXAS 77488

Copyright © 1981 by McGraw-Hill, Inc. All rights reserved. Printed in the
United States of America. No part of this publication may be reproduced,
stored in a retrieval system, or transmitted, in any form or by any means,
electronic, mechanical, photocopying, recording, or otherwise, without the
prior written permission of the publisher.

1234567890DODO8987654321

The editors for this book were William R. Newton and Virginia Blair, the
designer was Joseph Gillians, and the production supervisor was Paul A.
Malchow. It was set in Garamond by David Seham.
Printed and bound by R. R. Donnelly & Sons Company.


**Library of Congress Cataloging in Publication Data**

Koch, James H.
    Profits from country property.

    Includes index.
    1. Real estate investment. 2. Land use, Rural. I. Title.
II. Title: Country property.
HD1393.K57                 332.63′24                 80-15231
ISBN 0-07-035248-8

332.63
K811P

63191

*This book is dedicated to my wife, Anne-Marie Koch, who was my co-adventurer in several country property projects and whose questions suggested some of the research appearing here.*

# Contents

# Preface

From personal experience I believe that ownership of well-located raw land, a farm, or a residential property in the country has been one of the most reliable hedges against inflation during the past ten years. And country property is likely to continue to fulfill this valuable economic function, as real estate in the United States enjoys one of its great boom periods extending to the end of the century.

Certain commodities, such as precious metals and diamonds, have also done well during the last decade, but their future will be governed more by international politics than by their intrinsic value. Some collectibles, too, have proved to be good inflation hedges. But to profit from collectibles, one requires a high level of expertise that is beyond the education and natural talents of most investors.

Country property has the great advantage of being a popular investment medium as well as being a familiar one and within the reach of most investors—young, old, single, married, and city- or country-bred. Yet if you want to get the most profit from investing in country property, there are principles you should follow and pitfalls you should avoid.

I wrote this book to point out these basic principles as I observed them while publishing, during the past decade, *Country Property News,* a monthly newsletter for buyers and owners of all kinds of rural real estate. During these years I have had the enthusiastic cooperation of countless realtors and would particularly like to thank them for their suggestions and helpful information. Also, I am grateful to Eliot H. Sharp, founder and editor emeritus of *Investment Dealers' Digest.* He suggested that there was an international market for information on U.S. rural real estate, and he sponsored, with leading realtors, the early country property seminars which developed into a continuing newsletter. I would like to thank, too, my wife, Anne-Marie Koch, associate editor of *Country Property News,* for her wit and assistance on this long, fascinating project.

During the past years I have also found urban real estate a good medium for investment. Small towns and cities are being rebuilt; innovative and successful programs and techniques are encouraging the renaissance, recycling, and energy conservation in many old and new city buildings. Yet opportunities in small-town and city real estate are really the subjects for another book or two! As a way to produce a maximum personal profit for the investor—there are so many zoning, marketing, and political barriers that obstruct or limit an individual's profit in the city—it's simply easier to own country land.

The most rewarding real estate investment in these times for the average person or investor worried about inflation—you perhaps—is likely to be a parcel of country property, either (1) developed property, such as a primary or secondary residence, or (2) a working farm, or (3) raw land that has development potential. You may be single or married, have a family, have a partner or two, or own stock in a corporation that invests in these kinds of properties. Collaboration with other people spreads the risks and sometimes increases the reservoir of skills and talents for producing a greater profit. The person or couple willing to do the necessary homework, however, and pay for advice or expertise beyond personal knowledge and experience in specialized areas, will probably reap *greater profit by doing it alone.* For in sharing the risks you must also share the rewards, and in such partnership you can only maximize profit by common consultation and consent. A committee has never been known to share the rewards satisfactorily! Someone is always walking off with a lion's share of the cash or the fixed assets, or with the better part of the enjoyment.

For the ownership of country property bestows upon the holder a sense of satisfaction beyond the cash register or "the bottom line." Perhaps it is the wish in everyone to stumble across a private Eden or Shangri-la. This is a very deep, very substantial, personal profit, though not measured in money.

In the discussion of the financial aspect of ownership, do not for a minute believe that I have forgotten this personal benefit. I know very well that the satisfaction of owning country land can be so great that a property can actually stand still in economic value, or even decline, and the owner may still feel well rewarded. Yet in this book I emphasize a second aspect of profit—financial gain obtained from the creative use of capital. It shows you how you can get the most financial gain from your country property by using methods and ideas that have already helped many others achieve that goal.

As you use the various charts and statistics in this book, remember that there may be later data available from the same source. Use the credit lines and appendixes to identify sources; ask for later data if it will prove useful to you. The preliminary returns from the 1980 census suggest that the trend toward living and investing in the country has accelerated during the past decade. This trend reinforces the demand for country property and should make it a good investment well into the twenty-first century. The time to get involved, of course is now! Good luck on your own adventure in country real estate. May it reward you well.

*James H. Koch*

# PROFITS FROM COUNTRY PROPERTY

# Chapter One

# Profits You Can Expect from Different Kinds of Country Property

Profits—call them benefits if you will in this context—come from the intelligent use of an asset so that it produces a hard monetary reward and/or, in some cases, pleasure for the owner. Each owner of country property will have to make an allotment in his or her mind as to the balance between the tangible and intangible pleasure or profit that will be received from the property—whether it be a harvest of fruit, vegetables, and meat for the dinner table, or a harvest of dollars from produce sold, from rent, from depreciation of improved property as an offset against taxable income, or from an annual paper appreciation of the property's value.

Generating profit from a property requires optimism, alert thinking, and a willingness to take positive, intelligent action. If you are a realist, you will have to concede that the unseen satisfaction of ownership counts for something—but it does not put bread on the table. Just consider it a plus and go on to the actual operating profits and possible capital gains from your country property. Remember that you will own something that has proved itself as a hedge against inflation in the past, is likely to continue to do so, and has been a highly profitable investment for many informed investors like yourself.

This book, as outlined in the foreword, covers four different kinds of country property, which represent four different profit situations:

1 Country property—lots, small farms, and existing houses in rural villages bought essentially as principal residences.

**2** Rural second homes bought for weekend and vacation living.

**3** Raw land bought simply as an investment, *not to live on.*

**4** Farmland bought to work or to use as an investment.

These are artificial distinctions, to an extent, because the country property enthusiast usually buys additional pieces of property once he or she has success with the first venture. Yet different tax regulations and financing possibilities apply to different types of property and the way they are used. That is why it is so important to work with an accountant familiar with federal, state, and local laws affecting profits from real estate.

The following profit situations, with occasional examples to demonstrate applications and variations, should give you an idea of the different profit and use patterns you can enjoy as an owner of country property.

## PROFITS FROM DEVELOPED LAND OR IMPROVED LAND

If you *own* and *live* on developed or improved country property, such as a summer cottage or a year-round house or a farm in the country, a part of its profit comes from the shelter it gives you. How much is that worth to you? If you have no idea, find out what similar property is renting for in your vicinity and take that as a going rate for comparable shelter. Do not

**Table 1-1**   Estimated Profit from Improved Property

| | | |
|---|---|---|
| Rent saved | $_____ | |
| Rental earned (if any) | _____ | |
| Year's gain in value | _____ | |
| Year's amortization on mortgage | _____ | |
| Prorated tax shelter through depreciation of portion of property rented to others | _____ | |
| *Total income* | | $_____ |
| *Less expenses* | | |
| Year's real estate taxes | $_____ | |
| Year's utilities and water | _____ | |
| Year's maintenance and repair | _____ | |
| Year's interest on mortgage | _____ | |
| Interest not earned on equity because not invested elsewhere | _____ | |
| *Total expenses* | | $_____ |
| *Net profit* | | $_____ |

depend only on one other property in your evaluation. Check out several and possibly take an average. A local realtor may also be able to give you an estimate of rental value. Set up a statement, as shown in Table 1-1. If you rent out part of the property (live in only a part of it), add this income to your statement. Then subtract all the expenses you have per year.

*Example of Mr. and Mrs. Sam Skeptic*

The Skeptics and their two children moved to an old colonial home in a small, picturesque village in southern New Hampshire. With the main house came a carriage barn that had been remodeled into a garage, plus an apartment suitable for a couple to live in or for friends or relatives to use on visits. The Skeptics, when they bought the place, decided to rent this building aggressively for a number of years to help pay the mortgage. Then, they thought, they would redecorate it and keep it as a guest facility. They found they could rent it for $2,500 during the four summer months and on selected winter weekends to skiers for approximately another $1,000. In between it was a guest facility used for occasional visiting friends. At no time did the Skeptics occupy it themselves.

Their own, adjacent home had three bedrooms, two baths, a living room, a dining room, a kitchen, and a back porch that gave the family ample living space on their village lot. The property had been purchased for $65,000 a year previously, and comparable property in that town had been appreciating at about 20 percent a year. Current equity was about $16,000. Mortgage still owing was about $49,000 with amortization per year about $1,000 and interest $5,000 at eight percent. Real estate taxes were $875.

Insurance, utilities, and water cost $625. Maintenance and repair allowance was $1,000. The property had gained about $13,000 in value the previous year. Had the present equity of $16,000 been invested in a savings bank at eight percent interest, it would have earned $1,480. The Skeptics, after checking with their realtor, figured they saved the equivalent of about $6,000 a year in annual rent for the property. The portion of it that was depreciated (the guest apartment above the garage) sheltered income tax, so about $1,250 was saved on federal and state taxes. Thus the estimated profit of the country property was as shown in Table 1-2.

Note that the annual profit happens to equal approximately the year's gain in value. Other gains are offset by expenses.

Take these income and expense figures step by step so that you can estimate similar situations for yourself. You may want to ask your accountant for help in deciding what sort of income schedule you have or what are legitimate percentage deductions for depreciation. The categories given here are simplified; ratios of various expenses to income may

**Table 1-2** Estimated Profit from the Skeptic's Rented Property

| *Income* | | |
|---|---:|---:|
| Rent saved | $ 6,000 | |
| Rental earned on apartment | 3,500 | |
| Year's gain in value | 13,000 | |
| Year's amortization on mortgage | 1,000 | |
| Prorated tax shelter value | 1,250 | |
| Total income | | $24,750 |
| | | |
| *Less expenses* | | |
| Year's real estate taxes | $ 875 | |
| Utilities and water | 625 | |
| Maintenance and repairs | 1,500 | |
| Insurance (fire and liability) | 350 | |
| Interest on mortgage | 5,000 | |
| Interest not earned on equity if invested elsewhere | 1,480 | |
| Prorated depreciation on rentable garage | 500 | |
| Amortization of mortgage | 1,000 | |
| Total Expenses | | $11,330 |
| | | |
| *Net profit before income taxes* | | **$13,420** |

vary from state to state and will certainly vary from year to year. But these guidelines are here to show you how you should think of your country property in terms of profit.

**Rent Saved**   In addition to the sheer pleasure of living in a country place of your own, your ownership saves you from paying a certain amount of dollars each year in rent. You can estimate this figure based on going rents in your vicinity. Do not base your estimate on just one example. Rather, average out several, and if you are unsure about this important figure, ask your local realtor.

**Rent Earned (if any)**   Perhaps your improved property has an income-producing building on it. Perhaps you rent out a room, or sell wood-cutting rights, or let a neighboring farmer cut and harvest the hay on your five acres for a small income a year.

**Year's Gain in Value**   As with *rent saved*, this is a *most important figure*. It is based on the full value of your house, not just the equity you have in it. The leverage factor made possible by a home mortgage in the United States is what makes country property such a valuable asset.

Figure 1-1 shows the recent median price of an existing single-family home in the United States. To find out how your house is faring in this

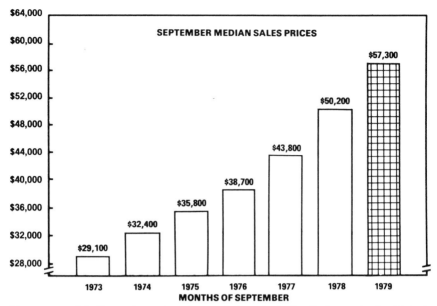

**Figure 1-1**  Median sales price of an existing single-family home in the United States for the month of September, 1973–1979. (*Source: National Association of Realtors.*)

market, ask a local realtor what you could get for your house and what the experience has been in estimating annual gains in value for your type of house in your area. Your bank mortgage loan officer can also give you some working figures.

**Year's Amortization on Mortgage**    This is both an expense and an income figure. You are reducing the principal of your mortgage and thus will not have to pay this amount of dollars in the future. Whether the sum comes out of your own pocket or is paid for by income derived from the property, no matter. Your debt is reduced by your payments.

**Pro Rata Tax Shelter Value**    The interest you pay on your mortgage is deductible from your taxes. If you have income-producing property, or part of your property produces income, you can depreciate it over its useful lifetime on a pro rata basis. The several or more thousand dollars you can legally deduct from your personal income may give you a substantial saving in your final income tax. Work out depreciation schedules with your accountant. Ask for a rough calculation on what your income tax would be if you did not have this depreciation deduction. The accountant will tell you, in the process, that the Internal Revenue Service (IRS) will want to tax this depreciation if and when you sell your property. Therefore, you will have to deduct from the original cost the amount taken in ordinary depreciation thus far and will have to add to the cost basis the undepreciated value of permanent improvements you have made. This affects the final capital gain; accelerated depreciation, on the other hand, is recaptured as ordinary additional income. In general, it will be to your advantage to set up with your accountant a depreciation schedule that is as rapid as reasonable. That enables you to shelter your personal income with as much real estate depreciation as allowed by the law. Your accountant has tables of typical and approved useful lifespans of different types of improvements and buildings. In practice, the IRS is not likely to challenge your depreciation schedule. If an examiner should pounce upon and challenge accelerated depreciation, use your claimed figure as a bargaining point. Perhaps you will have to pay a bit more in taxes, but it will be less than if you had not been aggressive about your depreciation.

**Expense—Real Estate Taxes** These are cut-and-dried expenses taken from your tax bill each year. Despite taxpayers' revolts, real estate taxes are the principal source of revenue for most localities. And certainly this is the case in country areas where village and town governments and schools and sanitary or sewer districts depend on property owners for revenue. Should property owners get some relief through these revolts, they will either have to do without services previously provided or these services will have to be paid for by alternative means such as state or local sales taxes.

**Expense—Utilities, Water Supply, and Sewers** You may have telephone and electric services supplied by local companies. You may not. If you generate your own electricity, there are continuing costs for fuel and maintenance. You may also have to maintain a septic system or its equivalent. Include sewer tax and expense if you have it in your locality. All these figures can be verified by your realtor or the supplier of services.

**Expense—Maintenance and Repair** Be honest with yourself on these figures. If your house is new, you probably will not have to spend much in maintenance and repair. But estimate generously for a reserve for such purposes. Also include heating expenses, either electric, oil, or natural gas. Perhaps you are burning wood or coal. How much do you consume each heating season and what is the total cost?

**Expense—Insurance** You probably will settle on a homeowner's comprehensive policy that covers fire and water damage, certain kinds of storm damage, and liability in case someone gets hurt on your premises. The latter coverage is especially important if you have tenants who might decide to sue you if they suffer hurt or loss through no particular fault of yours while they are residing in quarters owned by you. Another type of insurance expense you may be able to deduct is life insurance tied to the declining principal of your mortgage—so-called mortgage insurance. Ask your accoutant about these possible deductions.

**Expense—Year's Interest on Mortgage**  Most banks today will send you a year-end summary of interest paid on your mortgage during the previous year. The statement, often a monthly summary which starts over at the beginning of each calendar year, also includes your total principal outstanding. If you do not get this statement automatically, ask your bank for it. On this statement you may also find a summary of fire, and possibly other, insurance paid by the bank and your real estate taxes if the bank collects and pays them for you. Include in this expense possible late fees and penalties charged to you during the year.

**Expense—Year's Amortization of Mortgage**  These figures are the same as the income figures noted above. It is something paid out either from your own pocket or from a portion of the income of your property (if it has any). While this expense directly offsets the reduction of debt, it is a factor in cash flow. You have to pay it even though it is to your future benefit.

**Net Profit**  Subtract the total of expenses from the total dollar income and consider how lucky you are that you had the idea to buy country property! Note that the Skeptic family, with a current equity of $16,000, made a net profit of approximately $13,420. This was almost equivalent to the year's gain in value, but, in effect, it showed an 85 percent gain in equity through intelligent use of leverage. The Skeptic family cannot expect to double its equity every year, but it can make sizable annual gains during the near term. In a later chapter you will find how you can take advantage of this gain in value without selling the house. You can literally take out some of these profits, through refinancing, and not pay tax on them.

## TAXABLE GAINS ON DEVELOPED PROPERTY WHEN YOU SELL

If the developed property is your principal residence, and you or your spouse have reached 55, the Tax Equalization Law of 1978 allows you a capital-gains exemption of up to $100,000. At present, this is a one-time deduction; it cannot be carried forward by a divorced spouse to a new marriage and housing situation. As inflation continues, however, Congress may liberalize the law. It gives relief primarily to families who find themselves with large homes which are no longer needed after children have left and set up their own households. The "empty-nester" deduction comes as a blessing to older couples and has opened up a market heretofore locked-in for fear of sizable capital-gains taxes covering increases in value generated largely by inflation. There was considerable hardship for families whose principal wealth was in the family home, which had been well-maintained and cared for over the years, but who faced a nasty bite from the IRS if the home were sold outright. Of course, such gains can also be prorated over five years to equalize the income, or if a couple buys another house within 18 months or builds a new house within two years, the expense of the new house can be deducted from the gain on the old. If the new house is as expensive or more expensive than the old house, a tax on the gain can conceivably be delayed until estate taxes are paid on the final value of the last house at the day of death. Thus your heirs get a bit less through greater taxes, but you enjoy more while you are alive.

With the new law the transition from a large family home now worth, say $150,000, to a retirement cottage condominium in Florida worth $40,000 would run something like this:

| | |
|---|---|
| Sale of family home | $150,000 |
| Purchase of new condominium | 40,000 |
| | 110,000 |
| One-time exemption | 100,000 |
| Taxable gain | $ 10,000 |

The final $10,000 would be taxable at capital-gains rates, now a maximum of 29 percent for assets held a year or longer. Or it could be less if the total of your current annual income plus the $10,000 would put you in a tax bracket less than 29 percent. In any case, you would not have to pay *more* than $2,900 tax on the gain and depending on your personal tax situation, you may wind up paying much less or nothing at all. Here, as elsewhere in tax matters, it is best to consult with your accountant who may tell you that you can recapture any sums you took previously for depreciation of income-producing assets; at the same time, you can deduct from the selling price the undepreciated value of any improvements that you made as an owner and which have not yet been fully depreciated.

Naturally, if a part of your property produces income, it will be treated pro rata as commercial property; the part of your property you use as a family residence will not be affected by recapture regulations, since you were not allowed to depreciate it and deduct from income in the first place. As a general rule, you can only depreciate property you use less than two weeks a year. If you use it more than two weeks a year, your depreciation and the expenses deducted can total no more than the total income it produces. In other words, you cannot deduct depreciation and expenses in excess of the property's income *from your personal income*, unless you use that property less than two weeks a year. This is another point you will want to check out with your accountant to be sure you conform to tax rules that have been changing—and which may change again.

## PROFITS FROM A SECOND HOME IN THE COUNTRY

Some families or single people are fortunate enough to have a second home in the country that they use for relaxation on weekends and on vacations. They may have bought the property with weekend use in mind for the present and for possible retirement in the future. In the economic climate of rising prices for homes, and a limited supply of them, owning such a house can furnish much personal pleasure as well as investment profits, since you can rent the property to others when you are not using it or want to go elsewhere for variety during some of your vacations.

Your estimated profits, however, as shown in Table 1-3, will be based on components that differ somewhat from those affecting a principal residence.

**Table 1-3**  Estimated Profit from a Second Home

| | | |
|---|---|---|
| *Income* | | |
| Rental earned (if any) | $ _____ | |
| Year's gain in value | _____ | |
| Year's amortization on mortgage | _____ | |
| Prorated tax shelter through depreciation of part rented | _____ | |
| Total income | | $_____ |
| | | |
| *Less expenses* | | |
| Year's real estate taxes | $_____ | |
| Year's utilities and water | _____ | |
| Year's maintenance and repair | _____ | |
| Year's interest on mortgage | _____ | |
| Year's amortization of mortgage | _____ | |
| Interest not earned on equity because not invested elsewhere | _____ | |
| Total expenses | | $_____ |
| | | |
| Net profit | | $_____ |

*Example of Tom Skeptic and Mary Friend and Their Second Home in the Country*

Tom Skeptic, Sam Skeptic's cousin, was a commercial artist with a large advertising firm in Boston. He lived with Mary Friend, a copywriter for a retail chain, in an apartment they shared. On a visit to New Hampshire they fell in love with a small farmhouse and 10 acres on the outskirts of the village in which the Sam Skeptics had their old colonial home. Tom was impressed with the way land values had been rising in southern New Hampshire; Mary liked the rural quiet, where she felt she could get a lot of writing done. So they each contributed $10,000 to a down payment and the local banker gave them a mortgage of $45,000 on the rest of the $65,000 purchase price of the property, since both of them could prove steady incomes via their W2 forms and were willing to pay half a percentage point above the going mortgage-interest rate for residences. They were, after all, buying a second home and expected to rent it out part of the time for extra income. At the outset, they involved themselves in a property which cost the same amount as Cousin Sam Skeptic's: $65,000. But their financing was somewhat different and their use of the property was different, too. Table 1-4 shows what they could expect in profit after a year of ownership.

Note that the difference comes, in part, because Tom and Mary financed less of their property and because the rent savings was not as much because they were not living in the house much of the time. Their real estate taxes were lower, but because they were in the same country area as their cousins, the assessments were fairly uniform. Again, the net profit before income taxes amounted to about

**Table 1-4**  Estimated Profit from Rented Second Home

*Income*

| | | |
|---|---:|---:|
| Rental earned on property | $ 3,500 | |
| Weekend and vacation rent saved | 2,000 | |
| Year's gain in value | 13,000 | |
| Year's amortization on mortgage of $45,000 | 900 | |
| Prorated tax shelter value | 1,250 | |
|     Total income | | $20,650 |

*Less expenses*

| | | |
|---|---:|---:|
| Year's real estate taxes | $ 670 | |
| Utilities and water | 500 | |
| Insurance (fire and liability) | 275 | |
| Interest not earned on equity if invested | | |
|     elsewhere | 1,750 | |
| Interest on mortgage | 4,050 | |
| Amortization of mortgage | 950 | |
|     Total expenses | | $ 8,195 |
| | | |
|     *Net profit before income taxes* | | ***$12,450*** |

the same as the annual gain in value, which might vary from year to year. The figures show two somewhat different ways for holding property, having it pay for itself, and allowing the owners to enjoy its gain in value as general property values rose. In the case of the Sam Skeptics a cash investment of $16,000 showed a paper gain of $13,420 over the period of a year; in the case of Tom Skeptic and Mary Friend, a cash investment of $20,000 brought them a paper gain of $12,450 after the first year.

Both examples demonstrate the principle of leverage—as long as your property gains in value, its percentage of gain applies to the whole value of the property, not just to your cash equity in it (current market value less mortgage debt and improvement debt).

| *In the Sam Skeptic case* | | *In the Tom Skeptic and Mary Friend case* | |
|---|---|---|---|
| $16,000 equity gave control of property with a market value of | | $20,000 cash down controlled property worth $65,000 | |
| $65,000 | | $65,000 | |
| × .20 | Average increase in local real estate values | × .20 | Average increase in local real estate values |
| 13,000 | | 13,000 | |
| $78,000 | Value after one year | $78,000 | Value after one year |

These are approximate figures, of course, but they show how the principle of leverage can work in your substantial favor during rising real estate markets. If prices should actually decline, as they might temporarily in a recession, your equity would control less, but unless your timing is extremely unfortunate, it is a matter of reducing the paper profits amassed in previous years. Note, too, that these paper gains are not taxable until the property is actually sold, and the capital-gains tax can be postponed indefinitely as discussed in the preceding section.

## PROFITS FROM RAW LAND

The principal gain you can count on from raw or undeveloped land is capital gain as a result of increasing value year by year. If your land is farmland or cropland or is suitable for renting out as pasture, you may derive an income from it; you can sometimes sell water or mineral rights if the land is blessed with either natural resource and if a neighbor covets your property.

The usual reason for buying unimproved land for profit is with the idea of developing it—surveying it into smaller plots and either developing it into building lots yourself or selling it to a developer who has the necessary experience and wants to take the risk. In developing the land you are preparing it for a higher economic use and your reward sometimes can prove to be a handsome profit—perhaps double or triple the cost you paid for it. Your profit pattern then becomes one of listing the final sales price of all the lots. Then subtract the original cost of the tract plus all the costs on the way to the final sale—surveying it, possibly registering the subdivision, putting in roads, providing basic access to sewer, water systems, and telephone lines—and, finally, marketing the lots successfully to ultimate users.

Such useful and profitable development assumes that you have bought your original land in the path of growth and that development comes as a matter of fulfilling your profit dream. You may have to wait longer than anticipated, and meanwhile tax payments must be made. Your town or county board may require you to keep your fields mowed and noxious weeds suppressed (which they will do for you at a compulsory fee if you delay doing it). If you bought the piece of land from its former owner on a part-cash, part-mortgage basis, or on a land contract that includes the payment on principal and interest for a number of years, the interest on your debt will also continue as an expense against the paper gains you are making year by year.

Table 1-5 is a pattern balance sheet of possible profits on a piece of undeveloped land.

As you can readily see, the burden on profits for holding a piece of land falls heavily on annual appreciation unless you are fortunate enough to make an important mineral discovery on your land, or its unusually fine spring water can be sold to a local brewer or bottler, or perhaps to an

**Table 1-5**  Pattern Balance Sheet

| | | |
|---|---|---|
| Annual appreciation | $_____ | |
| Annual income from sale of rights | _____ | |
| Annual amortization (if any) | _____ | |
| *Total income* | | $_____ |
| | | |
| *Less expenses* | | |
| | | |
| Taxes | $_____ | |
| Interest | _____ | |
| Amortization | _____ | |
| Equivalent if equity interest were invested elsewhere | _____ | |
| *Total expenses per year* | | $_____ |
| | | |
| *Net profit before income taxes* | | $_____ |

industrial enterprise in the vicinity, or even to a neighboring rancher or farmer who needs more water for irrigation.

Of course, you can always improve the land by building on it and living there or by selling the finished house and its acreage. Then you will have to deduct the cost of improvements from the final sales price. In general, you may have to wait a few years before the rise in values catches up with the cost of your improvements.


## PROFITS FROM A WORKING FARM

When you own a *working farm,* you own a business and you had better keep business records, both for your own satisfaction in knowing your profits and, of course, for income tax purposes. Your accountant will help you set up the books and will work with you on taxes. An accountant can also give you worthwhile business advice if he or she has had experience with other farms. But you will find an accountant's advice especially useful on taxes, investment credits, and depreciation of buildings and equipment, and also on when it may be timely to incorporate, that is, when the tax-shelter features of your farm have diminished as it grows in profitability. The money you invest to improve the farm will probably cause it to furnish a profit rather than operating losses and depreciation that can be charged against your personal income. Incorporation will enable you to charge many operating and semipersonal expenses against income from the farm. With your accountant you may want to set up books so that part of the "salary" you draw from the farm is actually use of the farmhouse as a residence, as shown in Table 1-6.

Each category of income and expense shown in Table 1-6 needs a bit of expansion.

**Income—Produce from Farm**   A working farm suggests you are growing or raising a cash crop or product such as milk or meat. Perhaps you are raising chickens, goats, or beef cattle. Perhaps you have a herd of dairy cows. Or it may be an orchard of apples or of cherries. While you may also have a kitchen garden for vegetables and fruits your family can eat, you will derive most of your income from raising one or two specialties. Unless you are a great innovator and prefer to start from scratch, you will probably build on the income base of the previous farmer. The land, when you buy it, will come with a history of cultivation. The previous owner ought to be able to tell you what grows well in your kind of soil or, if for some reason he or she cannot, your country farm agent can tell you. It is possible from soil analysis to settle on the right crops, the necessary fertil-

**Table 1-6**  A Pro Forma Operating Statement for a Working Farm

| *Income* | | |
|---|---|---|
| Produce (milk, fruit, vegetables) sold | $_____ | |
| Estimated rental value of house owner lives in | _____ | |
| Possible rental from other farm buildings | _____ | |
| Possible lease of land to neighboring farmers | _____ | |
| Estimated savings on personal food by growing own | _____ | |
| Year's gain in value | _____ | |
| Year's amortization on mortgage | _____ | |
| Prorata tax shelter value | _____ | |
| *Total income* | | $_____ |
| *Expenses* | | |
| Year's real estate taxes | $_____ | |
| Hired help | _____ | |
| Your own labor | _____ | |
| Seed, livestock, etc. | _____ | |
| Interest on mortgage and equipment loans | _____ | |
| Year's amortization on mortgage | _____ | |
| Repairs | _____ | |
| Feed for cattle, fertilizer for vegetables | _____ | |
| Professional expenses | _____ | |
| Other expenses | _____ | |
| *Total expenses* | | $_____ |
| *Net profit before income taxes* | | $_____ |

izer, the proper cultivation technique, how much watering and spraying is required, and when and how to harvest and market your produce. Once you have the feel of your land, you can work with it and coax more yield from it through proper fertilizing, seeding, and cultivation. Presumably you will get to know the local seed and feed store proprietor and will compare the advice you get there with the farm agent's opinions and guidelines.

Frequently, there are marketing cooperatives in a specific farming area that will contract for crops and/or products and serve as suppliers of major equipment and services, insecticides, seed, and expert advice. In the Santa Inez Valley of California, for example, the tomato canners supply the farmers with plants, fertilizer, insecticides (and equipment for spraying them), and finally, mechanical harvesters. The farmers supply land and sweat equity for a price usually settled in advance. Needless to say, this contracting of crops takes much of the risk from the shoulders of the individual farmer. It assures the canner, who advances material and guarantees purchase, of a supply at harvest time, and also allows partial control of the costs for processing tomatoes. In many dairy areas there are capitalistic cooperative organizations, in which the farmers themselves may hold stock, that provide veterinary services (including artificial insemination) and all manner of advice. In addition, they may provide regular pick-ups of milk production, milk checks, and sometimes also pay an annual "patronage" dividend, or savings.

You can rest assured that your income from a working farm, at the start, will be less than you anticipated. At the same time, you can assume that whatever problems *you* have with your income, *your neighbors are facing or have faced the same problems.* Perhaps you will regard your neighboring farmers as your competitors rather than as friendly consultants. If so, you will have to approach the buyer of your produce more aggressively. After all, it will be to your mutual advantage if you both function profitably.

**Income—Rental From Other Farm Buildings**  Perhaps you have a second hay barn that you do not need that a neighbor can use to grow much more hay for a large dairy herd. Talk with your local farm agent to see if comparable barns are being rented out and, if so, what a typical rent is. Or just ask neighbors who rent out buildings what they get for them.

It is true that in some regions of the country (such as New England) your neighbor may object to personal questions about money, particularly from an outsider. That is why it is always a good idea to begin with the local realtor, lawyer, or banker. They may not identify who is renting to whom but they will probably tell you what the going rent is for buildings—and, for that matter, for land as well. It never hurts to ask. Since most farmers take out seasonal loans against crops or livestock these businesspeople are usually privy to financial statements. Thus, they may have a very intimate knowledge of another farmer's needs; in fact, they may even come up with a tenant for you.

You can also generate extra income by renting that second house on your property. Perhaps it was built to house help you no longer need. Perhaps it is an outbuilding, such as a horse barn, that could be remodeled for summer rentals to a city family who would like to live near or on a working farm. On many farms there used to be an apartment for hired men above the garage. With many kinds of specialized machinery now available, the owner of a farm usually finds it more economical to work with machines rather than with transient help. On many a Western ranch, these days, part of the old bunkhouse has become a series of guest apartments.

**Income—Lease of Land**  Especially if you are a beginning farmer, it may seem wise in the first years to buy more land than you plan to cultivate, simply to benefit from the growing value of the land. In many farmland areas, ambitious farmers seek to lease tracts of acreage. Possibly they have specialized in a crop, such as soybeans or corn, and have developed a production system that can handle far more land than they care—or can afford—to own. Land can be leased, of course, for grazing or for pasture, as well as for farming. You may, for example, lease an area of your land bordering on a neighbor's property to that neighbor for pasturing riding horses. You may even grant the right to build (or build it yourself) a suitable horse barn and paddock. If you lease out the property intelligently, you can amortize the improvement in a few years through the rent you receive. With more and more families moving to the country, you may often find that your neighbor does not particularly want to farm, but may want a place for riding horses or maybe an area for a kennel to raise dogs.

You can also lease a natural resource that you own but do not care to exploit, such as a pond on the edge of your property, to a neighbor who wants to raise ducks or try fish farming. You may have such an ample supply of well or spring water that you agree to sell some of it to a neighbor who needs more. This may be a resource worth considering if your land is in a region subject to drought.

Other resources you might rent or sell are harvest rights to woodlands and hayfields, or you can lease marshlands to a hunting club, or a lake and surrounding acreage can be leased to a local Boy Scout troop for camping privileges. There are, in fact, many possibilities for leasing and you should consider those appropriate for the land you are buying. You will frequently get a discouraging answer to your offer, but it is continually surprising these days to find people who prefer, for their own reasons, to rent land and/or its improvements, at least for a time, even though they know that land is going up in value and probably should be bought for the long haul rather than leased or rented. Sometimes it is a matter of supply and demand as well as convenience. In many cases someone is willing to rent because he or she is experimenting with a project, or does not expect to stay long in your vicinity. What is long? Five years or so. So the person rents for that period and then leaves. If one person will rent, and the population of country-property owners is increasing, another renter is likely to appear to prove that your original renter was not a freak. Accept it as a fact, in this day and age of high mobility, the chances are that someone who has a valid economic reason will appear and rent some of your country property rather than buying.

**Income—Estimated Savings on Personal Food by Growing Your Own**  You can easily overestimate this type of income. By and large you *lose* money growing your own food and enjoying it fresh in season and canned through the year. Your own labor costs more than the relatively few dollars you save on food.

You will, however, profit through pleasure in your own accomplishment—in that succulent tomato picked ripe from the vines and so red upon a bed of bibb lettuce you have also grown and picked fresh for dinner. Look upon the kitchen garden as a joy, a means of exercise, a point of pride, but not as a profit center.

Of course, an expanded market garden may furnish a modest profit if you specialize in a few vegetables and sell them at a roadside stand, or perhaps to a local supermarket. Fruits such as strawberries, apples, and raspberries, and vegetables such as sweet corn, tomatoes, and beans, lend themselves to seasonal emphasis, and you can perhaps bring in enough extra money to serve as a reward for the weeding, water, spraying, cultivating, picking, and shucking you do for your own kitchen table. Nowadays, unless you feel absolutely called to a vocation as a kitchen gardener, it is so much more efficient and economical to thaw out some frozen peas or lima beans, open a can of cranberry sauce, or boil a cup of precooked rice.

For most born-again farmers—out to make a profit on their farm—it is best to specialize in what can be grown most profitably and efficiently and buy or barter most of what else is needed for the table from fellow specialists. *What you can do more easily in the country than in the city is to pick up quantities of this or that meat, fruit, or vegetable at bargain prices when they are in season.* Then you can freeze or can your needs for the rest of the year and save several hundred dollars on your grocery bill, as well as have vine-ripened top-quality produce.

**Income—Year's Gain in Value**   During recent years the average percentage gain in value of an acre of U.S. farmland has outperformed all investment media with the exception of gold and diamonds. Table 1-7 shows the figures released by the U.S. Department of Agriculture's Economic Research Bureau, based on actual sales. You will probably find that this portion of your annual income will give you the most tangible rewards. Undoubtedly, your purchase of a farm involved a mortgage. Yet your annual capital gain (untaxed until you sell the farm, if you ever do), applies to the *whole farm,* not just to your equity in it.

For example, suppose you bought a 40-acre Wisconsin dairy farm for $195,000—$45,000 cash over a $150,000 mortgage. Wisconsin farmland has been making particularly good strides for the past several years. You can safely mark up your farm's value 12 percent each year. On $195,000, that is $23,400 the first year. It is more in the second year because it is based on $195,000 plus $23,400, or $218,400. The second year's gain,

**Table 1-7**

| Year | | Average price per acre* | Percent of increase over previous year |
|---|---|---|---|
| March | 1971 | $202 | 4.1 |
| March | 1972 | 218 | 7.9 |
| March | 1973 | 245 | 12.4 |
| March | 1974 | 303 | 23.7 |
| March | 1975 | 343 | 12.9 |
| February | 1976 | 390 | 13.7 |
| February | 1977 | 448 | 14.9 |
| February | 1978 | 488 | 8.9 |
| February | 1979 | 559 | 14.6 |

*Source:* U.S. Department of Agriculture.

then, would amount to $26,208. And so it goes, even though you may be amortizing as little as 1 percent (or $1,500) a year on your mortgage.

If Sam Skeptic were to buy into a farm situation such as this he might wail that the paper profit is all well and good but that it can only be realized if you sell the farm, and then a tax has to be paid on the gains. But there is another way you can cash some of the gains and not have to pay a tax on them. Based on its increased value, you can arrange to refinance the property. This is not always feasible and must be done with some care, as will be pointed out in a later chapter. Nonetheless, the possibility of doing this in many farm and other country-property situations makes ownership all the more attractive to a growing family.

**Income—Pro rata Tax Shelter Value**   With a farm you can take whatever investment credit is legal; perhaps 10 percent or so in any year. Your accountant will tell you the current percentage and will set up schedules for you. During the first years you own your farm, while you may still be earning most of your income from your trade or profession rather than from your real estate, the property can serve as an admirable tax shelter. For, aside from the housing it may give you (perhaps you and your family do not actually maintain your primary residence there), almost all other expenses are tax deductible, as your accountant will tell you and as the tax schedules will demonstrate. For you are living in the midst of a business. You are in the rare position in this world of having your business give you literal, as well as tax, shelter. The important thing is to get the details straight with the Internal Revenue Service and keep them that way. Your accountant can prove to be a manifold blessing in this situation.

**Expenses—Real Estate Taxes**   This amount will depend on local tax rates and your local assessor. There are many programs of tax reform that affect farmland and its evaluation. Farmland near a major urban area always has the potential for subdivision and higher economic use. As such, it will bring a much higher price per acre. But until it does, you do not want to pay taxes as if development were to take place tomorrow. You want to be sure you are assessed on the land's value as farmland, which is considerably lower in value per acre. You may have to sign up the land as part of an agricultural district and, in so doing, agree that you will not develop it or sell it to developers for a stated number of years. The laws governing these restrictions on agricultural land vary from state to state and you should find out exactly what kind of law is on the books in your state—or what kind of law the legislators are attempting to pass.

Because of the nationwide inflation in land prices, *all* states are likely to have a version of this law. It is only a matter of time and special situations before the assessments of comparable kinds of land will gradually fall into similar patterns throughout the United States, but because property taxes are *local taxes,* they will be the last to give way to uniform assessment and rates.

You will also find the manner of collecting taxes varies from locality to locality. In some places a village treasurer will act as the collecting agent; sometimes it is the town treasurer or other official. Sometimes you will be paying for the current year, sometimes for the past year. And there can be a partial payment by a specified date, with the balance due six months later. If you miss deadlines, you may find your liability sold to a larger government unit, such as the county treasurer, who may quite rapidly file a tax lien against you. This could result, in due time, in a threatened sheriff's sale of part of your property to satisfy the lien. You will undoubtedly have to pay additional interest on your unpaid taxes, and you may have to pay legal expenses as well. Your real estate taxes for a working farm may very well prove to be the largest single expense you will have to meet each year. Thus you should investigate taxes thoroughly for method of assessment, rates, payment-due dates, and penalties.

**Expenses—Hired Help**   This may mean part-time help by the hour or by the day in harvesting or planting. It may also mean full-time help. For the sake of this estimate, include an allowance for social security, disability, and unemployment taxes—running now, in all, to more than 16 percent of earnings. You may also have an arrangement whereby your help gets room and board, which should be assigned an arbitrary, annual value and prorated accordingly.

**Expenses—Your Own Labor**   You will want to include your estimated hours spent in active farming and the value you put upon them. Include whatever social security, disability, and unemployment taxes you may pay for yourself. Remember that you are not only a laborer on your farm, you are also its manager and should be paid accordingly. If your farm is actually profitable—and incorporated—it is conceivable that the corporation will pay you a salary. During the beginning years of operations, when the farm acts primarily as a tax shelter, you will probably do the work without compensation. But economic realism requires a figure for this very real input of human energy. So be generous in estimating this figure.

**Expenses—Seed, Livestock, and Other Supplies**   These expenses are readily supported by cancelled checks and/or bills of sale. You might want to set up a file with a folder for each of these tangible expenses. The file might also include promotion materials from sources of supply so that you can order quickly and also report defects or complaints to supplier's agents.

**Expenses—Interest on Mortgage and Equipment Loans**   If your loans are with a bank, you probably will get a bank printout of annual interest. But for purposes of estimating, simply figure the going rate against the loans you estimate you will have to carry for efficient operations.

**Expenses—Repairs**   It is hard to estimate repairs unless you have had years of experience in using farm machinery, buying replacement parts, and so on. It is possible that you can supply much of the mechanical expertise yourself. In that case, give yourself an hourly rate and use your experience with the family auto and other major equipment as a guide for estimating upkeep. Also keep in mind the rate and amount of depreciation you take on each piece of equipment. This will give you a rough idea of its useful life and of when the purchase of a replacement might prove timely.

**Expenses—Feed for Cattle, Fertilizer for Crops**   These are figures you will need to get from neighbors, your local farm agent, or the local feed store, where the owners, if they are worth their salt, will be able to tell you how much of most things you need per head or per acre and what the cost will be.

**Expenses—Professional Advice**   Include here the fees you have already paid or might pay to your lawyer and your accountant, and possibly to a business management consultant or a veterinarian.

**Expenses—Others**  These might include various fees for membership in local organizations, licensing fees for the farm truck, salary for a part-time bookkeeper (a family member, perhaps), office supplies, and other costs associated with the paperwork and record keeping for a farm.

## PERSONAL USE VERSUS MAXIMUM PROFIT

### Options and Trade-Offs

In the use of any capital asset or natural resource there is a wasteful and a conservative manner of consumption. The same is true of your country property. You can take much from it and put little back. In a period of inflation this may yield you considerable profit. You are, in effect, stripping the benefits from your property in a most profitable and ruthless manner. You can do this by planting crops that take heavy sustenance from the soil which you, in order to maximize profits, pay nothing to restore or build up through fertilizers, extra tilling, crop rotation, or resting the field every so many years.

Likewise, if you have a piece of woodland, you can cut off more trees per year than nature can replace at her leisure. You wind up with good receipts for your lumber, but no future for your crop of trees.

You can also subdivide your land for development in such way that lots are the minimum size allowed and are priced attractively so that many young couples who can afford only minimum accommodation buy them. In effect, you increase the density of population as far as the legal limit. Some tracts of land can stand this. Others can't. Some communities will tolerate this because it comes within their zoning limitation; others will go out of their way to foster a no-growth policy that insists on ever-larger sizes for building lots.

The farmer has a singular dilemma. If he or she can envision the day when the land in the path of growth will bring a high price from a developer, the tendency will be to hold back on expenses for conserving and improving the fertility of the land. Louis Bromfield, the novelist and pioneer in conservation of farm land, found to his dismay that his idealistic and advanced methods of organic farming often were not profitable, even though they were rewarding in knowledge gained and in a sense of accomplishment. He could not gain many converts to his organic farming methods because his neighbors, who were not best-selling novelists, had to think about the bottom line of their farm operations. This kind of experimentation continues, however, and it may be worthwhile to investigate current results.

As you farm you will have to reach some sort of compromise between financial returns from the land and conservation of the land. Louis Bromfield's experiments and fame caused the state of Ohio to declare his Malabar Farm a state park. Sections of the farm continue to grow crops, but most of it is a pilgrimage site where much can be learned about profitable and nonprofitable farming, as well as about conservation of the soil's fertility.

# Chapter Two

# Your Personal Pleasure and Living Goals

## THE CONTEMPORARY FAMILY—
## SHELTER NEEDS, WANTS, AND LIFESTYLES

Today's families, whether they live in the city or in the country, assert and express themselves in some ways that would seem alien to an earlier generation. Yet there is a core behavior persisting into the Age of Aquarius that even Victorian grandparents would recognize.

Predominant in this behavior are physiological needs centering on food and drink, sleep, and sex, in forms to satisfy one's natural desires. There are safety needs centering on shelter and warmth and a certain accommodation to environment. Then there are esteem needs—recognition from one's fellows in one's work, trade, or profession. Beyond these, there is the need for self-actualization—for developing the unique and expressive bundle of talents with which you arrived on earth. Finally, there are sheerly aesthetic needs that you, having satisfied the more basic needs, now have the leisure to enjoy. Abraham H. Maslow has identified this hierarchy of needs in detail in his profoundly humanistic study, *Motivation and Personality* (see Appendix B).

These needs make men and women tick, work, reach out—and buy country property. They are necessary for the humanistic fulfillment of each person's potential; they motivate an individual to move from mere being to essential selfhood. Along the way there are many wants that are optional variants to needs; they are the elaboration of basic needs. You can get along without satisfying wants, but an unsatisfied need can cause havoc with one's personality. Maslow points out that the more elemental needs, such as food and safety, must be satisfied before the upper hierarchy of needs can come into play. In other words, you can live on spaghetti although you may want a filet mignon, and you probably won't think very seriously about going to a country antique auction when your stomach is growling from hunger and the roof is leaking spring rain down on an empty kitchen table.

Whether to satisfy your shelter needs and wants in the city or the country is a choice you have. But rest assured, one way or another you will try to satisfy them. Your Victorian forbears customarily found a way to spend some time at a lake, the seashore, or in the mountains for part or all of the summer. If they didn't have a summer home in the country, they arranged to rent one or to go to a summer resort. Examine the sociological patterns of any large American city and you will find the remains of summer resort areas, usually within distance of a day's ride by railroad or horse carriage. This is the country property on which Victorian families relaxed one way or another. Thus, the recent rush to the country comes as nothing new, save the illusion in some young minds that they are doing something original and rebellious. What is new, perhaps, is the quixotic behavior of the young. The *me* decade of the seventies has been also the decade for being historically blind to what many generations have gone through out of economic necessity. The new pioneers in country property have similar economic needs but many of them move to the country not because they *need* to but because they *want* to. If they cannot afford a second residence in the country—in many ways the best of both worlds—they prefer to move entirely to the country rather than stay in the city with its current problems and discontents.

*Example of the Ridgeways—Teachers Who Grew Wine Grapes in Their Spare Time*

John and Ellen Ridgeway, graduates of a city college, wearied of the crises and pace of industry, went back to school to get advanced degrees in marketing, science, and English, and then emigrated to an old, run-down farm near Schenectady, where they both taught in the school system. There they raised their three children, an assortment of pets, and a small plantation of grape vines.

From their two teaching incomes they were able to improve and expand their wine plantation and accumulate the machinery necessary to make and bottle wine. They found, in consulting with their accountant, that they could take 10 percent off the additional investment as a credit against current income taxes. And there were the usual expenses for fertilizer, insecticides, and so on. The Ridgeways supplied their own labor. They began to sell their wine to neighbors and friends and joined the local winegrowers' association. A number of amateur—

grown professional—vineyard owners talk of forming a cooperative that will pool machinery resources and share marketing knowledge.

The Ridgeways find that their advertising and marketing experience may prove valuable once more in selling their wine.

In the small village to which spaceship earth has shrunk—as the electronic media have spread the good word and the new word—the challenges of the city have been cropping up in the country as well. At least some of the bright, fairly young, professional people who moved to the country to satisfy basic needs and wants more efficiently have come to realize, as they grow older, that higher needs are perhaps best fulfilled in the culturally rich city. And they are coming back, frequently rebasing themselves in the city but retaining that dream house in the country that seemed so important to them in their youth when they couldn't afford both places.

It is a supreme irony that the drinking water of New York City, time and again, has proven to be more pure than the drinking water of many country villages that have overpopulated themselves with refugees from the city, who add bathrooms to overloaded, often-primitive septic systems and then find bacteria from the effluent in their nearby water supply, and often on their beaches or in their recreational lakes and ponds. The big city had the same problem when it was a village decades or centuries ago. But it long ago met the challenge of a basic need for adequate food, water, and some safety from sewage pollution.

Many people who rush off to the country cannot imagine that they are running into their own arms and their own past, where many problems that the city has already solved will have to be solved. It is best to know what you are likely to find in the country before you rush out there.

Nonetheless, it usually proves healthy for a family to regain a close feeling for the soil and nature. This the country provides. It may very well be that excessive emphasis on fulfilling higher needs has created a certain nervousness and frustration because basic needs and the enjoyment in satisfying them have been neglected. Thus the back-to-the land movement is partly a back-to-basics movement. It is also part of the "greening of America," to a point where a healthy consciousness stays more in tune with both the urban and the rural landscape.

Because of the unusual, even unsettling, mobility of so many American families, a certain rootlessness can result. At worst, this can prove destructive, particularly to children who grow up without a sense of belonging to a place. At best, it gives a family many different kinds of friends in different parts of the United States and sometimes in foreign countries. When parents retire they can look forward to a nomadic traipsing from the home of one child or another and to all their friends in between.

Some families swear by the mountains, some by the sea, some alternate between lake and desert. Others find themselves at home in several environments, but tend to favor one over the other at different periods of their lives. These phases or passages in the life of a family cannot be predicted or prescribed; they vary in timing and in taste with each family. Fortunately, the country-property market is very active and liquid these days. You can buy and sell if your goals change. And you will probably make a profit, even if you have chosen the wrong environment and decide to put the place back on the market, provided you have bought and maintained it wisely. Probably the most realistic attitude to take is that your needs and your wants may change, and where once country property may have suited your family perfectly, a later lifestyle may require a move to another country place, or back to a small apartment in the city where maintenance is not such an individual burden.

An important aspect of the country-property market these days is its diversity. You can buy in a great variety of geographic areas and climates, from colonial austerity in Vermont to relaxed living in Florida to exotic living in Hawaii, if you want to stay within the boundaries of the United States. Of course, if you are more adventuresome and have your eye set on a villa in Tangiers or a ranch out back in Australia, these, too, are possible with the money and the right frame of mind. As you wander farther afield, remember it is a human need to have roots somewhere, especially in your later years. You will need to come home to root somewhere. In the United States 75 percent of retirees spend their leisure years in the same town, village, or city in which they worked. Keep that in mind as you accumulate profits from your transactions in country property.

## THE INVESTMENT THAT SHELTERS YOU AND YOUR EARNINGS

Real estate has traditionally been one of the most reliable ways for accumulating wealth. Provided it is well placed, in the path of urban growth or the shelter needs of a significant segment of the population, it has usually brought a good fortune to its owners. Of course, there are exceptions—the ghost towns that dot the West and surprise Easterners in their own backyard were based on dreams, usually mineral dreams, that thrived for a time and faded as did their populations. Figures 2-1 through 2-4 supply four different views of various real estate developments.

In these dreams and in sociological trends fortunes have been made in real estate, because it provides humankind with one of its basic needs— shelter or protection from elemental nature. The need for shelter is closely associated with basic needs for food and drink through the

**Figure 2-1**  Recreation facilities for young and old in a new town (Columbia, Maryland) in the countryside.

kitchen, bathroom, water supply, and sewer system. In the United States the laws have favored home ownership, and today 65 percent of U.S. families own their homes or condominiums; the remaining 35 percent rent. As shown in Table 2-1 ownership by family income shows relatively little variance. Ownership by age of head of household naturally shows a distinctive variance as young couples first rent, and then buy, expand, and maintain a family home for some years, and finally, perhaps when they become empty-nesters, think about renting once more. This cycle shows up in the cold statistics.

**Table 2-1**  Rent/Ownership Ratios
by Family Income and Type of Household

*By income*

| Income (dollars) | Homeownership rate (%) | Distribution of all households (%) | Distribution of owners* (%) |
|---|---|---|---|
| 7,000 | 48.5 | 23.3 | 31.1 |
| 7,000– 10,000 | 56.1 | 11.4 | 13.1 |
| 10,000– 15,000 | 65.4 | 21.0 | 20.7 |
| 15,000– 20,000 | 76.3 | 17.4 | 14.7 |
| 20,000– 35,000 | 84.3 | 20.7 | 15.9 |
| 35,000 | 89.3 | 6.2 | 4.5 |
|  |  | 100.0 | 100.0 |

*Number of owners in each income class divided by the number of all owners.

**Table 2-1**   Rent/Ownership Ratios
by Family Income and Type of Household
*By type of household*

| *Household* | *Homeownership ratio (%)* |
|---|---|
| Two-person (all) | 70.1% |
| Two-person (under 65) | 68.4 |
|    Husband-wife | 75.5 |
|       Under age 25 | 31.6 |
|       25–29 | 54.7 |
|       30–34 | 72.9 |
|       35–44 | 81.2 |
|       45–64 | 85.9 |
|    Other male head | 45.1 |
|    Female head | 41.9 |
| One-person (under age 65) | 32.0 |
| Elderly (65 or older) | 70.1 |
|    Two-person | 80.5 |
|       Husband-wife | 82.7 |
|       Other male head | 76.6 |
|       Female head | 71.3 |
| One person (65 or older) | 56.3 |

*Source:* 1975 Annual Housing Survey.

Although it is true that the current period of inflation makes more people consider renting as a way of getting more house with less capital tied up, the general American view is that the monthly payment on the mortgage gives you something in the end, whereas rent is just so much money spent with nothing to show for it. And years of rising home values have made a house such a very worthwhile investment that in increasing numbers singles and unmarried couples are choosing this route.

Within the American economic structure it is really only economical to rent when your capital can be earning more than 10 percent elsewhere and as safely (a rare possibility until recently), or if you know that you are going to stay in a place for only two or three years. Then, renting for the short term and bargaining with the landlord for decorating to suit your needs, will give you a personalized house or apartment that serves its purpose well and economically.

Certain middle-management and top executives for major multinational companies have found the hop, skip, and jump method to higher positions means buying and selling houses every few years. There are enough affluent executives doing this so that service businesses now pro-

**Figure 2-2**  Town square improvements—Hagerstown, Maryland.

vide help in buying and selling substantial properties for them. Execu-trans of Stamford, Connecticut, is one of these; the Corporate Service Division of Coldwell Banker, another. Realty divisions of chain stores (the Red Carpet Division of Sears, Roebuck, for example) also cater to this need. Given this help, even with remodeling done to suit the tastes of

**Figure 2-3**  Rehabilitation of water and waste system of a small town (Yakima, Washington), famous for its orchards.

**Figure 2-4** A whole, new town (Reston, Virginia) in the country.

the executive, profits can be made as the family passes from assignment to assignment. Customarily, employers help out with moving expenses and subsidizing increased interest rates, but there is a limit to the extent to which they will finance remodeling and improving property from which the executive will personally benefit. The handy executive, however, has every incentive to make a new home more appealing; it serves both as a status symbol and as a continuing accumulator of wealth. As long as an executive buys a house of value equivalent to the old one, taxes are deferred. And mortgage interest is deductible, as it is for every U.S. taxpayer.

Home ownership during the past years has proven to be one of the best investments a family can have. Compare Table 2-2 with whatever yardstick you use for investments in stocks, bonds, or a savings account.

As was pointed out in Chapter 1, ownership of real estate gives substantial financial leverage, with money borrowed at probably the lowest, most advantageous, commercial rates. The laws regarding financial banking operations tilt in favor of home ownership and cater to a basic need and want of the U.S. population.

You can deduct as an operating expense the interest you pay on a home mortgage. And with relatively low down-payments required—in some cases only 5 percent or 10 percent on FHA and VA guaranteed loans, although 25 percent or so is more normal—relatively little of the owner's capital, at first, is tied up in a house. Thus the amount mortgaged is maximized and so is the deductible interest paid.

**Table 2-2**  Existing Single-Family Home Prices, 1969–1979

| Month | 1969 | 1970 | 1971 | 1972 | 1973 | 1974 | 1975 | 1976 | 1977 | 1978 | 1979 |
|---|---|---|---|---|---|---|---|---|---|---|---|
| Jan. | $21,100 | $22,200 | $23,700 | $25,300 | $27,400 | $30,600 | $33,200 | $36,300 | $39,600 | $45,500 | 52,000 |
| Feb. | 21,000 | 22,500 | 24,200 | 25,400 | 28,000 | 30,600 | 33,900 | 36,200 | 40,700 | 46,300 | 51,900 |
| Mar. | 21,200 | 22,800 | 24,300 | 25,900 | 28,400 | 31,400 | 34,200 | 37,200 | 41,000 | 46,500 | 53,800 |
| Apr. | 21,500 | 22,900 | 24,600 | 26,300 | 28,500 | 31,700 | 34,900 | 37,700 | 42,000 | 48,200 | 54,700 |
| May | 21,600 | 23,100 | 25,100 | 26,900 | 28,800 | 32,100 | 35,200 | 37,600 | 42,200 | 47,800 | 55,900 |
| June | 22,200 | 23,300 | 25,100 | 27,300 | 29,200 | 32,900 | 36,200 | 38,600 | 43,400 | 48,400 | 56,800 |
| July | 23,000 | 23,700 | 25,400 | 27,500 | 29,900 | 33,000 | 35,900 | 38,900 | 43,700 | 49,400 | 57,900 |
| Aug. | 22,600 | 23,500 | 25,300 | 27,400 | 29,900 | 32,900 | 36,800 | 39,400 | 43,900 | 50,300 | 57,700 |
| Sept. | 21,700 | 23,100 | 24,800 | 27,000 | 29,100 | 32,400 | 35,800 | 38,700 | 43,800 | 50,200 | 57,300 |
| Oct. | 21,900 | 22,700 | 24,800 | 26,900 | 28,900 | 31,900 | 35,400 | 38,500 | 44,000 | 50,100 | 56,300 |
| Nov. | 22,100 | 23,200 | 25,100 | 27,000 | 29,700 | 32,100 | 35,700 | 38,800 | 44,500 | 50,700 | 55,600 |
| Dec. | 22,000 | 22,800 | 24,900 | 27,100 | 29,500 | 32,700 | 35,800 | 39,000 | 44,200 | 50,900 | 56,500 |
| | | | | | | | | | | | |
| Annual | $21,800 | $23,000 | $24,800 | $26,700 | $28,900 | $32,000 | $35,300 | $38,100 | $42,900 | $48,700 | 55,700 |

*Source:*  National Association of Realtors.

## TAX SHELTER FROM DEDUCTIBLE INTEREST

Although mortgage borrowers may complain about the high rates of their contracts, the amounts they actually pay is heavily subsidized by the U.S. government. Take, for example, the family that is in a 50 percent tax bracket and is paying 9.5 percent interest on a new, single-family dwelling that it bought for $125,000, with $25,000 down. Interest amounts to $9,500 a year, but because of the tax bracket, the family really pays only half that amount. The other half represents tax savings. And so the real rate of interest is only 4.75 percent, and that is paid with future dollars diminishing in value at about 10 percent a year. So you can knock off roughly another 0.475 percent from the effective rate of interest, and you wind up with a final rate of about 4.275 percent.

## TAX SHELTER FROM DEPRECIATION

You cannot depreciate personal property or parts of your own home, but you can depreciate the buildings and equipment of income-producing property. Your accountant can tell you what is currently acceptable with the Internal Revenue Service, but a typical deducation might be on a 20-year straight-line basis. Ideally, you will have access to the appraiser's evaluation of buildings and land—an appraisal that your lender will order for you, and that can serve as the basis for value against which you take depreciation.

Say you have a house and garage with a market value of $90,000 on an approximate acre of land that is worth $10,000. A conservative way to depreciate over 20 years is to take 5 percent of the $90,000 each year, or $4,500. Or your accountant may recommend an accelerated depreciation schedule, which allows a higher percentage to be deducted during the early years of the building's life. Of course, depreciation is an accountant's device to cover the wear and tear on a building through use. On the face of it, you would think that the building had to be rebuilt every twenty years. Fortunately for the owner of real estate, this is not the case. You *will* and *should* spend some of this money in prudent maintenance of the building, in replacing an old and faulty furnace, for instance, in replacing disintegrating shutters on a colonial house, in repointing masonry, in rebuilding a portion of the house where floor joints have shown dry rot, in putting on a new roof. Yet, in reality, these expenses and replacements— even if kept up on a high level as though you wanted to live in the house always and meant to upgrade it continually—do not amount to the tax-allowable depreciation each year. There is thus an actual incentive to improve and upgrade property each year and to use expenses and sizable depreciation as a deduction against your personal and/or professional income. Here are examples of a single doctor, two friends owning property jointly, and a business executive's family who made different kinds of investments in country property. Note how each fares with the IRS as a result of property ownership.

*Example: Doctor Albin Shelters His Substantial Professional Income*

Dr. Leonard Albin, a bachelor, was immersed in his work. Although he was only 35, his annual income was about $100,000. He had a regular investment program and one of his major investments was a working farm where he spent weekends and vacations. He liked to be in the midst of living things. Of course, he could not do much of the farm work himself; he paid a farmer $22,000 a year plus the use of a separate house for which the rental value was approximately $6,000 a year. Estimated operating income and expenses are shown in Table 2-3.

*Example: Two Professional Women Take It Easy On Their Ranch During the Summer*

Martha Bronson was a highly successful designer of women's leisure clothes and her friend Jane Atherton was a dean at a well-known university in the San Francisco Bay area. Together they earned $100,000 a year. They wanted to put some of their money into real estate. Because they both liked the outdoors—tall trees and

**Table 2-3**  Doctor Albin's Income

| | |
|---|---|
| Taxable income from profession | $100,000 |
| Farm income | |
| Crops sold | $ 12,775 |
| Farm expenses | |
| Interest on mortgage | $ 9,783 |
| Hired help | 22,050 |
| Seed and fertilizer | 5,500 |
| Real estate taxes | 4,788 |
| Repairs | 1,750 |
| | $ 43,871 |
| Operating loss | $ 31,096 |
| Less depreciation | $ 4,427 |
| *Taxable income before personal deductions* | $ 64,477 |

**Table 2-4** The Bronson-Atherton Ranch

| | |
|---|---|
| Taxable income from profession | $100,000 |
| Ranch income | |
| Rental of pasture | $ 2,000 |
| Expenses | |
| Cutting weeds | $ 225 |
| Interest on purchase-money mortgage | 2,476 |
| Real estate taxes | 2,313 |
| | $ 5,014 |
| Operating loss | $ 4,954 |
| Depreciation | none |
| *Taxable income before personal deductions* | $ 97,046 |

pine-carpeted forest floors—they bought an old ranch site of 20 acres across the Golden Gate Bridge in Marin County. Some of the old ranch buildings were in good enough shape to be used as a residence and a hobby shed. There was a neglected pasture that they rented to a neighboring farmer for $2,000 a year. Their estimated profit picture is shown in Table 2-4.

**Table 2-5** The d'Allesandros's Income

| | |
|---|---|
| Taxable income from profession | $100,000 |
| Income from property | |
| Summer rent from guest cottage | $ 2,950 |
| Expenses | |
| Cleaning of cottage | $ 555 |
| Repairs in cottage | 373 |
| Real estate taxes | 1,127 |
| | $ 2,055 |
| Operating profits | $ 895 |
| Less depreciation of cottage | $ 817 |
| *Taxable income before personal deductions* | *$100,078* |

*Example: The Herbert d'Allesandros Make Money on a Guest Cottage*

Herbert d'Allesandro, vice president of a leading Iowa food-processing concern, his wife Marie, and three teenage children owned two acres of land on Lake Winnemechong in Iowa. They had a guest cottage that they rented for $2,950 for the four summer months. They had no mortgage on the property; Herb had inherited it from his father. Table 2-5 shows how their profit expectations shaped up:

## TAX SHELTER THROUGH INVESTMENT CREDITS

Although the tax law changes from time to time on investment credit for expansion or improvements of business assets, this feature of the tax law also works in the favor of a farmer or investor in a working farm, for example, who regards the farm as a business that someday will bring a profit. It is intended as a profitable venture, not as a hobby, even though it is currently losing money on its day-to-day operations. Operating losses plus depreciation can be used as a deduction from your principal income. And you can plan your further investment according to the amount of money you might want to bury in your land. Perhaps you want to install irrigation, expand your orchard, build a new garage or shed for your tractor, or buy a new tractor or new milking equipment. Your accountant will give you the current percentage of these expenses you can deduct as an investment credit for tax purposes. Note that the single, doctor-farmer in the first example has a greater opportunity for this kind of deduction than the two professional women or the business executive and his family.

### The Shelter You Cannot Deduct from Taxes

The tax laws generally do not allow you to deduct depreciation for the part of a property that actually shelters you and your family, even if only for a small part of the year. Maintenance expenses of your main residence cannot be deducted, although local property taxes can be deducted on your state and federal income taxes. You can deduct interest on any mortgage, however, within certain limits. These deductions can also be made for a second home provided it is rented part of the year. If it is fully rented year-round, it is an income-producing property, not a second home. The cut-off point is two weeks. If you occupy the house more than two weeks of a year, you cannot treat the property as income-producing property. You can deduct pro rata expenses, however, up to the amount of rent actually received. Your accountant can fill in details for you and keep you in line with changing IRS rules.

Legislative trends in Congress suggest that there may be a gradual lopping-off of the tax-shelter possibilities in owning real estate. It is a part of the move to reform or even eliminate special privileges for certain kinds of investment. There has been continual legislative attention to investment credit—what counts, what can qualify, and what the current rate should be. As the Congress realizes that the capital equipment in the U.S. economy has aged, is often obsolete, and that spending for capital equipment can increase productivity and economic efficiency, it may grant larger investment credits for tax purposes and modify consumer deductions such as interest on a mortgage. Another change in tax strategy may allow renters to deduct from their own taxes a portion of their landlord's mortgage interest, thus making renting slightly more attractive than it has been in relation to owning. Since there is a broadening of conservative feeling in the United States, it is more likely that taxes will be simplified but not radically changed, and that the substance, though perhaps not the size, of the present deduction schedule for owners of real estate will continue. Of course, you will want to check out any plans you have for your real estate holdings with your accountant. Be sure that you know what your long-range goals are for earnings, lifestyle, and investment.

## WHAT YOU CAN EXPECT TO SAVE
## IN EXPENSES BY LIVING IN THE COUNTRY

**Air**  The pleasures of living in the country are environmental, physiological, and psychological. The air is probably purer in the country and you will save, in the long run, on respiratory diseases that thrive on urban pollution and its irritants.

**Energy**  Unless your country place is much further south, you will use about as much energy in heating, cooling, cooking, refrigerating, and TV watching as you did in your urban home. If you move far enough south, you may spend quite a bit of money for energy to air condition. Your clothes and home-maintenance bills may be less.

**Transportation**  Distances stretch out in the country, and except in essentially suburban areas, mass transportation is nonexistent. Bus service is inconvenient, at best; commuting on public transportation may save on nerves in heavy traffic to and from the city, but you cannot expect money savings unless you organize a car pool or switch from a car to a bicycle for short trips to and from the train or bus station and to and from your village shopping center. A study of energy use by rural families indicates that they use about the same amount of energy in the home but 42 percent more gasoline than their urban counterparts. It is a matter of longer distances to shop, to visit friends, go to the doctor, go to church, to a football game, even to a benefit supper, or to pick up the children after an extracurricular activity at school.

**Water Supply**   Water may be purer in the country than in the city, but do not take that for granted. Before buying have the existing water supply tested and the flow measured. If the well does not have good water or the supply is limited, drill a new well. It will only cost you more later and your health may be at stake. Believe it or not, water in the country does not come from a faucet (as does urban water with all those officials to watch over the purity and supply); it comes from your own well or spring. It has to be pumped, and that requires a small amount of energy each day as well as periodic repairs.

**Waste Disposal**   Unless you have a sewer system (as many planned rural communities do), you will have to dispose of your own wastes at considerable expense for a septic tank and leach bed, and for maintaining them with occasional pump-outs when the system is overloaded. If your surrounding land percolates well, that is, absorbs the moisture or the remaining effluent from the leach bed, you are fortunate. If percolation is poor, you may have to expand your leach bed, pump the tank more often, or if the leach bed is old and gummed with detergents—some of which coat soil particles in such a way that the saturated soil repels absorption of more liquid—you may have to dig and prepare a new leach bed at a cost of $1,000 or $2,000.

**Utilities**   Telephone and electric service may cost more or less depending on your section of the country and the policy of your state's public service commission. You will want to check these out for possible differences. Above all, be sure they are *available* for your particular property and that you will have no major expense in hooking up to a local supply. An alternative for electricity from a utility service is to generate your own with a diesel generator, a windmill, or a sensible (and expensive) combination of the two. By and large, you will not be able to generate enough electricity on your own, by any means, to match conventional electricity supplied by a utility. Someday refinements in solar energy may make this possible. If you are building in the country, you should certainly consider a solar energy installation as a supplement. (See books on solar energy listed in Appendix B.)

**Food** There is something appealing about having one's own chickens and eggs, a cow or two for meat or milk, perhaps goats or rabbits or beef cattle. Add a vegetable garden for fresh vegetables and fruits. From this type of operation you can save on grocery bills. But you will add to your equipment expense because you will need feed, fertilizer, seed, possibly a shed or coop or two, pesticides, and to your labor. Oh yes, poultry, rabbits and meat-supplying animals require someone to care for them, feed them, remove their wastes, clean their shelter, milk them, and see them through sickness, possibly with a veterinarian's help. Vegetables and fruits need feeding, cultivating, spraying, and harvesting. When you figure in all these expenses, particularly your own labor, you will find that growing your own will not result in much of an overall savings. You will have, though, *better-tasting produce* than you buy at the supermarket. And it may be a good hobby and exercise.

*Example: The Nelsons and Their Energy-Efficient Dome Home*

Ruth Ann and Leslie Nelson, who sell medical equipment for a well-known medical manufacturer in Wisconsin, found they could cut down on energy needed for heating by erecting a domed house, which exposes less surface to the weather than the conventional rectangular shape. They moved from West Allis, Wisconsin, to the Kettle Moraine country, west of Milwaukee, when they found that local regulations would not allow them to build a windmill to generate electricity on their urban lot.

Their geodesic-dome home is 44 feet in diameter; it cost $7,650 for the pre-cut lumber in a kit, including color-coded framework struts and interior triangular panels of chipboard and exterior panels of wood. The first floor has 1,450 square feet of living space divided into a living room (two stories in part), a bedroom, dining room, kitchen, bath, and mud area. With friends, the Nelsons put up the skeleton in two days and finished the outer and inner panels in another 14 days. They contracted out the plumbing, masonry foundation, and electrical work. Their foundation is of concrete blocks, excavated into the side of the hill, and the basement gives them a woodworking shop, a utility room, a garage, and a wood-storage space.

In the cellar is a wood-burning, forced-air furnace which can provide 160,000 BTUs an hour, which is more than enough to heat the home on cold winter nights. For fuel, they use trees cut from their own woods plus salvaged windfalls from the neighboring acreage. Leslie Nelson feeds the furnace twice a day during the winter and finds that it will hold a fire overnight. All told, the furnace requires 3.5 to 5 cords of wood a heating season. A fieldstone fireplace in the living room supplements the furnace as needed.

The Nelsons built the house on 4.5 acres of wooded hillside, overlooking a valley and three small lakes. They also have a chicken coop built from leftover construction materials, a 60-foot-square vegetable garden, plantings of herbs, grapes, asparagus, blueberries, and strawberries, and a 14-tree orchard of apples, pears, peaches, plums, and even an apricot tree. In another part of the acreage they have planted 350 white pine seedlings.

Now in their early thirties and after two years of work on their domed manor, the Nelsons next plan to add a wooden deck facing the sunset, a dome greenhouse, and—finally—the windmill power generator that they expect will furnish about 40 percent of their electricity.

## EARNING A LIVING IN THE COUNTRY

We have Ralph Waldo Emerson's assurance that if someone has good corn, or wood or boards or pigs to sell, or can make better chairs or knives, crucibles, or church organs than anybody else, a broad, hard-worn path will be beaten to the house, though it be in the woods. Emerson is supposed to have said something about a better mousetrap in much the same context in a speech remembered by a New England diarist and which has since become a common American folk saying. Naturally, if you possess the ingenuity to invent a better mousetrap, you may have solved with one stroke the problem of earning a living in the country.

About 1970 or so a Gallup poll showed that almost six out of every ten residents of cities would prefer to move to the country if they could make a living out there. Of course, many people *can* make a living there, particularly professional people who can bring a high level of personal service to rural areas. You may not find in the country the professional challenge and pace you know in the city, but it is entirely possible that you may *prefer* the quieter, less complicated ways of the country. You must, however, expect fewer support services in the country. The doctor will not have several nearby laboratories to make analyses; the lawyer may not have bright colleagues to consult at lunch, or sharp clerks who will look up precedents in the library; the accountant may not have a computer service handy to make analyses and to print out final reports. But it is surprising how many of these support services the persistent professional can find in the country, or by mail or sophisticated messenger services from the city. Any number of executive secretaries and people with office skills have *also* made the choice to live in the country, and if you want to take the lead, they are eager to follow. Simply spread the work around of your needs—or advertise in the local newspaper.

There is hardly a human activity, when you get down to some hard thinking about it, that cannot take place in rural parts of the United States. Even very professional entertainment is offered in reborn ghost villages that have refurbished an old-time opera house and revived period and even modern hits. So you really don't have to give up everything to live in the wilderness without electricity or running water. Of course, if that is your scene, you have that possibility, too!

What you *will* find in country villages and towns is a lower price level for most professional services. People will probably pay you more promptly, but they don't expect to pay so much for *any* type of professional service. But then, you will probably not have to pay big-city rates for clerical help or other personnel services either. Your lifestyle, undoubtedly, will become more modest, so you won't need as much income as you did before.

## MAIN INCOME OR SECOND INCOME?

In your dreaming and planning about living in the country, remember that it takes more self-reliance to live and thrive in the country than it does in the city.

So, if you must earn a major portion of your income in the country, you might better think twice before moving there. In a village where the president and part-owner of the leading commercial bank makes only $20,000 to $25,000 in salary, can you logically expect to earn much more *whatever* you do?

First of all, decide what you need to earn to maintain the lifestyle your research in country ways has led you to believe is possible and right for you and your family. Then decide if it is possible in the village or town in which, or near which, you plan to settle. Perhaps you cannot earn that kind of income in one place but you can in another. This is known as market research and it is well worth the extra effort. Any number of people have discovered to their delight and growing confidence that their highly developed professional skills and enthusiastic attitude would be more than welcome in the country. In so many professions and trades the competition and complexity of an urban practice gives the practitioner an unmatched, broadly based experience and confidence that will serve him or her in good stead in the country.

Your position will be easier, of course, if you only want to earn a second income at the start, that is, supplement your main income from the city with additional income, based on the same skills, from country clients. This is entirely possible in some commuting situations where you go to the city, say, several times a week and remain in the country some weekdays and most weekends. Your work style is what you make it, and in these days of telecommunications, electronic photocopying, and the computer, a great deal of work can be done by remote control.

One source of information that professionals should not overlook is their professional association, which may have figures on openings in various rural areas of the United States. This is also evident from local Sunday newspapers, with their weekly bulge of advertising and summaries of the business, commercial, and agricultural news of the region. You can get an idea of how your adopted rural area is thinking and acting, things you, as a newcomer, may have overlooked. Then, too, the local Chamber of Commerce could be of help, as well as business organizations such as Rotary and Kiwanis. Do not skip in your career research the people you probably have already met—the local banker, the realtor who sold you the land, a local lawyer and other businesspeople who may have sound readings of the business and professional activity in the area. Unless you intend to live as a recluse, you would normally want to know these community leaders anyway, and they may find in you a willing recruit for this or that community activity.

## STARTING UP A NEW BUSINESS

Many people who decide to pull up their city stakes and move to the country also want to *change* careers. Perhaps they have simply reached a point of boredom in the career for which they studied, perhaps their original career was chosen to please a domineering father or mother, but now they want to do what they always dreamed of doing—editing a small town newspaper.

The opportunities for such adventures are legion and so are the pitfalls. Since you already are abandoning the city for the country and may or may not have unhealthy (dangerous) illusions about greener rural pastures, you may be attempting too much by changing career as well. If you do insist on doing it, do it gradually so that your family doesn't have to suffer unduly until you find yourself, at long last!

If warning signals do not deter you, there are many opportunities for self-employment and new enterprise in the country, and the new environment may prove just the stimulus you need to get out of old ruts.

Here are 33 opportunities you may want to check out in the countryside you want to call your future home:

**1**  How about operating a franchise? Fast foods? Real estate brokerage with one of the nationwide chains such as United Farm or Strout? Simple printing, such as Sir Speedy or Postal Instant Press? Check local papers in the business opportunity section for other possibilities. The advantage of opening up a franchised outlet is the marketing skills and special training that the franchiser puts at your disposal. The disadvantage may lie in the amount of initial capital you have to put up and the continuing percentage of income you must pay to use the franchiser's name and expertise.

**2** How about getting paid for that craft you practiced as a hobby? Needlepoint? Woodworking? Pottery? Sewing? Decorating? Reupholstering? Candlemaking? Original work in stained glass? Repair of antiques?

**3** How about baking bread, cakes and cookies, and pies? You can sell them to neighbors as well as to your local supermarket, which might be delighted to offer some home baked goods among the shelves of standardized produce and packaged and canned goods.

**4** Can you cook three or four favorite family dishes? Let the neighbors know you will do their main dinner on a two-day notice. You may be going into competition with Colonel Sanders and Kentucky Fried Chicken. Be sure yours tastes as good or better and your ringing telephone will tally your success.

**5** Do you like to work with herbs? Grow them, or sell them as plants or packages of dried, ready-to-use leaves or seeds. Sell your know-how where the local customers can not only pay to eat and learn but may also buy some to take home. Try seminars.

**6** Can you manage large dinners with all the necessary apparatus, possibly chairs and tables, covering cloths, and personnel to set up and clean up? You might want to try catering for church suppers, business groups, school meetings, family picnics, weddings, and the like. There is *always* a need for someone who can bring in a delicious meal and serve it superbly, then fade away leaving the site clean and the people well fed.

**7** How about typing and bookkeeping? Many a country professional person will be glad to drop off dictation belts for transcribing into letters. Can you type speeches, reports, articles, minutes, and visit maybe once a week to go over the books? Much of the time you can do this in your own home.

**8** Do you like to telephone? Try telephone selling in your area for magazine subscriptions, for chemicals, materials for the home or plant, financial canvassing. Check help wanted ads in the local paper under sales help wanted, particularly telephone sales help wanted. You will discover what kinds of products already are accepted in your area. You may also want to get in touch with a business rep from the telephone company to learn about discount rates for a volume of calls.

**9** How about substitute or full-time teaching at a small college? Look for a small college or university town and teach that second language you know so well. Or provide one or more professional services needed part time by the college, from computer programmer to tutoring in zoology.

**10**   How about turning that camera hobby into a small photographic supply store where you also give seminars once a week in how to take better photographs?

**11**   If you are into arts and crafts, why not open a local arts and crafts center? Get your inventory from local craftspeople on a consignment basis and agree to sell it for them on a 40 percent commission or thereabouts. Encourage socializing with the artist at cider and cooky or wine and cheese parties; have the featured artist give demonstrations. This may turn out to be a seasonal business coinciding with the winter or summer tourist trade. So you might be free from the store for part of the year.

**12**   How about guest accommodations if your country house is large enough and you like company? There is always a danger that your friends and relatives will freeload anyway if you have the room and an open-door policy. Why not turn the tables and encourage everyone to come by reservation and for a good fee?

**13**   How about putting your expertise in antiques to good use as an appraiser, or an afternoon antiques salesperson, perhaps doing business from your own front room?

**14**   How about logging out some of the excess trees in your woodlot, or possibly planting other hardwoods so that you can enjoy a periodic harvest and extra income?

**15**   How about giving music lessons on the instrument on which you are proficient? There always seems to be room for another piano teacher, particularly if he or she is willing to drive to the pupil's home. This means less chauffeuring for mother and dad, and gives the pupil the confidence of playing on the same piano that is used for practice.

**16**   How about tutoring students through the local grade and high school in remedial work or in advanced studies in your specialty?

**17**   How about selling plants (seedlings and cuttings) from the excess of your hobby greenhouse? In all probability the nearest commercial florist will be miles away and then may not have some of the special plants you are able to slip or grow from seed and coax into luxurious bloom. A blooming plant still makes one of the most cherished gifts. So why not turn your green thumb into gold?

**18**   Why not organize a housekeeping service that will provide a thorough cleaning? Changing storm windows and screens is particularly needed in the spring and the fall. Housekeepers and working wives will welcome this extra-thorough seasonal cleaning, or a weekly service, too.

**19**   Why not organize and offer a lawn-care service that cuts grass, removes debris, and feeds and upgrades lawns with mechanical, time-saving equipment that the average householder would not want to buy? It is amazing how many neighbors duplicate their expensive and powerful equipment, run it maybe once a week for a few hours, and let it depreciate the rest of the time. Many are wising up and having a service do the heavy work.

**20**   Why not take part- or full-time employment in that new plant erected beside the new federal highway?

**21**   How about sewing clothes for your family and others? With a good and versatile sewing machine, these days you can do a better job of sewing than is seen in many of the dresses and suits found on the racks of even the most elegant stores. Don't compete with the jeans stores. Make dressy clothes featuring good materials that your clients may bring to you or that you have to show to them. You can earn quite a bit, too, in altering dresses that customers buy and want fitted, or in altering old but very fine garments to suit the current fashions. Put that handy needle and the new, fantastically versatile machine to work!

**22**   How about drying flowers and weeds and making original bouquets from them? Perhaps the nearest grocery or dry goods store will accept some on consignment. Offer to make custom displays for special occasions.

**23**   How about specializing in preserves, selling them to neighbors who like to eat them but don't want to take the trouble to put them up themselves? You can even take your neighbors' fruits and process them possibly taking part of your pay in kind, or as a quarter of beef in barter.

**24**   How about specializing in the management of rummage sales or country auctions or flea markets? Offer to handle the publicity, the tagging, the sale itself for a percentage of the money taken in. This might be a garage sale, a sheriff's sale, a charity benefit. The success of these kinds of markets depends heavily on a person who can organize them well.

**25**   How about turning that special recipe for fudge, brownies, salad dressing, or cheese cake into a supplementary income on a reservation basis? You can usually get your nearest grocery to give you some showcase space. The same goes for bread or rolls.

**26**   How about taking over a country store, guest house, horse resort, filling station, restaurant, motel, ski lodge or slope? This can prove even more than a full-time project and you need small-business management skills in order to succeed. In some popular areas of the country there are realtors who specialize in buying and selling businesses. Some are so good at it that they conduct seminars on how to run a small business in the country *(see Appendix C)*. A few such brokers will actually furnish consulting advice for a year or two to be sure you don't become entangled in the debris of shattered dreams.

**27**  How about part-time work at a nearby resort hotel that needs extra help for the summer season? The management of such a hotel is always on the lookout for part-time skills which can supplement the skeleton staff. You may get some pretty good meals as part of your reward. Maybe tips, too. And you won't feel tied down all year.

**28**  How about selling real estate? Once you have your own country place purchased and financed, full of the excitement of your transaction, you might apprentice yourself to a local realtor, get your license, and make your commissions as others like you arrive in the country. Having previous selling experience, no matter what kind, will help.

**29**  How about planting suitable fruit trees in one of your meadows? In several years you will be able to harvest crops of fruit for yourself, for sale, or for barter to neighbors.

**30**  How about raising chickens for meat and eggs for the family, for sale, and for barter to people around you? You could be the chicken specialist. Maybe a neighbor specializes in beef cattle, rabbits, or goats, and you can swap a year's supply.

**31**  How about bee keeping? You have to like the sweet little critters. They are relatively easy to care for and, once again, you will have something to sell or barter, or place in the local grocery. Your county agent can advise you on what type of bees to raise and where on your property is the best location for the hives.

**32**  How about writing articles about country living? There are a number of farm and regional magazines that want their part of the country covered. Examples are *Country Journal* and *Yankee* for New England; *New West* for that area. Consider, too, the editor of the Sunday real estate section for any large metropolitan daily newspaper. The Sunday real estate sections have swung toward articles written by people who "have done it," who have moved to the country and liked it, have moved back citing reasons why, have remodeled a house, have raised livestock or crops, have gone into business in the country—you name it. If there is a country setting, you have a growing market.

**33**  How about writing for the local newspaper, if that is your talent? You might specialize in a field such as recipes, crafts, business, social activities. Do not expect to be paid a lot—you might get more by selling advertising space and classifieds—but it is a good way to get acquainted in a new community. After all, the principles of getting a story apply any-place.

You might think these suggestions came off the top of the author's head. Actually they recall the experiences of people the author read about or knew enough about to realize that somewhere, someone earned money doing these things in the country. It is up to you to adapt these suggestions and others you have undoubtedly encountered.

With all these projects, be sure your local zoning regulations allow you to use a part of your house for a professional office, or possibly a shop. If not, take a little space in the nearest village. You will get in the swim of community and local business affairs and kill two birds with one stone.

*Example: Growing Mushrooms in Your Cellar*

Josie Watkins, who lived in the country, loved mushrooms, particularly *Agaricus bisporus,* the tasty white mushroom. She found the mushrooms she bought at the supermarket did not have the crunchy, nutlike flavor, or the succulent pride that dwelt within the homegrown mushrooms she enjoyed at the home of a friend.

Josie decided to raise mushrooms in her own cellar as part of a research project in her adult education course at a State University extension center in her county. Her experiment produced such good results that she decided to write a book about the culture of mushrooms that included careful instruction as well as a lot of recipes. Within a few years she was known as a mushroom expert. She sells her excess production and the royalties on her book give her some extra money for an annual vacation.

## WHAT YOU GIVE UP WHEN SELF-EMPLOYED

Remember, when you set up a business for yourself, you will be self-employed. You will, with the help of your accountant, have to keep timely and appropriate books for tax purposes. And you will be giving up some of the benefits of working with a big company: regular salary whether you are healthy or sick, a better credit standing based on a steady income, health and hospital insurance, social security payments (paid, in part, by your company), automatic pension and retirement plans, and the accompanying prestige and intangible sense of belonging to a large corporation. Rest assured you will work harder when self-employed than when you were on the company payroll. But your time *will* be your own to enjoy as you see fit. Some people, usually those who are self-reliant, self-disciplined, goals oriented, and tired of the bickering and politics of a large company, aren't really fulfilled until they are on their own. You may be one of those. Perhaps you are one of those natural self-starters who is out of place in the frequent mediocrity of an organization's structure. Presumably you have some strong motivations for moving to the country, and being "on your own" may be one of them. Many people before you have made this decision and are glad today they did.

## SCALING DOWN YOUR INCOME NEEDS

If you shop for a country home in the right places you probably can set up and run a household on less income than you needed for your city dwelling, where you had to keep up certain amenities and perhaps compete with the neighbors. In the country you will live more casually, but as pointed out earlier, if you want to transplant your city lifestyle, you may need an extra car or two and other such comforts may cost as much or more. You can save a lot of money by using the move as an excuse to simplify your lifestyle and its costs. You are likely to eat at home more often, and with all the family. Is that bad? It will save money for you and perhaps relieve that nagging sense of guilt that you are not with the kids often enough.

You will find, in general, that living fancy in the country will set you off immediately as a city slicker. There are elegant country colonies for people with that taste and perhaps you would be happy in one of them. However, if you settle in a village where the single car dealer specializes in Fords, put a Ford in your future, a family model with few frills. Skip the sportscar or the luxury sedan if you want to fit in, more or less. If you want something a bit different and serviceable, and which will meet the approval of your new neighbors, try a four-wheel drive. Or maybe a pickup or panel truck. The most useful family car will be a station wagon or panel truck in which you can haul kids and furniture, produce, and machinery about.

When you move to the country you may want to change your idea of "one of the best" schools for the kids. Rural schools often have dedicated and marvelously talented teachers. The sensible parent sees to it that unfortunate gaps in a child's early education are supplemented by the parents themselves, or possibly by special summer instruction at music, art, or sport camps. A child growing up in the country, and possibly joining the Scouts or a local 4-H group, will get better, more solid, down-to-earth vocational training, accompanied by better physical and mental health than a counterpart growing up in the city. There will be plenty of time in college to pick up the specialization and cultural events that may be lacking in the country. There is one exception to these country-school advantages. For the really gifted child, a country school will probably not offer enough challenge in *any* practical way. A gifted child should be sent to a special, private boarding school for at least part of the early years. However, you would have the same problem if he or she went to a public school, or even to a private school in the city. You would have to get the child into an environment of his or her peers as quickly and painlessly as possible before the extra gifts stagnated through nonrecognition or misuse. The retarded or disabled child will have a hard time, too, for country school systems just haven't got budgets for that kind of specialization. They are geared, and probably always will be, to the average child, although some localities *are* taking advantage of recent grants for this kind of special education.

## WHY NOT FARMING?

Full-time farming is not recommended to the city dweller coming into the country for the first time. The very young can get used to it and grow into it. For a middle-aged businessperson it may be slow suicide. Farming requires so much physical energy, even with the labor-saving equipment and devices, that it could literally kill and almost certainly discourage the person used to a desk job.

The other obstacle is the know-how. No matter how many books you read, how closely you communicate with your county agent or Farm Extension Service, the practical wisdom of a farmer begins when, as the child of a farmer, he or she learns that dogs can bite if teased while they eat, bees can sting, and cows or horses can kick. Not to mention goats. And that milk sours, that feed can spoil and poison livestock, that hay can rot rather than cure if not cut and raked properly, and that the hay fork will not lift it into the hay mow if it is not pitched onto the hay wagon correctly. And there are all the practical ways to fix machinery that breaks down. Of course, people like plumbers and carpenters bring much-needed skills to the country. These trades or hobbies will serve in good stead when you take up farming. But if *you are not handy* with tools and machinery, think three times about buying a working farm with the intention of farming it yourself.

For the wealthy nonworking investor, a farm *may* prove to be a fine investment, provided you also have a paid manager, who probably gets some of the profits to do all the actual farming. The manager may be a young farmer, the child of a neighboring farmer who wants to put to use skills acquired from the Ag School of the State University. These schools *do* produce people who specialize in farm management and are willing to work someone else's farm during their early years, simply because the wealth is there to develop a mere farm into an agribusiness. If you can afford to think that big, you solve the problem of know-how and sweat labor—you simply buy it and count the additional expense as a tax deduction from your professional income or other investments. Your working farm will undoubtedly increase substantially in value as the acreage produces ever more profitable crops and/or livestock through the expert management of an agribusiness. Your manager and your accountant will tell you when and where investment credits can be taken, and when it may be wise to incorporate the farm as a separate business entity in order to preserve certain deductions. In the beginning stages of ownership with a professional manager, you may be operating at a loss while you improve the place.

Another alternative is to lease most of your fields and facilities to a neighbor who knows how to farm and wants more acres but does not want to buy them. You can do this on cost-and-profit sharing basis.

If you must get your hands into the soil, cultivate a kitchen garden of, say, 40 by 40 feet. Cultivate it intensively for your own needs and then, if the labor suits you and you get used to it, expand to the point where you sell or barter your specialities with neighbors who have specialities in something else. Out of the hundreds who dabble idealistically at farming, very few stay at it long enough to make a good living from the land as agribusiness people.

*Example: Wagon Trek, or Going to the Country the Hard Way*

The trek began on April 1, and the fools numbered 38. They left Toronto, Canada, on a 2,960-mile trek to Alberta in the West and were led by an enthusiastic actor who recruited the train on a TV talk show. More than 5,000 applicants were winnowed and sifted out until a determined group of pioneers were ready to set out for the promised homestead land in the Golden West *via covered wagon*. For the Leader had in his possession several prairie schooners he had been renting to film makers for western shots. The whole project seemed a promotion natural, a media event, and a way to settle on country property at the same time. There were even some attempts to sell advertising space on the tented vehicles.

The company of pioneers were typical city folks, tired of city ways and open to the idea of going west to strike it rich as beef barons or land speculators. One dreamer expected the winter weather—occasionally it sinks to 60° below zero—to aid her bronchitis. She was spurred by relatively cheap land prices of $15 to $50 per acre—on a homesteading basis—whereas in southern Ontario, where she formerly lived, a building lot 60 by 100 feet costs as much as $60,000. (In Alberta, land is available for homesteading but the homesteader must live in this province a full year before he or she can buy it.)

A group of four young men pooled their limited savings, bought a wagon, joined the train and figured they could buy cattle at about $37 a head, fatten them, and become rich. (The fact of the matter is that fortunes have been made in Alberta cattle, but calves usually cost $250 a head and a minimum herd of about 75 is needed to turn a profit.)

Two weeks out on the trail, with police escorts getting more and more skeptical, the trek averaged 7 miles a day; old-time wagon trains usually managed 20. Impromptu promotions and donations helped to keep the train moving and illusions bright in the face of adversity. When one earlier Alberta pioneer heard the train was on its way, she sent a warning about her experiences in dairying 500 miles north of Edmonton. "My cows' udders froze," she wrote as she explained the end of her own dream.

Although the endings for the 38 dreams are not known in detail, the moral of the story for country-property buyers is this: You are living in 1980, save yourself a lot of grief—buy, first of all, a quick round-trip plane ticket to reality and back. *Then* make your commitment to country property *if what you see pleases you.*

## YOUR SOCIAL LIFE IN THE COUNTRY

Don't expect a Welcome Wagon representative to call on you shortly after you move to the country. You may get a formal welcome from one or two neighbors, and then again you may not. By and large you will probably have to take the initiative in getting acquainted with the folks in your new community. In buying your place you have probably met the local banker who gave you a mortgage, a local realtor who found the place for you, and a local lawyer who guided you through the legal aspects of your purchase. Already you have met three of the most important people in your community. Chances are one or more of them holds a minor political office in the town or village.

You will soon meet other small businesspeople as you go to the drugstore, meat market, grocery, and dry goods store. Perhaps there is a barber shop or beauty parlor where you will run into everybody sooner or later. Both are great clearinghouses for local politics. Gossip and scandal, too. If you have children of school age, you will shortly become aware of the local Parents-Teachers Association. And there are church groups, various lodges, business organizations, veteran's groups, historical societies, amateur theater groups, and even adult education programs that may tie in with the public school system.

*Example: The Bandleader Who Kept a Prize-Winning Rural Band in Practice During the Summer*

In a small town of 2,580 there are only so many children who want to play the clarinet, and a bandleader is lucky to find anyone who will try the tuba. Yet one enterprising bandleader in a village at one end of a popular vacation lake worried about the players "losing their lip" and the musical skills acquired during long winter months of practice. So a summer band was organized and older members of the community and summer visitors were encouraged to join the young regulars—some of whom drove in after a busy day of farm work, haying, or filling their silos. Needless to say, the band won many local music contests and the young musicians got a training seldom encountered in a village so small.

Sometimes a neighboring town has the kind of group you want to join. Once you have a car—your wheels—the federal highway system can put you in touch with a branch or outpost of almost any conceivable group or cult. Simply ask the group you belong to now where the nearest available chapter is in the village in or near which you will live.

In all probability you will also find new groups, of an entirely different sort, that you can join in your new village. Perhaps you will take up bowling, or maybe sailing if there is a lake nearby. Through benefit bridge parties you will discover the bridge sharks in your midst, and if that is your game, you may have new partners and friends.

One of the ways to meet a lot of potential friends is to volunteer for a community activity, such as collecting for the Red Cross or the local United Appeal. It gives you a natural reason for meeting people systematically and introducing yourself. In smaller towns and villages, just about everyone gives something to these drives. Choose the one that most closely matches your previous experience. You will have a natural reason for doors to open for you.

By and large country people do not go heavily into social time-wasters such as cocktail parties. They are too busy with serious business and with hunting, fishing, farming, gardening, or child-rearing. That doesn't mean they don't drink, although there are remnant packets of temperance and "dry" counties throughout the South and Midwest. The type of chatter you hear at cocktail parties is more likely to be heard over coffee or tea at a church benefit such as a pancake supper in the basement of one of the village churches, or in the case of men, at the village tavern across the street from the feed store. Sometimes, during the summer, one of the men's service groups may put on a bratwurst-and-beer festival, or maybe a raccoon roast. There are probably just as many alcoholics per capita in the country as in the city, but the problem is not regarded as lightly as in the city where sociable alcoholism seems to be taken for granted. The country alcoholic faces a more solitary, more guilt-ridden existence, with less chance of a sympathetic outpost of the AA nearby.

Do not expect gourmet restaurants in the country; do not expect gourmet cooking from your neighbors. Expect, rather, a lot of good food, plainly prepared, but costing much less than in the city. Yes, you can still get a Friday fish fry for about $3, and in many communities these bargain family rates follow through the week with other specialties such as a chicken fry on Wednesday, shrimp fry on Mondays, spaghetti on Tuesdays. The restaurant does a specialty well, makes a lot of it, and the people come. Because the menu is thus simplified, the prices can be mighty attractive too.

## COUNTRY CLERGY AND CURMUDGEONS

Some of the most delightfully literate and eccentric people who ever lived in the country were the English village parsons who attached themselves to the local squire's household. The parson and his wife, in alliance with the squire's family, could be generally counted on to set the cultural level of a happy rural seat.

Depending how far into the country you go, you will probably find today that the village churches and the people who run them are still cultural leaders, as are people associated with the local school and members of the older families who have always taken a lead in village affairs.

If you are going to enjoy life in the country to the fullest, you will want to know these people. They will be able to tell you a lot about your area's history. Learn to listen. You will find they are more interested in telling you about themselves and their locale than they are in learning about the city and its more sophisticated ways. You will generally find, in fact, that the local natives feel they have little to learn from the city and its anxieties or discontents. In the country many of the same problems exist on a smaller scale, but the local people have learned to solve what can be solved and to live with what cannot be solved. They have done that for generations without government analyses, grants, handouts, or supervision from welfare workers. And they often act as though they intend to do the same in the future for as long as they are able.

No matter how enthusiastic you are about your new country life, you may find the local people somewhat chilly in receiving you. New Englanders project this feeling because of their traditional reserve and concern for minding one's own business, and their ingrained distrust of the outsider. With the greater mobility of people these days, however, it seems certain that younger generations will grow up with people who are less angular and forbidding than those you may have as neighbors now. *You* will have to deal with *today's* generation and, as an outsider, you will just have to take them as they are. They may be unreformed, unregenerate, unsophisticated, often uncouth by your standards, but then that is the country and no one particularly *invited you* to live there. You will be the outsider who has to learn to give way, compromise, and walk the extra mile. You may find a few people who will reciprocate, but do not count on it. If you keep your own fences and walls in order and raise your own family well, you will certainly gain respect and perhaps gradual affection.

## RURAL POLITICS

Before you prepare to run for town supervisor, live in the town for a few generations. Many of the farmers who live in your rural area will remain names you read about a few times in the local newspaper, usually at the time of weddings and deaths. Yet these "hidden" citizens frequently hold the votes that will swing the election. You will be a nonentity to them, too, unless you provide the community with responsible leadership in the accepted volunteer ways, joining various political organizations and campaigns. Donate your time and talent, if you are looking for future office, rather than money. Everyone likes to have money, in the country as well as in the city, but a helpful hand and mind in the country goes a longer way toward getting you elected than mere money. Many farmers are wealthy in land, but they do not have a great deal to spend on luxuries that city folks take for granted. They lead a simple life and do not wave their wealth around. Most are also careful about maintaining a good credit standing and certainly expect you to do the same. If you don't, you can expect most of the area to know about your delinquencies and not give you much sympathy—or help. If you fall into such a position, accept the fact that you have made yourself a poor risk and defective character in their eyes—and shape up. After loose financial behavior, or after anything else that is somewhat scandalous, do not expect to win in running for a public office. The whisperers will prove an insurmountable obstacle in most cases.

In the country you will find remnants of the conservative, Protestant work ethic that is hostile to liberal ideas of welfare, minimum wage, strong centralized government, in fact, hostile to any government at all. The modern agribusinessperson is a breed apart; frequently he or she is the child of a small farmer who grew big through good fortune and a lot of hard work. So the individualistic ideas have a certain power behind them, although agribusinesses must maintain a relationship, however tenuous, with the government in Washington, which is constantly legislating land-use laws and overseeing and regulating commodity prices.

It is probably a good idea to steer clear of rural politics until you and your family have lived there long enough to know the lay of the land. You will eventually learn why the Democrats may have the best barbecues but the Republicans generally get elected, whatever their platform. Or vice versa.

## GOVERNMENT AGENCIES THAT CAN HELP

If you plan to open a small business—be it a shop in the nearby village or a small roadside stand—state, general, and local agencies can be of help, usually at no cost; they are a service paid for by you and other taxpayers.

If you have an idea for selling the extra produce of your kitchen or market garden in a picturesque roadside stand, you might check the long-range development plans of your state highway department. They undoubtedly have projected likely traffic patterns, highway improvements, and will recommend where to place your stand in relation to the existing road. It may be due for a widening. You may be required to have a drive-off spur and parking place.

Also on the state level, the business development department can help you with marketing statistics, the number of people in your immediate area, their median income, whether your marketing area is growing or declining, and what kind of people are moving in or out.

You will find many states with an environmental control department and, of course, a tax department. All of these can answer questions for you, but probably not all at one time. You will have to go to one and then the other. Use the telephone first. See what each has to offer.

Perhaps in Washington the most useful agency will prove to be the Small Business Administration, and maybe the Bureau of the Census, which is part of the Commerce Department. Through one or the other you ought to be able to find statistics on how many businesses similar to the one you are planning are already in your part of the state, or how many stores of your kind there are per 100,000 people on a national average. Some of the population and demographic statistics can give you an idea of your potential success (see Appendix C for addresses and additional details).

Probably the most helpful single person in your county will be the county agent of the Agricultural Extension Service. The Service generally has in each county, at least in each *rural* county, a county agent, a home demonstration agent, and once in a while a county forester as well.

County agents, you may be sure, are in touch with the agricultural colleges and the research departments in your state. They act as channels from various government-supported agricultural projects to you. The county agent can introduce you to other people in the state and federal government hierarchy.

Even closer to home is the town clerk or town administrative officer, who can explain to you the local land-use and zoning regulations. You should also check out your local Chamber of Commerce, if there is one. Every now and then you will discover a town or a village that has a sense of community and that will make available all the help it possibly can to an enterprise that seems useful and fitting to the town's past, present, and future.

Never, never forget your neighbors as a source of information and advice. Particularly those who have had families in the area for generations. They probably have stories to tell of all sorts of enterprises that were tried and failed. The ones that succeeded, presumably are still around to give you an idea of what the town or immediate area seems noted for. Does it have spring water to bottle? Is it popular for winter skiing? Summer boating? Is it dairy country and would a dairy store do well near a major highway?

Also remember that the U.S. Department of Agriculture has, at your and other taxpayer's expense, produced a gigantic library of useful how-to information on more topics than you would ever want to know about. Define your interest and request a catalog covering these topics from the Division of Publications, Office of Information, Department of Agriculture, Washington, DC 20505. Very often your county agent will have some of the more applicable pamphlets on hand. And if you hear of a special study issued by the Department of Agriculture or the Department of Commerce, you might ask your representative in Congress to get you a free copy. As you know, the modern representative usually maintains a working office in the district. You don't have to call Washington to get questions answered or to request booklets. Just look up the constituent office in your local telephone book.

## KNOW YOUR TURF AND ITS RESOURCES

Just as when you live in the city, you sometimes pass up some of the country's most scenic attractions or best restaurants simply because you have not made a thorough check of the resources literally at your own back door. Perhaps it is a meat market with the Middle West's best bacon and sausages. Maybe it is a small factory that fills mail orders around the world for great cheddar cheese, even though you never tasted it because it is not offered at local stores.

One of the most delightful drives the author ever made was a leisurely car trip down U.S. Highway 1 along the Pacific Coast from San Francisco to Santa Barbara and then inland to a ranch near Santa Maria. The owner of the ranch had told us where to pause at various places along the way to get clams (Pismo Beach) and wine (a small vineyard that only sold locally, and from which you walked away with half-gallon jugs you were asked to return). Still another small farm specialized in mushrooms. The farmer usually had some put aside in plastic bags in a cool refrigerator and didn't mind at all if you poked about in the sheds to see how such tasty succulence could be produced from such a humble fungus. The centerpiece of the dinner that celebrated our arrival on the ranch was a fat, tender, roasted hen from the ranch's flock. The local Chablis flowed plentifully with clams on half shell, mushroom and lettuce salad, and "poulet et champignons à la crème." For dessert there were fresh garden strawberries and more cream from the local dairy. Needless to say, the food itself was memorable, but the fun in collecting it from up and down the coast was a good part of the enjoyment.

Try such a story on your country friends sometime and you can be sure they will come up with similar tales from other parts of the country. You simply have to know what is in your own backyard before reinventing the wheel or wearing yourself to a frazzle creating a gourmet's Eden. Any gourmet cook will tell you, by the way, that half the success is the *quality* of the ingredients. One of the reasons for the legendary renown of the food of Lyons in France is the incredible agricultural wealth of this region. Family and commercial cooks can easily put their hands on some of the world's finest quality in poultry, fruit, vegetables, and dairy products at their local markets. And it has been thus for centuries. The people in the heart of the Beaujolais region and the burghers of Lyons have always eaten well; they expect to eat well; a restaurant cannot succeed for long if it does not cater to this natural appetite. This is a fine example of taking advantage of the natural wealth on your doorstep.

Somehow the food resources of a territory come to mind first because you associate good food with country living. As noted before, there is always a gardening decision to make when you move in the country. How much time and effort will you spend gardening it? This is a highly individual decision, but it may be made easier by checking out first what others are already doing.

Quite aside from the vittles from vine, bush, stalk, and hoof or foot that you may grow or buy from others, you may also uncover some first-quality country inns and restaurants to which you can take guests and to which you can treat yourself on a special occasion.

By checking out the territory you will know which restaurant has a salad bar where the lettuce and tomatoes aren't threatened by cold, boiled asparagus. Or which serves those delicious french-fried onion rings at the Friday fish fry. Or where that world renowned fish restaurant is two counties away (you have to make reservation several days in advance). Or where you can dine on geese with noodles and take home some of the cook's currant preserves.

Other sources of supply you will want to identify are feed stores, supermarkets, hardware stores, plumber, electrician, carpenter, septic-system maintenance (for repairs and pump-outs), and veterinary services. The obvious place to look for these is in the Yellow classified section of your telephone book. If you do not have a telephone, it is worth getting a local directory simply for this kind of listing. If you are planning a major remodeling job and worry about the credibility of any of the craft or tradespeople you will employ, check them out with your local banker. Check also with neighbors. They often have relatives whom they will be glad to recommend, but such a biased reference can be a mixed blessing. It is always a good idea to get signed estimates before telling anyone to go ahead with a project.

You may also find that your country place is near a village where the decentralized State University system has a unit where night courses are given. Or perhaps there is a technical school in a nearby town. Such schools inevitably are the nuclei for cultural events such as music, drama, and painting exhibits, in addition to providing training in all these modes of expression. Sometimes these institutions attract an outstanding artist for a year's residency. Your local newspaper can keep you posted about these opportunities.

And that is another resource you will want to have coming in your mailbox regularly—you will want the local paper, which is probably a weekly, for all the local news of meetings, changes in regulations for use of the nearest dump, the services and fees of the nearest volunteer (or professional) fire department. Also get the paper of the county seat for political news and for an idea of what can be bought in the stores—the sales and seasonal specials. The county paper also lists court actions and local disputes on which you may have to vote or come to a decision.

Then take, too, the nearest metropolitan daily, although you may dispense with that if you have TV that gives you the metropolitan, statewide, national, and worldwide news you want. Just because TV does this in many ways better than newspapers, the newspapers have become increasingly oriented to the family and home, with special supplements on real estate, decorating, sports, and the like. Country folk think nothing of driving a hundred or two hundred miles for a day at a football game in the fall. The price of gas may curtail the frequency of such events, but probably will make them all the merrier as friends and families pile into a station wagon or pick-up truck with beer and barbecue, and have a tail-gate party in the stadium's parking lot. So long as you have wheels and don't mind using them, the resources of your turf are little short of endless.

*Example: The Dream of Country Living . . . and the Reality—An Old and Frequent Fable*

The poet Quintus Horatius Flaccus, known to classical scholars as Horace, found a rich patron, Maecenas, who saw to it that Horace had a farm in the country and a certain income on which to live. On his Sabine farm, Horace wrote some of the most memorable lines in praise of country living. But he had a keen sense of irony, too, and satirized more than one eager city wheeler-dealer who came to the country to lead a "perfect" life and to make a lot of money. The following lines update, in a loose adaptation or imitation, one of Horace's most famous satirical sketches. Horace himself enjoyed country living enormously and knew what to expect and not to expect from it. In the sketch below, Al Morrison, a Wall Street broker, talks of a friend who lives a pleasant country life. Al mixes some of his own uninformed enthusiasm with descriptions of his friend's life in the country—a life style Al tries out for himself.

## THE JOYS OF COUNTRY LIVING
after *Quintus Horatius Flaccus*
*circa 30 BC*

*That guy's really got it made!*
*It's something . . . that farm in Riverhead*

*That boat he has for fishing off Montauk*
*A whole world away from Wall Street!*

*He took over an old family homestead;*
*He tells me he now owns it free and clear.*

*Worries? Not a one! Bankers are up tight*
*About the next recession, lawyers still panicky*

*Over Watergate. Not him! He doesn't*
*Have to lunch with clients at the Midday Club*

*Or buy tickets from old Street pals*
*To some tacky testimonial dinner or ball.*

*No, he's happy planting his fields,*
*His potatoes, pole beans, corn, his squash;*

*Or keeping book on the milk his cows produce—*
*Beautiful, those sleek Holsteins grazing—*

*Or pruning his roses, harvesting the new shoots*
*Of asparagus, or breeding the fattest of his geese.*

*Come Fall, he loads his roadside stand*
*With hybrid pears, tomatoes ripened on the vine.*

*At dinner the family always drinks wine*
*Pressed from local grapes, a salute to life,*
*Those country acres, and their fertility.*

*I should have it so good! He can take a nap*
*In his garden hammock, or simply stretch out*
*On the patio's lounge chair; or even flat*
*On the manicured lawn.*

　　　　　　　　　　*That creek in the woods*
*Murmurs, the mourning doves in their nests,*
*High on the blue spruce, croon to him.*
*The trickling fountain in the rock garden*
*. . . it's enough to set up anyone for a snooze.*

*And when it snows or sleets, he hunts deer*
*In this woods, or maybe squirrels or rabbits in his fields.*

*Or even ducks in his swamp as they cross*
*The Sound in their migrations.*

　　　　　　　　　　　*And in season*
*He dines on lobster or striped bass fresh*
*From his boat at Montauk.*

　　　　　　　　　　　*In the midst of such life*
*It's easy to forget the pace and push of the city.*

*He's twice lucky. He was smart enough to marry*
*A good strong woman with common sense,*

*Who does her share of running that country place*
*And bringing up the kids. She doesn't mind*

*Chopping and carrying in wood for the fireplace*
*Or keeping dinner hot when he arrives late*

*And bushed from the cattle auction where he sells*
*His pure-bred heifers at fantastic profits;*

*Or when he must direct repairs on the milking machine*
*And soothe the swollen tempers of his "girls" in the barn!*

*There's that sweetheart, waiting, setting out cider*
*From last year's harvest of McIntosh . . .*

*Served with the neighbor's prized soft cheese*
*On rafts of toasted home-baked bread.*

*Such a fortunate fellow needs no oysters*
*Rockefeller at Lutece or Windows on the World,*
*No escargots from France, no caviar from the Caspian.*
*Nothing is more tasty than peaches picked*
*From one's own orchard, lettuce from one's*
*Own kitchen garden and tea from the blooms*
*Of one's own linden tree . . .*

         *Or a piglet*
*Barbecued, perhaps for a weekend picnic*
*With the cousins. Or a duckling rescued just*
*Last May from a weasel and roasted now,*
*With dressing of celery, wild rice and a subtle sauce*
*Of hickory nuts, butter, Chablis, and cream.*

*In the midst of such content, it does one good*
*To look out the French doors at the heifers*
*Hurrying to their barn and Herman, the hired man,*
*(Who has the hang, now, of the milking machine)*
*And has plowed his last circle of the field*
*With the new tractor . . .*

        *In its air-cooled cockpit*
*The man rolls along to the barn and the milking chores.*

*It's pure pleasure, too, watching the sexy,*
*Live-in maids polish the silver heirlooms,*
*Dust ancestral oils, and the Chippendale chairs.''*

*Al Morrison, the well-known broker,*
*Said this in the bar of the Lawyers' Club.*

*He rattled on about his retirement and how*
*He had bought a working dairy farm*
*Like the one of his friend whose pleasures he was counting.*

*To buy the farm, Al sold out his shares*
*And his seat on the Stock Exchange, just before*
*Memorial Day.*

        *By the Fourth of July*
*He had returned, sun burned, blistered,*
*Looking for a chiropractor to put his back into whack*
*And for a lawyer to separate him from a bitter wife.*

*"I gave it a try," Al said. "I really did.*
*But an eager German beaver wanted to trade*
*This great Cezanne: 'Still Life with Peaches.'*

*I checked with Sotheby's on the painting's worth.*
*It looks like I'll make a bundle on the deal.*

*Under the circumstances," he winced in pain,*
*"It was an offer only a fool could afford to refuse."*

# Chapter Three

# The Current
# Land Boom in
# the United States

Owners of country property, no matter what their needs or wants in pleasure and profit, have a major economic trend working for them. Since World War II and particularly during the past ten years, the United States has enjoyed a major boom in land values. The reasons for the boom are many and interrelated and should continue, for the most part and in varying degrees, for the remainder of the century. Country-property enthusiasts should derive much support from this dynamic trend. It makes up for many an error in timing, for makeshift financing, and for reverses in other business activities.

Yet, within this general trend there are eddies and swirls which have caused variations in separate parts of the country and which translate into greater or lesser profits. You will profit most if you learn and apply all the economic factors at work. And there are *many* factors that affect the value of U.S. land.

## TREND UPWARD IN U.S. FARMLAND PRICES

As a beginning, consider the increase, as shown in Table 3-1, in the value of a typical acre of U.S. farmland since 1910. The U.S. Department of Agriculture has been keeping track of acreage prices for about 60 years now, and with the exception of one or two minor dips during the years of the Great Depression, farmland has shown continuing gains year after year, but particularly so during the last decade.

**Table 3-1** Average Value of U.S.
FarmLand Since 1910 (dollars per acre)

| | | | | | |
|------|------|------|-----|------|-----|
| 1910 | $40 | 1935 | 32 | 1960 | 116 |
| 1911 | 41 | 1936 | 32 | 1961 | 118 |
| 1912 | 42 | 1937 | 33 | 1962 | 124 |
| 1913 | 43 | 1938 | 33 | 1963 | 130 |
| 1914 | 44 | 1939 | 32 | 1964 | 138 |
| | | | | | |
| 1915 | 43 | 1940 | 32 | 1965 | 146 |
| 1916 | 46 | 1941 | 32 | 1966 | 158 |
| 1917 | 49 | 1942 | 34 | 1967 | 168 |
| 1918 | 53 | 1943 | 38 | 1968 | 179 |
| 1919 | 58 | 1944 | 43 | 1969 | 188 |
| | | | | | |
| 1920 | 69 | 1945 | 47 | 1970 | 195 |
| 1921 | 65 | 1946 | 53 | 1971 | 202 |
| 1922 | 57 | 1947 | 60 | 1972 | 218 |
| 1923 | 56 | 1948 | 64 | 1973 | 245 |
| 1924 | 54 | 1949 | 66 | 1974 | 303 |
| | | | | | |
| 1925 | 54 | 1950 | 65 | 1975 | 343 |
| 1926 | 52 | 1951 | 75 | 1976 | 390 |
| 1927 | 50 | 1952 | 82 | 1977 | 448 |
| 1928 | 49 | 1953 | 83 | 1978 | 488 |
| 1929 | 49 | 1954 | 82 | 1979 | 559 |
| | | | | | |
| 1930 | 49 | 1955 | 85 | | |
| 1931 | 44 | 1956 | 91 | | |
| 1932 | 37 | 1957 | 97 | | |
| 1933 | 30 | 1958 | 103 | | |
| 1934 | 31 | 1959 | 111 | | |

*Source:* U.S. Department of Agriculture.

## WORLD INFLATIONARY PATTERNS

Part of this increase stems from worldwide inflation patterns. Prices for most commodities have gone up as national governments tried to sustain the growth patterns achieved by recovery from World War II and the lesser wars that followed it, particularly the Korean war in the early fifties, the Vietnam war in the sixties, and the periodic Arab-Israeli flare-ups that resulted in the world-shaking rise since 1973 in the price of oil. For an industrialized civilization dependent on cheap energy for profits, the oil price hike couldn't have come at a more embarrassing time. But come it did, and it is a tribute to the underlying strength of the industrialized United States and other countries that between 1973 and 1975 they managed to absorb the shock and endure the worst recession since the Great

Depression of the 1930s. The lasting price of the struggle, unfortunately, has been inflation of a magnitude that has occurred before in world history, although not as often as one might imagine, and then always as a result of a major change in world outlook.

One of these periods occurred during the Renaissance and Reformation when exploration opened up new horizons. Gold and silver from the New World buoyed a great expansion in consciousness of spirit as well as in material goods. Another inflationary period occurred at the time of the Industrial Revolution, which raised the curtain to wealth from the machine and all of its ways of generating and transferring energy. In the postindustrial world following the World War II and its minor echoes, the developing nations of the third world have begun to realize the value of their raw materials and commodities for industrialized countries committed to an ever-higher standard of living and social welfare. Also contributing to this inflation has been the arms race and the competition to explore and obtain benefits from outer space. The fabulous wealth that a world civilization will eventually exploit derives from solar energy and space colonization. This will undoubtedly fuel another inflation, making the present one but a prelude to what will happen in the early twenty-first century.

In between these major periods, prices were relatively stable. This may seem strange to a generation that has accepted mild inflation as built into all its family decisions, savings, profits on investments, and style of living.

## Demographics—Trend to Urbanization Reversed

There are always undercurrents and surface currents in any wave. The major trend in the growth of the population of the United States has similar cross patterns. During the decade 1960 to 1970, the U.S. census figures show a substantial gain in the number of people who live in cities and a slight loss in the number of people who live in rural areas. That trend has now been reversed, as confirmed by interim census reports.

Figures 3-1 and 3-2 will give you an idea of where the gains and losses were most extreme. This will suggest which areas to avoid (those where people are leaving) and which are more attractive (those where people are arriving). People throughout history, have been notorious for their capacity of voting with their feet. They migrate habitually to greener, freer pastures. In the United States this was encouraged with homesteading provisions that attracted pioneers who settled in the West. Today, when one generation returns to the country, some of its offspring will trek back to the city, or sometimes maintain residences in both places. Thus country cousins become city cousins and reverse positions or, if financially able,

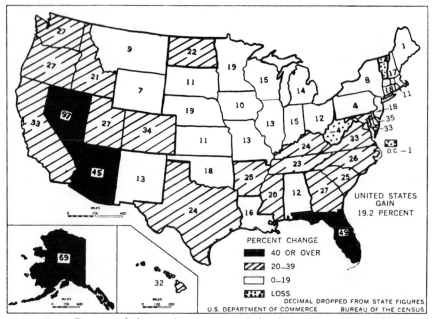

**Figure 3-1** Percent of change in urban population by states: 1960–1970.

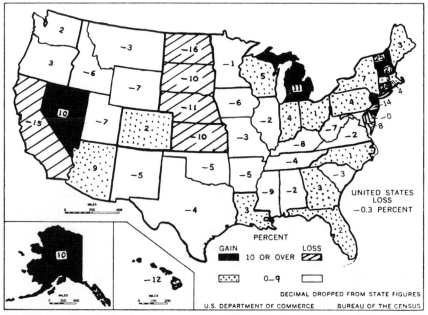

**Figure 3-2** Percent of change in rural population by states: 1960–1970.

play the game from both positions and then perhaps make a final choice when time comes for retirement. It is altogether likely—and often hoped for in vain—that the child will take over an old family home and thus continue a nexus of nostalgia for succeeding generations. Frequently this turns out to be the country place.

Today the long trend to mass migration from country to city that is still evident in the 1970 census figures has begun to reverse as employment opportunities and the chance to make a better living have opened up in rural California, in Nevada, Arizona, and Washington, in the Northeastern states (particularly in Vermont and New Hampshire), in Florida, in Alaska, and in some Southern states. *Urban* population also soared in Alaska (as a result of the discovery of oil there), Florida, and Arizona, where large retirement colonies have sprung up in the past twenty years.

The maps, with their blocks of shading, tend to oversimplify what has happened in each state: sometimes only a small area of any state became attractive to a group of the U.S. population.

One of the curious results of the new "greening" of the United States has been the suburbanization of the country. Where development encouraged large numbers of people to leave the city, they often moved not so much to the country as to a citified enclave in the country where the usual suburban services of water, sewage disposal, and recreation facilities

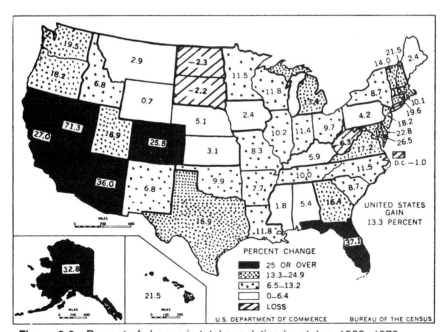

**Figure 3-3**  Percent of change in total population by states: 1960–1970.

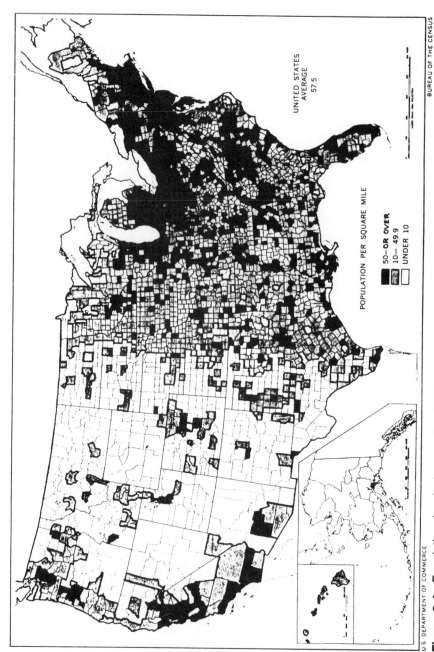

U.S. DEPARTMENT OF COMMERCE

BUREAU OF THE CENSUS

**Figure 3-4** Population density by counties: 1970.

were created at the same time the houses were built. Other country villages near urban areas have gradually brought in these improvements at considerable expense and have, in effect, become satellite sleeping suburbs of the city. Because of these different reasons for gains and losses in state populations, the buyer of country property has to investigate each situation to determine its continuing growth potential, climate variations, and all the factors that can affect pleasure in living or return on investment.

Figures 3-1 and 3-2 show where both city and urban growth has been most vigorous. Figure 3-3 shows the percent of change in rural population by states. Figure 3-4 shows where population is most dense. This may give you a clue toward pin-pointing where land values have increased the most and where, if the trends continue, land values will continue their ascent to the end of the century. In general, country-property values increased most strikingly where there were open spaces—attractive country residential potential—in the vicinity of densely populated urban areas. The population density by counties map (Figure 3-4) shows you some of these less densely populated counties (lighter shading) near the densely populated areas (darker shading). If this sort of analysis intrigues you, you can order the original, larger maps of this kind in colors from the U.S. Department of Commerce (see Appendix C for details).

Interim figures released by the Census Bureau since the 1970 Census indicate that since 1970 a million more Americans have moved to rural communities than have moved away from them, a strengthening reversal of the trend from previous decades.

## Historical Dreams of Land Ownership

Ownership of land has persisted as a part of the American dream and psyche. If some immigrants who came to the United States expecting to find the streets paved with gold were disappointed, most stayed, and in a generation or two made fortunes buying and holding the real estate that lay on either side of the city streets and country roads. It is part of the economic history of the United States that some of the earliest and largest fortunes were made through land ownership.

Early colonists were often enticed to a wilderness with the promise of land if they organized and financed a group of settlers. In return for services rendered and for adding lands to a European government's control, the settlers got their parcels free or they simply went westward beyond the settled boundaries and claimed their own land.

This form of land lure for pioneering and settling was institutionalized in 1862 with the passage of the Homestead Act, which made land ownership a reality for millions by giving every U.S. citizen over the age of 21 the right to claim 160 acres of public land and to acquire a deed to that land if it was farmed and a house built on it within a period of five years. A total of 270 million acres was settled this way. This represents, in one dramatic estimate, enough farms to make a strip of land 125 miles wide all the way from Boston to San Francisco. Land grants were also given railroads to encourage them to build the transcontinental rails of steel that bound the nation together.

Homesteading reached a peak in about 1913 when 11 million acres were claimed. But as late as 1937 two million acres were claimed under the Homestead Law. Thereafter, the amount of workable land diminished. This law has now been repealed for all states except Alaska, where it is only on the books in theory. In practice, few tracts are available because of the tangle of local claims and regulations.

Some people believe that there are still large tracts of public land available (there are) for homesteading (there are not—the law has been repealed). Thousands of letters pour into the Bureau of Land Management each year asking for free land. Advertising that you see offering government lands for very little money are usually legitimate, but you get what you pay for—very little. Yet many people buy this "waste" land.

When the Nevada legislature recently made a start toward special homesteading legislation that would open land to settling, so many people applied that the state officials declared a moratorium on further filings. They say frankly that the land offered is so marginal that estimated costs for development run into thousands of dollars per homestead.

With these free or inexpensive sources very limited, the market has been invaded by speculators who buy to sell at a profit a few years later. Nonetheless, the United States is not running out of farmland, even though about half a million acres of the cropland base of 385 million acres is lost to urbanization each year.

"The real threat to our agricultural lands doesn't come from individuals, who are usually just as happy to own a piece of land that's wooded or hilly; it comes from the haphazard expansion of metropolitan areas over the countryside," says Robert Otte of the National Resource Economics Division of the Department of Agriculture.

Norman McCain, president of United Farm Agency, a real estate company based in Kansas City, Missouri, that specializes in rural property and has sales offices in most states, says that today's rural land buyer is usually someone looking for woodland. "The important attraction is privacy. Most people seek it out by surrounding themselves with trees," he explains.

A competitor of United Farm is Strout Realty, a nationwide service based in Springfield, Missouri, that has catered to city residents who want to buy a place in the country. "What has changed over the years," says

Strout's president, D. R. Young, "is the amount of acreage people can afford. Buyers who 20 years ago wanted 100 acres will now settle for 20, which costs as much as the 100 acres once did. Also they're willing to travel a lot farther. It's not unusual for people to buy a piece of land that's five to six hours' driving time away."

In general, the more remote that comparable land is from a city, the lower is its price per acre. And buyers do not mind traveling long distances to their dream place in the country. Or even flying to it.

Also, in spite of steadily increasing prices and an energy crisis, the United States remains a place where a citizen can still find a few affordable acres to own. Today, the urge to own has never been stronger. Sometimes these dreams, however, manipulated by sellers of land, can become empty illusions.

Enticing potential buyers with free dinners and even free air trips and weekend stays on the site, supersalespeople trade on the dreams of potential buyers, who eventually buy a part of paradise that turns out to be a small parcel of Arizona desert or a piece of Florida swamp at inflated prices.

The recession of 1974 slowed down this type of sale, and a Federal Trade Commission crackdown on violations of the 1968 Interstate Land Sales Act also ended some of the most flagrant abuses. Many states, in the wake of federal leadership, toughened their procedures for reviewing the operations of land companies that sold in their states.

## THE NEW BOOM BUILDING

Expert economists say again and again that we are headed for a last, great land boom in the United States, a boom larger than any of the many that have preceded it. The recent behavior of well-chosen land—rising in value on the average of 15 percent a year—suggests the boom is in its early stages already.

There are sound reasons why this boom will be both large and sustained: (1) the war babies are at the nesting age, (2) environmental controls and zoning regulations regulate the use of land and make it more expensive to develop and improve, thus forcing up its price and putting a premium on its value, (3) the *amount* of energy input for building a house and its components has increased, and so has the *price* of energy, and (4) the resulting demand, relative to a modest supply of new housing at ever higher prices, has fueled the fires of inflation, and in the process has made people realize that their own home is one of the best shelters against inflation they can have.

## THE WAR BABY BOOM

As a result of the explosive burst of babies born in the 1940s and 1950s, the demands for housing is up sharply. These are the babies who fell like an avalanche on the U.S. secondary school system and then on the colleges in the 1960s, causing, in part, campus unrest as they sought a new world for themselves. Typically, their parents, emerging from the war years, left the cities and moved to suburbia, or sometimes even a bit further. Now *their* progeny are moving farther out, and because it was typical for families in the 1940s and 1950s to have four children, there are that many more people who have reached the home-buying age looking for houses now. The pinch caused by the severe recession of 1973–1974 and the ensuing inflation has deterred people, for a time, from buying the traditional, detached single-family home. Just as the rising cost of living has encouraged both husband and wife to work, it has allowed them to innovate in their choice of housing. Condominiums and mobile homes, plus duplexes, triplexes, and quadruplexes, because they offer economies in construction, have been attractive to younger couples and singles willing to experiment. In many places, these same people with willing and able hands have also spurred the "renovate-an-old-house" boom.

## ENVIRONMENTAL AND SPECULATION CONTROLS

Land use will never be the same in the United States since the environmental movement of the 1960s left its imprint on national laws and on regulations of federal bureaus. Laws have been passed by states, townships, and villages that often turn out to be obstacles to the land buyer out for a quick profit. In fact, states such as Vermont have passed laws that deliberately inhibit profit from dealings in Vermont land. And the state of Wisconsin taxes capital gains on any Wisconsin land sold at a profit, regardless of where the owner may reside and pay in other taxes. Some states reciprocate in these matters, so that a person does not, in effect, pay two state taxes on the same capital gain. In the case of Wisconsin, the gain cannot be prorated back or forward, and the owner-seller who does not know of this tax will be charged interest from the tax year of sale until the debt is paid in full, regardless of when the state notifies the tax payer that such a tax is due.

Thus it is important to know the local zoning regulations, and the ecological and environmental regulations, as well as the tax laws of the state and locality in which you intend to buy. Ignorance of the law is no excuse. You may get some sympathy, but no forgiveness.

Recently there have been frequent charges of elitism in some of these controls. In some enclaves of the very rich, zoning laws are passed setting the minimum size of building lots at one and two acres—or sometimes more than that—to build a house. Needless to say, this is well beyond the reach of most people in the United States. In other cases towns and villages come to a point of feeling "taken over" by outsiders and find their hospitality about exhausted. Their sewers, water supplies, school systems, and fire and police departments suddenly have to handle two and three times as many people as they were originally designed to serve. It would seem natural that the natives might finally protest. And they *do,* by passing local laws restricting additional growth severely or by adopting a no-growth policy that, in effect, makes the existing single-family home with its remodeling possibilities about the only shelter available on the market. This action puts a price premium on existing homes in these desirable and restricted localities.

Sooner or later such local restrictions may be tested in a court case, and the trend toward limited or no growth may be challenged as unconstitutional. The kicker in the argument will prove, however, to be the demonstrable fact that there is plenty of inexpensive land *elsewhere,* even though it does not have the amenities of the land so closely regulated. Unfortunately, it is not as desirable either in the eyes of potential buyers.

For it is a curious fact that the United States is by no means running out of land, and if people would only get interested in remote tracts and build entirely new towns in the desert or on distant meadows or plains, the various price pressures caused by clotting together where the population already is dense might be alleviated. The energy crisis, however, works against such a dispersal at present. Gradual development of solar energy will reopen the possibilities.

Perhaps foreign investors see something in U.S. rural land that U.S. citizens have passed by. They see it as investment potential, whether it is farmed or not. They know there will come a time when almost all the arable land in the world will be needed to feed an increasing population. They also know that the United States is a nation that respects the right to own property, and that it will probably protect the personal and financial values of ownership just as it has in the past. In other countries there is not this marvelous access to the land. In Austria, for example, foreigners cannot own land (although they can lease it). Even in the state of Hawaii, huge tracts of land are in the hands of a few private owners who lease smaller lots to a growing population. Now the land has become so valuable and the raising of lease fees has become so controversial that the laws have been changed to encourage the large owners to sell off their land gradually to present tenants. Many of the most avid buyers of Hawaiian land have been Japanese from the crowded Orient and sun-hungry Canadians from the western reaches of the North American continent.

## FAMILY FORMATION SUPPORTS PRESENT BOOM

In past booms, in Florida, Arizona, and California, for example, people surged to warmer climates. Earlier they had been attracted to the West because free land was available via the homesteading process. Or they were immigrants from Europe looking for opportunity. Or they sought wealth in the California gold fields or the Colorado silver mines.

The current land boom is different in its motivation. It is less pioneering and more investment oriented. No more land is available for homesteading. Snowbirds who want to stay permanently already have their favorite place in the sun. The latest natural resource boom bulged the population in Alaska, still the nation's ice-box and still unattractive for permanent settlement, except for the most hearty and adventuresome. The current land boom, quite aside from the lure of the country, has its base in the population surge following World War II. While it is true that the present birth rate is low, the number of family formations has never been higher. This reflects the high birth rate of the 1940s and 1950s. These births are the key to the surging demand for new houses and for the higher prices received for existing homes as they come to the market. Young couples in their twenties and thirties have traditionally been the largest single source of demand for housing. They have been the tide on which the housing industry floats. Regional waves may flow in somewhat different directions depending on additional motivating factors.

Those prolific households of the 1940s and 1950s have produced the young people who are now beginning to form their own households and, in doing so, will generate a housing and land boom unprecedented in U.S. history. It is simply a matter of the number of households in this crucial age group. The number of Americans aged 25 to 34 will increase in coming years by about 40 percent compared with the same number of people that age during the 1960s. Thus there is a strong tide flowing into housing, and because of the shortage of desirable existing homes, new houses *must be built.* That means buying land as a first step, and either developing it or dividing it into smaller lots on which the buyers will build.

## THE FINANCIAL BRAKES ON HOUSING

Housing starts and sales have always been bellwethers of the economy. They tend to dip at the start of an economic turn-down and are often the first major indicator to turn up from the trough of a correction.

Unfortunately, in the past this has often been a boom-and-bust situation and made the housing construction industry one of feast or famine. In the past, whenever an economic boom heated up and interest rates were allowed to surge upward by the Federal Reserve Board, the interest ceiling put on savings deposits by Regulation Q caused a slowdown in the rate of savings formation in the institutions that traditionally supply the bulk of the mortgage money for private residential housing. Not only did savings and loan associations have to raise mortgage rates in order to cover the increased amount of the money *they* had to borrow, they often also had to curtail sharply the amount of money they could supply to applicants. This meant a decline in new mortgages and often a drastic brake on housing construction and sales.

In 1978 the Federal Reserve experimented with a six-month savings certificate ($10,000 minimum) that savings and loan associations could offer to savers at a rate pegged a fraction of a point higher than six-month Treasury bills. This enabled thrift institutions to offer an alternative investment into which funds could flow when T-bills offered a good bit more than traditional savings rates on short-term investments. During less than a year of such offering, more than $100 billion flowed into these certificates. They effectively kept the windows open at the savings institutions, and they sustained the housing boom to the point where the Fed felt it required a correction. It revised the terms of the offer in March 1979; six-month savings certificates could no longer pay the interest rate differential if Treasury bills rose above 8.75 percent. Nor could savings and loan associations pay compound interest. This made the certificates less attractive and caused some money to flow elsewhere, thus cooling the housing market a bit. Because this applied the brake to housing in a more gradual way, the boom did not lurch to a sudden stop and cause consternation and dislocation, and suddenly shut out the thousands of young families who needed shelter but could not get financing that was normally available in another part of the economic cycle. This tinkering with interest rates will continue to affect the cost of housing and may increase the emphasis on timing in buying a house. In actuality, the component costs of a house have been such an overriding factor that the increased cost of a mortgage is no longer the greatest hindrance to buying a house. The whole bundle is a burden, and the mortgage rate, which can always be refinanced later when rates *may* be lower and money more available, is not the decisive factor in that bundle.

## THE TUG OF THE FUTURE

It was expected that a total of 17 million new houses, apartments, and mobile homes would be needed in the United States between 1975 and

**Table 3-2** Estimated Housing Needs for the 1970s (in thousands)

|  | Net increase in U.S. families | Total annual demand for new housing | Total new housing units |
|---|---|---|---|
| 1970 | 1,222 | 2,160 | 1,864 |
| 1975 | 1,430 | 2,551 | 2,725 |
| 1976 | 1,478 | 2,640 | 2,775 |
| 1977 | 1,538 | 2,720 | 2,825 |
| 1978 | 1,480 | 2,691 | 2,875 |
| 1979 | 1,450 | 2,697 | 2,920 |
| 1980 | 1,430 | 2,687 | 2,950 |

*Source:* Joint Center for Urban Studies.

1980 to keep up with the rise in demand for housing. That is an average of more than 2.8 million new housing units a year. And frankly, it was more housing needed each year than had *ever* been built. The top housing volume during the housing boom of the 1950s was about 2 million new houses, which were built in 1955.

Table 3-2 shows the projected estimated housing needs for U.S. families and the shortfall in new housing. Because the demand is not being met, the new households are competing for existing houses and they are also seeking new forms of housing that have not hitherto been available to young families. The demand carries over and is expected to remain strong well into the next decades.

## THE PRESENT DECLINING BIRTH RATE

The 1970s saw the emergence of another demographic trend that has affected the kind of family home sought today and will affect the number of homes sought by the next generation. The United States, unless the trend in birth rates unexpectedly reverses itself, seems headed for zero population growth about the year 2040. Thus, the great present population tide could gradually lose much of its surge.

Long before that, however, the land boom now aborning will probably taper off to a high plateau because of other factors that will tend to deflate moderately the prices of land. First and most important among these will be the growing realization that there is plenty of land available in the United States for farming and for residential living, provided people can develop it and are willing to live at a considerable distance from large cities. This is part of the greening process of the United States, in which new towns and new developments sprout as satellites of major urban areas, but at a considerable distance from them. The development of decentralized solar energy systems will encourage this movement. Rapid mass transportation will bridge the distance, supposedly, and a more civilized life may be possible as population density tends to decrease in the major urban areas. Population *losses* in New York City and other major urban centers in recent years indicate that this decentralization has already begun on a small scale. This spreading out of a mature population will modestly benefit the demand and value of contry property.

## SPREADING OUT THE POPULATION

Donating land to various conservancy projects, deeding it to towns and villages as a permanent recreation area, or placing blanket restrictions on it has the net effect of driving developers and individual buyers further afield, or even into nearby states where restrictions are not yet so stringent. This also spreads out the population, moderating the prices of heavily restricted land and driving up the prices of land that is not yet restricted. In the long run, the trend is toward more or less stable land prices in relation to similar opportunities throughout the country as this evening-out process continues for several more decades. The great mobility of people in the United States will have asserted and spent itself, and an aging and retiring segment of the population will put down roots in its chosen sections of the United States. The battles of certain areas about zoning and about discrimination by one elite of another will have smoothed out and rights will have been defined. Presumably, technology and research will have made large areas of land habitable that were not habitable before. Research and technology may help us colonize space, and at the same time, teach us how to coax shelter and nourishment from older and nearer environments on Earth.

## CHANGED LIVING PATTERNS

Although the number of households being formed has moved sharply upward, as previously noted, the number of children being born per couple has declined. That usually means fewer bedrooms per house and possibly more family living space, since square footage per dwelling, on average, has increased.

The following figures, compiled by the National Association of Builders, show that the average home built in 1972 had 1,555 square feet,

**Table 3-3** Changes in Physical Characteristics of New Housing

|  | 1972 | 1977 |
|---|---|---|
| Houses with air conditioning | 43% | 54% |
| Housing with two or more bathrooms | 53% | 69% |
| Houses with one or more fireplaces | 38% | 61% |
| Houses with full or partial basements | 37% | 44% |
| Houses with a garage | 61% | 73% |
| Houses using electricity to heat | 36% | 50% |
| Houses with 1,600 square feet of floor area or more | 38% | 51% |

*Source:* U.S. Department of Commerce.

whereas one built in 1977 had 1,720 square feet. Other major trends in physical characteristics of new housing during the 1972–1977 period, revealed by government statistics, are shown in Table 3-3.

During the year 1978 total housing starts reached the 2-million unit level for the second consecutive year, which made it the second most

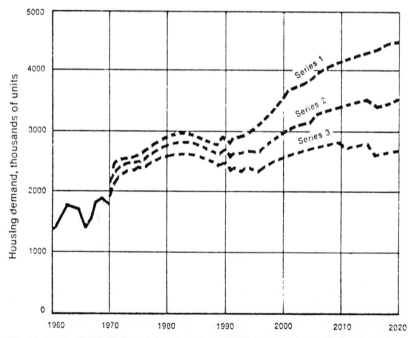

**Figure 3-5** Total demand for housing, 1960–1970, with projections to 2020. *Note: The above figures are based on the U.S. Bureau of the Census low, medium and high assumptions of the birthrate. (Source: National Association of Home Builders.)*

productive year for single-family home builders. Single-family home starts finished in 1978 at a total of 1.43 million, down about 20,000 units from the record set in 1977. There were about 586,000 apartment and condominium units started in 1978, including about 128,000 federally subsidized multifamily units.

Note that the total demand for housing, based on three different assumptions for the U.S. birth rate as shown in Figure 3-5, runs consistently higher than 2 million units a year. Demand strongly exceeds apparent supply.

## SHIFT FROM SINGLE-FAMILY HOMES TO CLUSTER HOUSING

Since 1971 the typical American family has had two children rather than the three or more which previously was the norm. In the first six months of 1971, the U.S. birth rate dropped to its lowest level in history, a level 10 percent lower than during the years of the depression. Although it is very difficult to predict how long this low level of childbearing will continue, its effect is being felt in housing construction, where three rather than four bedrooms for a family house are now the norm. Houses are tending to get more compact. Because they require less land but offer the latest facilities, so-called townhouses, garden apartments, and multifamily housing has become popular. In recent years the townhouse has made up as much as 15 to 20 percent of all new housing. In the country and suburban areas, the townhouse occurs in blocks or in clusters with green space around. Thus, though it relates to a city ancestor—the one-family row houses built as early as the colonial period in Boston, New York, and Philadelphia—it has adapted the building economics to a site in the country.

In the booming 1950s, the traditional one-family house on its own private lot accounted for roughly 90 percent of all new housing built and sold each year in the United States. Since then its share of the market has been falling. In 1970 only about 40 percent of all new units built each year were traditional one-family houses.

The great era of the traditional one-family house on its own lot, commonplace in previous decades, has all but ended as a dominant way of life in the United States. Exceptions continue, of course, among the wealthy who can afford the extra land for the sake of privacy, and for people who live in small towns or rural areas where land can still be obtained at relatively low prices. For potential buyers of single-family homes, therefore, the country still offers the lure of land at relatively bargain rates.

Suburban land, however, has climbed so strongly in value that it accounts today for about a quarter of the selling price of the typical new house. A new house priced at $80,000 would break down to roughly $20,000 for the lot and $60,000 for the house. In 1960, land usually made up only about 12 percent of the cost.

## THE GROWING POPULARITY OF MOBILE HOMES

One of the most popular alternatives to detached, single-family homes of the traditional sort is the mobile home, mass produced at a factory and delivered on a flatbed truck or on its own wheels, and then placed, usually permanently, on a foundation in a mobile-home park. Mobile homes, to an extent, solve the cost problem for couples willing to live in fairly cramped space. Because of the attractive price, a mobile home is often the choice of retired couples or single persons.

Another attractive feature of the mobile home is its gadgetry, and the fact that it arrives complete and ready for relatively quick assembly and positioning by a crew sent by the manufacturer. The owner can then move right in. In many states, a mobile home is still treated as a vehicle and is not taxed as real estate. Typically the owner of the vehicle leases space in a mobile-home park (which *is* taxed for its land ownership) and thus pays real estate taxes indirectly through monthly payment on the lease.

Although most mobile homes leave something to be desired in exterior appearance—they look for the most part like metal shoeboxes or perhaps a metal farm shed with windows and doors—their interiors can suggest a surprising sense of style. At once compact and neat, they often have luxurious appointments. They cost anywhere from $10,000 to over $100,000. The most expensive installations usually are two or more units on a single foundation. This gives much more room and allows for interesting variations such as private patios, atriums, and greenhouses, and all the luxuries of lavish ranch-style living.

Annual sales passed the 400,000 units mark as early as 1970 and are approximately 600,000 today. By the middle of the 1970s about five million U.S. families were living in mobile homes. Half of these were set permanently on private land, such as a lot; the other half were located in mobile-home communities or parks, with densities ranging from about six to twelve units per acre. When you consider that you can buy a well-appointed, fully-equipped, three-bedroom unit with central air conditioning for as little as $15,000 (land not included), you must realize that, compared to the median price of over $60,000 for a single-family detached home (with lot), the mobile home offers a distinct bargain.

## THE GROWING POPULARITY OF CONDOMINIUMS

Another alternative to single-family housing is the condominium in all its variations. A condominium, as its name suggests (con meaning *with* and dominium meaning ownership) is housing shared with others. It may be in a high-rise building indistinguishable, except in ownership and financing, from a rental apartment building. It may be a row of a dozen connected living units in the country. It may be four living units built on the same foundation and clustered graciously in carefully landscaped acreage. In most condominium developments, you own your own unit outright in fee simple and you share ownership and maintenance costs in public spaces and green woods with others. You may also share ownership of the recreational facilities and the land on which the additional facilities are built. Some of the pleasures and pitfalls of condominium living are outlined in Chapter 9 of this book.

Right now, you should know that federal housing authorities predict that by 1990 at least 50 percent of the nation's population will be living in multifamily complexes of one kind or another.

When you own a condominium, you and your family may very well own a new and more leisurely way of life emphasizing recreation and freedom from home maintenance tasks. The monthly maintenance fee, collected from each resident, provides professional maintenance and repairs for all systems and problems that develop *outside* your four walls, and this includes lawns and landscaping. You may want them to help you *inside* your four walls, too, at your personal expense; they are there—a trained staff of capable plumbers, electricians, carpenters, painters, and other maintenance people.

Most condominiums, known more familiarly as condos, offer such recreational facilities as golf courses, tennis courts, 24-hour security, and professional management. Some of the larger condominium complexes offer a gracious lifestyle at reasonable rates that few Americans could otherwise afford. They offer the luxuries of a private club, and some, designed for older residents, even have their own infirmaries, doctors, nurses, shopping centers, theaters, social centers, and mass transportation systems.

Siting may range from high-rise buildings in the city or the country, to townhouses, cluster buildings, or a mixture of low-, medium-, and high-rise buildings in a complex located in a parklike environment, possibly with a lake and wide expanses of greenbelt or meadow or woodland breaking up the developed portions and adding to the privacy and rural feeling.

Although condominium complexes, beginning in the 1960s, were first constructed with retirees in mind, it is now clear that with minor alterations of design they appeal to a much larger market and for the same reasons: greater security and more house and living facilities for less money than if separately purchased. Nearly all condominium developments now have elegant rooms for dancing, bridge parties, pool tournaments, and table tennis, and for older people, all manner of rooms and facilities for hobbies, crafts, and continuing education. They even have a few special party rooms wth adjoining kitchens for giving parties larger than can easily be accommodated in a single unit. Others have centrally located clubhouses, with gourmet meals served both to residents and passing visitors.

It is small wonder that single persons, childless couples, and couples only starting to have families find that the condominium offers them the best buy for relatively gracious living. Ironically, it is often the only kind of housing they can afford outside of mobile homes.

## THE COMING OF THE FOREIGN INVESTOR

The rush of foreigners to buy U.S. real estate has caused worry among farmers and U.S. citizens who wonder whether they can still afford their dream farm or house. These worries of the potential U.S. investor or family buyer, or the farmer who needs more land to support a growing agribusiness, are not shared by many U.S. businessmen. Realtors, lawyers, and all manner of intermediaries in the transaction welcome foreign investors who have large sums of money and seek guidance toward a profitable investment. These people are making a great deal of money and are inclined to pooh-pooh the foreign "threat."

"If foreigners could buy all the farmland available for the next ten years, they would not own two percent of the country's farmland," says one who advises farmers not to worry. Nonetheless a number of states—Connecticut, Indiana, Kentucky, Mississippi, Nebraska, New Hampshire, and Oklahoma among them—have laws barring nonresident aliens from owning land directly. Thirteen other states impose some limits. Almost all of these laws can be circumvented easily, however, through dummy buyers or by buying through an American subsidiary.

In an age of statistics and data, it is annoying that no one seems to know what part of U.S. land is presently owned and controlled by aliens. According to the Economic Research Bureau of the U.S. Department of Agriculture, 17 percent of recent land sales (per acreage) have been to foreigners. The Bureau is also conducting a survey to determine the extent to which foreign control has been established over U.S. land.

The examples of sales of country land to foreigners accumulates almost daily. In Montana, state officials reported that foreign buyers had already acquired at least 100,000 acres of ranch land. In rural Louisiana, a wealthy family from Italy bought and is developing a 27,000-acre cattle ranch. It also owns major ranching properties in North Carolina. In California's Central Valley, south of Sacramento, another Italian family bought a 2,100-acre peach ranch for $5.5 million. The selling family was pressured into liquidation because of the need to pay inheritance taxes after a father's death. In northern Iowa, a prospering farmer from West Germany bought 1,013 acres of farmland for $2 million. Another German family in the same vicinity had paid $3.85 million for another large farm three years previously and was happy with its purchase.

The foreign buyers have been satisfied, by and large, with their purchases. They are coming back for more and bringing friends with them. One realtor who specializes in ranches and in managing them for investors, explained "There is a lot of old wealth in Europe and these people know from experience that after wars and conflicts have ended, retention of farmland has enabled them to retain a net worth and get back on their feet. They are considering American farm properties because they feel this is the last place in the world where land will be confiscated."

In addition to a farm's value as *land*, it has the potential for growing food that can be sold to an ever-increasing number of hungry mouths.

## WORLD FOOD NEEDS

It has been established that by the year 2012 the world will have about 8 billion mouths to feed, just about four times the number existing in 1930. The population was about 4 billion in 1977, in case you doubt that it will double again in another 35 years. The challenge is to build twice as many houses and factories, train twice as many doctors and teachers, and raise twice as much wheat and rice as the world does today. And this will only maintain the world's present standard of living which each year results in more than 10 million people dying from diseases of malnutrition.

Sometimes it is said that the United States has no population problem for we are headed toward zero growth. Yet it should be noted that each U.S. citizen has an impact on the environment that is equal to that of about 50 Asians—50 times as much lumber, water, minerals, and fiber are consumed and about 50 times as much garbage and waste is created. Thus, approximately 220 million Americans have the ecological impact of

10 billion Asians. As developing nations reach for U.S. living standards, the worldwide impact on the environment *could* result in catastrophe.

## DECLINE IN WORLD BIRTH RATE

According to Lester R. Brown, a former official in the U.S. Agriculture Department and now president of Worldwatch Institute, there is evidence that there is a decline in global birth rates for the first time in recorded history. The rate dropped between 1970 and 1975 from 1.9 to 1.64 percent, which means that 5 million fewer people were added to the world's population in 1975 than would have arrived at the old rate. An apparent decline in China's birthrate was hailed by population planners.

The old idea that Asian parents want a large family as social security has become weaker, as indicated by new surveys. A poll in India reported that 70 percent of the adults who responded wanted smaller families. Yet only 15 percent of married women in rural areas admitted to any knowledge of contraceptives. On the other hand, within a mere six-month period last year, no fewer than six million people in India had vasectomies or tubectomies.

In the United States an average family with two children eats about 2.5 tons of food in one year. This demand is met by U.S. productivity and also by technological improvements that enable farmers and food processors to produce this food at a cost representing only 17 percent of a family's disposable income. Twenty-five years ago, the average family spent 23 percent of its disposable income for food.

One of the changes in eating habits that may take place within the next decades is a decline in the consumption of meat and an increase in the consumption of vegetables. Not only is a vegetarian diet adequate, but many doctors consider it superior in some respects to a diet abundant in meat and its unsaturated fats. Parallel to the health argument, there is an economic argument in favor of increased vegetarianism. Land used to produce food crops for human consumption feeds about 14 times as many people as when it is used to grow food for animals. Of the protein animals eat, only one-quarter is returned in milk; one-eight in pork, and one-tenth in beef. A vegetarian diet has been demonstrated to fulfill human nutritional needs. And since meat will probably become an increasingly expensive item at the supermarket, it is expected that the meat content of the American diet will gradually decrease. Meanwhile, the ever-ingenious food processors and food technologists have developed spinning and extrusion processes that produce textured and tasty products from soybeans, which taste like hot dogs, hamburgers, and beef chunks. It is expected that this technology will improve over the years to satisfy any lingering savor for old-fashioned meats.

## ROLLING WITH THE DROUGHT CYCLES

Drought cycles have now been identified for many regions of the United States and the world. Dry periods usually last about 13 years; then there is an interval of about 24 years before the next drought begins. The cycles have been measured on the growth rings of trees. Improvement in weather planning should smooth out the extremes between dry and wet periods.

One food systems futurist, Merritt L. Kastens, claims there would be much more food available if national governments directly attacked waste. Postharvest losses from spoilage, contamination, and insect infestation cause half the food supply to spoil in underdeveloped countries, he says.

In the industrial countries, too, known technology often is not applied. Techniques of processing, packaging, storage, and transportation, as well as the use of pesticides and preservatives, have not been introduced into the food supply systems in the case of developing countries and are underused in the case of the industrial countries. Available research and development projects are focused instead on gross yield from the field. All of these factors dramatize the need for more efficient production of food and the premium price that food-producing land will probably command in the future.

## THE FUTURE OF AGRICULTURE IN THE UNITED STATES

Whether you buy a farm or another form of country property, the value of your property will depend, in part, on the going price for farm acreage in your region. That is why it is important to understand some basic changes that are taking place within U.S. agriculture.

In general, the consolidation of small family farms into larger farms has been accelerating since the Great Depression. Since World War II these ever-larger farms, some of them owned by corporations, have been going through a period of transformation into agribusinesses. Unless you want to run a "hobby" or experimental farm where profit is not the primary goal, you will always have to contend with agribusiness as a competitor for the country land you want to buy. And in your part of the country, if the farmers do not yet consider themselves to be agribusinesses, such operations are nonetheless setting the price for farm land, or for pasture land and its rental. For, regardless of what you may hear about developers buying up land in the vicinity of urban growth, more than 90 percent of the annual transactions in farmland are *between farmers* and the land stays in agricultural use.

As the concept of agribusiness expands, more and more farmers, or their consultants, are becoming sophisticated in the methods of modern finance and marketing. They have the communications available to know what the cash and futures markets are doing in the commodities that affect them. They are large enough and control sufficient capital to take hedging positions in the commodities markets. They are more aware of export markets and alternative ways of storing, preserving, and marketing their produce during times of relative scarcity or glut.

In any specific year profits for farmers depend on the weather, on how much wheat, corn, and other feed grains the United States exports, and how many calves and pigs the farmers turn into their feed lots. When grain brings too low a price, the grain farmers move into feeding livestock instead of selling their grain. That is usually when cattle farmers make money; when grain prices are relatively low, their meat products can be offered at attractive prices.

But regardless of the surges and dips in the grain and livestock markets, the costs of running and maintaining a farm continue to climb as nationwide inflation continues. The gap between the prices farmers get for their products and the prices consumers pay for it has become so broad that farmers have regular protests and have even marched on Washington. But they have a more effective weapon—agribusiness and, most particularly, the cooperative organizations that have been vertically integrating large segments of U.S. agriculture. In so doing, farmers have cut out intermediaries and now deal directly with the retailer. Co-ops have also gone into manufacturing equipment and supplies for the farmer—and even into prospecting and drilling for oil.

Farmland Industries, a conglomerate of more than 2,200 farm cooperatives to which close to one million farmers belong, is an organization that does more than $3 billion in business a year and sells industrial goods to its members and farm products to retail outlets. It is now 75th in size of the country's 500 largest industrial concerns. It is the biggest provider of nitrogen feedstocks and probably the largest fertilizer maker in the nation. It also makes farm machinery and tires, operates insurance companies and investment systems, and produces tinned hams, bacon, and many other food products. Its grain elevator and other storage facilities give farmers the option of storing their grain if they decide not to sell it at current prices. The elevators also provide a marketing service that sells the grain eventually to domestic millers or to export houses, and increasingly, directly to foreign buyers. When they sell directly, they eliminate the exporter, an international broker who does not necessarily favor U.S. grain over the production of other countries.

It is not surprising that this conglomerate also offers its members computer services, runs a profitable printing concern, and engages in banking and investing for its members. It is a truly vertical and multinational organization and there are others sprouting in the same field. Needless to say, they already exert their international marketing and financial clout, and will have a stabilizing effect on farm prices as well as land values. As foreign and U.S. corporate investors—knowing a good thing when they see it and in an effort to diversify—put more and more money into country property, agribusiness will be in a stronger position to prevent prices from surging and dipping erratically. While land values may smooth out, the continuing needs of agribusiness for more land and for improving marginal land and bringing it into productivity, will assure a continuing, gradual increase in the value of land.

## TWO INDEXES TO WATCH

Because country property covers three main types of property: residential property either in or outside a village, or a farm that includes a resi-

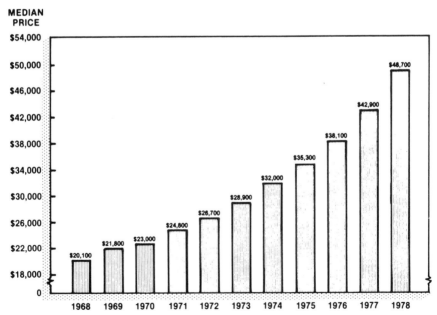

**Figure 3-6** Median sales price of existing single-family homes in the United States. (*Source: National Association of Realtors.*)

**Table 3-4**—Farm real estate values: Average value per acre of land and buildings and percent change from the previous year, by State, grouped by farm production region, March 1, 1973 and 1975 and February 1, 1977–1979

| State | March 1, 1973 | | March 1, 1975 | | Feb. 1, 1977 | | Feb. 1, 1978 | | Feb. 1, 1979[1] | |
|---|---|---|---|---|---|---|---|---|---|---|
| | Value | % chg. | Value | % chg. | Value | % chg. | Value | % chg. | Value | % chg. |
| **Northeast** | | | | | | | | | | |
| Maine[2] | $ 253 | 17 | $ 341 | 13 | $ 400 | | $ 441 | | $ 485 | |
| New Hampshire[2] | 404 | 19 | 564 | 14 | 661 | | 729 | | 802 | |
| Vermont[2] | 346 | 16 | 462 | 13 | 541 | | 597 | | 657 | |
| Massachusetts[2] | 766 | 11 | 961 | 10 | 1,126 | 8% | 1,242 | 10% | 1,366 | 10% |
| Rhode Island[2] | 1,124 | 16 | 1,500 | 12 | 1,758 | | 1,939 | | 2,133 | |
| Connecticut[2] | 1,229 | 11 | 1,525 | 9 | 1,779 | | 1,962 | | 2,158 | |
| | | | | | | | | | | |
| New York | 356 | 10 | 510 | 15 | 580 | 6 | 589 | 2 | 642 | 9 |
| New Jersey | 1,337 | 9 | 1,807 | 14 | 2,004 | 0 | 2,057 | 3 | 2,222 | 8 |
| Pennsylvania | 491 | 17 | 734 | 18 | 978 | 20 | 1,092 | 12 | 1,245 | 14 |
| Delaware | 645 | 14 | 971 | 20 | 1,340 | 16 | 1,500 | 12 | 1,725 | 15 |
| Maryland | 843 | 15 | 1,060 | 8 | 1,355 | 6 | 1,578 | 16 | 1,799 | 14 |
| **Lake States** | | | | | | | | | | |
| Michigan | 444 | 20 | 553 | 6 | 767 | 27 | 860 | 12 | 955 | 11 |
| Wisconsin | 328 | 20 | 434 | 12 | 583 | 19 | 690 | 18 | 807 | 17 |
| Minnesota | 269 | 12 | 429 | 27 | 652 | 25 | 730 | 12 | 854 | 17 |
| **Corn Belt** | | | | | | | | | | |
| Ohio | 505 | 15 | 706 | 13 | 1,121 | 31 | 1,263 | 13 | 1,516 | 20 |
| Indiana | 494 | 14 | 720 | 22 | 1,159 | 32 | 1,303 | 12 | 1,498 | 15 |
| Illinois | 567 | 9 | 846 | 18 | 1,431 | 36 | 1,581 | 10 | 1,786 | 13 |
| Iowa | 466 | 13 | 719 | 20 | 1,219 | 35 | 1,268 | 4 | 1,458 | 15 |
| Missouri | 294 | 13 | 396 | 3 | 526 | 18 | 602 | 14 | 674 | 12 |
| **Northern Plains** | | | | | | | | | | |
| North Dakota | 108 | 10 | 195 | 35 | 258 | 13 | 273 | 6 | 306 | 12 |
| South Dakota | 94 | 8 | 145 | 22 | 194 | 19 | 227 | 17 | 257 | 13 |
| Nebraska | 193 | 14 | 282 | 17 | 401 | 13 | 385 | -4 | 470 | 22 |
| Kansas | 199 | 14 | 296 | 17 | 376 | 14 | 380 | 1 | 437 | 15 |
| **Appalachian** | | | | | | | | | | |
| Virginia | 391 | 13 | 558 | 11 | 676 | 9 | 732 | 8 | 864 | 18 |
| West Virginia | 204 | 18 | 300 | 15 | 394 | 5 | 403 | 2 | 472 | 17 |
| North Carolina | 461 | 16 | 590 | 7 | 675 | 6 | 694 | 3 | 819 | 18 |
| Kentucky | 327 | 11 | 427 | 11 | 595 | 18 | 671 | 13 | 792 | 18 |
| Tennessee | 346 | 15 | 467 | 13 | 545 | 10 | 608 | 12 | 669 | 10 |
| **Southeast** | | | | | | | | | | |
| South Carolina | 336 | 7 | 467 | 12 | 529 | 9 | 543 | 3 | 635 | 17 |
| Georgia | 329 | 13 | 474 | 12 | 509 | 7 | 564 | 11 | 609 | 8 |
| Florida[3] | 464 | 15 | 685 | 13 | 777 | 7 | 838 | 8 | 930 | 11 |
| Alabama | 267 | 13 | 364 | 10 | 432 | 7 | 452 | 5 | 515 | 14 |
| **Delta States** | | | | | | | | | | |
| Mississippi | 270 | 12 | 379 | 11 | 404 | 6 | 464 | 15 | 520 | 12 |
| Arkansas | 337 | 14 | 419 | 3 | 521 | 12 | 571 | 10 | 691 | 21 |
| Louisiana | 403 | 6 | 512 | 9 | 581 | 8 | 669 | 15 | 763 | 14 |
| **Southern Plains** | | | | | | | | | | |
| Oklahoma | 219 | 13 | 302 | 15 | 365 | 10 | 402 | 10 | 442 | 10 |
| Texas | 196 | 13 | 243 | 1 | 286 | 7 | 316 | 11 | 354 | 12 |
| **Mountain** | | | | | | | | | | |
| Montana | 76 | 12 | 112 | 17 | 152 | 15 | 168 | 11 | 186 | 11 |
| Idaho | 229 | 12 | 339 | 18 | 412 | 12 | 445 | 8 | 485 | 9 |
| Wyoming | 55 | 15 | 80 | 14 | 101 | 7 | 105 | 4 | 119 | 13 |
| Colorado | 137 | 18 | 188 | 7 | 256 | 17 | 274 | 7 | 332 | 21 |
| New Mexico | 56 | 14 | 78 | 7 | 89 | 10 | 93 | 4 | 100 | |
| Arizona | 91 | 6 | 111 | 1 | 120 | 5 | 125 | 4 | 134 | [4]7 |
| Utah | 141 | 10 | 188 | 10 | 235 | 11 | 248 | 6 | 265 | |
| Nevada | 74 | 12 | 85 | 0 | 87 | 0 | 97 | 11 | 104 | |
| **Pacific** | | | | | | | | | | |
| Washington | 273 | 15 | 350 | 14 | 491 | 17 | 528 | 8 | 586 | 11 |
| Oregon | 205 | 10 | 250 | 7 | 278 | 5 | 303 | 9 | 330 | 9 |
| California | 509 | 3 | 653 | 15 | 673 | 1 | 761 | 13 | 936 | 23 |
| 48 States | 246 | 12 | 339 | 13 | 448 | 16 | 488 | 9 | 559 | 15 |

[1] Preliminary. [2] Average rate of change for the 6 New England States was used to project the dollar values for 1976 to 1979. [3] Values are based upon an index estimated from the average of the percentage change in Georgia and Alabama index values. [4] The average rate of change for irrigated and dry cropland and pasture land for the 4 Southwestern mountain States was used to project the dollar value.

dence and unimproved acreage, there is no particular composite and weighted index measuring these or any other types of real estate. U.S. Department of Agriculture's Research Bureau, however, does keep a count of acreage prices for farmland and the National Association of Realtors keeps track of the sales prices of existing single-family homes. Both of these indexes measure major components of the values of country property, and certainly the trends they indicate can provide reliable guidelines on the direction of country-property prices. As you can see in Figure 3-6 and Table 3-4 both indexes have been in a strong upward trend for the past decade and longer.

## SOLAR ENERGY

No matter how the U.S. government attempts to solve the energy crisis through conservation, deregulation of oil and natural gas prices, enlightened regulation of nuclear reactors, emphasis on more efficient extraction of energy from wood and coal, experimentation with wind and wave energy, the only real, long-term solution to the energy shortage and pollution threat is the development of solar energy—that endless, clean, and free supply coming down from the sun.

Solar-energy devices have been used for years in homes in places where there is plenty of sun, such as Florida and the Southwest, where people have used it to heat water for home use and for swimming pools. As of now, there are probably 2,000 to 3,000 solar-heated homes built and functioning around the country. And there are solar energy projects, sometimes financed by federal and state governments, for homes and apartments in almost all of the fifty states.

The federal government has announced a goal of 2.5 million homes with solar installations by 1985. It has set up a National Solar Heating and Cooling Information Center with a toll-free number (800-523-2929) that you can call to obtain technical details on solar power for space and water heating, lists of conferences on solar energy, and the names of companies offering computer analyses of need—for a fee.

The ultimate solution to the energy problems may prove to be solar energy captured and stored in space colonies and transmitted to earth as needed. Unfortunately, although the technology for doing this is already available, there has to be a decision on national priorities to justify the huge expense of such an energy-gathering system. It is probable that the many industrialized countries, faced with comparable problems, will form a consortium to launch such satellite colonies. That implies greater economic integration of national economies, but by the next century that too may have come to pass, just as the European Economic Community and the Common Market have recently added an ever stronger European monetary system.

There is one thing owners of country property can count on: The price of all fossil fuels will increase in the years to come as the supply of one and then the next is exhausted, becomes uneconomical to extract, or cannot be used because of environmental or governmental restrictions that cover extraction or use. Thus the trend will be toward ever more sophisticated building construction to use energy more efficiently and to conserve and re-use it whenever possible. In siting their houses and in building them today, country-property owners can reap future profits by recognizing these developments and getting ready for them. Chapter 8 on Remodeling and Renovation will discuss this further.

## IN SUMMARY

### Factors in the Next Ten to Twenty Years That Will Cause Country Property to Rise in Value

1 Worldwide inflation, spurred by the energy crisis.

2 Domestic and foreign investors seeking tax shelters and hedges against inflation.

3 The children of the post–World War II baby boom who are forming families in a record volume.

4 Governmental regulation of building and construction causing higher prices.

5 Go-slow and no-growth policies of local governments, which reduce supply of available land and cause prices to rise.

6 Worldwide demand for food and the unusual agricultural productivity of the U.S. farmer in growing agribusinesses.

7 New sources of energy that will support a spreading out of the population into the country, a natural inclination of people living in the United States.

### Factors in the Next Ten to Twenty Years That Will Tend to Cause Country Property to Decline in Value, if Only Temporarily

1 Temporary recessions caused by excessive periods of inflation.

**2**  Shocks in the energy crisis that may slow the move to the country.

**3**  Too rapid increases in property values of particular regions, which may cause a corrective decline—for a while.

**4**  Eventual lessening of the rate of increase in demand for housing as the decline in the birth rate lowers the rate of family formation.

# Chapter Four

# Where to Locate
# for Greatest Profit

## THE PERSONAL MOTIVE IN SELECTING A LOCATION

Where do you want to live in the country? Where the sun shines almost every day and the temperature seldom declines below 70°? Where all four seasons come and go with their typical colors, temperatures, and growing cycles? Where the sun is hot during the day, and the nights cool, and there is hardly any rain so that growing things can flourish only if given constant care and watering? Where the soil is fantastically rich for growing things, the climate is springlike the year-round, and you can count on some rain almost every day?

Positive answers to these questions might cause you to move to the leeward side of the Big Island of Hawaii, to Vermont, to Arizona, or to the windward side of Kauai in the Hawaiian chain.

For most people, moving to the country means moving closer to nature and the weather. The United States, including Hawaii and Alaska, has such a rich variety of climates that it is hard for a young couple or a single person to make a choice. Young or single people usually have more pioneering blood in their veins than older people, who are used to the conveniences and shorter distances of the city. Older people, if they move at all, tend to choose milder climates in the Sunbelt, where the sheer act of living requires less wear, tear, and expense of energy.

If you are actually going to live on your country property for part or all of the year, you had better be sure first of all that you enjoy the climate. There are many other factors to consider in making your choice, but climate undoubtedly is the most important of these for people who want to live close to nature for any length of time.

## THE PROFIT MOTIVE IN SELECTING A LOCATION

Remember, you want to make an eventual profit on your country property. That means you will always have to consider the country-property *market* situation in the area where you want to settle down or invest. Your personal idea of a Shangri-la may not coincide with the dreams of a significant number of other people. And thus you may create a beautiful retreat in the midst of a forest in the Maine woods, in the desert in New Mexico, or on a lonely northern lake in Minnesota. You will get all the privacy you may have wanted, but you may never be able to get your money out of your investment. In other words, you will have to choose a location that coincides with the choice of other people who have already begun to move there. You will have to make your choice partly on the basis of *where* people are going and try to understand *why* they are going there.

## METEOROLOGICAL MAPS

Sooner or later you will want to consult weather maps of your dream country. The maps reproduced here (figures 4-1 to 4-5) are the latest available from the U.S. Weather Bureau. Note that they include average annual rainfall, mean annual number of days with maximum temperature 90° and above, mean annual total hours of sunshine, mean length of freeze days, mean annual number of days with minimum temperatures 32° and below.

## POPULATION DENSITY

One other very important map (Figure 4-6) shows the counties of the United States visualized from the standpoint of population density. You can see at a glance where the people *are*. The most obvious places for areas of growth are at the fringes of the most densely populated areas. Most people who want to live in the country actually settle on the fringe

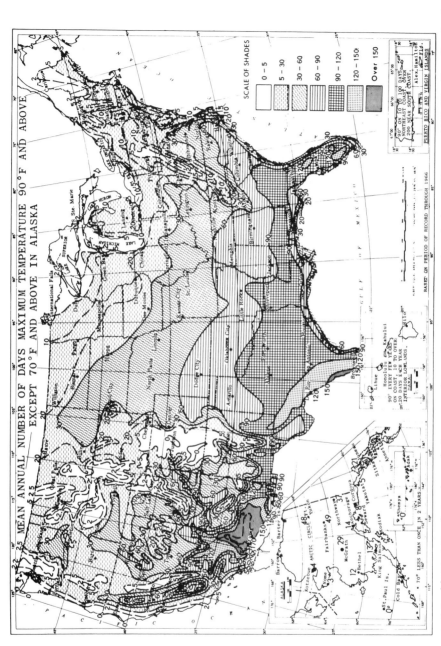

**Figure 4-1** Mean annual number of days—maximum temperature 90°F and above. (Source: U.S. Weather Service.)

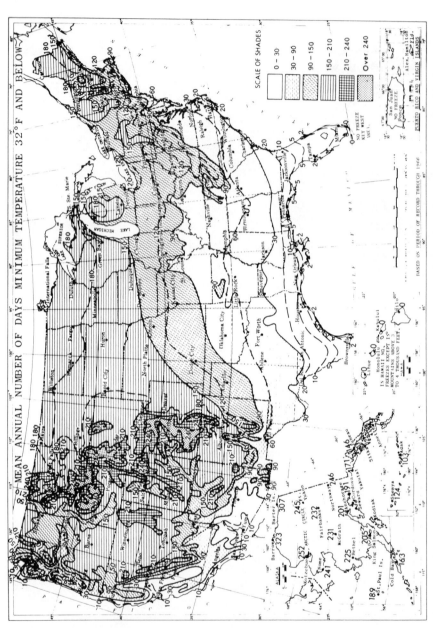

**Figure 4-2** Mean annual number of days—minimum temperature 32°F and below. (*Source: U.S. Weather Service.*)

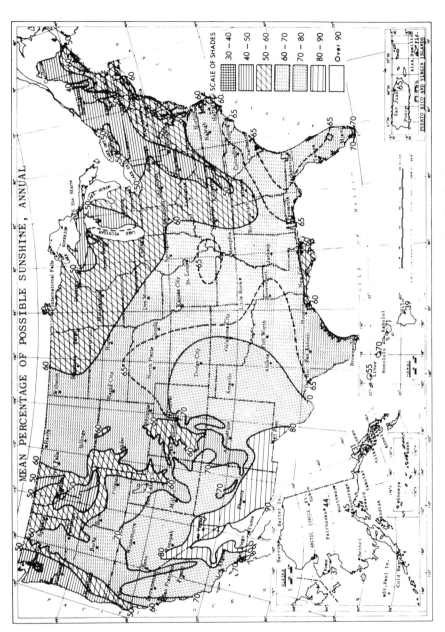

**Figure 4-3** Mean annual total hours of sunshine. (*Source: U.S. Weather Service.*)

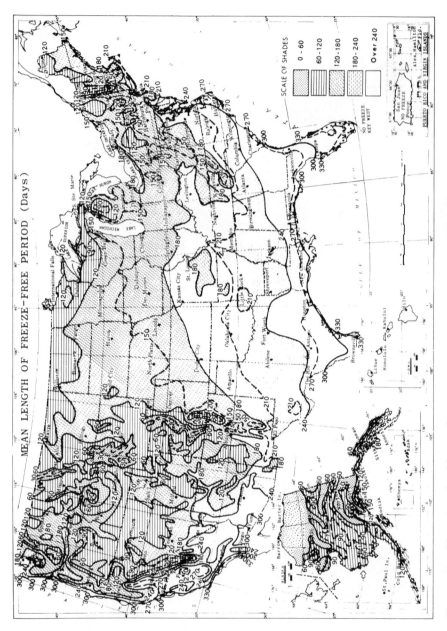

**Figure 4-4** Mean length of freeze-free period (in days). (Source: *U.S. Weather Service.*)

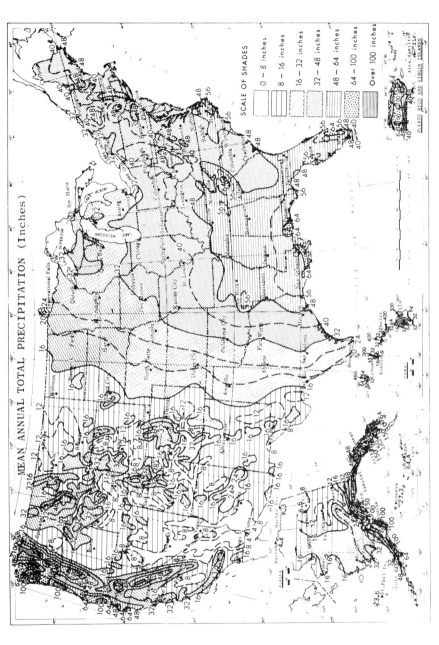

**Figure 4-5** Normal annual total precipitation (inches). (*Source: U.S. Weather Service.*)

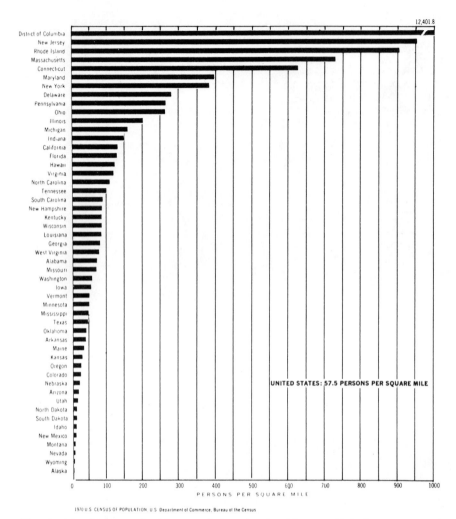

**Figure 4-6** States ranked by population density. *(Source: U.S. Department of Commerce, Bureau of the Census.)*

of a city area they know best. They are cautious and conservative and prefer to remain in a familiar region, with many other immigrants in similar background and experience.

This kind of moving, partly adventuresome, partly conservative, means an uprooting that takes a family to a different but nearby place in the country where people are not *entirely different*. Thus, while the step means change, the change has been partly hedged. It softens the shock for the emigrant-pioneer.

## WHERE THE PEOPLE ARE

Your best profit possibilities, by and large, are in *growing* country areas, adjacent to major metropolitan areas. Open spaces are fine for those who want to get away from it all, but most people like their rural escape property to have other people in the vicinity and where there is fire, police, and medical aid not too far away. That is why you have more profit opportunities in country property on the fringes of urban areas and in states where there already is a large population and where that population is growing. Figure 4-7 ranks states by population and will give you an idea of

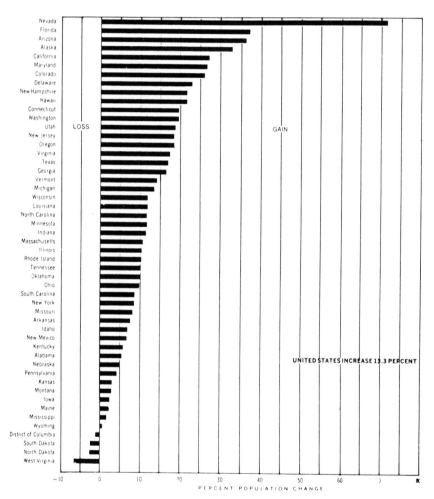

**Figure 4-7**   States ranked by total population. *(Source: U.S Department of Commerce, Bureau of the Census.)*

where the great masses of people have already settled. Look at Figure 3-3 to identify the states that have the most dynamic patterns.

Figures 4-8 and 4-9 rank states by *amount* and *percent* of population growth.

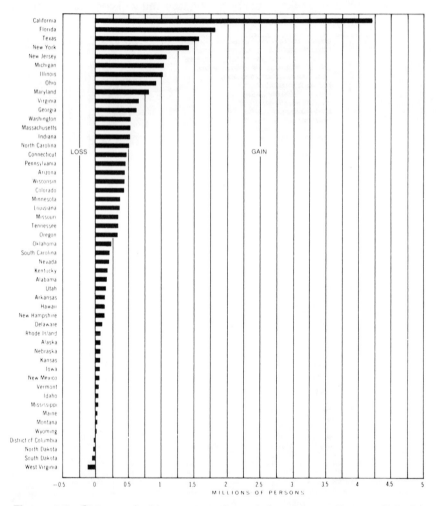

**Figure 4-8** States ranked by amount of population change. *(Source: U.S. Department of Commerce, Bureau of the Census.)*

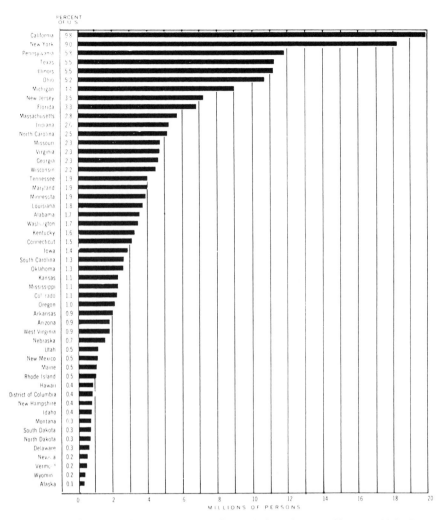

**Figure 4-9**   States ranked by percent of population change. *(Source: U.S. Department of Commerce, Bureau of the Census.)*

## THE FASTEST-GROWING METROPOLITAN AREAS

According to the National Association of Home Builders, the 20 fastest growing metropolitan areas in the country are as indicated in Table 4-1. They are listed by number of housing starts expected in 1979 compared to 1978 performance figures. Note that in both years Houston and Dallas–

**Table 4-1**   Housing Starts in Top 20 Metropolitan Areas

| | 1979 | 1978 | | 1979 | 1978 |
|---|---|---|---|---|---|
| Houston | 57,365 | 62,706 | Denver–Boulder | 21,000 | 23,400 |
| Dallas–Ft. Worth | 50,000 | 46,003 | Ft. Lauderdale– | 19,000 | 17,375 |
| Chicago | 43,000 | 44,000 | Hollywood | | |
| Los Angeles– | 38,000 | 38,500 | Minneapolis– | 19,000 | 19,700 |
| Long Beach | | | St. Paul | | |
| San Diego | 38,000 | 28,000 | Philadelphia | 18,290 | 20,160 |
| Seattle–Everett | 32,976 | 31,320 | Washington, D.C. | 17,000 | 21,149 |
| Phoenix | 32,000 | 40,000 | Palm Beach Co. | 16,900 | 19,254 |
| Riverside–San | 32,000 | 35,000 | Portland | 16,700 | 18,850 |
| Bernardino | | | San Francisco– | 16,500 | 17,500 |
| Anaheim–Santa Ana– | 22,500 | 22,500 | Oakland | | |
| Garden Grove | | | Atlanta | 15,500 | 15,600 |
| Detroit | 22,000 | 23,360 | Tampa– | 15,500 | 16,853 |
| | | | St. Petersburg | | |

*Source:* National Association of Homebuilders.

Fort-Worth headed the lists, with Chicago a poor third and Los Angeles and San Diego a poor fourth and fifth. But if you add San Diego, Riverside–San Bernardino, and Anaheim–Santa Ana–Garden Grove to the figures for Los Angeles, the southern California megalopolis is far and away the fastest growing area in the United States. In general the Sunbelt states are getting the bulk of the growth. Only one metropolitan area in the Northeast (Philadelphia) and three in the Midwest (Chicago, Detroit, and Minneapolis–St. Paul) made the top twenty. Country properties near these growth areas are likely to increase fastest in value.

*Example: Local Growth in a No-Growth State*
The Michael Egger family moved to the mountains of eastern Utah 10 years ago when Utah was not considered a growth state. It still is not growing rapidly according to the statistics released by the Census Bureau. But the Eggers, who were both college professors, were seeking a modest ranch of their own in the mountains where they could live quietly with nature during the summer when they both worked on books and articles. They were not particularly interested in growth; they wanted to get away from it in the city where they lived the rest of the year. But growth happened to follow them to Utah. Friends bought ranches nearby and ski-birds began to flock to a nearby ski resort. Eventually many of the skiers bought condominiums in the resort village and others bought ranches and acreage in the surrounding slopes and valleys. The Eggers benefited from the boomlet because the present value of their ranch has climbed considerably more than they expected; it was a bonus to the pleasure they found in mountain living.

*Example: Innovative Houseboat Living*
Suzy Eager and John Partridge lived an ocean apart but had the same dream—to

live on a river houseboat near the city and enjoy a few square feet of country living within sight of the city's bright lights at night. Suzy rented a houseboat on the Hudson as a lark and as a practical solution to her housing needs. She endured one winter of such living, arriving at her Wall Street office red cheeked, outfitted by several sporting-goods houses, in the throes of a series of severe colds, and with stars in her feverish eyes about the clear, clean air. She omitted to characterize the water. After one winter of such living, she wrote a witty article about it and found a cozy apartment in Greenwich Village with a river view.

John Partridge, near Nottingham, England, fixed up an old military boat which he bought as surplus material. After a summer of fixing it up, he settled down to a quiet winter in a backwater of the River Trent. During an autumnal rain storm the river rose a bit, lifted the boat from its mud bank, and caused some of the caulking in its seams to come loose. One day, when John returned home, he found that his boat had settled down on a deeper mudbank and that water was more than a foot deep in all his rooms. He, too, made other arrangements after this tentative pioneering effort.

Not all such creative shelter ventures end badly, but there are practical reasons why the mass of people do not rush to them. If you want to make a profit on your country property, do not expect to do it via far-out improvisations. The wave of the future will bring manufactured homes (formerly known as mobile homes) and condominiums; turn to them for unique adventures in living. Try, too, inexpensive solar heating and cooling innovations; houses built into a hill, for example, may have extra value for their heat conservation in winter and their cooler lower rooms in summer.

### Example: Proximity to a Thruway

Gloria Watson had recently been transferred from the headquarters of her insurance and financial company in San Francisco, to Baltimore, Maryland. In the Bay area she was familiar with the practical value of living near a freeway to facilitate quick commuting downtown. She was so used to the traffic flow on the freeways that the lesser traffic in the Baltimore area seemed an improvement. She asked her realtor in Baltimore about the relative value of living near a freeway, or thruway as it is called on the East Coast. The realtor remembered a study made in 1975 of several communities on the East Coast that had thruways within or near their borders. They were Bogota, New Jersey, North Springfield, Virginia, Rosedale, Maryland, and Towson, Maryland. The test made by *all four communities* showed that values can run as much as 15 percent lower on property adjacent to the thruway compared with similar property lying 150 feet or more from it.

Another part of the test, however, brought out that there was an offsetting value to all homes in communities serviced by an interstate highway. In North Springfield, Virginia, for example, houses less than 150 feet from the thruway showed an average loss in value of $2,100, but they also benefited from an average $2,955 gain in value because of the increased accessibility.

Gloria, with these figures in mind, bought a home on a country road, a half-mile and over a slight hill from the thruway. She maximized the gain from the proximity to the thruway but couldn't see it or hear the traffic. She was fortunate, too, in how that segment of the interstate highway had been planned. It paralleled an old country road in the area, so Gloria could drive locally on this access road without using the thruway at all.

## TYPES AND QUALITIES OF LAND

Figures 4-10 through 4-16 from the U.S. Department of Agriculture differentiate and demonstrate the various classes of land. They will enable you to talk sensibly about the type of land you want to buy—whether for cultivation or simply for residential use. As you might guess, land that is inhospitable to growing crops tends to lack an abundance of sun, drainage, water, or natural nutrients that support life. The difference between human beings and plants is that people can radically alter their environment; they can make up for just about any lack—at a price. But it is important to know what you are starting with. If you are going to buy *farmland,* have the county agent check it with you. Have it evaluated for its good and poor points. Find out also what similar land is selling for per acre in your vicinity. You will want to know the agent for later advice. When you are ready to buy, the agent can serve as an expert in matters where a realtor would not be entirely competent and would, in any case, be disinclined to identify weak points of the land for sale. The county agent can suggest and may perform soil tests, such as for average depth of top soil, acidity, and alkalinity. Based on local experience, the agent will know what fertilizers should be added and what poisonous pesticides may have been used that may have a residual effect on your soil, and can also tell you about local weed and insect pests and the best way to control them.

### Good Soil

Soil textures—gravel, sand, loam, and clay—usually come in varying combinations. Loam consists of approximately equal parts of sand and clay. This makes for a crumbly soil that tends to let water through quickly and has a tendency to leach out valuable minerals and nutrient chemicals, which all drain away in water that flows quickly through sand, gravel, and other large-particled components. Clay, composed of small, compacting particles, holds the water. If there is too much clay in your soil, it can prevent adequate drainage. Clay soil can be loosened up with additions of humus, such as peat moss and compost. Soil that is too porous can be improved by adding soil that has a high clay content. In general, the best quality of soil has a top layer of humus about 14 inches in depth, and then

**Figure 4-10**  Class I land. *(Source: U.S. Department of Agriculture.)*

a loamy layer of subsoil on top of a layer of one to four feet of various types of clay, which acts to slow the drainage of water and nutrient materials. Below that, there may be varieties of rock.

Because of poor soil management practices during several centuries of land exploitation, many tracts of farmland in the United States have eroded, and the top soil and even the subsoil has been stripped from what was once good farm land. What is left is a combination of clay and sometimes rock on which very little can grow.

## Class I Land

Class I land retains water, has good drainage, and endures little wind or water erosion. It is ideal land for grain, corn, and most vegetable crops.

## Class II Land

Class II land has soil characteristics similar to Class I land but is more vulnerable to erosion. To cope with water erosion, particularly, the land can be plowed in a contour pattern. Strip cropping can slow both water and wind erosion.

**Figure 4-11** Class II land. *(Source: U.S. Department of Agriculture.)*

## Class III Land

Class III land will give you problems with its wetness. For efficient farming, drains have to be installed and kept in repair. Even then, if you want to raise cash crops, you may have to favor those which like water, such as rice or taro root.

**Figure 4-12** Class III land. *(Source: U.S. Department of Agriculture.)*

**Figure 4-13**   Class IV land. *(Source: U.S. Department of Agriculture.)*

## Class IV Land

Class IV land may be level or sloping. Usually its soil will not erode, but it is too wet for the efficient growing of crops and cannot be effectively drained. If you use it for farming at all, you will have to use it for livestock when it is dry enough for them to graze it.

## Class V Land

Class V land has soil on which crops cannot be grown effectively. If it has the right rainfall, it can be used as a grazing meadow or an orchard.

**Figure 4-14**   Class V land. *(Source: U.S. Department of Agriculture.)*

**Figure 4-15**   Class VI land. *(Source: U.S. Department of Agriculture.)*

## Land of Mixed Classes

Mixed classes of land occur in hilly or mountainous regions of the country or in wet-dry areas where some of the land, because of excess moisture or the lack of it, cannot be used for agricultural purposes. While these drawbacks in a portion of land may not bother a large farmer, the small farmer

**Figure 4-16**   Land of mixed classes. *(Source: U.S. Department of Agriculture.)*

usually avoids buying land that has not been productive in the past or has no potential for conversion to a more profitable use. In Figure 4-16 the land in the foreground, used for farming, buildings, and roads is considered Class II, while the high slopes in the background can be used for nothing except grazing at certain times of the year. The hilly soil is considered Class VI land.

You can readily see that soil characteristics such as seasonal flooding that prevent profitable growing of crops also would prevent effective enjoyment as a residential site. Thus it would not be suitable for a rural residence or for development. The characteristics of the land you want to buy can be identified by the previous owner or your county farm agent. You should know what you are buying and what its drawbacks are as land for farm and other uses—those potential uses, or lack of them, will determine its profit potential.

## IMPROVED OR UNIMPROVED LAND

*Improved* or *unimproved* are flexible terms. Improvements can be as small and unimportant as a cattle feeding area on 1,000 acres of grazing land, or they can be barns, machine sheds, roads, walls, drainage, homes for the owner and farmhands, and anything that would normally be sold with the land and can be depreciated if used for business or to produce income. Improvements do not generally include machinery and equipment that can be sold separately. Of course, these, too, can be depreciated if used for business, but they do not necessarily belong to the farm or land as such.

When you buy improved land and use it for business purposes, you can begin the process of depreciation for tax purposes all over again, regardless of how much depreciation the former owner has taken and regardless of how you have financed the property. An exception would be the purchase through a land contract or any other conditional sale that prevents title from passing to you until the entire series of installments has been paid in full. Until that time, you *can* deduct the interest built into the financing agreement but you *cannot* deduct depreciation. The seller (the person who is still technically the owner of the place), deducts depreciation from his or her income and is liable for real estate taxes under installment-payment purchase contracts.

In general, you will make more profit when you buy substantially improved country property. There is a reason for this. Buildings, particularly highly usable farm and residential buildings, are rising in value at a rate at least as rapid as land, *and often are rising faster*. The second reason lies in the ability to take depreciation on income-producing assets such as buildings and equipment. You cannot depreciate land, although you may write off expenses for improving its fertility or drainage, or for surveying and registering a planned development.

## TIMING YOUR INVESTMENT IN COUNTRY PROPERTY

Consider yourself lucky if you are ready to buy your country property at a time when there is a slight dip in mortgage rates. Or if there is a recession and prices of property pause in their rise and thus enable you to shop around a bit and perhaps to bargain with the seller. Other things being equal, it is not worth waiting for a dip in rates and certainly not for a dip in prices. Although there have been dips in mortgage-interest rates (see Ta-

**Table 4-2**  Change in Mortgage Rates, 1960–1978

| Year | Federal land banks[a] | | | | Life insurance companies[b] | | | |
|---|---|---|---|---|---|---|---|---|
| | Quarter ending | | | | Quarter ending | | | |
| | Mar. 31 | June 30 | Sept. 30 | Dec. 31 | Mar. 31 | June 30 | Sept. 30 | Dec. 31 |
| 1960 | 5.98% | 5.98% | 5.98% | 5.98% | 6.08% | 6.12% | 6.11% | 6.05% |
| 1961 | 5.73 | 5.60 | 5.56 | 5.56 | 5.95 | 5.82 | 5.85 | 5.81 |
| 1962 | 5.56 | 5.56 | 5.56 | 5.56 | 5.84 | 5.84 | 5.78 | 5.78 |
| 1963 | 5.56 | 5.56 | 5.55 | 5.52 | 5.75 | 5.76 | 5.72 | 5.76 |
| 1964 | 5.52 | 5.52 | 5.52 | 5.52 | 5.72 | 5.74 | 5.74 | 5.73 |
| 1965 | 5.51 | 5.50 | 5.54 | 5.54 | 5.74 | 5.74 | 5.81 | 5.82 |
| 1966 | 5.54 | 5.60 | 5.96 | 6.00 | 5.94 | 6.16 | 6.47 | 6.64 |
| 1967 | 6.00 | 6.00 | 6.00 | 6.08 | 6.68 | 6.60 | 6.73 | 6.88 |
| 1968 | 6.64 | 6.71 | 6.81 | 6.81 | 7.06 | 7.26 | 7.54 | 7.62 |
| 1969 | 6.93 | 7.41 | 8.15 | 8.38 | 7.74 | 8.20 | 8.72 | 9.27 |
| 1970 | 8.66 | 8.72 | 8.71 | 8.62 | 8.98 | 9.48 | 9.37 | 9.40 |
| 1971 | 8.22 | 7.80 | 7.71 | 7.70 | 8.75 | 8.42 | 8.45 | 8.87 |
| 1972 | 7.51 | 7.42 | 7.39 | 7.38 | 8.31 | 8.32 | 8.26 | 8.39 |
| 1973 | 7.35 | 7.35 | 7.48 | 7.75 | 8.29 | 8.49 | 8.70 | 9.01 |
| 1974 | 7.82 | 7.88 | 8.28 | 8.57 | 9.22 | 9.35 | 9.68 | 9.85 |
| 1975 | 8.67 | 8.67 | 8.68 | 8.76 | 10.29 | 10.00 | 9.70 | 10.11 |
| 1976 | 8.75 | 8.67 | 8.59 | 8.57 | 10.02 | 9.78 | 9.77 | 9.62 |
| 1977 | 8.43 | 8.37 | 8.32 | 8.27 | 9.35 | 9.29 | 9.26 | 9.27 |
| 1978 | 8.23 | 8.26 | 8.35 | 8.58 | 9.26 | 9.52 | 9.68 | 9.84 |

*Source:* U.S. Department of Agriculture.

[a]Straight average of district rates. Does not include charge for 5 to 10 percent stock requirements.
[b]Estimated by ESCS. Number of companies reporting interest rates varied over the period, ranging from 10 to 20 representing over 90 percent of all farm real estate lending by the life insurance industry.

ble 4-2 for rates over the past 19 years), they have not been large enough to offset the additional rise in the price of the property while the buyer waited for a change. Not only do prices rise, but interest costs are based on a higher principal. Remember, too, that the government *subsidizes* your interest payments because you can deduct the interest *you pay on your home as well as on income-producing property* on your income tax return.

Unless laws governing property and its tax-shelter possibilities change radically, the best timing signal for buying country property is the finding of a property that suits your needs and wants or your investment goals. The sooner you begin to own such a property, the sooner you will have a hedge against inflation and an investment that has proven itself a medium for capital growth.

## THE CHALLENGE OF INFLATION

Your worst competitor or enemy at present in making a profit from your country property is inflation. The dollar profits you earn from your real estate operations come at a time when their worth is declining in purchasing power at a rate between 9 and 10 percent a year. Although this rate hopefully may vary toward the lower side of its recent range, it is not likely that the U.S. government, or any one government, can slow it down significantly. It is a worldwide problem, caused partly by the rise in the price of energy, and particularly in its oil-based components, partly by the increase in the prices charged by third-world countries for the other vital commodities the industrial world must have for its intricate manufacturing processes and technologies, and partly by governments mismanaging their economic responsibilities.

Unfortunately the sources of energy have been politicized. The long-term economic future of the United States has been put into jeopardy by short-term solutions benefiting special interests.

It is probably best to look upon the current bout of inflation as an annoyingly large ripple on the top of the wave. Even if the ripple recedes, the wave will continue to erode currency values throughout the world in relation to basic commodities to supply personal and industrial needs and wants. *So despite what the politicians say, they do not have the will or the way to do much about inflation, except modify its degree at any one time.* The beleaguered investor simply has to protect earnings by being alert, innovative, and ready to take reasonable risks in financing, maintaining, and improving country property as a profitable alternative investment. If bought well and mortgaged well, country property—with its recent record of appreciation of about 10 to 15 percent a year—should keep the investor *ahead* of inflation most of the time.

## BUYING FARMLAND OR A FARM

The most profitable way to buy farmland is to buy an existing farm from a farmer who wants to retire for one reason or another—age, lack of heirs who want to take over, or perhaps financial distress. When you buy a working farm with improvements on it, you will at least have the basic buildings for the type of farming suited to the land in the past. You may have some ideas for improvement and your county agent may have others, but at least you will buy a farm which has the potential and the tools to produce something: dairy products, poultry, crops, or meat.

You will have to decide what your long-term plans are for the farm or the land. Will you work it yourself with your family's help? Is it the kind of large farm that will support your family as well as a tenant farmer? Or will you simply live in the main house and lease the land and buildings to a neighboring farmer for use? Or do you plan to discontinue the active farming and eventually sell some or all of the land to a developer?

There is an advantage, in most states, to keep the land classified as agricultural land; the tax rates are lower. Your county agent can tell you about the local program and can tell you, too, what has been the classification of the land you intend to buy.

### Living on a Small Working Farm

Despite all warnings, every year a growing trickle of people, primarily pioneering couples, buy farms and intend to make a living at small-scale "family" farming. Even with the best of intentions, sweat equity, and intelligence, only a few succeed. The agroeconomics and politics of the United States are tilted to large-scale farmers, the agribusiness people who account for the bulk of the food grown each year. Because food production is such a crucial factor in the economy of the United States and the world, it is likely that small farmers will continue to suffer from benign neglect—until they make the most of what they have and succeed by sheer endurance and intelligent self-reliance.

According to Karl Schwenke, a successful small-scale farmer in Vermont who has written a most useful book, *Successful Small-Scale Farm-*

*ing,* "governmental help for the small farmer is virtually nil. Homesteading belongs to history, and subsidies, price-support programs and other giveaway gimmicks belong to mass-production agriculture. If small-scale farming continues to grow in this country, it will owe its success to the native grit of the small farmer, not to the politician." Books such as Schwenke's are must reading for the would-be, first-time farmers.

*Example: Farm Survival Seminars Bring Extra Income*
Peter and Grace Petrides bought 75 acres of pasture and woodlands and farm buildings that enabled them to keep cows, chickens, horses, rabbits, and to grow a limited amount of feed crops. Both were professional people, Peter an economics professor at a nearby college and Grace a lawyer with clients in Knoxville, about twenty miles away.

After a year or two of gathering experience in farming, they hit upon the idea of encouraging people—singles, and couples with children—to come to week-long seminars on farming and getting the most out of country life. They fixed up an old equipment shed as a meeting place and classroom. An abandoned hay barn served as a dormitory. Classes covered buying land, gardening, raising farm animals, poultry, and crops, maintaining farm equipment, food preservation, and even beekeeping.

They encouraged one of the children of a neighboring farmer to help out with the cooking and serving. During the spring, summer, and fall months a limited number of people came each week. The charge was $150 for adults and $50 for each child under 14. The guests got three meals a day and plenty of time just to relax. They were told to bring their own bedrolls, which they could stretch out on hay in the dormitory. Or they could bring tents and campers to suit themselves.

Weekends the Petrides saved for themselves.

Quite aside from the stimulation of passing on a way of living, the Petrides got a lot of help, some of it amateur, of course, in caring for and developing their own farm and *were paid for giving others the privilege of working for them.*

## Hiring a Manager for a Large Farm

If you are going to be a substantial investor in farmland or in a farm, it would be worth your while to have an appraiser (see Appendix C for details and the names of other useful farm-buying and management services) check out the land for you before you close on the purchase. These organizations also manage farms and ranches and can find a tenant farmer for you and guide the work, if that is the kind of help you need.

In general, you will have to decide whether you are going to be a small farmer doing most of the work yourself with somewhat old-fashioned tools, often powered by sweat, or whether you are going to put several hundred thousand dollars—even a million or more—into the farm for starters: buying the land and upgrading all the buildings, and buying the modern equipment necessary to run a modern agribusiness. Such a venture will support a hired manager who earns a salary plus, perhaps, a share of the profits. All of these business angles (and expenses) can put the investor into agribusiness on a profitable scale, but expert advice, at a price, is highly recommended.

*Example: Fable of the Seducer, Idealist, and the Farmer*
There was once a country girl—call her Terry for the purpose of this fable. Terry was a beautiful, simple girl besieged by proposals of marriage and assorted adventures. Terry's trouble was her lack of experience. Which suitor would be best for her?

Would it be Charlie, a rich, handsome fellow from the city? Charlie talked up a whirlwind of promises and purported pleasures. When Terry expressed some doubt about whether that was what she wanted, Charlie wanted to force his plans upon her with little regard for anyone's gain but his own.

Would it be Sam, a lithe, brilliant college graduate and environmentalist, also from the city, who told Terry that Charlie had ruined a lot of girls and that Terry ought to be on a pedestal where she could be appreciated, planned for, but not touched? This attitude, though flattering to Terry, relieved Sam of many responsibilities. Terry, a healthy, maturing young lady turned to a third suitor, George.

George was a no-nonsense farmer, not particularly handsome but kind, gentle, and strong when strength was needed. He took the trouble to find out what Terry expected out of life and promised he would do his best to help her get it. They married and Terry worked hard with George during their entire life together. Her experience with her three suitors, Terry passed on to their many descendants.

From Charlie, she said, she had learned to beware of great schemes motivated only by money. From Sam, the idealist, she had learned the appeal but eventual sterility of idealism carried to an extreme. From George, she had learned common sense, caring, and the husbandry of mutual resources.

## BUYING LAND WITH THE IDEA OF DEVELOPING IT

Unless you are experienced in buying raw land or farmland with the idea of developing it, you had better get professional help. There are many factors which increase the value of raw land but they are all variations on moving it up to a higher and better use. Idle land is the least valuable. The following is a list of common uses for country land. The uses are listed in order of general value based on use:

1  Industrial park

2  Shopping mall

**3**   Condominium development

**4**   Resort hotel

**5**   Small lots for single families

**6**   Large lots for single families

**7**   Recreation-vehicle camping ground

**8**   Working farm

**9**   Cropland leased out

**10**   Pasture land leased out

**11**   Woodlands and/or wetlands

**12**   Hilly or mountainous acreage

*Example: Vast Trinchera Ranch in Colorado Developed into 5-Acre Lots for Roughing it*

Some years ago, when Malcolm Forbes, publisher of *Forbes* magazine, bought the huge Trinchera ranch, covering 260 square miles in Colorado near the Sangre de Cristo Ranches in the foothills of the Rockies, he may not at first have planned to develop it. But selling the land gradually over a period of years—sharing it with others who liked the climate and the view, and who wanted a chance to rough it in one of the great natural vistas of the West—proved highly profitable.

With careful land planning, parts of the great ranch were reserved for wilderness and parts were opened to purchase in the form of 5-acre lots or multiples thereof. The first lots were sold for as little as $3,500 in the section known as Sangre de Cristo Ranches. Lots with better views went for $5,000, $7,500, and $9,000, and at the start payments could be made in installments with *no interest charged.* Sales went well, interest was instituted on installments, the market was able to bear a rise in prices, and over several years, with the help of a professional advertising and direct-mail marketing campaign, most of the Sangre de Cristo sites were sold. Then another part of the ranch, on somewhat higher ground— 8,350 to 10,000 feet—was opened up and that is still selling today for prices beginning at $3,500 for a 5-acre site.

The newsletter for the development, *The Roundup,* indicates that the lure of the place is the remoteness; the buyers are either land investors or people who are *not* looking for the total-recreation community or recreation-home approach, with organized social events, clubs, tennis courts, and swimming pools. There is no electricity, sewers, swimming pools, casino, or beach—the buyers build their own homes within certain specifications, must drill their own wells, and provide for sanitary facilities. The success of the Trinchera ranch venture indicates a certain strong market for nature lovers and those who want to own a piece of valuable raw land in the West—a kind of investment in the American past as well as in its future.

## Buying Raw Land in Quantity Reduces the Price per Acre

You may want to accumulate an inventory of land so that you can sell it gradually at a later date when it has increased in value. Note in Tables 4-4 to 4-12 how smaller tracts bring premium prices compared with larger tracts of the same grade of land.

**A Checklist for Comparing Tracts of Land**   Table 4-12 is designed to be used for comparing tracts of land rather than appraising them. You can make several copies of it on a photocopying machine and then fill out one for each tract of land you have under consideration.

**Table 4-3**   Approximate Land Values in Selected Counties in Pocono Mountain Area, Including Pike, Monroe, Wayne & Susquehanna Counties of Pennsylvania and Western Sullivan & Delaware Counties of New York

| Acres | Good unimproved land per acre |
|---|---|
| 5– 10 | $1,200–3,000 |
| 11– 20 | $1,000–2,000 |
| 21– 40 | $800–1,500 |
| 41– 60 | $700–1,200 |
| 61–100 | $600–1,000 |
| 101–200 | $500– 800 |
| 201–500 | $400– 600 |

The above acreage parcels are considered basically unimproved, that is, without major building improvements. They would have paved or gravel road frontage, and in some cases views, streams, pond sites. All property would be from 1½ to 2½ hours distance from New York City and be within 30 minutes driving distance of many Pocono Mountain year-round recreational facilities.

### Pocono Mountain Vacation Home Sites

Usually in lake or ski communities. Home sites from one-third to one acre in size:

*Priced by category based on location*

| | |
|---|---|
| Lake front home sites | $50,000 |
| Lake view home sites | $7,500–20,000 |
| Back lots | $5,000–10,000 |
| Exceptional view lots | $7,500–20,000 |

Courtesy of Davis R. Chant, Milford, Pennsylvania.

**Table 4-4**  Approximate Land Values in Northern
Fairfield and Southern Litchfield Counties, Connecticut

*Redding and Ridgefield areas (southern portion of Fairfield County)*

Building lots (2 acres) in Redding —$16,000–20,000
Building lots (1 acre) in Ridgefield—$12,000–13,000

Parcels of unimproved land (10 to 100 acres)—approximately $2,500 to $3,000 per acre.
(*Note:* Parcels over 100 acres are rare but, if available, per acre cost would be somewhat
lower.)

*Danbury, Bethel, Brookfield, Newton areas (northern portion of Fairfield County)*

Building lots (¾ to 1½ acre)—$8,000–11,000

Parcels of unimproved land (10 to 75 acres)—approximately $1,800 to $2,500 per acre.
(*Note:* Parcels over 75 acres in this area are very rare but, if available, per acre cost would
be somewhat lower.)

*New Milford area (southern portion of Litchfield County)*

Building lots (¾ to 1½ acre)—$6,000–9,000

    Parcels of unimproved land (10 to 100 acres)—$2,000–2,500 per acre
                         (100 acres and up)—$1,500–2,000 per acre

*Lakefront Property (Lake Candlewood)—$225–300 per front foot on lake.*

(*Note:* There are very few unimproved building lots on lake front available.)

*Note:* Values increase with proximity to New York City metropolitan area.

Courtesy Emil J. Morey, Danbury, Connecticut.

**Table 4-5**  Land Values in Northern
Mendocino County, California

| *Typical tract sizes (in acres)* | *Range of total prices* | *Average price per acre* |
| --- | --- | --- |
| 5 | $ 25– 35,000 | $6,000 |
| 10 | $ 20– 40,000 | $3,000 |
| 20 | $ 25– 35,000 | $1,500 |
| 40 | $ 35– 45,000 | $ 937 |
| 60 | $ 40– 60,000 | $ 833 |
| 80 | $ 50– 75,000 | $ 781 |
| 160 | $ 75–100,000 | $ 546 |
| 500 | $125–250,000 | $ 375 |
| 1000 | $300–400,000 | $ 350 |

    Land is good unimproved hilly land with spring water and gravel road access. Common
cover is Douglas fir, pine, oak, madrone, bay, and redwood. The tracts lie about 2.5 hours
north of San Francisco. Terms are usually 25–40% down with seller financing at 10%.

Courtesy of Lorne Strider, Laytonville, California.

**Table 4-6**  Approximate Land Values in Eastern Long Island, New York

| | Improved Land (per acre) | Good to exceptional unimproved land |
|---|---|---|
| *Building plots: $8,000–25,000* | | |
| *Acres* | | |
| 1– 4 | $6,000– 10,000 | $3,500–6,000 |
| 5– 10 | $3,500– 8,000 | $3,500–8,000 |
| 11– 50 | $3,000– 5,000 | $3,000–7,000 |
| 60–400 | $3,000– 5,000 | $3,000–5,500 |
| 15–200 | Agricultural rights only | $1,000–1,750 |

*Waterfront property*

| Located on: | Per front foot |
|---|---|
| Inlet | $250– 350 |
| Bay | $400– 600 |
| Long Island Sound | $300– 450 |
| Ocean | $1,000–1,500 |

Courtesy Val Stype, Mattituck, New York.


**Table 4-7**  Land Values in Otsego, Delaware and nearby Chenango and Broome Counties, New York

| Acres | Excellent unimproved land (per acre) | Fair to good unimproved land (per acre) |
|---|---|---|
| 1– 10 | $1,000 | $600–800 |
| 10– 20 | $1,000 | $600–800 |
| 20– 50 | $350–500 | $300–500 |
| 50–100 | $400–500 | $300–400 |
| 100–300 | $350–400 | $250–350 |

These figures apply to land only, with no buildings. A similar chart 10 years ago would show values one-half of these.

Courtesy of Tom DeMulder, Sidney, New York.


**Table 4-8**  Approximate Land Values in Sullivan County, New York

| Acres | Excellent unimproved land (per acre) | Fair to good unimproved (per acre) |
|---|---|---|
| 1– 10 | $1,000– 5,000 | $500–2,000 |
| 10– 20 | $1,000– 3,000 | $450–1,500 |
| 20– 50 | $1,000– 2,000 | $400–1,000 |
| 50–100 | $1,000– 1,750 | $350– 750 |
| 100–300 | $1,000– 1,250 | $325– 600 |

Courtesy Marty Schwartz, Livingston Manor, New York.

**Table 4-9**  Approximate Land Values in Chenango County, New York

| Acres | Improved land (per acre) | Good improved land (per acre) |
|---|---|---|
| 1 | $1,000 | $10,000 |
| 5– 20 | $700 | $1,500 |
| 20–100 | $500 | $1,000 |
| 100–200 | $200 | $400 |
| 200–400 | $200 | $300 |
| Over 400 | $200 | $300 |

Courtesy of Irmin A. Mody, Norwich, New York.

**Table 4-10**  Approximate Land Values in Southeastern Vermont in Windham and Rockingham Counties

| Acres | Good unimproved land (per acre) |
|---|---|
| 5– 10 | $1,400–3,000 |
| 11– 20 | $1,300–2,800 |
| 21– 40 | $1,200–2,400 |
| 41– 60 | $1,000–1,800 |
| 61–100 | $500–1,500 |
| 101–200 | $400–1,300 |
| 201–500 | $400– 900 |

Any improvement, such as old farm buildings, would generally be a positive factor in relation to the above per acre prices. Southeastern Vermont lies 3 to 4 hours from New York City and 2 hours from Boston and thus has experienced the strongest demand in New England for recreational land over the past eight years. Generally, the land as noted would be within 30 minutes of major ski facilities.

**Table 4-11**  Approximate Land Values in Cheshire County in Southwestern New Hampshire

| Acres | Good unimproved land (per acre) |
|---|---|
| 5– 10 | $1,000–3,000 |
| 11– 20 | $1,000–2,700 |
| 21– 40 | $900–2,500 |
| 41– 60 | $800–2,200 |
| 61–100 | $700–2,000 |
| 101–200 | $600–1,500 |
| 201–500 | $500–1,000 |

Demand just east of the Connecticut River has been well behind that for Vermont land for many years. However, rising prices in Vermont and the basic attractiveness of New Hampshire have had an influence toward higher prices this past year and this is continuing strong. Proximity to lakes is good as compared to Vermont land, and the location is the same as Vermont in relation to Interstate 91. The price range for acreage pertains to raw land or old farms and would not be lakefront or lake oriented.

Courtesy Freeman, Everett & Co., Brattleboro, Vermont.

**Table 4-12**  Land Evaluation Chart

Parcel Name or Number _____

Location _____   Ownership _____   Date _____

| Characteristic | Point score and determining factors | | | | Score—this Parcel |
| --- | --- | --- | --- | --- | --- |
| | 4 | 3 | 2 | 1 | |
| Dist. from major pop. centers | Under 50 mi | 50–100 mi | 100–150 mi | Over 150 mi | |
| Dist. from major highway | Under 10 mi | 10–20 mi | 20–30 mi | Over 30 mi | |
| Dist. from major airport | Under 10 mi | 10–20 mi | 20–30 mi | Over 30 mi | |
| Major recreation areas within 20 mi | More than 4 | 2–4 | 0–2 | None | |
| Distance to lake or ocean | Under 5 mi | 5–10 mi | 10–20 mi | Over 20 mi | |
| *Score*—General Factors (maximum 20 points) | | | | | |
| Dist. from access road | Thru Site | Under 1 mi | 1–5 mi | Over 5 mi | |
| Condition of access road | Paved–Good | Paved–Fair | Gravel–Good | Poor | |
| Acreage (total) | 1000 | 500–1000 | 250–500 | Under 250 | |
| Topography (general character) | Gentle | Rolling | Hilly | Mountainous | |
| Extent of slopes over 20% | Less than 25% | 25–50% | 50–75% | Over 75% | |
| Woodlands (extent) | Over 75% | 50–75% | 25–50% | Under 25% | |
| Woodlands (type and condition) | Excellent | Good | Fair | Poor | |
| Extent of tract with good soils | Over 75% | 50–75% | 25–50% | Under 25% | |
| Rock and ledge occurrence | None | Occasional | Frequent | Extensive | |
| Water (pond and/or brook) on site | Good | Small | Possible | None | |
| Gravel—distance to source | On site | Under 1 mi | 1–5 mi | Over 5 mi | |
| Existing buildings | Excellent | Fair | Poor | None | |
| Electric power | On site | Within 1 mi | 1–2 mi | Over 2 mi | |
| Public water supply | On site | Within 1 mi | Over 1 mi | None | |
| Public sewers | On site | Within 1 mi | Over 1 mi | None | |

*Score*—Physical factors (maximum 60 points)

| | Over 75% | 50–75% | 25–50% | Under 25% |
|---|---|---|---|---|
| Percent of tract usable | | | | |
| Zoning controls | None | Limited | Average | Rigid |
| Subdivision controls | None | Limited | Average | Rigid |
| Environmental controls | None | Limited | Average | Rigid |
| General character of land | Attractive | Pleasant | Average | Poor |

*Score*—Miscellaneous factors (maximum 20 points)
Result of preliminary environmental impact study (minor impact—no change; moderate impact—deduct 20 points; substantial impact—deduct 50 points)

_____

*Total score* (maximum 100 points)

Rating—Highly desirable = 75–100%
       Good      = 50–75
       Poor      = Under 50

Suggested highest and best use:
Residential _____ Single-family units _____

Condominium _____ RV camping _____

Resort hotel _____ Recreation center (type) _____

Other use (describe) _____

Courtesy Lord-Wood/Lardson Associates, Incorporated, realtors.

# Chapter Five

# Buying with Professional Help

## WORKING WITH YOUR BANKER

The country banker knows as much as anyone about a rural area, its history, its land values, its potential future growth. That is why a banker may prove to be your most reliable source of information about the land you want to buy. Bankers also can recommend other professional people who can assist you as you buy, finance, maintain, and remodel, and possibly later sell, your country property. Why the banker rather than the realtor? Because a banker deals in mortgage loans, he or she will give you a more conservative opinion than a realtor who will want, above all, to sell you the property. Also, the banker knows the relative credit and performance record and most of the business and professional people in the community. When you ask for the names of competent professionals, the answers will take into consideration what the bank's experience has been with these businesspeople. You can exect the banker to handle these situations in a positive manner. That is, if you ask for the name of a good lawyer, realtor, or insurance agent, you will likely get the names of several so you can make a final choice.

## WHAT YOUR BANKER CAN DO FOR YOU

After serving as a point of reference, invaluable if you are new to the countryside, a banker can serve as a lender of money. In all probability this will mean a mortgage loan, either of the conventional type or one guaranteed by a government agency.

Your country banker can also guide you throughout the entire financing of your property. A banker has the money and the judgment to know where it can be prudently invested—and it could be in *you* and your projects.

As you establish credit with your banker, remember that the extra trouble you take in presenting your case can result in many doors opening for you in a new country community.

## ESTABLISHING YOUR CREDIT WITH YOUR BANKER

You will usually establish credit with your banker by applying for a loan to buy or to remodel your property. Mortgages or home loans come in two categories: conventional loans in which the real estate property—usually improved real estate—is the security that payments will be made on a timely basis. There are also loans made with the cooperation of federal agencies such as the FHA and the VA.

Banks give loans under regulations that are monitored by the federal and state governments. The law in your state undoubtedly limits interest rates that can be charged, how long a loan a bank may write, and the required minimum down payments.

Most contemporary home loans fall into the conventional category. Most are amortized or paid back in equal monthly installment payments over the life of the loan. Payments include interest on principal and an increasing amount of principal. Set up this way, your mortgage loan will eventually be paid up in full and your banker can arrange it so that the date parallels some other personal goals you may have—such as retirement. By dealing directly with the bank and its officers you will save time processing your loan application and you will close more quickly.

### Federal Housing Administration Loan Guarantee

The FHA and the VA encourage other types of loans but these, too, require cooperation between you and a recognized lender, usually a bank.

In the case of the FHA, the borrower (you) pays a mortgage-insurance premium of ½ of 1 percent of the amount of loan outstanding each year to insure the loan. The money goes into an insurance pool administered by the FHA. The insurance covers the lender, not the borrower.

Because this insurance reduces risk, the bank or other lender can accept a lower down payment. The schedule in Table 5-1 shows a typical pay-out plan. These change, however, with regulations, and it is best to ask your bank for the current figures.

**Table 5-1**   Typical Monthly Repayment
Schedule—$100,000 Loan at 13.50%

| | Years | Monthly payment | Annual constant |
|---|---|---|---|
| | 10 | 1.522743 | 18.28 |

| Yr | Annual interest | Annual principal | Year end balance |
|---|---|---|---|
| 1 | 13.193316 | 5.079599 | 94.920401 |
| 2 | 12.463507 | 5.809407 | 89.110994 |
| 3 | 11.628844 | 6.644071 | 82.466923 |
| 4 | 10.674261 | 7.598654 | 74.868269 |
| 5 | 9.582528 | 8.690386 | 66.177883 |
| 6 | 8.333942 | 9.938973 | 56.238910 |
| 7 | 6.905966 | 11.366949 | 44.871961 |
| 8 | 5.272826 | 13.000089 | 31.871872 |
| 9 | 3.405045 | 14.867870 | 17.004002 |
| 10 | 1.268912 | 17.004002 | 0.000000 |

| | Years | Monthly payment | Annual constant |
|---|---|---|---|
| | 15 | 1.298319 | 15.58 |

| Yr | Annual interest | Annual principal | Year end balance |
|---|---|---|---|
| 1 | 13.366361 | 2.213462 | 97.786538 |
| 2 | 13.048343 | 2.531480 | 95.255059 |
| 3 | 12.684634 | 2.895189 | 92.359870 |
| 4 | 12.268669 | 3.311153 | 89.048717 |
| 5 | 11.792941 | 3.786881 | 85.261836 |
| 6 | 11.248863 | 4.330959 | 80.930876 |
| 7 | 10.626615 | 4.953207 | 75.977669 |
| 8 | 9.914966 | 5.664857 | 70.312812 |
| 9 | 9.101071 | 6.478752 | 63.834061 |
| 10 | 8.170240 | 7.409583 | 56.424478 |
| 11 | 7.105672 | 8.474151 | 47.950327 |
| 12 | 5.888153 | 9.691669 | 38.258658 |
| 13 | 4.495708 | 11.084115 | 27.174543 |
| 14 | 2.903204 | 12.676619 | 14.497925 |
| 15 | 1.081898 | 14.497925 | 0.000000 |

**Table 5-1** Typical Monthly Repayment
Schedule—$100,000 Loan at 13.50% (continued)

| Yr | Years<br>20 | Monthly<br>payment<br>1.207375 | Annual<br>constant<br>14.49 |
|---|---|---|---|
| | Annual<br>interest | Annual<br>principal | Year end<br>balance |
| 1 | 13.436484 | 1.052012 | 98.947988 |
| 2 | 13.285337 | 1.203159 | 97.744828 |
| 3 | 13.112474 | 1.376023 | 96.368806 |
| 4 | 12.914774 | 1.573722 | 94.795084 |
| 5 | 12.688671 | 1.799826 | 92.995258 |
| 6 | 12.430082 | 2.058414 | 90.936844 |
| 7 | 12.134340 | 2.354156 | 88.582688 |
| 8 | 11.796108 | 2.692388 | 85.890300 |
| 9 | 11.409281 | 3.079215 | 82.811084 |
| 10 | 10.966876 | 3.521620 | 79.289464 |
| 11 | 10.460909 | 4.027587 | 75.261878 |
| 12 | 9.882248 | 4.606248 | 70.655630 |
| 13 | 9.220448 | 5.268048 | 65.387582 |
| 14 | 8.463564 | 6.024932 | 59.362650 |
| 15 | 7.597935 | 6.890561 | 52.472089 |
| 16 | 6.607938 | 7.880558 | 44.591531 |
| 17 | 5.475703 | 9.012793 | 35.578738 |
| 18 | 4.180795 | 10.307701 | 25.271037 |
| 19 | 2.699842 | 11.788654 | 13.482382 |
| 20 | 1.006114 | 13.482382 | 0.000000 |

Courtesy: The Thorndike Encyclopedia of Banking and Financial Tables.

## Veterans Administration Loan Guarantee

You can get a mortgage loan through the Veterans Administration if you are a veteran of World War II, the Korean war, or the Vietnam conflict. Under the VA plan, loans can be made for the full value of the property up to 30 years. The borrower pays no insurance premium and the VA limits the charges and fees to the veteran. The VA guarantees the mortgage lender that a percentage of the principal will be returned in case of default. For this reduction in risk, the lender is supposed to offer the loan at a lower rate of interest than on a conventional loan. In fact, the federal government puts a ceiling on the maximum interest rate a lender can charge the consumer under the FHA and the VA plan. It also puts a ceiling on the maximum amount that can be borrowed.

**Table 5-2**   Graduated-Payment Mortgage Plan

$55,000 sales price; mortgage amount: $52,750; down-payment: $2,250
HOA graduated payment mortgage plan
30 year term; 2 years of level payments; with 10 years of payments increasing 6% per year
Contract rate: 9.5%
Income to Qualify: $18,000[a]

| Year | Monthly payment | Annual mtg. insurance premium | Amount of principal paid in year | Loan balance at end of year | Estimated value of home[b] | Loan to value ratio | Owner's net equity |
|------|------|------|------|------|------|------|------|
| 1 | $316.57 | $266.60 | −$1,266.59 | $54,016.59 | $57,200 | 94.4% | $ 3,183.41 |
| 2 | 316.57 | 273.22 | − 1,392.30 | 55,408.89 | 59,488 | 93.1 | 4,079.11 |
| 3 | 335.57 | 279.96 | − 1,292.37 | 56,701.26 | 61,868 | 91.6 | 5,166.74 |
| 4 | 355.70 | 286.14 | − 1,168.22 | 57,869.48 | 64,342 | 89.9 | 6,472.52 |
| 5 | 377.04 | 291.64 | − 1,017.00 | 58,886.09 | 66,916 | 88.0 | 8,029.91 |
| 6 | 399.66 | 296.30 | − 833.90 | 59,719.99 | 69,593 | 85.8 | 9,873.01 |
| 7 | 423.64 | 299.99 | − 616.03 | 60,336.02 | 72,376 | 83.4 | 12,039.98 |
| 8 | 449.06 | 302.49 | − 358.52 | 60,694.54 | 75,271 | 80.6 | 14,526.46 |
| 9 | 476.01 | 303.60 | − 56.33 | 60,750.87 | 78,282 | 77.6 | 17,531.13 |
| 10 | 504.57 | 303.09 | 296.13 | 60,454.74 | 81,413 | 74.3 | 20,958.26 |
| 11 | 534.84 | 300.69 | 705.05 | 59,749.69 | 84,670 | 70.6 | 24,920.31 |
| 12 | 566.93 | 296.10 | 1,177.33 | 58,572.36 | 88,056 | 66.5 | 29,483.64 |
| 13 | 566.93 | 289.95 | 1,294.15 | 57,278.21 | 91,579 | 62.5 | 34,300.79 |
| 14 | 566.93 | 283.19 | 1,422.62 | 55,855.59 | 95,242 | 58.6 | 39,396.41 |
| 15 | 566.93 | 275.76 | 1,563.81 | 54,291.78 | 99,051 | 54.8 | 44,759.22 |

[a] For a $40,000 mortgage, the income needed to qualify would be about $15,000.
[b] Based on 4 percent appreciation value per year. Despite the negative amortization in the early years of the mortgage, an appreciation rate of only 2.5% in the value of the house will still result in positive equity build-up and a decreasing loan to value ratio.

*Source:*   NAHB Economics Division.

In an effort to make housing available to families with incomes ranging from $15,000 to $24,000 a year, at a time when the median price for an existing single family house is close to $60,000 and is increasing yearly by a double-digit amount, the FHA, working with banks and the Department of Housing and Urban Development, in 1979 devised and has been offering a graduated-payment mortgage plan. A typical mortgage of this type might require an income of $18,000 to qualify, a down payment of $2,250, and two years of level payments. Over a period of 15 years it would work out as seen in Table 5-2. Chapter 6 gives further details on government aid in financing private homes.

## SHOPPING FOR THE BEST BANK DEAL

Do not believe for a moment that you must get your bank loan from the most obvious bank in your rural area. It may be the largest local bank but for one reason or another, it may not offer the best mortgage deal available in your country area. Traditionally, a savings bank or a savings and loan association will be most liberal in its lending policies. But the bank regulators of any specific state can limit the amount lendable to any one person, and the amount of money you need may soar well beyond that limit. You must then go to a commercial bank. In rural areas, commercial banks get more actively involved in farm and residential mortgages than banks of similar size would in the city. A federally chartered commercial bank may very well have more liberal lending limits than a state-chartered bank. Because of widespread changes within the U.S. banking system— and the increased competition for business—it pays to shop for your mortgage deal, just as it pays to shop at the supermarkets for bargains.

Here are the main questions you should ask in order to decide where you will get the best deal:

**1** I am in the process of buying a country property for $\$$_____. *If, after investigation, my credit and your appraisal of the property prove out, will you be able to lend me $\$$_____ against this property?* Get this money commitment from the banker first. If there are limitations on the amount that can be lent on a property, this question will identify the limitations and perhaps eliminate any further steps if the banker can't handle your request.

**2** *What is your current rate?* Banks may charge a quarter to a half a point more for a second residence or an investment property than they will for a primary family residence. That is, if the bank's rate is 10 percent for a mortgage on a family residence, it might be 11 or 11.5 percent on a second residence or investment property. Be sure you have an understanding about this. Most country bankers assume you will be asking about a primary family residence because that is the bulk of their business.

**3** *For how many years will you give the mortgage?* The usual length of time is 20 or 25 years. In some instances you can get a 30-year mortgage. On the other hand, you may want the mortgage paid off at a specific date in the future, when you plan to retire, for example. By stretching out the mortgage, you reduce somewhat the amount of the monthly payment. You pay back less principal per month, but the amount of interest is higher because of the longer time period. Of course, this interest can be deducted from taxes and the *smaller* amount per month may seem attractive to an eventual buyer. In general, a potential buyer will be looking for a maximum amount of mortgage at a low interest rate.

**4** *What penalties, if any, are there for prepayment?* Most banks charge a penalty for prepayment of the full amount. Many banks will allow you to pay as much as 20 percent *without penalty* in anticipation in any one year. For reasons of your own, you may want the privilege of prepaying the entire amount without penalty. If so, ask for this privilege.

**5** *Is the interest rate variable or fixed?* Be very sure about this difference. It is something that may be spelled out in small print these days, as it is to the bank's decided advantage to be able to raise the rate of interest on its mortgages if money becomes tight and prime rate goes up. This raise may play havoc with *your* financial planning. Try to avoid a variable rate mortgage. True, it will benefit you if prime rates decline and the bank decides to lower its rate. But this happens more often in theory than in practice.

**6** *Up to what percent of appraised value will you lend?* In some ways, this was covered in your first question, when you put your specific case on the line. Ask the question this way to get the general policy of the bank. The bank's appraiser may make a higher (or a lower) appraisal than you might expect. The fact that you are paying a certain amount of dollars for the property will weigh toward an appraisal near that amount. If there has been talk with the seller as to the appraised value of the property, try to identify the local person who made the last appraisal. If the figure seemed right for your plans, try to get the appraisal brought up to date. Perhaps that person does appraisals for one of the banks you are considering doing business with. Do not be surprised if different appraisers come up with substantially different amounts. This occurs often when there have not been many recent sales of comparable property. Then, too, some appraisers are more conservative than others, and a bank, depending on its lending policies of the moment, may favor one philosophy or the other.

**7** *What are your closing costs? And who is responsible for what cost?* These will vary with the bank. By law banks must spell these out for you, but not necessarily at this shopping stage. From the banker's point of view, these closing costs are obstacles to a deal, as well they might be from *your* point of view if they are out of line with what you can get elsewhere. Typical items of closing and settlement costs are shown in Table 5-3. Not *all* of these costs apply to your settlement but many of them probably will. Go over them one by one, as a kind of checklist, with the banker

**Table 5-3** Typical Closing and Settlement Costs

| | |
|---|---|
| [ ] Application fees | $_____ |
| [ ] Credit report | _____ |
| [ ] Survey | _____ |
| [ ] Title examination | _____ |
| [ ] Mortgage title insurance | _____ |
| [ ] Owner title insurance | _____ |
| [ ] Attorney fees | _____ |
| [ ] Origination fees | _____ |
| [ ] Preparation of documents | _____ |
| [ ] Closing fees | _____ |
| [ ] Recording fees | _____ |
| [ ] Transfer taxes | _____ |
| [ ] Escrow fees | _____ |
| [ ] Termite inspection | _____ |
| [ ] Other closing costs | _____ |
| *Total closing costs* | $_____ |
| [ ] Loan discount payment | $_____ |
| [ ] Real estate taxes | _____ |
| [ ] FHA mortgage insurance premium | _____ |
| [ ] Special assessments (if any) | _____ |
| [ ] Other prepaid items | _____ |
| *Total prepaid items* | $_____ |
| *Total estimated settlement costs* | $_____ |

you are interviewing. Use the same procedure with other banks on your shopping list. Then compare what each bank is offering you and choose the deal that best suits your profit goals.

## WHAT THE BANK EXPECTS FROM YOU

The bank naturally expects your full cooperation in getting credit information, and also access to the property so that the bank can examine it and have its appraiser do likewise.

You should have the following information ready to turn over to the bank and ready to help you fill in its application form if you get satisfactory answers to the preliminary questions you put to the bank:

1 Proof of your income, such as W 2 forms for the last two or three years. If you are self-employed, the banker will want to see copies of your federal income taxes for the past year at least.

2 You will be asked to identify your commercial bank account, your savings accounts, credit cards, and any lender who has extended substantial amounts of credit to you in the past. This could be a previous mortgage holder, a landlord, a commercial bank that has lent money to you in the past.

3 You will be asked to construct a balance sheet of your personal finances so that the banker can determine what you have coming in, what you owe, and what expenses will be payable monthly. Perhaps you expect to enjoy an income from your property. You will then want to make a pro forma statement of what income you expect, and what expenses will reduce that income.

As you supply this information, remember that the banker will check it out or will have a credit information service check it out. The credit industry is so organized these days that central credit files will almost certainly turn up any judgments against you, any tax liens, or slow or disputed payments. It is best to tell the banker right away about problems you may have had in the recent past. If these things turn up in the credit check there may be a question as to why you suppressed the information. By and large, bankers are in business to make loans and earn the going interest rate without assuming unreasonable risk. They will probably overlook past problems if you can convince them that they have been solved and that they won't become *present* problems.

## INSPECTION OF LAND, LOT, AND BUILDINGS

The bank will expect its appraiser to inspect the land and buildings you want to finance, and probably any architectural plans you may have had prepared for improvements. This inspection is for the *bank's benefit*. It is not necessarily by a professional engineer—a separate inspection you may want to have made for *your* benefit. The value of this separate inspection will be discussed in a later part of this chapter.

Although the bank's appraiser and inspector may *not* tell you the appraised value of your property, the banker may be willing to tell you. The appraiser may have volunteered other information about the property that influenced its valuation. Perhaps the bank will give you a copy of the appraisal. It could be valuable to you when you refinance the property or if and when you want to sell it for a profit.

## SURVEYING YOUR PROPERTY

Perhaps the seller of your new property has a recent land survey and is willing to turn it over to you. The seller may be able to point out surveyor's marks, stakes, or pipes. If there is doubt in your mind as to the reliability of the surveying office, the banker will undoubtedly recognize the surveyor and can give you an opinion. If you or your banker feel it is necessary, you can call up the same office to reconfirm the survey and perhaps have it reviewed or possibly redone to cover changes that may have taken place since the last survey. Land may have been added or subtracted, or building or zoning regulations may have changed, thereby altering one or another measurement. If, for example, you want to position a garage or outbuilding as close to a lot line as possible, you will have to know the current regulation governing the nearness of buildings to lot lines and you will have to *be sure* of where the lot line runs. This could be a crucial decision if your neighbor, the fellow on the other side of the lot line, does not particularly want to see a building there, or if it otherwise annoys him. These matters become more important in a rural village than way out in the country, but then your "out in the country" survey may have been done haphazardly, with reference to "a large oak tree" or a shoreline that may no longer exist, a center of a creek that may have dried up, or the bank of a brook that may have changed its course.

When you have your land surveyed, be sure the surveyor anchors the points of reference in something with some permanence. Should you want to improve your property, subdivide it, for example, or sell it to a buyer who is as thorough and cautious as you are, you will want to refer quickly to these permanent markers. Identifying these markers when you buy will save you time (and money) at a later date when you may want to take your profits from the project. If, by chance you find that the person who sold the property to you has overlooked a violation and that the title is actually in default, you can have him or her correct the flaw before you actually close on it. That is why it pays to use the time between contract and closing for these investigations, that which the bank may not require but which you, as a prudent buyer trying to assure yourself of maximum profits, will want to verify. Years hence you or your heirs will be glad you did.

## OTHER SERVICES YOUR BANKER CAN SUPPLY

Many banks require you to pay, in addition to your monthly principal and interest on a mortgage, a pro rata installment on your fire insurance and your real estate taxes. This works out to the bank's advantage in two ways: (1) it allows the bank to monitor your personal paying habits, and (2) it assures the bank that these important payments are made on time. Late payments or nonpayment, of course, can entangle the property in liens, in the case of taxes, or may result in a fire insurance policy cancelled for nonpayment of premium. The second advantage for the bank is the opportunity to act as a custodian of the flow of funds from month to month until such time as payments are due. Your own payments may add up to only a few thousand dollars. But consider these few thousand dollars multiplied by the number of the banks' customers, and you have a sizable float that the banks can invest and earn interest on until the actual payments for premiums and taxes become due.

This procedure has become feasible in the age of the computer, but it is not necessarily foolproof. You will have to check, at least at the start, that the bank actually makes its payments. Through no malign intention of its own, the bank may omit payments through oversight or because a special situation was not programmed into the computer. The computer, these days, is blamed for many an error that bank management should have eliminated from services offered to the public. Most of these services *are* consumer oriented to save you time, money, and worry, but it pays to ascertain whether the service delivers the convenience and savings it claims. As you shop around for the best deal, ask your banker about voluntary or involuntary collection of fire insurance money, taxes, and any other payments required in addition to the conventional interest and principal payments.

Most banks will *not* require credit life insurance, but you may find it to be an inexpensive and worthwhile term insurance covering the unpaid balance of your mortgage. If you should die before the mortgage is paid off, this type of insurance would take care of the mortgage. You could possibly arrange to have this premium paid in monthly installments with the mortgage.

Finally, since the bank is investing your credit and the feasibility of your entire project, you may want to finance, from the outset, some of the improvements you intend to make immediately. The banker and the appraiser can consider how much value the projected improvements will actually give to your property. The bank may be willing to finance these when you are ready to go ahead with them.

## WORKING WITH YOUR LAWYER

Unless you are a lawyer yourself or feel confident in becoming one after reading a do-it-yourself book, you had better work closely with a local lawyer. There is an old saying that one who represents oneself in court has a fool for a lawyer. You are, of course, not going to court with your real estate closing. The purpose of having everything in good legal order is to prevent anything from going to court because of a disorder discovered later. Are you willing to risk your potential profit on your limited knowledge and lack of local experience?

The several hundred dollars a lawyer may charge you when you buy your property will seem relatively little when you consider the peace of mind it gives you at a later date. Yes, bone up on what the do-it-yourself books outline and *minimize* the amount you pay an attorney. You can save by having the lawyer review what you have done, what research you have made, and the rough papers you have drawn to cover the verbal agreements you have made with the seller. The attorney can then add the precautions and provisos that are necessary and "legalize" the language. Many of the self-help books outline standard agreements; if you follow them as a pattern, you will have most of the fine legal phrasing already in position and will save your lawyer time and yourself some money in fees.

One of the main reasons for bringing local lawyers into the act is to benefit from their experience on what documents are in common use in their local area. They can also expedite the need for rulings, changes, and legal interpretations because they know the local officials. And if you bring them in at the start, they will be inclined to remedy errors and answer questions at no further charge. The burden of proof or correction falls on their shoulders rather than yours.

You will find that a lawyer, wisely used in buying, will probably eliminate the need for one in selling, save for a quick review and perhaps a brief session of explanation with *your buyer's* attorney. When you are selling and use a realtor, the realtor will usually represent you. When you are buying, however, count on the realtor representing the seller primarily. No one will make any money unless the property is sold, so the realtor will go a long way toward getting the place sold to you at the asking price. A realtor will not be inclined to lower the price or make any other kind of monetary concession which will reduce or delay the commission, and will not be looking out for your short- or long-term interest in the property. Of course, a realtor is not out to cheat you because she or he would hope to be the realtor you use when you take your profits by selling the property once again in several years.

## WHAT YOUR LAWYER CAN DO FOR YOU

In the first place, the lawyer can take your hand and walk you through all the legal ramifications of the sale. But that is the most expensive way to use a lawyer and is probably not necessary unless you feel utterly incompetent in the field of real estate. But if you *feel that way,* why are you in it expecting to make a profit? Truly, you may have heard opportunity knocking but, frankly, it was not for you. Of course, if you inherit some property—if it literally falls into your lap and you are the Walter Mitty type—you had better turn everything over to an attorney to handle, but be sure you establish a fee before you wash your hands of your daily concern about the property. Your lawyer's fee for this management service will probably eliminate a good share of the operating profits, but eventually a buyer will be found, and then *you* will enjoy the probable substantial capital gains.

What is more likely in your case is that you will do as much of the investigating and negotiating toward a contract and closing as you think lies within your area of competence. Then you will turn the matter over to the lawyer to be carried on. Naturally, the lawyer will begin by reviewing what you have done thus far.

Your lawyer can also help you in the bargaining to establish a final price for the property, and to sort out the closing expenses and deciding who will pay for what. Very often you, as buyer, may find yourself in a relatively embarrassing position as you face the seller and the real estate agent. You perhaps know one or both too well, or you may have had past experiences that left a bad taste in your mouth. Your lawyer can act as a cushion, a replacement, or stand-in, and thus you will avoid some awkwardness or the reopening of old wounds. Then, too, if you are asking for a figure or a concession that the seller thinks outrageous, you can modify your stand and save face by presenting a more liberal offer than your lawyer did at the start. Lawyers are accustomed to this kind of scouting and representation of their client's proposals. Do not hesitate to use them that way. True, the lawyer you have chosen, though entirely competent, may not relish such ticklish situations. Some lawyers do and some don't, and that is why you should choose a lawyer—if you have a *choice*—that fits your individual situation best. You may find, too, that the lawyer you have chosen doesn't seem to get anything done because there are too many clients pressing him or because he or she may simply be lazy. There are two ways out of delays. One requires *coaxing* the lawyer to do what has been promised. The other requires finding a new lawyer who is more alert, more aggressive, and more willing to be of service.

This working relationship is particularly important if you plan to buy and sell country property with some *frequency.* This will mean more money for the lawyer and more interest in you as a client. If, on the other hand, you are likely to have only the one transaction it is best to outline with your lawyer just what you want done and when you want it done. If you don't know exactly what has to be done, get the lawyer to explain it to you, make an outline of it, and include a timetable for what each party must provide.

## An Outline and Timetable of Services

Such an outline might include the following services:

1  Drawing up or confirming a contract of sale.

2  Final negotiations with the seller and his agent.

3  Checking title for possible adverse easements, rights, liens, delinquent taxes, quirky strictures dating back to an earlier time that have never been removed from local laws or zoning regulations or from properties affected. This involves checking the abstract of title, which should give a history of the property from the date of the original owner.

4  Touching base with the seller, the realtor, and possibly the seller's lawyer, and also the bank, which will want certain papers in order so that the mortgage can be closed.

5  Setting a mutually suitable date for the closing.

6  Telling you what checks to have ready, in what amount, and in what form. Telling you what papers you will have to sign and, in brief, what they mean.

7  Guiding you through the steps of the closing and answering your questions along the way.

8  Filing papers that must be recorded with various public officials.

9  Presenting an itemized closing statement and a bill—both useful for tax purposes.

10  Giving counsel on the property as problems arise when you appear on the record as the new owner. Problems *may* arise in the tax area and both your lawyer and your accountant can help you, the lawyer with practical advice about local tax and legal procedures and the accountant in matters of tax shelters, investment credits, and the like.

Because this process of contract and closing has a vital influence on your subsequent profits and on the smooth management of your property, it is of paramount importance that you understand each part of the process. That is why the quality and honesty of your lawyer are so important. A lawyer *must* be alert and on the lookout for *your* best interests; this is worth the fee provided it is within the range of fees charged by other lawyers in the area. It is up to you to ask your lawyer what the charge per hour is and how many hours the complete service will take.

In the discussion of these several steps of the contract and closing process, remember it is a well-known routine to a lawyer, even if it may seem rather complicated or even incomprehensible to you. Ask your lawyer to explain the steps. At the same time listen carefully. A lawyer is there to clarify, not to give you a many-hour seminar on real estate. You should bone-up on transactions through reading a book such as this *before* you make use of a lawyer's services.

Here are three rules to follow as you work with your lawyer toward a closing and transfer of the real estate you want to buy.

### A Three-Step Working Procedure with Your Lawyer

**1**  Reduce all agreements to writing. Usually, all agreements pertaining to the sale and what has to be paid by whom will appear in the contract of sale and be repeated in the deed at the closing.

**2**  You and your lawyer should transfer all monies via checks on which purpose and amount are clearly stated. If possible, a summary receipt should be signed, acknowledging receipt of amounts paid by each party to the sale, the purpose of payment, and the date.

**3**  Ask your lawyer about words or concepts you do not completely understand. Although there has been improvement during the past years in putting real estate documents into understandable English, the tradition of property law is very strong and certain phrases and words mean something specific in courts of law, whereas contemporary paraphrases of them do not. For example, in the state of Hawaii some of the land can be bought in fee simple, an English concept which amounts to outright ownership of the land, as distinct from feudal use of it or leasing of it. In Hawaii there is much land still held by large land trusts dating from the days of the first white settlers and their descendants and, in some cases, from Hawaiian royalty. These lands can only be leased. This is equivalent to renting the land but owning the house you build upon it. Although words such as fee simple and leasehold may seem confusing, they actually refer to ancient procedures for controlling land. But the details vary from country to country. And certainly the person buying land in Hawaii must know the exact difference and what it will cost.

### THE CLOSING

The following are common and ordinary facets of a real estate closing. With each of them a lawyer can be helpful and in some cases crucially necessary. Apply the three principles suggested before. Put everything into writing, get receipts for all the money paid, with descriptions as to the purpose of the payments, and have your lawyer explain anything that seems unclear.

## Taking an Option to Hold a Property

A simple procedure for holding the property for a limited period of time is to take an *option* on it for a week, 10 days, or perhaps a month. This, too, should be a signed agreement stating price and expiration date, with a brief outline of what is included in the property under option. That is, the option should detail what the property includes beyond the land and obvious buildings. Certain tools and equipment, machinery, and furnishings may be included in farms and other improved rural property. The money you pay for an option characteristically amounts to a token, at most a few hundred dollars, and it is almost never refundable. That is why it can be so small and informal. It gives you the privilege of freezing the status of the property for a short while so that you can clear the decks of other possibilities and possible snags in financing. In short, you are buying time for other matters to work out.

## Drawing Up a Sales Contract

The next step in the process is a major one—the signing of the *sales contract* which, for the first time, outlines in complete detail the respective obligations of the buyer and the seller and describes the property. By the time you sign a sales contract (or purchase contract as it is sometimes called), you will have obtained a mortgage commitment from your banker, and it will be written into the contract that the sale is subject to obtaining a mortgage on the terms you have arranged. During the course of drawing up the contract, which usually takes about a month, all the serious investigation into your credit takes place and your lawyer can check out the property to be sure the title is clear and the items to be purchased are exactly as represented. After you have signed a sales contract you cannot bargain any longer with the seller. So be sure you have covered everything in the contract, which is signed by all the parties involved (including the spouses of the buyer and the seller).

The following are items that may or may not be involved in your sale. Check them over with your lawyer to be sure. They have been prepared in the form of an extended checklist with comments for your convenience:

[ ]   **The survey** of your property should be part of your sales contract. A copy of it will also interest your banker or other mortgage lender. It

summarizes the property's details and shows its exact dimensions, boundaries, often its elevation with respect to sea level, its relationship to an existing river or lake shore. In some rural areas the property acres have never been surveyed and boundaries exist only in informal relationships with neighbors, who have agreed over generations that the lands are adjacent to one another with a lot line running in the vicinity of some natural landmark, sometimes a creek, sometimes an old tree or rock, and then, by sight lines, to another landmark. You will be fortunate if the territory has been officially surveyed and there are benchmarks from the National Geological Survey on which a surveyor can base measurements. From the survey you should know your boundaries and know how many acres they encompass. A survey should describe your buildings and where they stand in relation to your boundaries. This placement can be very important in relation to existing zoning laws. Sometimes you will find that the buildings could not be placed as they are, if built today, because of a contemporary zoning regulation that prevents buildings that close to another building or to a boundary. Zoning laws cannot, fortunately, be made retroactive. Owners with existing buildings in violation of the current zoning laws are protected by "grandfather" rights. That is, what existed when the regulation was passed may or may not conform but it is *legal* via this prior right. New additions, however, *may not be legal* and thus could be a limit to your profit if you plan to improve the property further. For example, if a one-car garage is already too close to a boundary and you want to enlarge it to a two-car garage, you may have to obtain a variance to go ahead with your remodeling work. And it is conceivable, if a neighboring villager objects strenuously, that you will *not* get the variance

[ ] **Date for moving in**   The date when you can take possession of the premises should appear in the contract. This is not so important if you are buying raw land, but it could involve squatter tenants or even neighbors who have been informally using some of the land for grazing their cattle. You should demand (and get your guarantee in writing) full and uninhibited use of the property you buy. If there is something sticky to clear up, such as a tenant's lease that runs beyond the date stipulated for purchase, the seller should guarantee possession or, as an alternative that a reasonable amount of money will be paid to you should you have to take court action or simply wait until the tenant leaves or other encumbrances to the property are cleared up. A property may be in the process of improvement. Perhaps the owner was remodeling the kitchen, resurfacing a road, building a shed, or perhaps extending an access road that would facilitate sub-

division. Be sure to specify whether you expect the seller to complete the work. If it is not done, you can ask to be compensated. At times, too, an important piece of equipment, such as a pump, obviously does not operate satisfactorily. Its condition should be noted and repair obligations sorted out. Once in a while, as you go through these many bargaining points, the seller in rising exasperation may say, "Enough! I have stated my price. Not everything is new, some things need repair. But I am selling the property as is. Take it or leave it." You may counter through your lawyer with an estimate of what it would cost to put everything in working order, and then suggest that amount as a reduction from the price. The seller may not take kindly to your suggestion. Your lawyer may tell you as much, and then you will have to decide whether you will accept the property as is. The shrewd seller will certainly put into the contract for his or her protection that the property is being sold "as is," so you cannot come back later with law suits because the septic system does not function and a new $2,500 leach bed has to be dug. The time to try to make these adjustments in price is *before* signing the sales contract; doing it later will only lead to bad feeling. Your lawyer can tactfully bring up items that come to light between the contract and the closing, but it is better if you are aware of the defects in the property before signing the sales contract and include solutions to problems within this document.

[ ] **Taxes and special assessments** ordinarily will have been paid by the seller, and your lawyer will verify this. Outstanding obligations of this sort should be identified in the sales contract with a phrase added to the effect that all other obligations have been paid. In case an obligation turns up later, you can then hand the bill over to the seller. If, on the other hand, tax payments for the full year have been anticipated and you take possession prior to the end of this period, the seller is entitled to a pro rata reimbursement of the excess taxes paid. Remember, the financial institution that grants you a mortgage will want all these matters spelled out and settled as far as possible before it will supply the mortgage money.

[ ] **Insurance** can prove to be a ticklish matter for the period between the date you sign a purchase contract and the date you close and take possession. What if a fire occurs or there is storm damage? Once you have signed the purchase contract, as buyer you are the party who will have to sustain the loss in most situations. That is why you should bring up the subject of insurance with your lawyer to be sure that adequate protection exists for you. If it does not, you should get in touch with your insurance broker and establish some interim or

permanent protection. Your broker can also tell you whether the coverage is large enough and sufficiently comprehensive.

[ ] **The property defined**  Because of the legal importance of the sales contract, you and your lawyer must see to it that the legal definitions of the property, as outlined in the survey, are spelled out in writing in the contract. Specify the number of acres included in a tract of land. Specify the exact number of acres on which your colonial house stands in its village. Should a dispute arise, most courts will let you claim only the specific number of acres mentioned in the contract. If by chance there is no existing survey of the property, your lawyer will probably suggest one be carried out before closing. Meanwhile, the definition in the contract should be reworded in such a way that the purchase covers all the property offered by the seller in that specific parcel within the given boundaries—however vague—representing plus or minus a stated number of acres *subject to verification by a survey.*

[ ] **Fixtures and equipment included in the property**  You cannot claim anything not mentioned in the sales contract. Thus when it comes to pieces of equipment fastened on the soil, or if there is a house, fastened down in that house, these should be specified by name. You may be surprised what your seller may attempt to haul away—items that you know belong and function only on the property, such as a windmill, a water pump, an electric generator. Probably they *do* belong to the property, but not legally if they are not mentioned in the sales contract. You and your lawyer can construct such a list. Make it longer rather than shorter than necessary. A few extra lines of type can save you some very bitter arguments, or even expensive lawsuits over relatively small misunderstandings.

[ ] **The delivery of the deed**  Although usually done at a closing, it may be illusive in complicated cases. Your lawyer will know how to put a timing phrase in the contract to void it if the deed is not delivered by a specific date, with no extensions unless by mutual consent. This will prevent a hang-up which could occur if the title for the property is complicated by previously unacknowledged old liens or old claims by heirs which surface once the property is contracted for sale. Another situation also develops sometimes: the seller, as a result of advertising and promotion gets a higher bid from someone else *after* the initial agreement with you and is tempted to stall the closing on your purchase contract and sign with the higher bidder. If your lawyer is alert, many of the possibilities for delay can be prevented by planting a relatively short time fuse in the contract compelling the

seller to resolve all issues with dispatch. This gives a minimum of time for wheeling and dealing elsewhere.

[  ] **Payment on contract**  Money changes hands at the closing, but the signing of the contract usually requires 10 percent of the price of the property or some other earnest money, some or all of which may or may not be forfeited if the contract fails as a result of a flaw caused by the buyer. This money is customarily in addition to the binder or any option fee paid. Your lawyer must be very specific about this payment. In some cases, this may amount to the entire down payment you will make on a heavily mortgaged property.

[  ] **Payments on closing**  At the closing the major part of the money changes hands. In your case, as the buyer, this may amount almost entirely to putting a mortgage in place to cover the gap between the sum of your initial payments and the full purchase price. In addition to the financing of the property itself, there are several fees to be paid for title search, title insurance, recording fees, transfer of tax equilization payments, attorney fees, and miscellaneous application fees. Your lawyer will have to specify who pays what and whether it will be in ordinary checks, certified checks, cashier's check, or by some other guarantee that the money is good. Once in a while the seller may accept another property in exchange, or perhaps will want cash, gold, a foreign currency, or a check made out in a special way to a partnership, a corporation, or a variant of the seller's name because of the way he or she is formally known at his bank. All of these details can be cleared by your lawyer *in preparation* for the closing rather than have these petty issues come up for argument at the closing.

[  ] **Existing obligations** may or may not be a matter of public record. Thus, a routine search by your lawyer may not discover that the seller, as a result of a previous transaction, may owe money to a relative or a friend in the form of a second mortgage that may have the property as implied—but not recorded—security. This sort of situation might become a problem if the seller and the creditor were in the midst of a feud and the creditor forced a way legally into the sale situation to be sure the money was paid. The lawyers could work it out so that a specified payment was reserved for the "hidden" creditor at the time of the closing, with a clause in the sales contract that the seller assumes sole obligation for any other liens or debts with which the property might be indirectly encumbered.

You, as a buyer, may *want to pick up existing debt* as a way of financing your purchase. In that case the lender or creditor will want to check out *your* references. If you increase the amount loaned, either as a formal first or a second mortgage, you will want to have your lawyer verify the agreement, the amount owed, and the unpaid interest, if any. If the situation is rather ticklish, the lawyer can find out how the lender feels about transferring the debt to you and possibly increasing it.

[ ] **Repairs and remodeling before closing**  When you buy a property, you may have some ideas about immediate improvements before the closing, before the title is delivered to you, or before you take it over. By and large, it is better to wait until you have title to start construction, build roads, install utility lines or pipes, and the like. In some circumstances you may want to rush ahead, but then have your lawyer specify that the improvement belongs to you and can be taken away, or that the seller will compensate for your costs should the deal fall through.

Sometimes the seller is in the midst of an improvement. In such case you will want your lawyer to have it spelled out in writing just what is going to be delivered to you. Will the project come "as is," or will certain further steps be taken toward its completion? Your lawyer will want to determine how the improvement project is going to be paid for and what commitment has been given (preferably in writing), so that you know what your obligation is to complete the project and pay for it. There are many ways to skin these kinds of cats, but there should be a written agreement covering all the details of the work in progress.

[ ] **Abstract of title**  Normally your lawyer will stipulate in the purchase contract that title will pass free and clear of all encumbrances except those specifically noted in the contract. Those noted can usually be solved in one way or another, so the contract outlines the way out of the encumbrance and who should do what to clear the title. There will normally be a stipulation, too, that if these obstructions are not carried out successfully and the encumbrance is not eliminated, then the contract will be void, there will be no closing, and all deposits, prepaid fees, and the like will be refunded to you, the potential but frustrated buyer.

Your lawyer may obtain or compile an abstract of title as a result of the search of the records. This will carry back the history of the property to all previous owners and often back to the time when the land was a grant from colonial times, perhaps from a government homesteading program. Subsequent owners, easements, legal entanglements, and other agreements affecting the clear title of the property will appear, including passage of ownership through wills, execution of wills, outcome of suits, and the like.

In addition to this search, you may want your lawyer to have the title insured by a title guarantee insurance company. That kind of company will issue a policy that offers protection against surprises that are not yet a matter of public record. If and when they surface, they could cause havoc to your plans. This puts the burden of research on the insurance company and relieves you and the lawyer of much responsibility and worry. The company insuring will usually guarantee, too, that the land you have seen and the land as represented in the purchase contract is, in fact, the land you will eventually buy. These investigations, if they have not been previously made in such depth, will pave the way for a later profitable sale *by you* with much less fuss and scurrying at that time.

One of the levers you have for obtaining a good purchase price is how clear the title is. You have the seller at a psychological disadvantage if you can say, "You didn't tell me there was this easement you gave so that neighbors might connect with the county road over your property. I had no idea these people could connect to the road if they decided to build on their wooded acres. If they do, that means it will prevent me from using some of my land. This calls for a reduction in price of $2,000." You may work the seller down that way, particularly if you catch that this relatively minor fact has been suppressed. Here again, your lawyer can make preliminary negotiations, then you can compromise on whatever gap in understanding or agreement remains.

[ ]  **Income owing you as buyer**  Perhaps the property you are buying has tenants, fields under lease, an existing arrangement to buy water or to drill for oil or explore for minerals. Rents and royalties, once you have bought the place, are due to you. Your lawyer will have to review and revise all agreements of this sort and a date must be set when the income, on a pro rata basis, will come to you instead of to the seller.

[ ]  **Delivering and accepting the deed**  The deed describes in careful detail the property that is being transferred from seller to buyer. It should contain all the agreements and provisos of the purchase contract. As far as you are concerned, it gives you the right of ownership and is a final statement of all the negotiations you have carried on with the seller. Needless to say, this is not a do-it-yourself document. With all the intelligence and good intentions in the world, you may, in trying to formulate the correct legal sense, make mistakes that could haunt you later. The deed should spell out in writing, as clearly as possible, using whatever legal phrases are necessary, exactly what you own, what tangible property, what intangible rights.

The deed should be made out in your name—as a buyer—or possibly in the name of your spouse, or in the name of a corporation or partnership you have formed to hold the property. Normally, to define the property, the completed survey will become part of the deed. In legal terms, the deed must be "signed, sealed, attested, acknowledged, and delivered." Your lawyer will tell you about each of these steps and will see to it that each is carried out properly.

The kind of deed you accept will usually be a warranty deed. The seller warrants or promises to defend your title to the property and also obligates agents or heirs to the same task. Another kind of deed, often used, is the quit claim deed in which the seller turns over to you the property and that is the end of it; the seller is "quit" of all liability. With a warranty deed, you may also find you have come to the end of it if the former seller, despite promises, has neither the means nor the inclination to defend the title when a surprise claim against it surfaces. That is why your lawyer should come up with a comprehensive survey and title insurance with a reputable firm. If trouble arises, the insurance company will take over for you.

[ ]  **Restrictions of use**   Your deed may contain restrictions of use that are not known by the seller. Some earlier owner, perhaps a teetotaler, may have sold the land with the restriction that "spiritous liquors" may never be sold from a building on that property. That means no subsequent owner can open a tavern or bar. This may seem far-fetched, particularly for a country place. But the clause in an abstract, and subsequently in a deed, will be carried forward, presumably for centuries, and the rural area, particularly if it is on the outskirts of a city, may become a main street in a suburb. The opportunity to sell liquor from a tavern, restaurant, motel, or hotel has increased, and if some neighbor or group of neighbors objects to this use, that clause in the abstract could very well be the anchor on which an alert lawyer will base a case. It will be uphill all the way for the business developer to get a variance on this restriction. As a buyer you should be aware that it exists—you can't do much about it—before you close. Upgrading the property for business use, of course, is one way to make a profit on it. Your lawyer can tell you what the chances are for getting a variance on this or that restriction. Presumably the lawyer knows the ropes in such situations and can evaluate the chances of profitable change for you.

Contemporary zoning restrictions take precedence over the unlimited use of the property you may think you have purchased. In general, zoning is a good thing for property owners. In an orderly way, it designates specific parts of a community for residential, manufacturing, commercial, or mixed use. This tends to stabilize property values. With sensible zoning regulations in place, property owners can plan for the long term, make improvements, and remain fairly confident that their neighborhood will not change radically. Some localities, unwilling to welcome vigorous growth, have voted to restrict severely the kind of development allowed. In fact, the requirements for the number of acres needed to build a single-family house, and the approximate value and quality of any house built, can be placed so high that it effectively discourages most people from moving in. Changing the zoning in an area to benefit your own investment or to benefit the entire community usually is up to the citizens. Many *vote* on zoning changes and are disinclined in the case of strict regulations to relax them for an individual variance. Fortunately there are communities more hospitable to growth and profit making.

The local building code may also prove a stumbling block. If you have plans for the profitable development of the property you have just bought, you had better be sure beforehand that they conform to the applicable building code. You may find that your planned garage would fall too close to a lot line. Or you may find that the house you plan to build does not have sufficient floor space to meet local requirements. Or that it must have a basement twice as large as the one you wanted. Or that it is too modern for the colonial character of the community.

Do not depend on buying your way out of a dilemma once you have the property and are moving ahead with plans. Perhaps you think you can buy 10 extra feet from your neighbor to fulfill regulations. The neighbor may decide to take advantage of your predicament and double the normal price for the extra land. And in trying to get a variance, you may have to launch a campaign among the local townspeople so that they will vote for the exception. Considering the conservative nature of most country folk, you may find yourself spitting into a strong wind. They wouldn't have put the restrictions on the books in the first place if they didn't think them worthwhile and for the general mutual benefit of the neighborhood. Why should they make an exception for you who seem out to defeat their original purpose? After a strong try—and defeat—be sensible and profit minded. Either change your plans or move on to another property. The important thing is to recognize all these limitations on your action *before* you sign a purchase contract and before you are saddled with a deed that frustrates your plans. Beware, too, of easements or rights of way that you may need or that a previous owner may have granted. Often these lie dormant for decades but surface finally to vex a contemporary owner who was unaware they existed.

They may include giving the right to a utility company to erect a pole in the front of the house, a pole which may or may not be allowed to support a decorative street light.

When all of these details have been researched, adjustments made, and the necessary papers drawn up, you are ready to actually close and receive your deed. You will close sometimes on the premises of the seller's lawyer, or perhaps on the premises of your lawyer, but more often at the bank that is giving you a mortgage and has probably been acting as escrow agent or holder and monitor of deposits and papers. When all is ready, the seller will sign the deed and then your own lawyer will verify all is in order. Then your lawyer will give it to you—along with a bill for services rendered. If you are alert, that bill will cause no surprises. Before hiring your lawyer you should have gone over exactly what was going to be done for you and what the charge for the services would be. After going through all of these procedures you will probably agree that it was worth the fee. *If it wasn't,* so much the worse for you and your lack of judgment in not retaining a first-rate lawyer.

There is one final step to take. Your lawyer must file the papers in the county clerk's office so that there is a formal record of your ownership.

## WORKING WITH YOUR REALTOR

All real estate brokers must be licensed to practice their professions, but state laws do not require the extra exams that lead to the title of realtor. It is up to you to decide what category of professional service will suit you best. Fees do not necessarily run parallel to titles and sometimes the extra designation is really not recessary for the job in hand.

As a buyer, you will normally have to deal with the realtor or the broker who is handling the property for the seller. You can count on that broker-seller relationship to be closer than the broker's relationship with you, even if you sought the broker out as a possible finder of a property. Of course, in the case of a personal friend, the picture would change considerably. If you are coming into the country, however, and dealing with local people, the broker is more likely to be a personal friend of the seller. That is one reason why your choice of an attorney to represent you is so important. Someone familiar with the local situation but independent of the sale ought to be on your side.

Now, there is always the possibility that the seller's broker is a great person and quickly inspires confidence in you, and that your attorney also recognizes her or him as a thoroughly honest and competent person.

Then, and only then, should you accept favors that may be offered to you in order to induce you to buy quickly. Yes, let them arrange for a survey of the property at a bargain rate; let them bring in an appraiser; let them rough out an easement or a second mortgage agreement between you and the seller. Insist, though, that your attorney read over these documents and approve them.

Particularly in the country you will probably find a lower ratio of realtors to licensed brokers than in the city. Anyone can become a broker simply by working in the business for a while and passing a state examination. Brokering is a favorite second source of income for many people. Of the close to one million licensed real estate brokers in the United States few can depend on it for all of their annual income. Many combine it with selling insurance or acting as developers or builders, or sometimes as appraisers. A realtor is a licensed broker who is also a qualified member of a local real estate board and a member of the National Association of Realtors. A realtor usually has a stylized letter R—a registered trademark— displayed in the office, in advertisements, and on business cards. Most realtors who take the trouble of further qualification and membership are in the business full time and have that much more commitment to the business. In the process, they are likely to be more experienced in sophisticated financing and land use for greater profit.

Selecting a country broker requires as much looking around as you did for a lawyer or a banker. It pays to shop for a broker who can become a business friend. Later on you may want him or her to sell your property at a profit.

Remember, many properties for sale in the country, as in the city, may or may not be exclusive listings. Co-brokerage arrangements and commission splitting is possible through many multiple-listing services. Therefore you may have access to the property through several brokers or realtors. Nonetheless, before you let a broker show you a property, and thus make an implied commitment to buy it, scout around a bit for the right broker for you. You can check out local brokers through telephone calls to the local Chamber of Commerce, or similar businesspeople's group, the local bank, or a local lawyer. Then look at the real estate advertising in the local newspapers. Which broker seems to lead the pack? Certain names will come up again and again in your investigations and they are probably the leading and most respected brokers of the region. You are most likely, then, to answer an ad and begin to look at properties. Since you are doing this, presumably, to make a profit, you might as well give the broker extra-thorough scrutiny. Can you do further business with this firm? Actually the broker will be of more use to you in selling the property at a profit than when you buy it. As mentioned earlier, when you are the buyer, the broker or realtor handling the property is working primarily for the *seller*. Therefore, find a broker with whom you are comfortable in business dealings.

You may find that the realtor or broker is also an attorney who will offer to do all necessary legal work for you at a modest fee. This may be the most expensive "bargain" that was ever offered to you. What you need is your *own* lawyer to ask the pesky little questions that may irritate the broker but may save you a good deal of worry and later expense.

About all you can expect as buyer from a real estate agent, broker, or realtor is a finder's service and a question-answering service. Very often the man or woman who goes out with you to see the property is merely a salesperson with *no particular qualifications* for selling real estate. The salesperson must work under the supervision of a licensed real estate broker or agent. But who is to know how thorough is the supervision? If you feel uneasy about the answers to some questions that seem important to you—if the salesperson tells you, "that isn't important in this case" or "I don't know, but I think so; with all the sales I've made (and there may have been none), this problem has never come up," and gives other responses in a similar vein, remember to put the questions again, in as tactful a way as possible, to the licensed broker personally. And if the boss doesn't give a straight answer, and it becomes very important, either give them the brush off or have your attorney bring up the matter as a last resort. Sometimes you may feel you have been getting so many evasive responses that it isn't worth pursuing the property further. Something must be (and probably is) wrong.

## WHAT YOUR BROKER, AGENT, OR REALTOR CAN DO FOR YOU

As a buyer, you can expect brokers, agents, or realtors to find a property for you, give you the terms of sale, answer questions clearly and competently, and serve as quick and honest go-betweens in relations with the seller. But do not expect them to look out for your interest: they are looking out for the interests of the seller, who pays the commission.

But with these caveats in mind, you can find *any* broker or agent helpful in steering you toward a bank that can offer you a mortgage loan or to an insurance agent familiar with houses in the vicinity. The broker may sell the insurance. The knowledgeable agent can steer you to an appraiser whose estimates will coincide, more or less, with the appraised value the bank will accept on your property as security for a mortgage loan. This is important.

There is nothing more vexing than to plan on a mortgage of a certain size at a certain rate, subject to an appraisal, and then have the bank say later that the amount must be less because the appraisal came in much less than expected. A good real estate broker can help you find a continuity of appraisals and mortgage sources.

A broker can also outline for you possibilities, based on experience in the area, for improving the property within local zoning regulations, rental demands, the market for remodeled houses, and the like. In other words, you can get ideas for making a later profit on your property. Naturally, in time, a broker will be glad to sell it for you again and earn another commission. Take the ideas with several grains of salt. If something is mentioned that seems particularly interesting and on which you would like to rely in order to make a later profit, check out the possibilities immediately with the help of your lawyer. Not only will you protect yourself as a buyer, but you will establish the credibility and usefulness of the broker for later business. Remember, it is not beyond the imagination or the capability of a broker—not an honest one, to be sure—to get you trapped into something so that he or she can later get you out of it and, of course, earn a second commission. That's known as getting you coming and going.

On the other hand, if you have gone into the country property for the purpose of making money through buying and selling, perhaps keeping some for the long term, there is nothing so helpful as an alert, conscientious realtor who earns the brokerage percentage on some very valuable properties by identifying the potential for profit in each one of them. When a good realtor gets this "feel" for property that is going to move upward in value, he or she is just as worthwhile for you as a money manager who gets a better return for your investment than a competitor. Such a person will find it advantageous to make money for you, because a broker always gets a percentage of it, and perhaps gets too the business of some of your friends who can also be guided toward profits in country property.

Probably the most useful service any realtor can supply to a buyer is the matching of needs with supply and the solving of problems that stand in the way of a clean and profitable sale. The broker is the person of experience on the spot. Of all people concerned with the transaction, the broker is the person who will earn the most immediate money from services rendered as the real estate negotiator and expert. The banker, the insurance agent, and the lawyer may know quite a bit about real estate but they are not highly motivated to *move* the property. Your lawyer is there to *restrain* you from doing something rash. Usually only the broker will come up with ideas for making more money for both of you. So if you have a fine relationship, run with it. You both can make good profits.

## WHEN PROPERTY IS SOLD WITHOUT A BROKER

In country areas you may find a lot of sellers who prefer to try to sell their property themselves. Sometimes they give a property to a broker but also reserve the right to try to sell it themselves. This can get sticky because the broker naturally expects the commission to be protected when referring a prospect to the seller.

Trouble can arise when you buy without a broker, because the seller, unknown to you, may have made a commitment to a broker. The broker may later claim part or all of a rightful commission. You may not be liable for it, but the subsequent suit could take up some of your time and possibly some of your lawyer's time.

One of the dangers in buying property directly from the seller is the difficulty of negotiation. It is a one-to-one relationship, and if the seller has overpriced the property or is trying to hide some encumbrance or market flaw, it will be the seller's word against yours, unless you let your lawyer do the negotiating for you. A reputable broker will either talk the seller out of an unreasonable price or have the property represented with all or most of its attractions and defects showing, and will act as an efficient go-between. The broker will usually more than earn the fee.

There is one negotiation ploy *you* can use as a buyer when the seller is handling the sale directly. When you have come to an agreement on all major points, you can say that by saving the broker's fee, which would normally be 6 percent, you are entitled to a reduction in the price by that amount. This could work, particularly if the seller has the property listed legitimately with brokers at the same price. If you have found a way to approach the seller without going through a broker, possibly because you heard of the property by word of mouth or saw it advertised by a broker at a price you think attractive, you might make an offer to buy at that price minus the normal broker's fee. Understand, though, that the seller may counter your proposal with the argument that he or she has had to do some of the normal work of the broker and is entitled to some kind of compensation. You may claim that you have had to take the initiative. You may also find that you will have to do some work, such as getting details for the later drafting of a purchase contract.

This type of negotiating and sparring around is particularly difficult if you know the seller or, worse yet, if the seller is a relative of yours. In situations such as these, the first thing that comes to mind is to eliminate the third, experienced or professional party. In doing so you *do* save on commission or fees. But what strains you put upon your friendship or your family tie! For one thing, you may blunder into foolish mistakes which can prove a source of embarrassment for the rest of your life. And you will have no one to blame but yourself. For another, you may *not* get the best deal available under the circumstances.

*Example: The Realtor Who Outsmarted Some Shrewd Relatives of a Seller.*

Tom Chambers was about to sell some inherited property—a small house and lot in Sausalito, California. Tom's relatives, who had nearby property, wanted him to be sure to get a suitable residential buyer or they would buy it themselves in order to protect their own holdings and to profit from the rising values in the neighborhood. They smelled a possible bargain. Tom, knowing that the advice given was not entirely altruistic or unselfish, agreed to offer the property to them at a minimum acceptable price because "there would be a savings on the brokerage commission." He suspected that the relatives would come up with a buyer or buy the property themselves after further price reductions. So a time limit was set and a well-known realtor in the vicinity was found who would be glad to try to sell the property at a price 10 percent higher than the one offered by the relatives. This would more than cover the commission. The relatives found excuses as the deadline approached. Their list of interested friends evaporated. They, themselves, fudged at the price and said they would "run it through the computer" again within three months. The seller turned it over to the realtor who was thoroughly competent, and within six days the property was sold to a completely qualified professional family who fit right into the neighborhood and the community. The price was the one asked: $135,000, 10 percent more than the price offered by the relatives. The broker took 6 percent of the price in commission and certainly earned it by eliminating paperwork and sales time for Tom Chambers.

Of course, not all stories end as happily as this one. But more can end happily when you use professional services. And, as you try to make a profit on your country property, no one can help you as much as your realtor.

## WORKING WITH YOUR INSURANCE AGENT

If you own country property to make a profit, you will want insurance protection but you do not want to be overinsured. You undoubtedly have life insurance, and if you are happy with your insurance broker, ask for recommendations for insurance needed on your country property: fire, personal liability, and possibly theft insurance. You may also want mortgage life insurance and other special insurance, such as flood insurance subsidized by the U.S. government.

The bank that finances your property will probably require fire insurance up to the point where the value of improvements are covered. Insurance companies require that you get a minimum coverage of 80 percent of the replacement value of the house. Coverage can be extended upward beyond that. Many advisers recommend up to 100 percent coverage of replacement value in the case of fire. The bank will usually be satisfied with less than that. If you are living on your property, you will probably want to insure yourself to the maximum amount available for hazards such as fire, with extensions covering the natural catastrophes that have a habit of affecting the region. These may be hailstorms, tornadoes, wind erosion, or earthquakes—and inflation!

If you are buying and selling property quite actively, but not living on it, perhaps minimum insurance is sufficient to protect buildings. You will have to take a business risk in these cases.

There have been enough rulings in court to establish precedents that in the case of loss the person *in possession* of the premises is liable for the loss. That person must insure the loss even though title may not have passed, through a technicality or through mutual agreement. Thus, if you agree to buy a place and the seller lets you move in before title has passed, that is all well and good, but *take out the insurance you think you need immediately.* If you have good relations with an insurance agent, you simply need to call and give a description of the property. You will get immediate coverage as of a stated time and date and can follow up later, if necessary, with a revised policy based on a final survey. At least you are covered for the interim.

## WHAT YOUR INSURANCE AGENT CAN DO FOR YOU

In the first place your insurance agent, although not as important to your profit as your lawyer, broker, or banker, is another of those professional consultants who can save you from losses as a result of mistakes and can often point the way to greater profit.

The insurance protection you will probably *have* to consider immediately is *fire insurance.* The institution that lends you money will probably insist on that, and will normally ask you to arrange to have a copy of the policy, with a duplicate of the premium notice, sent to the institution so that it can monitor payments—or delinquency and cancellation notices. In fact, some banks, both commercial and savings and loan, will figure in fire insurance payments with their required monthly payments, and *they* will make the payments to the fire insurance company. They will do this, too, with real estate taxes. Sometimes this "collection" by the bank is optional. You will have to decide whether it is a convenience or an imposition for you.

Your insurance agent will explain to you that you cannot insure the land on which your buildings rest but that you *can* insure the buildings up to their replacement value at current prices. The agent will also make a survey based on current market values, so that you will have practical and economic coverage even though the policy is not written for total coverage. With regular and volunteer fire departments as efficient as they are today, it is unlikely that your buildings will be totally lost in a fire.

Of course, it pays to shop around for the right insurance, but it is best to shop for an *agent* first, a person who knows his or her business and sells the insurance of a well-known company or companies. You will have to tell the agent what your financial objectives are—whether you are going to be interested in the property for the long term as a place of personal residence and on which you will make improvements from time to time, or whether you are going to hold it for a short-term profit and want minimum but prudent coverage. Most insurance agents will then recommend one or more policies to cover your situation. If you live on your property, you will want to check out a homeowner's comprehensive policy, which will include a package of coverage, including fire insurance, burglary and theft, and personal liability coverage.

Your normal property insurance will protect your improved real estate in case of loss or damage stemming from smoke, fire, theft, storms, explosions, riots, aircrafts or autos, and vandalism. These types of protection, in addition to fire, are known as *extended coverage.*

You will want *liability insurance,* too, if other people expect to live on, cross, or otherwise use your property. This will protect you against suits as a result of accidents that happen to people while they are on your property. In general, this kind of insurance is inexpensive. Do not be surprised if your insurance agent recommends a policy for several hundred thousand dollars, depending on the neighborhood and the history of accidents in the region.

You can save money by accepting higher deductibles on your policy. Contemporary insurance policies have deductibles structured for many situations. Only your insurance agent can give you up-to-date details and advice. But you could perhaps save as much as 20 percent if, for example, you increase the deductible on your basic homeowner's policy from $50 to $250.

Remember, premiums for risk insurance are based on past losses for categories of risk. The more "business risk" you assume, the less insurance expense you will have. You insure yourself against *two* aspects of risk: (1) that you will have *any* loss or damage; and (2) that the damage will be *major* or *minor*. By paying for minor damages, you may save yourself a substantial on-going expense in insurance premiums.

Another type of insurance policy that may intrigue you and protect your profit is *mortgage insurance.* This is term insurance that starts out as an amount equal to your mortgage. The covered amount then declines in tandem with the principal of your mortgage. You can get this at a very attractive rate, depending on your age. If you should die, the insurance company will automatically pay the mortgagee the remaining principal outstanding and lift that burden from your property. This will seem especially worthwhile to you if you live on your property and it is heavily mortgaged. As the mortgage gets lighter, you may want to discontinue the insurance, since it usually bears a level premium that is inexpensive in relation to the total mortgage at the start but relatively expensive toward the end of the term. Of course, if you are active in the real estate market, buying and selling with several mortgages on several properties, you might be better off to have your insurance agent write a term policy that reflects the blanket value of all indebtedness and also your financial planning for it. It could be on a gradually declining basis or it could remain level, as any ordinary term policy. At a later date, as you eliminate debt from your holdings, you might want to eliminate the cost of your term insurance policy as well. It has served its purpose. Because of the many ways you can insure complex risks, you ought to have a frank talk with your insurance agent about the plans you have for your property.

## WORKING WITH AN APPRAISER

One of the most frequent questions you will hear from prospective buyers of your country property is, "Well, what is the property worth? What was a recent appraisal?" This is a favorite question of buyers because appraisers in country areas tend toward conservative estimates. Their primary customers are banks and institutions that prefer to have a property turn out to be worth more than appraised rather than less. It is simply a prudent business attitude. The *assessed* value is something else again. It is set by a local tax assessor and can be subject to all manner of political quirks. Residential property habitually is underassessed. Appraisals are usually based on the latest sale of the property itself or of comparable property. If these "comparables" do not exist in your immediate area, you will probably get an assessment and an appraisal lower than actual market value.

The habit in many parts of the country is to assess residential property at a fraction—50 or 75 percent—of its market value. In these inflationary times, the equivalent square footage of a new building often is appraised and assessed at a much higher value than an old building. This has led to tax inequities and a trend in many rural areas to reassessment. At the same time, appraisers are now—because of the activity in country property—more aware of current market values for both existing single-family dwellings and new buildings. But, unless reevaluation has been done in your vicinity or the resale market has been active, both assessment and appraisals will be lower, often much lower, than the current market value. How to answer the question "What did the latest appraisal show?" If you fudge the answer, the buyer will be suspicious that you are asking much more. Since the buyer can always get an appraisal for a modest fee, perhaps the best strategy to use is to pay the modest fee yourself, if there has been no recent appraisal, and find out what the most liberal appraiser in the area judges the value of your property to be. Your realtor can identify such an appraiser for you. This appraiser will probably do a lot of work for the bank with the most liberal lending policy in the region. You will then have a dollar value in hand to answer the appraisal question. You will also have some proof for the bank when it comes to financing a subsequent purchase or the refinancing of your property. You will know about how much additional money you can ask for. The appraiser's fee is well worth this knowledge.

When a dispute arises about the appraised value of a property, it is common practice for both the buyer and seller to have an evaluation made by the appraiser of choice and average the difference. Banks are not that accommodating. You will have to take the appraisal a bank sets. But you can always find out from your realtor which bank is the most liberal in lending. It will probably have the most generous appraisers working for it.

Any knowledgeable buyer will know that appraisers tend toward conservatism. The buyer will probably want a generous appraisal so that a large part of the purchase can be financed. And that is a comeback weapon for you when you have had an appraisal made. Talk in terms of *mortgages possible* rather than of the full cost to the buyer. A generous appraisal is a good selling tool. A stingy one is not. The distance between could even out if you can persuade your potential buyer to use an average of several appraisals.

Somewhere within the range of the appraisals lies the true present market value of the property. It is up to you as a seller to persuade the potential buyer that the fair price is on the higher side. As a buyer, you will want to persuade the seller that it is on the lower side. The difference, of course, affects your potential profit. In some markets, in some areas, the supply of property may be so slim that it hardly meets demand. In that case, appraisals have less relevance. It is a seller's market and the prices will run with the price tag put upon each property by the seller. If you are the seller, you are lucky. If not, you might want to think twice before buying to make a profit in such a situation. You could very well *make* a profit in the long run, but you will probably have to wait longer.

Fees for appraising usually are a percentage of the value. Ask your appraiser, if *you* rather than the bank will pay for the work, what the fee is.


## WHAT YOUR ACCOUNTANTS CAN DO FOR YOU

You have undoubtedly noticed references to "your accountant" all along. There are so many financial situations where accountants can help you make a profit within the tax laws that their services have been suggested because they seemed useful. Here is a summary of these services. Look for discussions of specific profit and tax situations in Chapter 1 and in Chapter 6.

**Profit Planning**   Your accountants presumably have a working knowledge of your personal finances and know how much income you may want to shelter. They also have a working knowledge of tax laws in your state, and of course, the latest IRS rulings. The accountants may *not* know the tax laws in another state where you have property, but will know how to get the special information needed. Since they know you are interested in profit from real estate deals, they will assign someone in the firm who has special knowledge of real estate matters. If the type of real estate buying and selling you do has no special complications, the matter will probably be handled by the person who usually does your tax work. The point is, just as you need a lawyer with real estate skills and experience *in the area where you buy property*—and that usually means a local lawyer, you should have as your accountant the person *who does your usual taxes*. For other business reasons, you have probably selected an accounting firm that has the special skills you need. A real estate expert is probably on its staff.

Have your accountants set up (or show you how to set up) pro forma schedules of operating income and costs based on the property as if it were actually owned by you with your usual income. Once your accountants have set up a pattern statement, you can plug in figures to suit the several situations your potential property represents. The figures do not have to be elaborate or accurate down to the last penny—rounded amounts will do. They will give you an idea of the relative profits or tax shelter you can expect from differing situations. Refer to the simple income statement shown in Chapter 1.

**Tax Planning**   Proper tax advice can maximize your final after-tax profit; accountants are indispensable for such advice. The recent changes in the tax laws have made your accountants very important consultants as you pursue profits in country property. For the big profit opportunity given to you by owning country property is (1) its financial leverage, (2) its long record for steady increase in value, and (3) its generous tax-shelter possibilities. Your accountants can help you on all three fronts.

First of all you will want to discuss with your accountants *how* to figure the profit on your property. This means both paper and realized profit. Sometimes the most spectacular profit you will make will stay "on paper" if you *decide to hold* the property. In so doing, your property may double, triple, or quadruple in value. You will be getting value from it through use or by taking out cash through refinancing—all the time charging against income the interest on your mortgage and your real estate taxes, and taking full advantage of depreciation possibilities. Whether you buy property for a quick turnover or for the long haul, be sure you work out your plans carefully with your accountants. Of what benefit is it to make a large profit on country property and then have to give up a great deal of it to the IRS?

### When You Buy Property as a Residence

1  You may want to put it in the name of your spouse or in trust for minor children, so that taxes would be minimized if you should die as possessor of a particularly valuable property. Careful planning can prevent untimely splitting up of the property or what amounts to a forced sale because no one heir can take it over from the others and the group cannot agree on what to do with it. Ask your accountants in what name—private, corporate, or trust—it would be best to carry the property.

2  Depending on the mortgage rates, decide what is the maximum amount of mortgage you should try to carry based on your salary and tax position. In times of inflation, particularly the double-digit variety, and provided you are already in a high tax bracket, the U.S. Treasury subsidizes your purchase on credit because you will be deducting from taxes all the mortgage interest you pay, even if it is on a single-family dwelling in which you and your family live. Your accountants can show you that your mortgage loan is probably the cheapest, safest loan you can make, because with inflation and your growing success in your profession or business you will probably be earning more both in real as well as in inflated dollars. Particularly if you are a young executive with a family, you will want to ask your accountants how to set up your property with maximum leverage at the most reasonable interest rate available. Once you have set up such financing, based on tax planning, you will have established a good credit record and can use the property over the years as security for refi-

nancing to raise money for expansion of the buildings, for a possible down payment on a second home or on investment property, and for educational funds for the children.

### When You Buy Income-Producing Property

**1**   Talk over with your accountants the way in which you own the property, in whose name you take title, and whether it should be held by a corporation.

**2**   Discuss the leverage of financing with your accountants. The same principles apply as in the case of your own residence.

**3**   Have your accountants set up depreciation schedules consistent with your financial planning. If you do not plan to hold the property for a long time, you might find it advantageous to use accelerated depreciation where possible. For long-term holding, you might want to reserve more of the depreciation for later years, when your interest payments normally would be less and you would want relatively larger deductions from other legal shelters.

**4**   Check with your accountant about investment-tax credit for improvements you plan to make. What limits are allowed by the current law? This has changed often during the past 10 years and it may change again. At last report it allowed 10 percent of the improvement up to a total of $2,000.

**5**   Check with your accountants on whether your property can be certified as historical under the terms of the Revenue Acts of 1978 and 1976, and whether your planned rehabilitation qualifies for special amortization provisions, tax credit, and accelerated depreciation.

## WORKING WITH FARM AGENTS AND OTHER GOVERNMENT SOURCES OF INFORMATION

It is highly recommended that you meet and keep in touch with your local representative of the *Cooperative* or *Agricultural Extension Service* of the U.S. Department of Agriculture. The advice is expert, the cost is nothing, and if you are interested in building your basic profits, you should know what government benefits and aids are available to you.

Through the government you can get particularly good advice about crop culture, livestock, insects, plant or animal diseases, and advice on your soil, as well as special loans and grants available to qualified families.

Some pesticides are for restricted use only and you must be certified before you can purchase or use them. Your county extension agent can sort out for you the do's and don'ts of pesticide use, as well as explain new and alternative methods of controlling pests.

You will find the location of the county extension offices in the telephone book under the name of the land-grant university in your state or listed as Cooperative or Agricultural Extension Service under your county government.

**The Soil Conservation Service (SCS)**  The Soil Conservation Service supplies advice usually through a local soil-and-water-conservation district. It can help you evaluate your land and water resources and suggest ways of upgrading them in order to encourage better crops, to build up wildlife, to increase the supply of water, and to use existing resources to increase your income. It can also help solve flood, drought, and other problems involving the natural resources of land use. You can usually find a SCS field office in your county seat. In the telephone directory it is usually under U.S. Government, Department of Agriculture.

**The Farmers Home Administration (FHA)**  The Farmers Home Administration makes loans to farm and nonfarm families to aid home ownership and improvements in rural areas, which is classified as the countryside and towns of up to 20,000 in population. Loans through this agency are for upgrading existing homes to adequate standards, including the installation of wells, waste disposal facilities, and inside plumbing. Loans are also made to improve home insulation.

To be eligible, families must prove income levels; direct loans are for low- and moderate-income families that cannot obtain conventional credit, although the agency, from time to time, may guarantee loans by commercial lenders to above-moderate-income families. Do not expect a loan for landscaping an existing home, for gardening on a noncommercial scale, or for improving acreage that is not essential to the homesite.

Students may get loans on their own signature for projects undertaken as members of a youth organization such as 4-H or Future Farmers of America, or for classes as part of a school curriculum. Also business loans are considered for rural families who want to become entrepreneurs. Many kinds of farm loans are available to those families working as farmers for a substantial part of their living.

The Farmers Home Administration has 1,825 county offices. In lightly populated areas, one office may serve more than one county. Local telephone directories carry listings for these offices under U.S. Government or alphabetically. You can also find them by asking at any other identified U.S. Department of Agriculture office in your locality.

You will want to get in touch with the *Agricultural Stabilization and Conservation Service (ASCS)* if you want to take part in any federal farm program, in cost-sharing assistance for soil and water conservation practices, or in loans for farm storage facilities. In crisis situations, the ASCS can supply emergency feed for livestock, help restore farmland, make payments for field crop losses, and make indemnity payments for pesticide losses to beekeepers. Again, you can find this agency in the telephone book, listed independently under U.S. Government or sometimes under your county's name. Obviously you can call *any* U.S. Department of Agriculture listing and it will probably be able to tell you the nearest office of *any* of these services.

When you are talking to these people, ask them whether your *state* government has any equivalent rural-aid agencies. Ask too, whether your local U.S. Department of Agriculture unit puts out local newsletters, does columns of advice in local papers, broadcasts advice on radio or possibly, even, on TV stations in heavily agricultural areas. Leave no stone unturned, in other words, in ferreting out these free services. They are free in the sense that you and others have already paid for them with your taxes, and the personnel are only too happy to give you the benefit of their accumulated experience. One of the ways to make the most in profit is to learn from the mistakes of others, and if possible, make as few of your own as you can. Your neighbors, respecting your privacy, and sometimes out of a certain malicious enjoyment in watching others struggle with problems, may not tell you what they have learned, but you can be sure your county agents will tell you what they know—and often will relay to you what they have learned from what *your neighbors* have learned.

Needless to say, you can learn a lot about rural living by reading the many books, including the yearbook of pictures and essays on country living, published by the U.S. Department of Agriculture and available from the U.S. Government Printing Office, Washington, D.C. 20202. Ask for a list of publications appropriate to the areas that interest you. Many are free and the prices for others are nominal. (See Appendix C for additional sources of government, and other, information.)

## WORKING WITH A PROFESSIONAL HOME-INSPECTION SERVICE

When you buy property in the country, you had better have it inspected by a professional if it has buildings on it. A surveyor will define the boundaries of the *land* for you and will locate the buildings involved, but will not give you a diagnosis of the land's or the buildings' flaws. Your county agent can help you with the land. An inspection service will analyze the buildings. Perhaps you can *see* some of the repairs that have to be made. It is better to have a professional check out with a trained eye, with tests, and with measuring apparatus the various systems of a house.

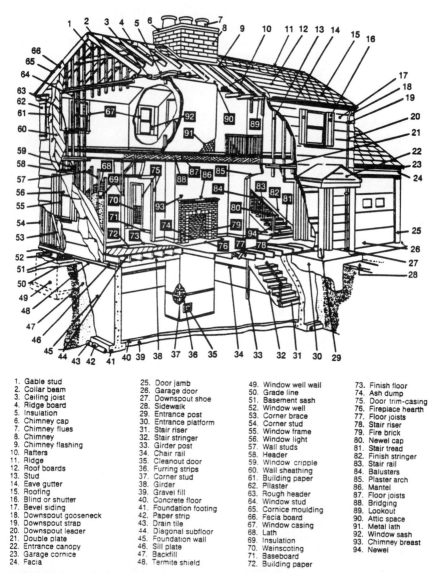

| | | | |
|---|---|---|---|
| 1. Gable stud | 25. Door jamb | 49. Window well wall | 73. Finish floor |
| 2. Collar beam | 26. Garage door | 50. Grade line | 74. Ash dump |
| 3. Ceiling joist | 27. Downspout shoe | 51. Basement sash | 75. Door trim-casing |
| 4. Ridge board | 28. Sidewalk | 52. Window well | 76. Fireplace hearth |
| 5. Insulation | 29. Entrance post | 53. Corner brace | 77. Floor joists |
| 6. Chimney cap | 30. Entrance platform | 54. Corner stud | 78. Stair riser |
| 7. Chimney flues | 31. Stair riser | 55. Window frame | 79. Fire brick |
| 8. Chimney | 32. Stair stringer | 56. Window light | 80. Newel cap |
| 9. Chimney flashing | 33. Girder post | 57. Wall studs | 81. Stair tread |
| 10. Rafters | 34. Chair rail | 58. Header | 82. Finish stringer |
| 11. Ridge | 35. Cleanout door | 59. Window cripple | 83. Stair rail |
| 12. Roof boards | 36. Furring strips | 60. Wall sheathing | 84. Balusters |
| 13. Stud | 37. Corner stud | 61. Building paper | 85. Plaster arch |
| 14. Eave gutter | 38. Girder | 62. Pilaster | 86. Mantel |
| 15. Roofing | 39. Gravel fill | 63. Rough header | 87. Floor joists |
| 16. Blind or shutter | 40. Concrete floor | 64. Window stud | 88. Bridging |
| 17. Bevel siding | 41. Foundation footing | 65. Cornice moulding | 89. Lookout |
| 18. Downspout gooseneck | 42. Paper strip | 66. Facia board | 90. Attic space |
| 19. Downspout strap | 43. Drain tile | 67. Window casing | 91. Metal lath |
| 20. Downspout leader | 44. Diagonal subfloor | 68. Lath | 92. Window sash |
| 21. Double plate | 45. Foundation wall | 69. Insulation | 93. Chimney breast |
| 22. Entrance canopy | 46. Sill plate | 70. Wainscoting | 94. Newel |
| 23. Garage cornice | 47. Backfill | 71. Baseboard | |
| 24. Facia | 48. Termite shield | 72. Building paper | |

**Figure 5-1** Schematic diagram of a home—check points. *(Source: National Home Inspection Service.)*

Most of the people who actually come out to inspect for such a service are engineers or architects, people trained to spot trouble and who know what to do about it. Lacking such a service, you might have a friend in these professions look at your buildings. You may have talked to an architect, even chosen one, to make design improvements on the house. The advantage of a service is that it will give a report in writing and sometimes make a form of guarantee covering defects that were not identified. Figure 5-1 pinpoints the important structural details of a house. Naturally you will want such an inspection *before* your closing so that the seller can remedy these discovered defects or possibly make adjustments in the asking price. You can find home-inspection services listed that way in your local Yellow Pages or as Building Inspection Services.

Another possibility for guaranteeing condition and workmanship is the relatively new Homeowners' Warranty program sponsored by the National Association of Home Builders. This relates to a new building, particularly a residence, which may be covered for malfunctions or defects in construction for a period of 10 years. So, if you buy a relatively new building, you will want to ask the seller whether it is registered in the HOW program and ask, too, what other guarantees or warranties are outstanding on any recent new equipment or construction. It is best to get the names of the contractors who installed or built anything recently for *they* are the ones you will want to call first if anything goes wrong.

# Chapter Six

# Financing
# Country Property

Frankly, the way you finance your country property makes all the difference in the world in the profits you can reap. With first mortgage money in recent years costing from 9 to 14 percent, and second mortgage money as well as finance company loans costing 14 to 20 percent and sometimes more—you can readily see that your net profit before depreciation and tax-shelter calculations can be wiped out by the amount of interest you pay. A net operating profit of 9 to 14 percent before taxes on any investment these days, of course, *may* not keep you ahead of inflation. Fortunately, with country property, as with most real estate, you are in good position for capital *appreciation,* and your tax bracket will determine your degree of shelter as you deduct interest paid on borrowed money. If you are in a 50 percent tax bracket, for example, that 12 percent mortgage interest is actually costing you only 6 percent; the rest is paid for by Uncle Sam, a subsidy you might say for risking your money in real estate. Then there is the depreciation factor if you do not live on your income-producing country property, or if you live on it only part of the time.

At the end of this chapter you will find some composite case histories of how different investors and different families financed their country property and how they made out in profit. But first, you might want to figure out how much *you* can afford to pay for country property; how much of it you can hold, based on your other financial resources, where you can get your down payments, where you can shop for mortgage money. You will also want to learn the benefits that lie in refinancing, and in buying more than you need for personal use with the idea of selling part of it later at a profit that will help liquidate the financing of the part you keep.

## FIGURING WHAT YOU CAN AFFORD TO BUY AND HOLD

You may be fortunate in having a lump sum you can invest in country property in addition to your present residence. This money may now be in savings, in stocks or bonds, or in some other relatively liquid investment that you can use as the down payment. If you are going to use your country property as *your principal residence,* however, you have to consider the same rules of thumb that apply to the family looking for a house in the city or the suburbs. Your country home is likely then to be the largest single investment you will make in your life. If you structure the purchase wisely, it can bring you personal pleasure and profit throughout the years.

Now, if you are in the category of the home owner who wants to make an additional investment in country property, you will be interested in these calculations, too, because you will have to pay something on your mortgage every month, or perhaps quarterly or yearly. You will want to know how large a mortgage you can afford to carry.

As a good rule of thumb, most middle- and lower-income families can handle a home priced at 2.5 times their gross annual income. If your total gross annual income (if both husband and wife work, count both incomes) is $24,000, you can safely consider buying a country house priced at $60,000.

Another way of expressing this rule of thumb is: allot up to one-third of your net monthly income (take-home pay) or one-quarter of your gross monthly income for housing expense. This includes interest on your home loan, payments to reduce principal of your home loan, taxes, insurance, and upkeep.

You can budget your allowance for housing by using a chart suggested by the American Bankers Association (see Table 6-1). If you are paid weekly, multiply your take-home pay by 4.3 to settle on your monthly take-home pay. If you are paid every other week, multiply your take-home pay by 2.6.

Compare the two figures: your effective monthly income with your total actual or projected monthly housing expense. Usually your monthly housing expense should not run more than 40 percent of your effective monthly income. If it is much more, you are probably trying to commit too large a part of your monthly resources to housing or real estate investment. You would be more comfortable with one-third (33.3 percent) of your net monthly income flowing into this type of investment.

**Table 6-1** Effective Monthly Income versus Total Monthly Housing Expense

| | | |
|---|---|---|
| Monthly take-home pay | | $_____ |
| | | |
| Less fixed monthly expenses | | |
|   Car payment | $_____ | |
|   Boats/other | $_____ | |
| | | |
|     *Total fixed monthly expenses* | | $_____ |
| | | |
| Effective monthly income | | $_____ |
| | | |
| Actual or projected monthly housing expenses | | |
|   Principal and interest | | $_____ |
|   Hazard insurance premium | | _____ |
|   Real estate taxes | | _____ |
|   Maintenance allowance | | _____ |
|   Utilities | | _____ |
|   Others (such as condominium fees, mortgage insurance premium etc.) | | _____ |
| | | |
|     *Total monthly housing expense* | | $_____ |

Of course, you may have a special situation that will alter these rule-of-thumb figures. And you may have an outside income in addition to your take-home pay from your job or profession. If that is the case, your required housing expenses may wind up to be a much smaller percentage of your total effective monthly income. Be sure to take into consideration the fact that taxes apply to your outside income, and only add to your available monthly resources a net-after-taxes figure. Although it is only natural to think in larger terms with outside income available, it too requires tax deductions, and many people delay this crucial computation until tax time and then find they have not set enough aside. They simply spend what comes in and drift into the tax season with nothing ready for the extra taxes. In the past two decades you would have been happy with the increase on any money put aside into country property. You might even have said it justified some of the pinch you felt when mortgages and taxes had to be paid. Your consolation lay in the fact that your property was increasing 12 to 15 percent in value each year *on average*. Although it is likely that country property will continue its substantial annual gains, it may not do so at quite this advantageous a rate. So don't get yourself into a liquidity pinch by biting off more country property than you can comfortably pay for in mortgage installments each month.

## SOURCES OF DOWN PAYMENT

When you plan the purchase of country property, you must keep four figures in mind: *the total asking price,* the likely *mortgage available,* about $1,000 to $2,000 in *closing costs* of one kind or another, and the amount required for *down payment.* Some of your closing costs will have to be prepaid, including the earnest money that may be asked. Earnest money, naturally, will be included in the total cash credit you have laid out and will be so indicated at the time of your closing. But you do have to have the money in hand. The remainder of the money you will finance in one way or another.

Say you have seen a property listed at $110,000. You believe you can get it for $100,000. The owner wants $20,000 down, asks you to finance the rest, and will help you with a purchase-money mortgage if you can't get a first mortgage for $80,000.

You apply to your bank and learn that closing costs will require an out-of-pocket expense to you of about $1,500. So in reality you need $21,500 cash. You get a commitment from the bank for a first mortgage of $70,000, providing the property is appraised at $80,000 to $85,000. You have in your savings and securities only about $15,000. That means you are short $6,500 in cash. The seller suggests that you settle on a price of $105,000, with a purchase-money mortgage for $11,500 for five years. In that time you will be able to establish your good payment record at the bank and can look forward to refinancing to pay off the remaining pur-chase-mortgage principal and get some extra "take-out" cash besides. This is the way the required final money requirements will look:

| | |
|---|---|
| $105,000 | purchase price |
| 1,500 | out-of-pocket closing costs generously estimated |
| $106,500 | |

Here is how you will finance the package:

| | |
|---|---|
| $ 15,000 | cash from your savings or from securities |
| 11,500 | 5-year purchase-money mortgage, |
| | 10% interest, 2% amortization annually |
| 80,000 | 25-year first mortgage from local savings |
| | bank, 9% interest, 2% amortization annually |
| $106,500 | |

Now figure out roughly how you will fare with this financing after the first year of ownership and residence. Consider that the house increased in value by 14 percent, a conservative average gain based on existing family-home sales in your state. You had interest payments as follows:

| | |
|---|---|
| $  1,150* | on your purchase-money mortgage |
| 7,200 | on your first mortgage |
| $  8,350 | total interest |

You amortized or paid down on the principal as follows:

| | |
|---|---|
| $    230 | on your purchase-money mortgage |
| 1,600 | on your first mortgage |
| $  1,830 | total amortization |

You have paper profits of $106,000 times 14 percent, or $14,700. Against these are expenses of $8,350 for interest (which is deductible on your federal income tax). That means you made, on paper and before operating expenses and real estate taxes, $6,350 on your cash investment of $15,000. In addition, you paid $1,830 on the principal, which you will not have to pay back in the future. That means a gain in your paper equity of $8,180. Compared to your initial investment of $15,000, that means a net equity a year later of $23,180, a paper gain over the year of about 54.5 percent. You might want to subtract from the $8,180 gain, the $1,200 you might have earned on that $15,000 invested elsewhere at 8 percent. You still come out $6,980 ahead, which amounts to about 46.5 percent. Your housing expenses and your tax situation will affect the final net profit, and you will want to go over with your accountants the way they recommend that you consider this "investment." If you are in a high tax bracket, you may discover that Uncle Sam is heavily subsidizing your financing through the interest you can deduct from federal income taxes. Note that if you live in the house most of the time, you cannot deduct depreciation. Your accountant will guide you in situations where your property is producing income year-round or for part of a year.

*For purposes of this example, the interest rate is applied on an annual basis. In reality, most banks will apply one-twelfth of the rate monthly. As a result, your annual interest charge will be slightly less than the above figures and your monthly amortization slightly more.

## ALTERNATIVE SOURCES OF DOWN-PAYMENT DOLLARS AND FINANCING

In the example outlined above you saw the most familiar, conventional sources of money at work. There are other sources, and if you use them, you can probably save interest expenses. This might mean a lot to you *if you are not* in a high tax bracket and interest deductions do not mean as much to you. Some sources, too, may not be as demanding or hard-headed about repayments as are commercial and savings banks that threaten foreclosure, occasionally at the least lapse of prompt payment. The following are some common and uncommon sources of money you may want to consider:

### Savings Bank Loans

In these days of double-digit inflation, money in a savings bank simply loses its purchasing power even if it compounds at an annual rate of, say, 9 percent. As a practical businessperson and property owner, you will certainly want to keep some money in a savings account, enough to cover you for six months of crisis if you lose your income from your job or profession.

The rest of your savings had better work harder than the bank will allow in a passbook account. True, there is no government agency to insure your investment in country property. But most state laws make foreclosure by banks a long and drawn-out procedure. You will have a long time to remedy a default. It is perhaps because current regulations tend to favor consumers, or borrowers, that aggressive savings banks have little patience with late payers or those who default. If you feel you have overextended yourself on your country property and run into difficulty because you lost your job, or if a recession comes along and cuts your self-employment income, it is best to tell your savings or commercial banker right away, before you start paying slowly or default. It is possible the banker can restructure the mortgage so you will be paying less per month.

But there are other sources of bank money. Some people save large amounts via certificates of deposit (CDs). The best rates go to the largest saver. If you have $100,000 or more in CDs earning the maximum rate (negotiable), you would be ahead to use the CDs as collateral for a loan at 8 to 9 percent, maybe less. This could be temporary money for you, per-haps, until you can get a 25-year first mortgage at more reasonable rates. Such a loan can increase your down payment, reduce your monthly mort-gage payments, and give you more control on the money you owe. In the examples outlined above, the negotiations in which the seller suggested a

$5,000 increase in price in return for a convenient purchase-money mortgage at 10 percent could have been eliminated had the buyer, beside the $15,000 in passbook savings, been able to borrow, say, $30,000 with a CD as collateral. The interest at 8 percent on $30,000 would amount to $2,400 a year the first year, less than the total of interest on the purchase-money mortgage, the $5,000 extra on the price, and the loss of interest on the $15,000. Your savings through this alternative method of financing for the first year would amount to about $550.

|              |         |                    |                     |
| ------------ | ------- | ------------------ | ------------------- |
|              | $2,400  | $30,000 at 8%      |                     |
| *compared to:* | 1,150 | $11,500 at 10%     |                     |
|              | 450     | 5,000 at 9%        |                     |
|              | 1,350   | 15,000 at 9%       | invested elsewhere  |
|              | $2,950  |                    |                     |

This not only represents a hypothetical savings but it also gives you a much simpler financing structure over which you have greater control. If you have a CD for $100,000 or more, conceivably you can *borrow* that entire amount from your savings bank, using the CD as collateral and using the interest it pays you as part payment on the loan you take. Here, too, you eliminate the purchase-money mortgage and some of the closing costs, such as the bank's survey of the property. If you are fortunate to have as much as $100,000 in savings, you can, of course, simply withdraw it and buy the house for cash. But consider what this will do for your profit by eliminating the leverage on your money which is possible through a mortgage:

|        |         |                                                      |
| ------ | ------- | ---------------------------------------------------- |
|        | 0       | interest to pay on $100,000 put up in cash           |
|        | $14,000 | earned on paper through capital appreciation         |
| *Less* | 9,000   | representing $100,000 at 9% invested elsewhere       |
|        | $ 5,000 | net profit                                           |

The $5,000 represents a 5 percent net earnings on your cash put into real estate as an all-cash purchase. You see how unfavorably that compares to the 45.4 percent you earned when you carried a mortgage and obtained leverage—a minimum amount of cash and the rest in other people's money. Think about this example when you are tempted to pay all cash for country property, *particularly if that property produces income and can be depreciated.* For you can depreciate and create a tax shelter on the *whole amount,* not just on your equity in it.

Some of these variations in financing will make more sense than others, depending on your tax situation. Again, ask your accountant for advice.

## Credit from Your Commercial Bank

If you are a businessperson with an established line of unsecured credit, you can borrow your down payment on a short-term note, say for 90 to 120 days. Depending on your credit record and your line of credit, you can stretch out this loan. If you sell your property, or part of it, in less than a year, you can pay this loan off with the proceeds. Yet, even if you are a preferred customer of your commercial bank, you will still be paying rates of interest beyond the usual mortgage rate. When mortgage rates are running about 10 percent, you could well pay 13 or 14 percent on this kind of loan. Its purpose, of course, is to help businesses over a seasonal situation—for example, a need to purchase inventory that will carry a business through an entire season. The savings possible through timely discounting and quantity purchase will offset this loan if taken for business. You will have to justify the increased rate of interest if the money is used for a down payment on real estate—or for any other investment purpose, by the increase in value of the investment made. Did it increase, within your tax situation, at a rate well beyond the interest rate of the money borrowed to pay for it? In a real estate situation, with its high leverage, the *entire* property, not just your equity in it, will increase at the going rate. (The national average is about 14 percent a year for an existing single-family dwelling.)

In planning to use this kind of loan, you will want a clear idea of when the income from the property—or other income—will arrive to pay off this relatively expensive loan.

*Example: Financing that Solves Several Family Problems at Once*
Bill Fitch, Senior, wanted his son, Bill Fitch, Junior, to get his feet wet in Kansas real estate. Bill Senior was 60 and wanted to retire. He had accumulated growth stocks worth about $175,000 toward that purchase. Trouble was, if he sold it, he would have to pay a capital-gains tax all at once. And there was a large potential capital gain because Bill Senior had bought the stocks years ago for a total of a bit less than $35,000. With his accountant's advice, Bill Senior worked out a deal whereby he sold these stocks to Bill Junior for $25,000 down and the remaining $150,000 due over 20 years at an interest rate of 7 percent. This meant an annual income for Bill Senior of $10,500, much more than the dividends he was receiving on his growth stock. He could spread his capital gains over a period of 20 years. Bill Junior, on the other hand, sold all of his newly bought stocks. He lost on a few, made something on others, so that, in the end, there was no gain on which to pay taxes. From the proceeds he made good on his promise of a down payment, paid his father monthly on the remaining amount, and put the proceeds of

$150,000 into a limited partnership that bought and managed a country motel and adjacent farmland. The partnership was expected to yield 8 percent a year in cash distributions, plus an annual gain in value because of the buildings and farmland owned of about 15 percent.

So Bill Senior wound up with his gains taxed only lightly because of the stretch-out, and also had the satisfaction of seeing Bill Junior get right into the middle of a rural business project. At the same time, the venture furnished Bill Junior with a good profit that supplemented his salary as a science teacher at the local high school. Here is how Bill Junior made out:

| | |
|---|---:|
| Income from partnership: 8% of $150,000 | $12,000 |
| Payments to father on stock sale: 7% of $150,000 | 10,500 |
| *Profit* | $ 1,500 |
| Annual gain in value of property: 15% average | $22,500 |
| *Total paper profit after first year* | $24,000 |

This was not bad for an initial investment of $25,000 cash.

## Refinance an Existing First Mortgage

Suppose you have had a first mortgage on your residence for the past 10 years and have a good payment record. You now want to buy a piece of country property that will eventually serve as your retirement home. For the time being it will be a second home for use on weekends. It is conceivable that your principal residence has doubled or tripled in value during the past 10 years and that you can get a *substantially larger mortgage* on it, which will enable you to buy the second home with little strain. It is conceivable that the bank will rewrite the mortgage so that you preserve the lower rate on the amount you still owe and pay the going rate for the amount you are now about to borrow. The bank, because of your good payment record, may also be the same bank to approach for the first-mortgage money on your new property, even if you decide not to refinance your first mortgage. The bank *may* want to rewrite the financing into one uniform package with *both* properties as collateral. Work with your mortgage banker on this package so that it is structured to suit your individual family financial planning.

## Take Over an Existing Mortgage

If your seller has been an alert trader in country property, a commitment may have been obtained for a new first mortgage, or an extension or possibly a refinancing of the old mortgage. The seller may have had the property appraised or have obtained an informal commitment from the lending bank based on the bank's reappraisal of the property. (The bank, after all, had the original appraisal made; presumably it has kept in touch with the values of the properties on which it holds mortgages.) Because the seller has taken the trouble to arrange for this tentative commitment, you may take for granted that probably $5,000 to $10,000 more is being charged for the property than if it were not readied for a smooth sale. The seller, in effect, is doing some of the preparatory work you might normally be expected to do.

This kind of preparation of a first mortgage may extend to an offer of a purchase-money mortgage to cover whatever cash you cannot raise for a down payment.

### Example: A Farm as Part of an Estate

The Jens Johnson farm in southern Ohio had been in the family for two generations, but the current crop of children went to the state university and had studied other professions. Don became an accountant and Nan, a designer, married a druggist. So when Jens Jensen, after a lifetime of improving the farm, died at the age of 58 of a stroke, the survivors had a problem on their hands.

Jens left the farm to be shared equally by mother, son, and daughter. Mrs. Johnson wanted to stay in Ohio near her friends and neighbors for at least part of the year. She and Jens had been fortunate enough to find a hired man to take care of the livestock during two of the worst winter months, when they rented a place in Florida where they also had friends. Mrs. Johnson hoped to move there now, but also wanted to keep one of the cottages she and Jens had built and rented along the river that ran through the 200-acre farm. Don and Nan and Nan's husband wanted to sell the farm and use the proceeds to invest in their careers. None of them wanted to worry about the farm and its operations, which had given them a modest living over the years but not enough to finance their current projects.

A neighboring farmer was willing to buy the land for $1,125 an acre ($225,000), plus $50,000 for buildings, used farm equipment, and livestock. Outstanding was a mortgage with a principal of about $90,000 still to be paid. It had been needed for financing equipment and the college educations of Don and Nan. The potential buyers, approved by the bank that held the mortgage, proposed to pay $275,000 for the farm—cottages and all. The neighbor was willing to let Mrs. Johnson have her cottage and road access, plus an acre with river frontage, for $10,000. The bank would finance $120,000 for the new owner, who still needed a purchase-money mortgage of $90,000 to make up the difference between the cash on hand, $65,000, and the purchase price.

The three partners in the Johnson Estate went to the family lawyer and banker and, working together, they hammered out a solution as follows:

| | |
|---|---|
| Cash down | $ 65,000 |
| Second mortgage to buyers | 90,000 |
| First mortgage | 120,000 |
| | $275,000 |

The partners got $95,000 from the cash down and refinancing of the first mortgage. This covered their immediate needs for capital. Mrs. Johnson bought from the new owner the cottage and acre along the river for $10,000. The lawyer worked out an agreement with the three heirs to liquidate the partnership they had in the estate. The buyer gave each of the three heirs a separate five-year note for $30,000 at 8 percent interest with the farm as collateral. Thus, each could use the note as he or she saw fit. Mrs. Johnson could consider it a good investment. Don Johnson sold his note at a discount, used the cash for investing in an accounting partnership, and charged off the discount on his taxes. Nan and her husband used her note as collateral for a loan to purchase new equipment for their businesses. Thus each seller's goals were served, and the land continued as a farm operated profitably by the new owner.

In general, when you buy country property, you will want to get as much leverage on it as possible; when *selling,* however, it is a good idea to take as much cash out as possible. That is, arrange for a bank or similar institution to hold all or most of the mortgage. Offer a purchase-money mortgage (for a relatively small amount and at a good rate of interest) when it will help smooth the sale of a fully priced property. If this kind of package is *offered to you as a buyer,* you can assume that the property is priced accordingly. But it may be the only way you can finance the deal; it may mean stretching a bit in order to get into a good market. You will have to make an investment decision based on your long-term financial planning. Keep in mind, always, that the easier the seller makes it for you to buy the *more* you will pay. In the case of raw land, this may be a disadvantage and a hindrance to future profits; it requires a longer period of holding and that much more risk that the current annual appreciation may tail off in the next five or ten years. In the case of income-producing property, you are in a better position when you perhaps "overpay" a few thousand dollars in the total price because of convenient financing packaged for you by the seller. For you will be using income (which presumably can be raised gradually) from the property to pay off your fixed amount of debt with dollars worth less every year.

In accepting mortgage loans from private sources, be sure the mortgage has a definite rate of interest (not variable—in the current market variable rates work to the disadvantage of the borrower and to the advantage of the lender, for they are more likely to go up than they are to go significantly downward, even in a recession).

## Take a Second Mortgage on Property You Own

This is another way to take advantage of your good credit and to take out in cash the equity on a property you already own. Taking a second mortgage, however, is more expensive in interest (always deductible whether for a residential or for income property); it is, however, a quick and convenient way to raise up to about $25,000 on prime property. You will have to shop to see what finance companies specializing in second mortgages can offer you. Do not be surprised if the effective interest rates run to 14 or 18 percent or more. There may also be "points" to pay and a fee for writing the mortgage. When you shop for a second mortgage, try to bargain with the lender into agreeing to prepayment of the entire obligation without penalty and without additional fees. This is easier to do with a private property or with your own commercial bank, which may hold the first mortgage. If you do not have these resources to tap, you may have to talk to one or more of the nationwide finance companies that operate pretty much on cut-and-dried regulations and policies. While they are usually polite and more than willing to work with you if your credit is satisfactory, they are usually the lender you will approach as a last resort because of the high interest rates.

If you are friendly with any realtors in the area of your purchase, you might ask if they know of an investor eager to place some second-mortgage money. Look also in your local newspaper in the real estate section. The ads you see in newspapers for second-mortgage money are usually for substantial sums with *commercial* property as collateral. Still, it may not hurt to call one or more of these advertisers. If they do not lend on the kind of country property you are buying or that you already own, they may know someone else who does.

## Sell or Exchange Property You Already Own

If you are buying country property because you will make it your primary residence, you may finance it advantageously by selling your former home in the city, a single-family home, a condominium, or a cooperative. As long as you buy an alternative worth as much or more within 18 months or build within 24 months after selling the old house, you can delay indefinitely the capital gains you might have had to pay on the sale.

It is a fact of home ownership these past years that considerable equity builds up for the owners (1) through repayment of the principal of the mortgage, and (2) through the 14 percent or so a year the home appreciates in value. Thus, if you sell your old family home in order to buy a property in the country, you might structure the purchase with the tax law in mind. You will want to keep in touch with your accountant about this. It is conceivable that you can deliberately buy extra adjacent land in addition to the property you want to keep. In other words, you may want to "cover" completely the sales value of the old house with its sizable and taxable gain. At a later date, perhaps when your tax situation makes you less vulnerable (the trend in legislation after some years of "punishing" those who invested capital is to tax capital gains less in an effort to stimulate capital formation), you can sell this extra property or the adjacent guest house and pay taxes on that portion. You may be in a situation at that time where a sales contract will give you some income over a period of years and minimize your tax gains even further. Of course, you will do this with the advice of your accountant whose business it is to keep up on tax law changes and possible new opportunities to minimize taxes.

If you take the sales route and create a potential tax liability, since the passage of the tax law of 1979, you also have the opportunity, if you are 55 or older, to take advantage of a "homestead sale" deduction of $100,000 in capital gains. This could apply if you sell your principal residence with the intention of buying a smaller condominium or a residential property for your retirement.

A better way, perhaps, than both these processes, is to exchange the property, with your realtor's help, so that you incur no tax liability at all. This takes more time, is difficult if the properties are at a distance from one another and cannot be handled by one realtor or by participating realtors. As national chains and affiliations of realtors develop in the United States, however, exchanges should be easier to accomplish. Realtors will have more experience with them and swaps will become more routine.

The principle behind an exchange is the time-honored custom of swapping with no money changing hands. Tax law allows barter, exchange, or swapping of like commodities, and parcels of real estate are considered as such. Thus you can swap one property for one or two others with a total equivalent value. This is particularly helpful in the case of income-producing property on which you do not live and where you cannot take the "residential" tax-shelter benefits mentioned above. Sooner or later you (or your estate) may have to pay a tax on the final appreciated value of the property that you (or your estate) hold. Meanwhile you have accumulated more and more property without the nick usually taken by taxes as you buy and sell.

The challenge, of course, is to exchange the property you already own for something you want to buy. The seller of that second property, unless you are unusually fortunate, may not want to take your property in exchange. You will have to find a third person or entity to act as intermediary. Here is where realtors can come in handy. They might know such a third party, who will buy the property you want and exchange it with the person who wants your present property, who, in turn, for reasons of his or her own is willing to buy the property *you* eventually want to own and then swap it with you. You see why this method of exchange, intriguing as it is from a tax standpoint, *may* run into delays and complications. Still, in a very active market and with an alert realtor, such exchanges can be worked out for the benefit of all concerned. The realtor is usually in line for one commission and one or more barter-arranging fees.

## Borrow on Your Life Insurance Policy

Your insurance agent may not think very much of this source of down payment, but your insurance company, by law, must make it available to you at a low rate of interest, usually 5 or 6 percent as stated in your policy. Check any life policy you have with a cash surrender value and you will also find a guaranteed loan value after so many years and usually at a specified rate of interest. Many companies will process such a loan in a matter of a few days and will accept the request by telephone. This is a most convenient and a quick way to raise money for the purchase of a property at a very low rate of interest. Better still, you need never pay back the principal. Of course, you will continue to pay interest, but that too can be added to the loan if payback becomes a problem. The only catch is that if you die, your insurance payoff will be the face value minus any outstanding debt. But, in compensation, you have in your estate a property worth, in proportion to investment, more than the decrease in insurance coverage. For the property increases in value more rapidly than the cash value of your insurance. Now, naturally, in your financial planning you will not want to wipe out a good part of your insurance protection. In most situations you will only be able to borrow a relatively small fraction of the face value of the policy, although that amounts to most of the cash surrender value. The difference continues to protect you as before and you get your share of dividends as before, depending on the face value of your policy. You can instruct the company to use dividends to pay back the loan, or at least the interest on it, and thus eliminate build-up of the loan.

## Loans from Relatives and Friends

Among relatives and friends it is wise to remember the advice of Polonius to Hamlet, "Neither a borrower nor a lender be"! The tie of blood and friendship is *not* the best basis for money transactions, despite what your natural inclinations might be. Sibling loyalty and the tenuous idealistic feelings of true friendship are particularly vulnerable to loss of money or diminished expectations from an investment. It is no wonder that the principal basis for quarreling in a marriage and the most frequent cause of divorce revolves about money disagreements. Nonetheless, young couples starting out may have better-than-average fortune in surviving loans from older relatives and friends. There is a tolerance for mistakes made by younger siblings; there is a certain margin of generosity in the face of error by older patrons and lenders for younger protégées. Therefore, if you sense this might be the case and you are the younger party in such a relationship, do not hesitate to ask for money. You may very well get it at a nominal rate of interest. The special relationship *may* cause you to be extraconscientious in making the investment work out profitably. After all, not only are your profits at stake, there is a certain pride in performing well in the eyes of a friend or someone who has witnessed your growth and increasing prosperity.

If you negotiate a loan in such circumstances, be sure to follow the line of financial prudence and put everything in writing. Have a lawyer draw up and keep a copy of the agreement. Sometimes the principals in such an agreement hit it off well, but the heirs of one or more of the parties may not. Then, if the agreement gives you unusual advantages because of your special relationship, the heirs may dispute the fairness and give you a hard time of it, particularly if the agreement is not in writing and has not been drawn up carefully.

## LESSER KNOWN BUT AVAILABLE SOURCES OF FINANCING

In the United States, the primary loan market has institutional and noninstitutional components. Institutional participants include savings and loan associations, commercial banks, mutual savings banks, and life insurance companies.

Noninstitutional lenders include mortgage finance companies, private individuals, and nonfinancial organizations such as unions, pension funds, and the like. They lend the money directly to the borrower and take back a mortgage with the property itself as security.

The most obvious lenders are savings and loan associations, which account for about 53 percent, or more than half the number of residential mortgages given in any one year. Commercial banks are a distant second with about 18 percent.

With the less obvious lenders, you have to use a bit of ingenuity; you have to seek them out and find out whether they would be interested in financing your country property. In general, institutional lenders will consider financing property in their immediate region, but they prefer property with improvements on it. They shy away from financing the purchase of raw land as a speculation. People buy it because they have a reason to believe it will increase in value through improvement or through its position in a situation that will eventually be interesting to a developer.

The unhappy fact of the matter is that most institutional *and* noninstitutional lenders shy away from financing raw land. You should face this fact immediately and encourage the seller to give you a first mortgage and enjoy the going rate of interest. At a later date, when you have made improvements, built houses, barns, and so on, your project will be more attractive to commercial lenders.

## Commercial Banks

Loans are most often given for buying a building or remodeling a *house*. Loan officers respond most favorably when the money will go into a sensible improvement or an improvement that will bring an income. You will probably find that state-chartered banks are more liberal, as a whole, in their lending policies than federally chartered banks. If your property is in the country and if it is a farm or if it brings commercial income, try your local commercial bank. If your property is essentially residential, try the local savings and loan association first. In many rural areas, you will find *only* a commercial bank and it should be your target.

## Mutual Savings Banks

These come in the same shape and sizes with the same requirements as loans from savings and loan associations. Mutual savings banks are located primarily in the Atlantic and New England states, where they developed in place of savings and loan associations.

## Mortgage Companies or Mortgage Banks

These lend money under regulations from the state in which they operate. In general, they are the most liberal of lenders. They investigate your credit, close the financing, and collect your payments, but they actually sell, or discount, their notes to insurance companies, commercial banks, savings and loan associations, and government lenders such as the Government National Mortgage Association (Ginny Mae). Their function, as far as you are concerned, is the same as the local bank. They see to it that you pay your monthly installment, your taxes, and your insurance, and that you keep the property in good shape. They charge the buyer of the note a management fee of about ½ percent on the outstanding loan balance. Sometimes you may run across a mortgage broker or mortgage "finder," whom you might confuse with a mortgage company. The broker or finder simply matches potential lenders with potential borrowers and performs no on-going services. By simply pocketing a fee, the broker adds to the overall cost and price you have to pay. Sometimes, however, such a broker can find money for you where you and others have failed.

## Insurance Companies

As pointed out above, insurance companies generally buy mortgages from mortgage companies that administer and manage the portfolio for them. They also sometimes invest directly in large ($500,000 and above) first mortgages to agribusinesses and developments. Their investments are subject to the state regulations governing investments by insurance companies. There are limits to the amount of money that can be loaned with one property as collateral, or the percent, usually about 75, that can be loaned against appraised value. A few insurance companies will make small loans only on properties that are guaranteed by the FHA or the VA. An insurance company is also likely to request or require that you take out a life insurance policy for at least as much as the unpaid principal of your mortgage. You are likely to average less, however, on the interest rate compared with the rate on the open market.

### Credit Unions

These are a good source of relatively inexpensive loans, but first you have to join one or, if it is in an open-charter organization, be recommended by a friend who is already a member. Credit unions sprang up in the last century as a mutual financial service for people who worked for the same employer, or had the same ethnic roots or the same sports or cultural interests. When you are looking for a loan, it is a little late to organize a credit union, but they can be incorporated by just a few people, provided there are about 200 more who have an affinity of interest, that is, work or play under some common umbrella. With credit unions you are likely to get a lower rate of interest, and perhaps a higher ratio of loan to appraised value. The union, after all, is looking after your financial welfare and is not seeking to make a maximum profit. On the other hand, don't expect it to wander too far from a conventional type of mortgage on an existing single-family home or the new home you want to build. One of the innovations for savers usually offered by credit unions is the share-draft privilege—checks written on a credit union savings account—a pioneering advantage that conventional savings banks and commercial banks have begun to offer.

### Realtors, Brokers, Lawyers, and Accountants

All of these professional people are possible sources of temporary mortgage money or, for example, seven-year second-mortgage money. The way you structure the loan is up to you and your lender. Most certainly there will be some sort of written agreement based on a note with the property as security. People close to or in the real estate business frequently have funds available for investment, and because they know well the property offered as security—even if they do not know *you* that well—will lend generously against it for the sake of making a deal. They are most likely to know the local courts and the foreclosure process, too, and will not hesitate in taking back the property if you default. On the other hand, once pleased with your project, its concept, progress, and your prompt payments, they can be the source of later loans with a lot less fuss and investigation than if you went to commercial sources.

Remember, too, that lawyers and accountants often have access to the investment *funds of others* who would like to make a private placement in real estate that might turn 11 to 14 percent annually on money invested. This could apply to family residential property, as well as to something that produces income, such as a country inn, a ski slope, or a small country shopping center with a theme. Perhaps the lawyer or the accountant knows a group of other professionals, such as doctors, who are anxious to form a limited partnership and put money into a venture that you will manage and gradually buy from them as you amortize the loan.

## Federal Land Banks

Federal Land Bank Associations, of which there are more than 600 throughout the country, bring to local farmers and would-be farmers, the loan services of the Farm Credit System and its Federal Land Banks. The system is a federal agency set up in 1933 to help agricultural development and financial stability in the United States. It continues today to furnish about one-quarter of the total financing of farms, farmland, and farm buildings.

To qualify for a loan, you must be a member of your local association. When you borrow from a land bank, 5 percent of the amount you borrow goes for the purchase of shares in the association, on which you are entitled to dividends as they are declared. The system generates its capital from the sale of these shares as well as by issuing farm-loan bonds.

Loans from a Federal Land Bank Association are made for up to 70 percent of the appraised "normal agricultural" value of the farm. Four factors enter into the figuring of this "normal agricultural" value. They are (1) the market value of the property, (2) the income the property produces, (3) your outside income, if any, and (4) a pro rata value of the property as your family home. A weighted combination of these factors will establish a base for loans to buy additional acreage or to improve buildings and soil already owned. Usually the association will come up with a loan equivalent to about 60 percent of the market value. In the case of forest land, the base of evaluation will depend on marketable timber, plus a residence—your house in the woods.

The loans today have a variable rate. You are guaranteed the current interest rate for three years, after which it can be raised or lowered depending on the mortgage market. Customarily there is no prepayment penalty and the amortization period runs from 5 to 40 years.

## Federal Housing Administration Loans

This federal agency, a subsidiary of the Department of Housing and Urban Development (HUD) continues a program of mortgage insurance that protects lenders and thus enables them to extend to you more liberal terms than are available from institutional lenders. The rates change from time to time, and at present are running at 11.5 percent interest for 30 years. The loan can be up to 90 percent of appraised value. Most of the FHA-insured loans go to urban housing, but there *are* FHA loans for purchasing property in outlying areas. Also, you may be surprised to find that your country property is in one of the acceptable "urban" areas—usually on the fringe of a major metropolis.

You will quickly find out if your property qualifies for FHA insurance by making an application. You apply for a loan at a commercial lending institution. It will arrange for an appraisal, check your credit history, employment, and current bank account, and send this information with its proposed lending terms to the local FHA office. You, as borrower, pay an FHA application fee of $35, a lender's service charge of 1 percent or less of the loan; you pay for the title search and the title insurance policy premium, for the FHA appraisal, for the credit report, and for the fees charged to prepare, record, and notarize the deed, mortgage, and other documents involved in a standard closing.

There are, in fact, several FHA programs that could apply to your venture into country property. You will find a brief description here. It would be wise to first ask your local FHA offices for a pamphlet on the type of help that suits you best. It will give you latest regulations, rates, and availabilities.

**The Mutual Mortgage Insurance Program**   This program is the most familiar one offered by the FHA and provides for the purchase of family homes. You can borrow up to $35,000 for as much as 30 years. The loan-to-value ratio depends on whether the house was originally built under FHA approval and how old it is. If built under FHA inspection, a house over one-year old can possibly get a maximum insured mortgage of 97 percent of its value up to $15,000, plus 90 percent of the value between $15,000 and $25,000, plus 80 percent of the value over $25,000 to a maximum loan of $35,000.

**Outlying Area Properties Loan**   Of all the plans, this offers most help to country property buyers. FHA insures mortgages on nonfarm as well as new-farm housing on five or more acres adjacent to a highway in communities of less than 10,000 inhabitants. Construction requirements are relaxed in comparison to urban property loans. The maximum loan permitted is 97 percent of the appraised value of the property, up to a maximum of $16,200. Any higher amount has to be supplied by the buyer. Amortization can be scheduled for a period between 10 and 35 years.

**Unsubsidized Cooperative Housing Loan Insurance**  This has particular use for a commune or a group of people who want to buy property together. You have to set yourself up as a nonprofit cooperative intending to build five or more dwellings. This kind of loan is often used by developers who want to launch low-cost cooperative housing. The program does not cover the purchase of land; your group will have to buy the land first and then get the loan for the construction of houses. Check with your local FHA office for latest requirements and availability of funds.

**Experimental Housing Mortgage Insurance**  This can be obtained from the FHA for housing that features new or experimental construction concepts aimed at reducing housing and energy costs. Again, you have to pay for the land. The FHA will help you with the building if you can persuade it that your design tries out new and worthwhile ideas. If you are ready to experiment with a solar-heated and electrified home, or with wind applications, you should not have to put too much pressure on the FHA to help you out. Ask the local FHA office what it considers experimental and make your presentation accordingly. As you stress energy-saving experiments, make a mental note of how the cost of these might be written off, following recent tax law, and your income taxes diminished. The program does not cover the cost of land. It will go as high as $25,000 on its loans, and terms are from 10 to 35 years.

**Condominium Housing Insurance**  This can also be used by a group building a project on land already purchased. The program was originally designed to encourage investors to develop condominiums, but you can organize a group of not-for-profit investors and apply to build four or more dwelling units. After the housing has been completed, you would normally sell a unit to each member of the group, and the group, as a whole, would continue to own the land and recreational facilities in common. Payments toward the purchase would be used to amortize and pay interest on the original FHA-insured loan. The FHA, under this program, will lend as much as $75,000 for a period of 5 to 35 years.

**Insured Title I Mobile Home Loans**  These bring the entire FHA program up to date by insuring the purchase up to $15,000 for a two- or more-unit mobile home that you buy as your principal residence. You can expect to pay this back over a period of 15 years. The units you buy must meet FHA standards of construction for a single- or a multifamily home.

**Property Improvement Loans**   These are underwritten by the FHA to finance repairs and improvements of existing structures on your country property. At present, the loans can run as high as $15,000 and are repayable much like an installment loan at a local bank. Effective interest rates, however, because of the FHA guarantee run lower than the usual installment improvement loan.

## Veterans Administration

VA or GI loans help out in much the same way as FHA loans. The VA guarantees repayment up to a certain amount for purchases of homes and farms, for constructing homes, and for remodeling and improving existing homes.

In order to qualify for these loans, the borrower must have been a World War II veteran who served in active military service for at least 90 days between September 16, 1940, and July 25, 1947, or a Korean war veteran who served on active duty for at least 90 days between June 27, 1950, and January 31, 1955, or a veteran who served on active duty for a period of 181 days, any part of which occurred after January 31, 1955. Persons now on active duty who have not been discharged since January 31, 1955, and have been on active duty for a period of two years or more are also eligible.

Once a veteran is eligible, there is a $25,000 "entitlement," which means that that amount can be borrowed from a commercial bank or other financial institution and the VA will guarantee it. Of course, the loan you take may be larger than $25,000, but the VA will guarantee only up to that amount. If you are a World War II or Korean war veteran, your entitlement is valid until used. If you are a veteran discharged after 1955, you can take advantage of a GI loan only up to 20 years after you have been discharged. *You can use this entitlement in joint ventures with other veterans or with nonveterans.*

The maximum maturity on a VA loan is 30 years for a house and 40 years for a farm. There is usually no prepayment penalty. Maximum interest rates are set by law and are usually below the prevailing market rates because of the VA guarantee.

A practical procedure for taking advantage of the VA availability is as follows:

1   Obtain a Certificate of Eligibility from your local VA office.

2   Find the country property that suits you.

3   Make a deposit and agree to sign a contract contingent on your getting a VA loan for a stated amount.

4   Submit to the commercial lending institution where you expect to get a loan, a legal description of the property and a survey or diagram of the boundaries plus your VA Certificate of Eligibility.

The VA will then appraise the property itself and send a Certificate of Reasonable Value to the lender you have approached. If the lender's credit committee decides favorably on the loan, it obtains the necessary guarantee from the nearest regional VA office and gives you the money. The VA, as noted, will go only as high as $25,000 on an individual guarantee. The lender assumes the risk on the remainder of the loan, or at least on that part of the remainder they think it prudent to lend to you.

On a VA-guaranteed loan you must pay certain fees: an application fee, which includes $45 for the appraisal and $25 for the credit report, and a processing fee of 1 percent or more to the lender. This is considered a "point" fee, which helps to make up the difference between the interest rate the VA sets and the going market rate. Sometimes a lender may try to charge you more than 1 percent in points; technically, the extra points should be paid by the seller. If you make an issue of this, however, you may find the seller will pay the points but add the extra cost (and maybe more than that) to the price of the property. Having the seller participate this way in the financing, simply reduces the profit on the sale, so you cannot get too angry about a rise in price. However, this changes the structure of the loan as first contracted, so you might find it cheaper to pay the "points" yourself and keep the financing as originally outlined in the contract.

**Direct Loans From the VA**   These can also be obtained in some cases where the conventional lender is not willing to approve the request for a loan. Requirements are the same as any GI loan and the upper limit of the loan is $25,000.

Veterans should also look into the direct-loan possibilities available from states. Again, low interest rates make this an advantage worth asking your local VA office about.

## THOSE PESKY "POINTS" REQUESTED BY LENDERS

Whenever you go through the FHA and the VA insuring or guaranteeing procedure via a commercial lender as required, you will find the commercial lender invariably will talk about points, or a bonus fee, for writing such a loan. Even though part or all of it is insured and there may be almost no risk involved, the vexation of agreeing to a loan that has a lower-than-market mortgage rate stands as a challenge. Hence the "points," or bonus, which make up the difference. In some localities, it hardly pays to go to the extra trouble of the waits and additional investigations by the FHA and the VA. In the long run you pay as much through the subterfuge of points. Because of the fussiness of these loans, they have a tendency to dry up in times of tight credit. Many banks just decline to make them at all, rather than put themselves into jeopardy by changing points higher than the law allows.

The same points system enters the picture when state law slaps a usury ceiling on interest rates. The ceiling sometimes turns out to be lower than the going market rate. Then the points charged make up the difference. They are all loaded on the front of your contract, or written into the overall loan, but deducted from the proceeds to you. On a $100,000 loan, for example, if you have to pay two points, you sign a mortgage for $100,000 but get from the bank only $98,000.

Although usury laws vary from state to state, their general purpose is to protect the consumer from rapacious lenders. In recent years, however, during credit crunches and semi-crunches, potential buyers have been so aggressive that they have paid what the lenders asked simply *to get a loan*. The relatively short supply of new and existing single-family housing has helped to create this inflationary market. The reluctance of legislators to raise usury ceilings, *although they have been raised in some states*, usually makes any raise too little and too late, and the poor buyer soon bumps against the next credit ceiling. That is why you read so frequently about rate changes in ceilings for all manner of government-sponsored or guaranteed loans. The more aggressive buyer knows that extra fees make up the difference between the regulated rates and the going market rate.

As you can see from the various government programs outlined above, there are many of them, some with specific and limited purposes, which may enable you to get some money you might not get any other way. So, depending on your goals for buying country property, you will want to examine these financing possibilities carefully. Check them out with the appropriate office in order to get current policies, lending limits, and rates.

### Special Loans From the Farmers Home Administration (FHA-USDA)

These are special loans *not* issued by the Federal Housing Administration (FHA–HUD). They are officially for farm families and other people in rural areas and in small communities of 10,000 persons or less. The purpose behind them is to enable people living in rural areas to improve their shelter and to encourage others to move to those areas.

The loans are direct to the borrower, but you must agree to try to refinance them with a conventional lender after a specified period of time. The loans, for the most part, are for small dwellings of modest size and are for people who have been turned down everywhere else. Suitable purposes to qualify for such a loan are to buy an existing house, or to buy a parcel of land and to build a house on it, or to build or repair a house on land you already own. You can buy forest land if you can show you intend to farm it for an income or use it for some kind of income-producing recreational enterprise. The agency will work with you in trying to increase the income from the property.

In the case of a family farm, there is a maximum amortization-rate period of 40 years. Current interest rates are 8 percent a year. The rate for a loan on a nonfarm dwelling is 9 percent. Prepayments can be made without penalty and can be considered a reserve to be applied in periods of low income when payments become difficult to make or *cannot* be made.

When you ask the FHA–USDA for a loan on a farm, you may have to be certified by a local loan supervisor as having the capacity for operating a farm. This means farm experience or training. If you have dependable sources of income *outside* the farm, the inspectors will probably be lenient on this point.

The FHA–USDA also conducts a self-help housing loan program under which money is made available to a group of people for buying building sites and materials. The majority of the actual construction, then, is done by the families themselves under the supervision of an FHA–USDA construction expert. These, too, are expected to be homes of modest design and cost, usually no more than $25,000. Limits and availabilities may not be uniform across the United States. It is best to check your local U.S. Department of Agriculture office about these special loans.

## A CAUTION ABOUT GOVERNMENT LOANS

The general motive behind government-sponsored direct loans and the insuring or guaranteeing of private or institutional loans is to encourage home ownership among low- and middle-income families. You cannot really expect the FHA, HUD, or the U.S. Department of Agriculture to get enthusiastic about insuring a luxury suburban home, a lavish ranch, or a plantation in the country. That is why the loan program often seems to have ridiculously low "top" limits for lending and insuring. True, the limits have been rising with inflation, but they still barely cover the lower echelons of contemporary housing. Do not be surprised if your package is criticized as being too big to qualify for the government aid. Take what aid you can get, provided it doesn't create more delay and trouble than it is worth. And go to the commercial market for the rest of the money you need.

## LENDERS OF LAST RESORT

In the business pages of almost any metropoligan newspaper you will find a business opportunities section where financing and business loans are advertised. These are for the most part private lenders who will gladly charge you an arm and a leg for the privilege of lending you money to buy your dream property in the country. If you have a modest income and correspondingly modest dreams, the government-aid route is certainly what you should try first. The private-loan sharks will normally not be interested in you, and you should *not* let them dazzle you with their jaws of gold. It is much better for you to wait a while and accumulate the extra down-payment money you need. Or you should find less-expensive property in the country.

Once in a while you may discover one of your business acquaintances in this financial line. Do not accept the usual exorbitant rates. Who knows, approached the right way, you *might* get the equivalent of a commercial loan with much less trouble than it takes to go to a bank. With business or personal friends, remember, however, the sayings "Borrow today for sorrow tomorrow," or "Get him to lend and lose your friend." Of course, *you* may be *just the person* to *prove the adages wrong*.

# Chapter Seven

# Maintaining
# Country Property

Good maintenance of your property, with an eye toward eventual profits, requires a program of doing a *little all the time,* so that no system of your house deteriorates before it has completed its normal useful life. If Americans would treat their homes as well as they treat their cars, with periodic check-ups suggested by the manufacturer, they would have homes that last longer and provide less troublesome replacement costs.

When it comes time to make replacements, you may want to consider more durable modern materials than those which recently wore out. For example, in some climates anodized aluminum siding, doors, and window frames may function for a much longer time than wood replacements. It pays, of course, to get competitive bids on such a maintenance project. With wooden houses, one of the best maintenance programs includes regular painting with a good paint that suits your climate and the material you want to protect. Some of the best stains and paints are developed locally for local conditions. You simply have to begin with a knowledgeable *painter,* if you are not one yourself, and get the maintenance started. Sometimes you can uncover a team of college students or local teachers who make a specialty of earning extra money during the summer by painting houses. Check them out by contacting previous clients and ask about their know-how, reliability, and prices. Also, be sure you have liability insurance in case of accidents. If you are a do-it-yourselfer, you can fill in from year to year. If the job gets behind, you may want to call in the pro again. Or, if painting is not your scene at all, you will want to bring the pro back periodically, usually every five years.

In addition to a painter, you will need a reliable *heating expert*. Often the local heating fuel company provides the service on a subscription or fee basis, accompanied by a guarantee to supply additional labor during the heating season if anything goes wrong. You don't pay for service calls, in other words, but you may have to pay for new parts. The idea is to have an expert check out the system at least once a year to assure that it will probably function for another year without untimely breakdowns during the coldest days of winter when the repair people cannot get through the drifts or are at holiday parties. You also need a reliable carpenter, electrician, and a plumber.

## DIFFERENT MAINTENANCE PROGRAMS FOR DIFFERENT TYPES OF PROPERTY

The above remarks assume that you are living in a home in the country, or that you have an income-producing property, such as a farm, that includes buildings, or buildings occupied by tenants. Yet, even if you own raw land, the county in which it is situated may require some maintenance by owners, such as cutting weeds to a certain depth along country roads. If you don't provide this service in a timely manner, the county may do it for you and send you a bill. There is a chance that the county can do it for you for less money and trouble than it would cost you. So you simply make a deal with the county highway department to maintain the roadway's shoulder regularly every year and send you the bill.

The type of maintenance will also vary with the climate. If you are in the "termite belt," you simply have to watch out for the critters, even though a preliminary inspection shows them absent and your buildings have foundations of stone or cement where the wooden portions do not touch the soil. In northern climates, frost and freezing can cause heaving of the ground, and some of the cement portions of your house may develop cracks and displacements that may allow water to enter in places it could not get into before. Then, if the water freezes, further damage can occur. You will have to be alert with a caulking gun and asphalt filler.

## SYSTEMATIC INSPECTION PAYS OFF

The adventures of the astronauts, checking that all systems are "go," gives the country-property owner an image of what must be done for a space mission to succeed. Systematic maintenance checks are just as necessary for profit from your country property.

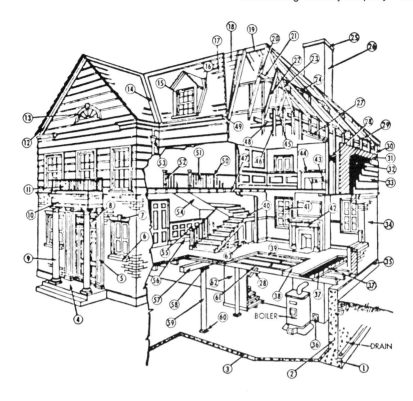

Items to check in maintaining a house

| | | |
|---|---|---|
| 1. Footing. | 22. Jack rafter. | 43. Rough sill. |
| 2. Foundation wall. | 23. Hip rafter. | 44. Mantle. |
| 3. Basement floor. | 24. Purlin. | 45. Ceiling joists. |
| 4. Porch floor. | 25. Chimney cap. | 46. Studding. |
| 5. Pilaster. | 26. Chimney. | 47. Floor joists. |
| 6. Window sill. | 27. Header. | 48. Ribbon. |
| 7. Key stone. | 28. Bridging. | 49. Gutter. |
| 8. Transom. | 29. Plate. | 50. Handrail. |
| 9. Column. | 30. Corner post. | 51. Balustrade. |
| 10. Entablature. | 31. Sheathing. | 52. Newel. |
| 11. Balustrade. | 32. Building paper. | 53. Leader head. |
| 12. Cornice. | 33. Siding. | 54. Stair soffit. |
| 13. Fan window. | 34. Brick. | 55. Wainscoting. |
| 14. Valley. | 35. Water table. | 56. Base. |
| 15. Dormer window. | 36. Cleanout door. | 57. Girder. |
| 16. Flashing. | 37. Subfloor. | 58. Column cap. |
| 17. Shingles. | 38. Finish floor. | 59. Basement column. |
| 18. Roof sheathing. | 39. Hearth. | 60. Column base. |
| 19. Ridge. | 40. Stair landing. | 61. Joist. |
| 20. Common rafter. | 41. Casement window. | 62. Partition. |
| 21. Collar beam. | 42. Fire place. | 63. Lath. |

**Figure 7-1**  Diagram of a house key places of wear and tear.

Probably the best way to consider this subject is system by system: structure, windows and doors, electrical and heating systems, insulation, plumbing supply and waste lines. To follow the accompanying checklists and comments, note Figure 7-1. It identifies the key places of wear and tear of a colonial house in the country. Presumably you checked out these systems carefully when you bought the house. If you didn't, there is no time like the present to get started. Remember, benign neglect may work in politics but it doesn't work in owning country property for a profit.

Perhaps the best place to start is the **roof system:**

[ ] **Shingles** If wooden, have they begun to rot and let the water through? If composition—such as asphalt—have they remained intact? Of metal or slate, have some fallen off? Do some shingles need replacing? Does the entire roof need replacing? Most roofs in harsh climates last only about 20 years.

[ ] **Flashing and Valleys** They are usually of copper or similar durable metal and serve as a conduit for roof water at angles in the roof or where dormers nestle into the main slope of the roof. If they have been damaged, punctured, or torn, they might let water leak through. Flashing around a chimney is particularly vulnerable to corrosion and deterioration. Check, too, the mounting of a TV antenna to see whether it has possibly damaged the flashing or shingles into which it is fastened.

[ ] **Flat Roofs** Do they feel squishy under foot? Are there bubbles, or separation of roofing felt or paper? After rain, are there large puddles which take a long time to evaporate and threaten to leak through?

[ ] **Gutters** Inspect them to be sure they are draining properly, are not filled with silt and decayed leaves, and that they do not leak. Depending on your climate, you may want to have de-icing cables looped along the eaves. If installed, they will require periodic testing. Downspouts sometimes clog. Sometimes they need a length of heating cable to stay functional during alternating winter freezes and thaws. A backed-up gutter and downspout system can cause havoc during freakish winter weather when melting snow on the roof, rather than running off, seeps into shingles and joints in the eaves.

Next, **attics and ceilings:**

[ ] Check for water stains in wood or plaster. They are a simple and natural warning that the roof system may be leaking and require attention. If your attic has no natural light, you sometimes can find leaks in the roof by entering the attic (and putting a cardboard tempo-

rarily over the ventilation louvres) and looking for spots of daylight showing through cracks or joints. Check carefully around the chimneys and under valleys and gutters if you have a gabled roof with dormers.

[ ]  Note whether there are wasps nests in your attic or evidence of squirrels or mice nesting there. Wasps can be deterred with vespicides; they usually come in through cracks in the eaves or through ventilation louvres that have no screens. Mice and squirrels sometimes get in through these same gaps and can cause endless nervous harassment to you or to your tenants. Once they get into the attic, they can gain quick access to walls, make nests, raise families, and multiply at your considerable expense. They can raise havoc with your insulation system. They may even gnaw old-style electrical wires and cause a short circuit, and possibly a fire.

[ ]  With contemporary construction techniques, water vapor sometimes becomes a problem because it cannot escape. As it gets into the attic, it may condense and cause water stains even though there are no leaks in the roof. That problem is usually solved by strategically placed vents that let moisture escape (some heat, too), but to compensate there is insulation in walls and ceilings to prevent heat escape from below. Because moist, warm heat rises, the problems accumulate in the attic of a steamy house, and it is particularly important to have proper ventilation if you have dishwashers, laundry equipment, a greenhouse, or a solarium with many plants. Remember *the plant watering you do:* most of the water you put on your plants is breathed out by them, and if too much gets into the air there is likely to be "rain" somewhere. You can see this principle in action in a terrarium or in your bedroom on a cold morning. Notice the steam or frost on the inside of the cold window pane? And how bedroom window sills eventually crack and peel due to this recurrent condensation? This happens on a grander and more destructive scale in your attic when it is not properly ventilated and there is an imperfect vapor seal.

Then, **walls and windows:**

[ ]  In older houses it is often easy to tell what insulation went into the attic ceilings because the joists are exposed. It is hard to know what went into lower secondary ceilings and into the walls. Years of opening walls to rewire, place strategic electric outlets, intall TV aerials, additional telephones, and the like may have seriously impaired the insulation system and caused a great deal of heat loss. That is why, in

older houses, you may want to look into possible renewal of the insulation system with blown-in material.

[ ] Again, if very much moisture is generated in rooms such as kitchens, and there is no vapor seal in the wall, the moisture may condense within the walls and cause the outside finish of paint to peel.

[ ] Conversely, if your walls are masonry and there are cracks or faulty pointing (the mortar between the bricks, or blocks), you may have water coming in, particularly if a wall is exposed to the driving rain or prevailing winds. Such a condition may require repointing of the mortar and waterproofing of the building blocks or bricks with a silicon solution.

[ ] Windows and storm windows require painting and occasional reputtying to be sure cold winds do not literally blow through cracks and crevices. The new, aluminum, double- and single-pane window systems with storm and screen inserts are a boon to home owners with aging backs, and who lack patience to deal with stuck window sashes and finicky painting of mullions. If you have colonial windows with the necessary mullions, you might consider the aluminum inserts for screens and storms only. Get the inserts finished in white and preserve your colonial style with no need to paint.

## Floors

[ ] Aside from maintaining the finish of floors, replacing tiles, and occasionally scraping to eliminate stains or warping, you may encounter sagging floors, which put everything at a tilt. This may require substantial rebuilding, such as positioning a steel beam or lally column on a new concrete base. In the country, such sagging may be caused by dry rot or termite attack on the support system of your building. If you see a widening of floor cracks, you had better call in a contractor or engineer right away. Poorly built foundations or erosion of natural support may cause a whole section of your building to sheer away from the rest. Timely correction of the fault can prevent an extensive and costly catastrophe. Sudden changes in floor behavior usually signal a shift in the foundation, an uneven settling of your building.

[ ] If by chance your building has cement floors that have been covered by flooring or asphalt tile, check carefully to be sure there is no moisture accumulating in the flooring material. The cement will not let spills or leaks run off property; if the moisture accumulates, or if surface moisture is allowed to seep through to the cement, you will

soon have warping of your expensive flooring. Parquets on cement are especially vulnerable to this subtle and costly deterioration. Vinyl tile will also loosen.

[ ] If termites get into your house and floor joists, or other floorboards fall prey to their jaws, you might some day have an expensive collapse that could not only damage a large portion of the building but also expose you to negligence suits by tenants. Be sure you inspect regularly for termites if your structure is partly wood and is in the middle or lower tier of states, where termites have been known to survive the winter. Unless you know all about termites and have fought them successfully in the past, better have a professional exterminator look at your suspected visitors and see what can be done. Then, perhaps, you can learn how to continue the treatment.

**Stairways and Halls**

[ ] If these are not well lighted or have loose treads, you are asking for trouble with tenants, and if you are living with these unsafe conditions you may have a serious and expensive accident, such as a child or senior citizen falling down a stairway and getting a concussion or breaking a limb. In some old houses the stairways are steeper, and the treads less wide than in modern houses. Strangers in the building, not used to the difference, may slip. It may be negligent of you not to post or otherwise emphasize the danger. Be sure you have a secure railing, so that the young and the old can help themselves up and down unfamiliar territory.

**Basement**

[ ] In the basement of the house you may encounter any number of failing systems. The lowest toilet or sink of a building is the one where back-ups will occur first. Sometimes if the house is hooked up to a sewer, there will be a trap or cleaning outlet *outside* the house. This is the place to enter the line to free it of roots or other obstructions.

[ ] Sniff the air of a basement and check if anything seems to be leaking, such as heating oil, sewage, or possibly gas, if you use that for fuel.

[ ] Check to see that floor drains in the basement floor have not overflowed—you will see stains on the cement or other flooring. They are the lowpoint of your interior drainage system and give a clue to a possible obstruction in the system. Sometimes they have been installed improperly and have no gas trap—an elbow filled with water

that prevents methane gas from the sewage system from backing up into a house. This can happen with septic systems as well. The best septic or sewer systems are situated below the level of the house so that backed up liquids have a chance to announce their presence through traps outside the building. Failing that, they will back up into the basement.

[ ]  Foundation walls, often around windows, may show cracks caused by excessive or uneven settlement. You may also find evidence (mud tunnels) of termites, or growing fungus, which would suggest rotted floor joists.

[ ]  Examine the lower part of basement walls and all the floor for possible floods in the past that may have left their waterlines. If you were not there for the actual flood, or it predates your ownership, try to find out what caused it so that you can prevent a recurrence.

[ ]  Check wooden support pillars and makeshift reinforcing to be sure they can continue to give reliable support.

**Heating System**

[ ]  If your home is heated by oil, be sure that the storage tank does not leak and that pipelines into the house do not cause smelly and dangerous puddles of oil on the basement floor. Many oil suppliers, these days, offer a low-cost checkout service to be sure that all valves and controls are in good working condition. The checkout should include recommendations for dealing with soot in the chimney, if any. At the beginning of the heating season, a check of all heating ducts and radiators should be made to be sure that heat reaches throughout the house.

[ ]  If you have hot-air ducts through which a fan blows air, be sure that the fan is in good working order and that the vents in each room are not obstructed.

[ ]  If you have heat pumps, air conditioning, or varieties of solar heating that use liquid to transfer heat, be sure all pipes are sound and are not dripping—either because of leaks or because of condensation of moisture. Be sure to insulate all pipes that carry cold water for they will show condensation on warm, muggy days. If there is enough condensation, water can begin dripping and cause damage wherever it collects.

[ ]  You will want to examine the water heater to be sure it is functioning efficiently and that it has sufficient capacity for the family or families inhabiting the building.

**Plumbing System**

[ ]   If one after another pipes crack and leak excessively, you may find it less expensive to prevent future water damage by replacing much of the plumbing with copper or brass water pipes, or with the new plastic pipes that have been certified by local building codes. Be sure that the change does not violate vapor seals or your insulation system.

[ ]   The waste water system, if old, can cause problems by backing up or by overflowing the leach bed and producing smelly puddles in the lawn. If there seem to be mysterious troubles that you cannot trace, call in a septic system contractor. Often the overflow can be stopped, at least for a while, by pumping out the septic tank, which a contractor will do for you. A contractor will also check the system for any clogging, and will flush it out.

[ ]   The water pump should be oiled and greased regularly, and all valves should be checked by the plumber, who should check, too, to see whether the pump is bringing up the volume of water for which it is designed. You may become aware that the pump seems to be working overtime. The cause may be a defective pump that is not bringing up enough water, or it may be a storage tank that is too small for the amount of water used daily by the building. It may also be caused, in a pressure storage system, by a storage tank that is "waterbound," that is, it has lost its air cushion and there is no pressure left to force the stored water through the system. Learn from the plumber how to drain the storage tank, at least partially, so that you can restore the air cushion. The plumber can easily do this for you, if necessary.

**Electrical System**

[ ]   Unless you are yourself an electrician, you had better let a pro check out your building's electricity to be sure you have sufficient wiring, that the circuits are properly fused, and that you have a central control panel with circuit breakers or fuses properly identified. You may yourself overload your electrical system from time to time. Or an appliance may short-circuit and cause a fuse to blow or the circuit to break. These interruptions are caused by *something*. Find the source of trouble before putting in a new fuse or resetting the circuit breaker. You have to be a detective for this. If electrical detecting is not your thing, better call in an electrician.

Also eliminate multiple cords feeding from a single outlet; be sure that ceiling light fixtures have a wall switch hand to an entrance.

**Exterior Walls**

[ ] If these are painted wood, they will need painting about once every five years with perhaps midterm touchup of the side most exposed to the weather. Excessive peeling or flaking usually indicates a moisture problem—see if you can trace it to inadequate ventilation of an interior room, or perhaps a leak in the water system within the walls. A good paint job will not peel or crack on a sound wall; rather it will turn dull and "dust" off gradually.

[ ] Most buildings of any size present too many problems for the amateur painter: scaffolding, brushing and scraping, repairing windows, recaulking around metal fixtures, and handling shutters—if that is the style of your house. Choose the best paint available; have a pro tell you what it is. Then observe how the pro goes about painting. Perhaps the next time you can save money by doing part of it yourself. It has become popular summer work, and college students and teachers often form painting crews. They are often good painters, and it is a way to help them through school, particularly if they are relatives of some friends. But they are *not* professionals, and *you* should learn some of the tricks of the trade first so that you can give adequate supervision. Kids have the strength for the job and often the neatness, but they don't always have the method for putting paint on so that it will last for five years. Be sure you have liability insurance to cover painters and other workers or visitors to your place.

[ ] If your house or garden walls are brick or building blocks or tailored stone, you may have a problem with the mortar—particularly in an old installation. The mortar may have to be repointed, that is, partly scraped out and replaced. A mason can do that for you; it is also easy, these days, if you want to do these chores yourself, to get prepared mixtures of mortar to which you add water. If the bricks need a complete stripping, and you will have to put up scaffolding, better call a mason or a painter. One or the other can also waterproof the entire facade for you with a silicon solution that will keep the wall intact for an even longer time.

## GETTING RELIABLE REPAIR PEOPLE

When something goes wrong, you can always run to the Yellow Pages of your local telephone directory and call someone. But this is not the way to get the best service and make the most profit.

Ask around among your neighbors which electrician, plumber, and heating contractor they think is the best in your area. Ask several people and beware of relatives recommending relatives. Yet, do not be put off *just because* someone is the cousin of a neighbor. The person recommended may be the best in the line. And "being cousins," you know is a country commonplace and custom. But just get another recommendation or two that supports the quality of the work. Then get estimates. Have the person come to size up your problem and give you an estimate of how much labor, how many parts, and how much material will be required. Get two or three such estimates, and then give the job to the company that seems both competent and reasonable. Get the contract terms in writing and explore the question of guarantees and on-going maintenance. Get those details in writing, too.

This may seem a lot of fuss for minor repairs, but wait. This screening will serve you in good stead later when you may need a backup for a repair person who may be on vacation, retired, or just too busy. Good workers, these days, in the country as well as the city, seem in as much demand as brilliant surgeons. They know their worth and sometimes it goes to their head. That is why it is a good idea to try a person out on a small repair job. You may find someone who, during a slack season, can help you remodel, construct an additional room, an outbuilding, or whatever you may decide will increase the usefulness and value of the property as an asset.

## Landscaping and Grounds

Growing things such as trees, shrubs, and flower gardens, and grounds and improvements, such as pools, picturesque bridges, driveways, and shorelines, all require attention. All require maintenance and all, when in good condition, enhance the value of a country property. Let them deteriorate over many years and you will have costly repairs, rebuilding, or replanting. If you decide to sell instead of making extensive repairs, you will get less for your property than if it were in first-class condition.

Most people, if they live on their country property, will want to keep it up as a matter of personal and community pride. You may be upgrading the property to produce income or simply holding it as an investment with the hope of selling it later at a profit. It is then a matter of conscience as to how much maintenance you want to do, how much will be required, what sort of citizen you want to be. True, in the country, your buildings are at a good distance from critical eyes, and you may not have to keep maintenance at quite so high a level as you would in a village. In the recent rush to the country, city folk often seem to seek out the picturesque, the somewhat delapidated building. They expect to buy it for less, of course, and then fix it up and restore it to the color and condition they think it ought to enjoy. On the other hand, as the owner of that dream property you might want to think of selling and taking your profit rather than undertaking substantial repairs and remodeling. If you plan to stay there, though, and pass the property along to your heirs, you will undoubtedly want to keep the place well maintained.

## Maintenance on the Farm

Not everyone who wants to buy a farm realizes how much it costs to keep it operating—until the tractor konks out and the local mechanic says it needs a complete overhaul at a cost of several hundred dollars. Or until a storm knocks down the electric wires to the barn and the milking machinery stops working—there is no light and the cows seem to sense that much is amiss. It might be enough of a nervous shock to them so that they temporarily produce less milk and thus a little less profit for you.

That is why farming is such a commitment and such a hurdle. It can require back-breaking work, as well as many mechanical skills that the neophyte may or may not be able to master quickly enough to keep the farm in the black rather than in the red. For the family that has in it a natural mechanic or two, farming becomes more feasible. You will sense when to make a minor repair that can prevent a major one at a later date.

On the farm, the wintertime is traditionally the time to fix up the machinery, sharpen the blades of the reaper, replace the housing of the milking machine, rebuild the chicken roost, put a new floor in the machinery shed, and replace a stanchion that has become worn and rusty and could wound one of your best milking cows.

The problems of maintenance on a working farm are something you either know about because you have been brought up on a farm, or you learn about by trial and error, from the county agent, or from neighbors—often at considerable expense. When you buy a farm you ought to have another farmer or your county agent outline for you what you have to do and when it should be done. Have one of them evaluate for you whether the existing machinery is in sufficiently good shape to do its job, or whether it needs reconditioning or should be junked and a newer model bought. Your county agent can also advise you on the upkeep of field drainage systems and how to maintain soil fertility by crop rotation and the addition of fertilizer.

## Maintenance for Investors Only

Even if you are an investor who puts money into a farm, ranch, or raw land and does not live on it, you will be faced with the challenge of maintenance. Suppose in the case of the farm or ranch that you have a competent manager. The manager will have to make maintenance decisions that will cost you continuous sums of money. The manager will tend to want the machinery, equipment, and buildings in better shape than you might. You are not there looking at it most of the time as the manager is. The best way to prevent excessive improvements at your expense is to work out a profit-sharing deal with the manager as part of the compensation package. Then your manager will keep a sharper eye on the bottom line—it will belong to both of you.

One of the attractions of investing in raw land is the limited maintenance it requires. It will have its natural attraction that will continue to flourish season after season. You may be unfortunate as to have an insect blight emerge after you buy it. Then you will have to decide, with the county agent's help, what controls you will want to use. Or maybe you will just let the pest pass through in hope that its natural cycle and predators will control the damage. Another threat may be fires, particularly if your land is in the West where dry seasons and careless campers or hikers often start a blaze.

Another fact of natural life to remember is that forest and woods go through cycles, which may or may not produce replacements for that lordly oak grove you feel gives your investment in land its character and principal attraction. Better to see to it that you have some smaller oaks started to take over when lightning strikes one of your specimen trees, or it just dies of old age. Even Sherwood Forest, near Nottingham in England, has had to have the help of man to survive as an oak forest.

A commonsense rule of thumb to follow in maintenance of raw land is this: Keep alive and attractive the main features of the property. If there is a pond on it and a path to the pond, keep the pathway clear and be sure the little streams that feed the pond are kept open and trickling. If someone put up an earthwork dam to form the pond, be sure that leaks do not develop after a hard winter or after a local snowmobile club tracks through your property on one of its rallies. What seems safe for the land when it is frozen can be devastating during a seasonal thaw when the land becomes mud for a time and can be chewed up and mangled disastrously by sport fanatics and their vehicles. That is one of the risks you take with raw land—you are not there to watch and supervise its use by local people who might hunt, fish, and otherwise trespass and poach upon your posted acres. This is a risk every absentee landowner (and tribe) takes and has taken since the beginning of recorded time.

The point is, if you become aware of threat or danger, you can try to do something about it. You can repair the damage before it gets worse, even though you may not be able to get the culprit to pay for the destruction caused.

## THE PRINCIPLE OF CONTINUING MAINTENANCE

You will learn from owning a country house that an owner with an eye for eventual profit has a continuing challenge of repair and replacement. You can keep your costs lower if you *use* your building and equipment in a more conservative way. Each checkpoint of a house has its characteristic wear and tear, but you can see that it gets *least* wear and tear by adapting your personal and family habits.

This applies to operating a farm as well as to using your raw land for camping or for fishing and hiking. You can *use* or *abuse* your land and buildings. But the greater profits usually come to those who use their property with common sense and are not distracted on their way toward the benefits they expect.

The maintenance manual of your car—or any other appliance—will give you an idea of the way a profitable maintenance program can work out on country property. Such an inspection of key systems will, first of all, get you acquainted with the property and its buildings, and with their strengths and weaknesses. You may discover old repairs, badly made, that ought to be done over in more durable fashion or using another technique (makeshift roof repairs and patches are an example) in order to prevent a more serious breakdown at a later date.

Early in the ownership of a house, if you have not already had it inspected by an engineer or an architect, you would do well to have it done and get a written report. Going around the premises with the inspector will help you learn what to look for in the way of telltale signs of trouble. Ask the inspector to suggest what maintenance routines would give longer life to the various systems in your house. Take notes and make a schedule of the suggested routines and their timing. Put them on a piece of cardboard or have them typed and put in a glassine folder in a looseleaf notebook. Keep them in a drawer in your office, kitchen, or workroom. In the same drawer you can collect ads from stores for various materials and suggestions for good maintenance—just as another person in your household might collect recipes and cookbooks. On a similar sheet or cardboard, keep the names and addresses of your principal repair and service people. When something goes wrong, you simply have to reach for this listing and telephone the appropriate person. Sometimes it is worthwhile to jot down what that person charged for various jobs. It will give you an idea of what system on your property—electrical, plumbing, or heating—is cutting the most into your profits. It may give you a sense of timing and proportion as to when an appliance or a system requires replacement.

## WARRANTIES AND SERVICE CONTRACTS

If your country property investment is a home or farm, you undoubtedly have bought equipment and appliances for it, with guarantees of performance of one kind or another. Keep these in one place. They can save you money on repairs required before the lapse of the guarantee. In fact, a prudent farmer would make a point of inspecting any new machinery a reasonable time *before* the warranty ran out, just as you would check out the family car before its parts performance warranty runs out. The manufacturer owes you a usable machine or tool, not a temperamental lemon that causes more expense than it is worth. If you are an investor in country property, but do not live on it, you will want, nonetheless, to keep track of these guarantees. If you have a property manager, insist that they be kept on file.

Sometimes various appliances such as dishwashers, electronic door openers, and the like come with optional service contracts. Well-known brand-name manufacturers and major merchandisers offer these contracts; in some cases they are worthwhile. But you will have to feel out whether they actually save you money. Try out one or two of the most attractive offers, on an appliance such as a dishwasher or on the automatic door opener of the garage where you keep your farm machinery. See whether you get your money's worth out of such a trial service contract. Then, perhaps, extend your use of them.

## LEASING EQUIPMENT

Particularly if you have income-producing property and, with your accountant, you have set up your tax schedule so that all expenses can be deductible, you may find it advantageous to *lease* some equipment, such as a pick-up truck for a farm or a small lawn tractor to keep the acreage around your country home trim while your back stays comfortable. There is often the possibility of a big savings through a leasing contract that requires the lessor to keep the machine running satisfactorily. When leased equipment konks out, you simply call the lessor, who will come to fix it, usually at no charge (if that is what is spelled out in the leasing contract—and be sure it is!).

Quite aside from the service you get on equipment that is leased, you can write off the expense as it occurs. You do not depreciate it over many years; you take the tax write-off right away as you use the leased equipment. This may be particularly attractive to owners of country property who do not intend to hold on to the property for any length of time. Unlike land and buildings, most of this equipment (with the exception, recently, of a mobile home) declines in value like a family car. The decline in market value roughly parallels the depreciation. Land with buildings and mobile homes (lately) have actually been increasing in market value, although for tax purposes you still can take depreciation on them if they generate income. With farm implements and machinery costing so much these days, you may find it more worth your while to lease them. They will *not* be worth more in the future, and the tax and service advantages of leasing are considerable if you have short-term plans. Talk this over with your accountant to determine how this can possibly improve your profit.

## KEEPING ADEQUATE RECORDS OF MAINTENANCE EXPENSES

Your accountant can suggest the property records to keep, but you will find two basic tax situations with country property and two kinds of records to keep.

### For the Country-Home Owner

As IRS regulations now stand, you can deduct interest paid on mortgage loans for your principal house and on fixtures and equipment you use in your house. (There are some situations where you cannot deduct interest, such as interest on money you might directly borrow to buy tax-exempt municipal bonds. But these are tax refinements that you will want to discuss with your accountant.)

Therefore, you will want to keep track of your mortgage payments. Most banks send an annual summary of interest and principal payments. Banks from which you take personal loans usually will give you a summary of the same thing; if they do not automatically do so, put in a standing request for an annual statement for tax purposes.

## For the Person Who Has a Second Home in the Country

If you use the home on weekends and holidays, with the thought of retiring there one day, *but do not rent* out the home at other times of the year, you can take the same interest deductions as you would on your primary residence. But keep the two separate so that it is clear you have two properties. Otherwise, the larger-than-average interest deductions, as though for one house, may cause an audit by the IRS.

*If you stay in the second house less than two weeks of any year* and rent it the rest of the time, you are entitled, for tax purposes, to deduct all maintenance and other expenses, interest, real estate taxes, and the usual depreciation. Usually, on this kind of most-of-the-year rental, the IRS will expect you to show an operating profit in two out of five years. Otherwise they may consider it as a "hobby" and not run seriously for profit. This means an operating profit before depreciation is taken. Because of the high original cost of many country properties, the depreciation figure, based on a 20-year straight-line schedule, can amount to a sizable deduction. Say the original cost of the house was $84,000; this means a depreciation deduction of $4,200 in each of 20 years. By then you may have sold the property to one of your children, who can begin taking depreciation all over again based on the price paid for the house.

*If you stay* in the house more than two weeks of *any tax year,* you have still another kind of tax situation. You may take all the maintenance expense deductions as in the preceding case, but only up to the amount of rent you get. In effect, you zero out the income from the property, but you cannot deduct additional sums from your personal income. Thus you "waste" most of the depreciation. Therefore, it is important that you stay less than two weeks of any year if you want to take full tax advantage of your second home. Or that you benefit from it by living there a much larger part of any year. The point is that three or four weeks of living there (the one or two extra weeks) change the rules of your tax situation. Depending on the cash flow of the property, you may lose considerable tax advantage. Talk it over with your accountant to be sure you know what those few extra weeks of use are costing you, and when you risk running a "hobby" rather than a business for profit.

### *The Rattners Buy a Second Home in the Country*

The Rattner family bought a second home on the Jersey shore not far from Asbury Park. In talking to their accountant one day they said they thought the new tax rules were unfair; they were building up that second house for retirement and were spending a lot of money on maintenance and improvement. The maintenance expenses were written off in the years the expenses were made; the improvements, along with the basic house itself, were depreciated on a straight-line schedule over 20 years. The accountant recommended a long, even period of depreciation because the Rattners said they intended to hang on to the house for their eventual retirement. The Rattners were perplexed. They had bought the house to use it, but couldn't really afford to spend every weekend and their vacation at the new house. Both were working, and they wanted to take as many tax deductions as they could during the years when they were putting money into the maintenance and improvement of the house. They even started a peach orchard that would only begin to produce heavily five years in the future. On the peach orchard they could take capital improvement deductions. Table 7-1 shows what they figured out with their accountant's advice.

Note that in both cases the expenses the Rattners had were the same. By living in the house for three summer months, they took in $1,000 less rent; in effect, they "paid" $100 a week for their stay in the house. But from the standpoint of taxes, they could deduct only $4,000 instead of the $8,067 they could have deducted had they stayed two weeks or less. That hurt a bit. The peach trees, as capital improvements, could be deducted in both cases and were not that great a factor in any case—only a 10 percent tax credit for the $200 to $300 they spent each year on planting new trees as they expanded the orchard. They did their own digging and planting.

They found, too, that it would be hard to get a tenant, even a very friendly one, willing to vacate the premises for three months of their stay. It was fairly easy, however, to get a tenant who would agree to take a vacation sometime during the summer and leave the house for the Rattners to enjoy and to do a lot of the repairing and improving themselves.

**Table 7-1**

| Two weeks or less | | | More than two weeks | | |
|---|---|---|---|---|---|
| Income from 50 weeks at $100 per week | | $5,000 | Income from 40 weeks | | $4,000 |
| Expenses | | | Expenses | | |
| Heating | $ 875 | | Heating | $ 875 | |
| Real estate taxes | 1,150 | | Real estate taxes | 1,150 | |
| Electricity | 485 | | Electricity | 485 | |
| Fire insurance | 212 | | Fire insurance | 212 | |
| Mortgage interest | 2,465 | | Mortgage interest | 2,465 | |
| Parts and Repairs | 126 | | Parts and Repairs | 126 | |
| Depreciation | | | Depreciation | | |
| ($54,000 ÷ 20) | 2,700 | | ($54,000 ÷ 20) | 2,700 | |
| | $8,067 | | | $8,067 | |
| Total expenses deductible against income | | $8,067 | Total expenses deductible against income | | $4,000 |

They did go up to their country village on some holidays and weekends, but made arrangements to rent from various friends who were on vacation and appreciated having their homes watched. Sometimes they bartered the rent for some repairs that Tom Rattner agreed to make. The rent expenses the first year came to only $735 out-of-pocket. They looked forward to the day when their joint salaries would grow to the point where they didn't have to calculate where every penny went and didn't have to make so many decisions based on tax considerations. Their accountant agreed with their plans but said they would always have to think about taxes in any property situation. And the accountant warned that tax situations could change—that the trend was gradually *against* second homes providing a tax shelter.

The Rattners used their tax shelter in an intelligent way. They were working hard to build up their property. They learned from the realtor who had sold it to them that a year later similar properties were being sold for 15 to 20 percent more. This, in a time of inflation, made for a good investment and was worth the sacrifice the Rattners were making—and their tenants appreciated having someone else worry about repairs, taxes, and improvements while they enjoyed the house.

*The Walter Wandt's Disaster*
The Walter Wandt family bought a farm near New Paltz, New York, used it as a weekend retreat for many years, paid off the mortgage, and improved the farm systematically. It had an orchard that they cultivated and upgraded and on which they took capital improvement deductions on their income tax.

By the time they were ready to retire to their handsome, old stone, country house—parts of which dated back to colonial times—they had completely revamped the heating system, replaced parts of the magnificent wide-board floors, added an extension, put in a vegetable garden, and built a guest apartment in the old barn so that the children and grandchildren could visit. From years of summer residence, they were known in the community and felt completely at home. They had no great maintenance problems so, one year, they left for their usual Christmas visit to their son's family in Florida.

In Florida, they read about the warm weather followed by a cold snap up North and were glad to be where it was sunny. When they returned home to New Paltz they were sorry they had left. The Walkill river had overflowed, as it often did at that time of year; however, this time it had gone a bit higher than usual and seeped into their basement to a depth that swamped the oil burner, caused short circuits, and in effect, knocked out the power of the house. Since they had a hot-water heating system, the water in the pipes froze and split the pipes; and then, during the thaw of the next days, the water trickled out. It caused severe damage to the wallpaper, warped the floors, and ruined the rugs on the main floor. It all happened so quickly that neighbors who had also been away for a few days came back to the same disaster in their own home. They remembered that the Wandts had given them their key to check their house and they did. But it was too late.

The weather had been unseasonably warm, then unseasonably cold, a freakish situation—but it had happened.

Of course, the Wandts had the insurance necessary to cover the damage. After about a year of repair and meticulous cleaning and painting, the house looked again as though nothing had happened. There was something new, though, an automatic pump in the cellar that would take care of any unforeseen drainage water. And there was a maintenance contract with the heating-oil people to check out and clean the heating system each year, as well as a promise to stop by the house every day in case of freakish weather when the Wandts were away. With their neighbors they made a mutual "we'll watch your house and you watch ours" pact.

It took one disaster to make the Wandts complete their security and maintenance planning. They had a good insurance policy: comprehensive homeowner's protection. But they had no pump, even though they knew the river occasionally flooded in winter. It just hadn't happened to them and so they thought they were safe. Their arrangement with the neighbor was a step in the right direction, but it was not definite enough. Wherever water pipes and water-heating systems can freeze, you must have someone responsible for checking the oil burner and the rest of the heating system. You can buy electronic devices that will light up if the interior temperature goes below a certain point. But the best solution is a maintenance agreement with a professional, your regular repair or service firm in the vicinity with the know-how and responsibility to sense approaching danger and be ready to handle it.

Then, too, always leave a telephone number where you can be reached if a crisis occurs. That way if you read in the newspapers that there is a reason to worry, you can trust that your watchman will call you if anything goes wrong and needs your attention. This is the marvelous blessing of today's telephone communications. Even if some disaster threatens, if you laid contingent plans, you will often find that your support system of service people and contractors will swing into action and *you do not have to return* from your business trip or vacation. The main thing is to stop the destruction and then *wait* for the insurance appraiser. Your support system can take the first step, and in most cases you might as well wait wherever you are until the time you meant to come home or until the appraiser is ready to make an inspection.

## WHAT ABOUT THE "HOW" PROGRAM?

For most of the history of home building in the United States the buyer took a major risk on the property bought. You could have the building inspected by a professional architect or engineer before closing, but it is *only recently* that such precautions have been actually taken seriously on a large scale.

Since 1975 there has been growing emphasis on insurance and warranty plans that protect the buyer against defective plumbing and wiring, roofing and structural defects, as well as against malfunction of some built-in appliances. These agreements vary, but most involve a one-, two-, or more-year guarantee against defects, spelled out in contract format. If one of these flaws or malfunctions should occur, the defect is repaired at no further charge, or for a minimum fee. There is a set premium, usually a few hundred dollars. The company issuing the policy generally inspects the house before writing such a contract.

The contract, if offered by the seller, is a decided plus for a property. It implies that an inspection has been made and, in any case, that it will become the seller's responsibility to fix undiscovered flaws. From the seller's standpoint, this is an extra burden in getting the house ready for sale. The inspection may turn up the need for major and costly repairs. If you, as potential seller, have been practicing good maintenance, however, you should not have any big surprises. The fact that a warranty against defects is in place should help you sell the house at a premium price. If you are the buyer, you can rest easier about stretching a bit. Usually one of the worse worries in buying a new or an existing house is that something will go wrong shortly after the closing and that thousands of dollars will be needed for a new room, for example, or a new heating system. More than a million such warranties are now in effect in the United States. They cover both new and old homes.

The National Association of Home Builders has developed in recent years a warranty covering *new* homes. Known as the Homeowner's Warranty (HOW) program, it provides protection against major structural defects for up to 10 years. The buyer and the builder both sign the HOW documents, either when there is a closing or when the buyer moves in.

During the *first* year, the builder agrees to fix defects caused by faulty workmanship and materials at variance with HOW standards. For the *second* year of coverage, the essential warranty continues as a protection against defects in the house's electrical, plumbing, heating and cooling systems, as well as for structural defects that turn up. The Insurance Company of North America takes over the responsibility for this. For the *third* through the *tenth* year, a national insurance plan directly guarantees the home buyer against major structural defects.

The rationale is to give the builder a year to make good on mistakes, and then pass the responsibility on to an insurance company. If a dispute arises over whether something is or is not covered by the plan and the buyer and builder cannot settle it between them, the problem goes to a local HOW council that appoints a disinterested person to try to settle the difference.

If all these preliminary attempts fail, or if the homeowner loses patience during this period, the problem is placed with the American Arbitration Association. During the last nine years of the warranty, when the builder has been removed from the prime position of responsibility, the buyer makes a claim for major structural defects directly to the local HOW council or to the insurance company issuing the guarantee.

*Example: A House with a Bad Basement*
The Terry Kelly family, a mother and three children, moved into a house that behaved well during the first year, but developed cracks and water leaks in the basement late during the second year. The house was covered by a HOW guarantee, and by the third year it was apparent that something basic was wrong.

Mrs. Kelly, a single mother and head of the household, got in touch with the local HOW council—who knew the builder had gone out of business—and notified the insurance company to send an appraiser. The appraiser inspected the home and found that its foundation did not take into account the underground water flow in the immediate neighborhood. This caused the basement to flood and the foundation to settle unevenly. In turn, this produced cracks in the wall and warped floors. Repairs were estimated at about $10,000. These included reworking much of the basement—with reexcavating and repouring walls to prevent water damage.

*Example: The Hellers and Their Homeowner's Warranty*
The HOW (Homeowner's Warranty) program is a 10-year warranty insurance plan on new homes, with its own complaint-handling procedure which provides HOW home owners with three opportunities to work out problems with their builders. First, it tries to get the buyer and builder to work out the problem on their own. If this fails, the buyer can request that a conciliator be appointed to meet with both parties in order to resolve the dispute. The third and final step, if all else fails, is the appointment of an arbitrator. Either the buyer or builder may request arbitration, and both parties must agree beforehand to comply with the arbitrator's decision. Recently, the program had its first case of arbitration settled. All previous cases had been settled either by buyer and builder reaching a mutually satisfactory agreement or by agreeing to conciliation.

The case in point involved the Heller family, who settled in a new home only to discover a sour odor that seemed to come from several walls. The builder attempted to eliminate the odor by washing the walls with a baking soda solution and by placing deodorizers in the house. This failed and the Hellers asked the builder to remove all the drywall and completely replace it with materials of "new and good quality." The builder thought this was asking too much. Communications broke down even though a conciliator was called in. The builder was a participating member of the HOW program. The case went to arbitration handled by the American Arbitration Association, a private nonprofit association.

The arbitrator in the case was a professor in the building construction department of a local university. He analyzed the situation and consulted with an architect, two drywall contractors, and a staff member of the International Association of Wall and Ceiling Contractors. The arbitrator decided that the Heller's request was excessive. He proposed an alternative and less-expensive solution. To eliminate the odor he proposed to (1) remove the wallpaper and wood paneling, (2) prime the wall and partition surfaces inside the house with pigmented shellac, (3) repaper the walls and reinstall the wood paneling as called for in the original plans, and (4) repaint all wall and partition surfaces that had originally been painted with two coats of first-quality latex paint. The arbitrator estimated the value of these repairs at $3,030. Under the HOW warranty agreement the builder had the option of either paying the assessed value of the repairs or making the repairs. In this case, the builder chose to pay the cost of repairs.

Most home buyers' complaints under the HOW program have been settled before reaching arbitration and without the need of going to court. The Kelly case demonstrates that the program works, even if the builder goes out of business. HOW warranties available on single-family houses, condominiums, and townhouses, cost $2 per thousand dollars of the cost of a house, with a mininum charge of $50. The cost is paid by the *builder,* although this is undoubtedly figured into the cost of the house. More than half a million houses are covered by HOW warranty in the United States, and over 10,000 builders are now part of the program in most states and the District of Columbia.

Your local HOW council—and these are multiplying and spreading throughout the United States—can give you good maintenance tips, regardless of whether you are part of the program or not. Most builders will *tell* you they are part of the program, because it is a sales incentive for you to buy the house they have built. In advertisements, many builders include a HOW logotype. It always pays to ask the seller, however, whether there is a warranty on the house or its appliances and equipment. Sometimes, in the heat of the sale, these details may be forgotten. The HOW warranty can pass along from one buyer to another until it expires in ten years. It is definitely a plus to have one on your property, both from the standpoint of lower maintenance charges and of greater resale value. The whole HOW program, of course, encourages better construction techniques by builders who cannot afford to have their colleagues review too many of their mistakes. Because the HOW program was an idea of the building industry and is being promoted by it, the whole concept of warranteed housing should grow by leaps and bounds during the next decade, so that home buyers in the United States *should* live in houses that function more efficiently. This is a trend which should make your country property all the more valuable as you participate in the improved quality of housing construction.

# Chapter Eight

# Improving
# Country Property

If you are at all handy with tools, you will find that improvements in your country property can give you great personal pleasure, as well as increase the profitability of its operation and its asset value. If you are not handy, well, there can still be joy for you as you have improvements made by skilled people and see the value of your property increase.

Yet there are improvements that will increase the value and longevity of your property and there are some that will not—although they give enormous satisfaction to you and your family.

## IMPROVEMENTS FOR PERSONAL RESIDENCES

While you may very well want to have a swimming pool in your yard in a residential area where there are none (because there is a lake nearby), even though you will be able to swim in the pool for only three summer months unless you heat it and close it in, do not expect your pool to increase much, if at all, the price you can get for your property. It will, by and large, sell for about the same price as comparable poolless property in your neighborhood. If you have remodeled a $100,000 property at a cost of about $10,000 to $15,000, you *may* get that additional sum from a buyer, but not much more. A buyer will look at the price as something that the house will achieve over a period of years. But then all houses in the neighborhood that are kept in good condition will increase in price by approximately the same percentage, whether or not they have been re-modeled or improved.

In most cases it is foolish to remodel or substantially improve a house with the idea of selling it at a higher price right away. You *may* make a profit if you supply your own labor—labor accounts for about one-third of most remodeling projects—but if you pay going rates for contractors and materials, you will be lucky, after you pay them, to make a cent on the improvement right away. The list price of the house will go up, but you have to deduct from that rise the cost of improvement.

You will be further ahead if you plan your improvements for the immediate pleasure and benefit of your family. If you need a new kitchen, build one. New kitchen equipment? A new counter sink in the bathroom? Put it in. An add-on to the bedroom wing to increase the size of the cellar for a workshop? An additional bedroom plus their own bathroom for your two growing children? Add on that two-story wing. These improvements will make the house a better place to live in. Forget about the gold-plated fixtures in the powder room, the extraneous swimming pool, the elaborate wetbar in the family room, or an add-on library and studio. These are items your family might enjoy, but you cannot expect to profit from them on the resale market. On the whole, buyers will pay a little extra for anything in a neighborhood that is on the way up; they will pay a little less for anything in a neighborhood that is visibly on its way down. You may or may not be able to do anything about your neighborhood. From the standpoint of profit, however, it is unwise to do extensive remodeling of your house if the neighborhood is deteriorating and the situation is pretty much out of your control. On the other hand, if you move into a neighborhood as a kind of pioneer and are committed to living there for a long time, you can over the years help to upgrade the entire area as you remodel your house, and you can find a rewarding investment as the area enters a more prosperous cycle. Your paper-profit situation implies a lot of your own caretaking and labor—and the persuasion of others to upgrade their properties.

*Example: Depression Necessities Turning into Post-World War II Gold*
The Webbers moved to the country in 1932 in the midst of the Great Depression. They bought a neglected summer house from a relative who no longer wanted to keep up a family house in Milwaukee plus a summer place in the lake district to the west of that city. The cost was $3,000 for the old farm house, a hay barn, and about an acre and a half of land, stretching from a dusty country road to a swamp that edged a shallow bay of a lake. Both of the Webbers were handy with tools, and they liked the idea of creating something new out of an old family place. They began with the plain, run-down Victorian farmhouse with no architectural features worth saving. It had three bedrooms, one bath, a family room, and a summer

kitchen. Over the years, with help from carpenters from time to time, they tore down the unheated summer kitchen and substituted a stove and screened porch with a bedroom above. They added a modern, heated kitchen, with a master bedroom above. A second bathroom was added, made from one of the small old bedrooms. They ended up with four bedrooms and two baths upstairs, a living room, a laundry, bathroom, family room, dining room, kitchen, and the screened outdoor room opening into the surrounding woods. They gradually relandscaped the grounds, filled in the swamp, built a boat house on the edge of the lake, and made a second, or guest house, from the hay barn. Now, 50 years later, the dusty old road is asphalted, there is a regular garbage pickup, and a sewer system has just been built to alleviate the poor percolation of the relatively wet, clay-heavy soil.

Neighbors in the 1930s and 1940s had also sold their summer places to a younger generation, and most of the people on that country road now live there the year round—the Webbers were among the first to do so. The former colony was definitely in the country—three miles away from the nearest village—but the building boom spreading west from Milwaukee has made it now almost a suburb of the metropolitan area. There is talk of the township in which the Webbers live becoming a fourth-class city to support more services and to protect itself from increasing annexation by nearby cities and villages. Although it is still a township and contains many working farms, the population explosion has made it the fastest growing county in Wisconsin. About 50 years after the Webbers bought the place for $3,000, and after much labor and community efforts to upgrade the region, the Webber place with its improvements on about 1.5 acres is worth about $350,000. Each year the value goes up another 15 percent or so. In the Webber's case, sensible and gradual improvements meshed well with the rise of the neighborhood, and the work proved worthwhile on the wave of post–World War II prosperity. Timely mortgages with a local savings bank financed the remodeling and part of the schooling of the young Webbers; the increasing value of the house was always good security and the Webbers maintained a good credit reputation over the years. Today, they hope that one or more of their children or grandchildren will take over the old country homestead.

## WHAT IS WORTH IMPROVING

You presumably went through some sort of physical inspection of your house when you bought it. If not, it might be a good idea to have your entire place inspected by an architect or an engineer before you go ahead with extensive improvements. There may be some basic defects that can be corrected at the same time. There may be also defects that will *have* to be corrected so that the planned additions are workable, that is, work with the present electrical, heating and cooling, plumbing, and sewage disposal systems.

Assuming that your house is sound, or is about to be made sound, you then have choices to make regarding improvements that will cost a certain amount of dollars and will add (1) to your personal and family pleasure, and (2) to the market value of your house.

Selective home improvements offer a tangible and gradual way to upgrade your investment in country property. You may own the property and live in it as a principal residence, you may use the second house as a weekend retreat or for income from rents, you may own and operate a farm, or you may simply be an investor in a commercial building in a country village. The same principle applies: You can *protect* the value of your investment with adequate preventive maintenance and you can *build* it up with appropriate improvements. The question of *what kind* of improvements is a relative one, based on neighborhood or regional lifestyles and the prevailing prices of typical homes or farms. If your house is on a lake, an adequate pier, marina, or boathouse will probably add to the value of the house, if most waterfront properties have one or more of these additions.

On some remote sparsely populated lakes, however, a boathouse may be an oddity, an additional building that will not increase the profit potential of the property. In fact, if you try to sell, your possible buyer may tell you, "Who needs a boathouse? We weren't planning to race around in a motorboat. If we wanted to do that we'd buy on a lake where there are lots of sailboats and motorboats." This sort of remark is a ploy to get you to reduce the value of the property. Unfortunately, you are vulnerable. A boathouse on that lake is just not worth another $10,000 on the price.

On a well-populated lake, however, where new zoning makes new boathouses impossible to build because the lots are too narrow, an existing boathouse could well be worth an additional $15,000, particularly if it has a working marine railway, a rack to store boats during the winter, a heater, running water, and toilet hooked up to the septic system.

For a country-property owner on a lake that is highly developed for water sports and entertaining, the boathouse might even have decking on the roof or porch area for giving parties. In this situation, a boathouse can be improved considerably to become a major entertainment area in addition to a place for docking and sheltering boats during the summer and for storing them during the winter. You might very well justify the expense of $25,000 or more in that boathouse, possibly with a guest apartment, because the neighbors have the equivalent or better. A good rule of thumb might be this: Your profits are assured if you go a long way toward keeping up with the neighbors, but try not to get very far ahead of them. Now, if you have a crystal ball and can foresee that all the neighbors will have barbecue patios within 10 years, you might want to lead the pack now at costs that assuredly will be less than they will be 10 years from now. You

**Table 8-1**  Home Components as a Percentage of Total Value

| Roof | 7% | Heating Systems | 5 to 10% |
|------|------|-----------------|----------|
| Walls | 16% | Hot air | 6% |
| Electrical system | 5% | Hot water | 10% |
| Floors | 12% | Electric | 5% |
|  |  | Plumbing | 5% |

can speculate on improvement very successfully and profitably if you have a reliable crystal ball. But who owns one of those, nowadays?

The field of planning improvements has been well plowed by many consumer consultants. A number of tables and charts are available for use as rules of thumb as you consider improving your home to increase its value and profit potential.

Table 8-1 indicates the value certain common features in a house possess in relation to the value of the whole house. Of course, this adds up to only about half of a whole house; there are also many minor items to consider. But the percentages for these major value centers will give you a handle for your planning.

Figure it out this way: Suppose you want to buy a country house that would cost $45,000 to replace as a new building. It is on land worth $10,000. The price for the land and the house as offered to you is $32,000 because the house needs work and is advertised as a "do-it-yourselfer's special." This means the house alone has a price of about $22,000. Compared with its replacement value of $45,000, this means you have about a $23,000 rule-of-thumb figure for remodeling to justify the economic feasibility of your planned improvements. That is, once you have paid $32,000 for the house and the lot and you put in about $23,000 worth of improvements, you will have a home (with land) worth about $55,000, which is the going rate for that kind of home, in good condition, with traditional features, in that neighborhood. Always remember the neighborhood. There is no profit in building a palace in the midst of nice, middle-income houses on half acre lots.

Translating the required dollars, based on the percentage components in Table 8-1, you get the figures shown in Table 8-2.

This budget figures out to about one-third for materials, one-third for labor, and one-third for the contractor's profit. That would mean that if you do most of the work yourself, you can save two-thirds of the cost of remodeling—the labor and the contractor's profit. But be careful before you plunge ahead. If you botch the job, you are probably worse off than if you had let well enough alone. For a botched job shows up either in appearance or in obvious malfunction. An alert buyer will probably have an

**Table 8-2** Dollar Allotments for Home Components

| Component | | Dollars of remodeling budget |
|---|---|---|
| Roof | 7% of $23,000, | or $1,610 |
| Walls | 16% of $23,000, | or 3,800 |
| Floors | 12% of $23,000, | or 2,760 |
| Electrical system | 5% of $23,000, | or 1,150 |
| Heating systems | | |
|   Hot air | 6% of $23,000, | or 1,380 |
|   Hot water | 10% of $23,000, | or 2,300 |
|   Electric | 5% of $23,000, | or 1,150 |
| Plumbing | 5% of $23,000, | or 1,150 |

inspector go over any building that was remodeled recently, particularly if it was remodeled by the owner.

Remember, the percentage figures given are average, rule-of-thumb figures. You might spend less in one category; you might want to spend more in others.

Take the *roof,* for example. The percentage allotment is for an entirely new roof beginning with the frame. There are many different kinds of roofing materials: wooden shingles, asphalt shingles, tar paper, and asphalt roofing compound, plus flashing for the valleys formed by gables and dormers, if any, and gutters for the eaves. Get estimates on the cost in terms of dollars per square feet for the roofing, and cost per lineal foot for the gutters, flashing, and downspouts.

And the *walls* could be done over entirely, if sections require it. This may be the case with concrete or stone walls. If you use expensive interior coverings, you will want to increase this percentage a bit. You may want wood paneling, for example, or a fine, washable vinyl fabric on the inside walls. Outside walls, of course, can be repaired simply by reinforcing them, by installing new siding, or by repairing the siding, which would then be painted. Or they can be stuccoed, or you can finish them with weathered shingles that do not need painting. Get estimates for concrete work in cost per cubic yard; for the stucco work, get the estimate in terms of square yards; for interior paneling, ask for cost per square foot.

With *floors,* the percentage figure applies to complete replacement. Most floors may need a board or two replaced, or perhaps a joist splintered or a lally column installed to correct sagging. The most usual improvement for floors is a scraping and refinishing job. Or it might mean a wall-to-wall carpet in the living room, or perhaps vinyl tile in the children's bedrooms or in a family room. Ask for estimates in terms of square feet, and be sure all labor costs (such as the charge for laying the tiles or carpet, and taking away all debris) are included.

For *electrical systems,* the percentage allotment covers complete replacement of all controls, wiring, and outlets. In many cases this will not be necessary because houses built since World War II, for the most part, have wiring adequate to carry most modern appliances, with perhaps the exception of a central air conditioning system or individual window conditioners of large capacity. These often require separate circuits of higher voltage (220 volts instead of 110, the normal house circuit voltage). Unless you are a competent electrician yourself, you had better leave this work to a professional contractor. The life you save may be your own, and you will not need to worry that an incompetent splice made by you may short and cause a fire. Your electrician will know about the number of outlets to attach to one circuit and will bring the circuit into a master control panel with circuit breakers (that konk-out when there is an overload). The same effect can be accomplished by a master panel with fuses; in this kind of system you see the telltale blow-out signs in the fuse. Then you have to remove the cause of the blow-out and replace the fuse to restore the circuit to function. Be sure the electrician gives you a diagram of the circuits so that you know what outlets are on each circuit. This is frequently arranged by room and by major appliances, such as the furnace, air conditioner, pump, water heater.

Have the contractor give you an estimate for necessary equipment, fixtures, wiring, controls, and labor. You may want to buy the fixtures, such as ceiling illumination, chandeliers, and attached wall lamps, yourself to be sure that you get the style and quality you want. But start with your electrician, who may have a supplier who will meet your needs. The electrician can buy in quantity at a discount, and perhaps pass some of the savings on to you.

*Heating systems* have been allotted a percentage to cover an entirely new installation. Here again, you will seldom find you need a completely new system. There will be some usable ducts and some usable pipes in place. Have your heating contractor check out the existing system and ask for a recommendation. Does the furnace need replacement? Does the chimney require cleaning and reconstruction? Do you have adequate thermostats and fuel-saving controls? This is another job that you should not plan to handle yourself unless it is your line. It is too important to family health, consumes too much of your valuable time, and requires too much practical knowledge and technical skill. You could better spend your time upgrading the insulation, which is particularly important if you have an electric heating system. There is no merit in "heating the outdoors" as they say in the country. That is what you do when your windows need reputtying, the frames of doors and windows need recaulking and weatherstripping, when storm windows and storm doors are needed, and when walls have been pierced for electrical outlets and the tunnels thus cleared have not been repacked with insulation.

You will have a major insulating problem if you buy a summer house and convert it to year-round use in a northern climate. The house was *not built* for year-round living, but rather for natural cooling during the summer. Thus, the screened porches with their counterweighted windows to keep out rain, the thin walls with no insulation, the careless accumulation of makeshift wiring, and the like, make extensive rebuilding necessary to accommodate a modern heating and plumbing system, as well as rewiring for modern appliances and efficient living. That summer house may have character and good Victorian lines, but aside from space, charm, and not always a sound roof—you could always put a pail under a leak for that occasional violent summer thunderstorm—the house has little else to offer for modern living besides a lovely setting on a lake or seashore, or a view from halfway up a hill or in the mountains. In some cases, the house lacks charm even though it has a superb location. In such a case, it might be best to tear the thing down and start over with a modern foundation that makes efficient use of contemporary materials, that positions the furnace efficiently, and that uses modern construction techniques. Many old homes are worth remodeling and restoring. A few are not. If you have already bought one of the latter and have determined that it is not worth your, or anyone's, while to preserve—tear it down. Start with a new building in the style you prefer. You can probably make a profit on the venture over the years. With the old Victorian lemon, you would wind up profitless and probably a masochist as well.

The plumbing of a house can prove more crucial to your comfort than you expect, particularly if you are used to city living and move to the country. Many ordinary household tasks depend on a quick supply of hot and cold water and rapid draining of waste waters. In the country, pipes clog, pumps wear out, fuses blow, wells run dry, septic tanks back up into the basement, toilets back up and flood the floor, and septic systems grease up and do not percolate effectively. Then the leach bed becomes a smelly swamp with telltale tufts of prodigiously green grass or weeds that advertise to the neighbors that all is not well with your septic system. That bright green reminds you, too, that something has to be done. It will probably be one of the few silent nags you will ever have to endure in your life from *grass*. But nag it does on a leach bed that is not percolating properly. Fortunately the nag is silent—except for children and malicious friends who voice amazement at how green your grass is and wonder "Why does it seem to have a pattern just there?"

All this can easily be avoided with good plumbing. If you have pipes replaced, be sure they are copper, or the new plastic pipes that are so much easier, quicker, and less expensive to cut and fit. You may have to order, for your new bathroom, fixtures such as a toilet, lavatory, bathtub, or shower. Have the plumbing contractor estimate costs of these, as well as labor, materials, and removal of old fixtures. You will want to call in one or two septic-system specialists to check what to do about your septic tank and a possibly malfunctioning leach bed. Ask how much cast-iron pipe it would take, how many feet of trenching, how many cubic feet of gravel, and whether the system requires a new tank or not.

You *can* do some of these chores yourself, but mucking around with the sewage system may not be very pleasant. Perhaps you can dig some of the trenches. The specialist, remember, can bring in a trenching machine and do the job in a matter of a few hours. This may save you an alienated back or a dislocated sacroiliac, much discomfort, and a small fortune in medical bills not covered by your insurance.

## ALWAYS OBTAIN COMPARATIVE BIDS

Presumably you have heeded the advice in the previous chapter and gotten in touch with *several* contractors in the same line of business. You might want to alternate in giving them work so that more than one contractor of a kind is familiar with your property. Then, in a repair emergency, if one cannot come, you can fall back on the other. This method of selection and trial will assure competent and quick repairs. It makes an excellent reference list, too, for choosing contractors to do your building, remodeling, or for installing improvements.

Get two or more *signed* estimates for any major job. In the process get the recommendations of each contractor as to how to *do* the job or solve the problem. Sometimes a different point of view can simplify the solution and save money.

## FOR ANY MAJOR REMODELING TAKE AN ARCHITECT

It used to be that most country carpenters could build and remodel houses according to two books of designs widely popular in the Victorian period: A. J. Bichnell's *Detail, Cottage, and Constructive Architecture,* and William T. Comstock's *Modern Architectural Designs and Detail* (see Figures 8-1, 8-2, and 8-3). You cannot count on building contractors to know these styles, even though they can build a thoroughly creditable contemporary home with the usual features. You may, however, want something a bit more unusual than your contractor's idea of design. So get an architect whose homes you admire and who is thoroughly familiar and enthusiastic about the style you want your house to be. An architect can give you

**Figure 8-1** Advertisement from A. J. Bichnell's "Detail, Cottage and Constructive Architecture," 1873, New York.

# MODERN

# ARCHITECTURAL

# DESIGNS AND DETAILS

*CONTAINING EIGHTY FINELY LITHOGRAPHED PLATES,*

SHOWING NEW AND ORIGINAL DESIGNS IN THE

## QUEEN ANNE, EASTLAKE, ELIZABETHAN,

AND OTHER MODERNIZED STYLES,

GIVING PERSPECTIVE VIEWS, FLOOR AND FRAMING PLANS, ELEVATIONS, SECTIONS, AND A GREAT VARIETY OF MISCELLANEOUS EXTERIOR
AND INTERIOR DETAILS OF DWELLINGS OF MODERATE COST    ALSO, A NUMBER OF

### *DESIGNS OF LOW PRICED COTTAGES*

IN THE VARIOUS POPULAR STYLES, ADAPTED TO THE REQUIREMENTS OF

Seaside and Summer Resorts, and Suburban and Country Places.

ALSO, SEVERAL DESIGNS FOR

MODERN STORE AND OFFICE FRONTS, COUNTERS, SHELVINGS, ETC., ETC.,

COMPRISING ORIGINAL DRAWINGS BY A NUMBER OF PROMINENT ARCHITECTS OF DIFFERENT LOCALITIES,
PREPARED EXPRESSLY FOR THIS WORK.

———

*ALL ELEVATIONS, PLANS AND DETAILS TO SCALE.*

———

NEW YORK :
WILLIAM T. COMSTOCK,
SUCCESSOR TO BICKNELL & COMSTOCK,
ARCHITECTURAL PUBLISHER,
194 BROADWAY.

**Figure 8-2** Advertisement from William T. Comstock's "Modern Architectural Designs and Details," 1881, New York.

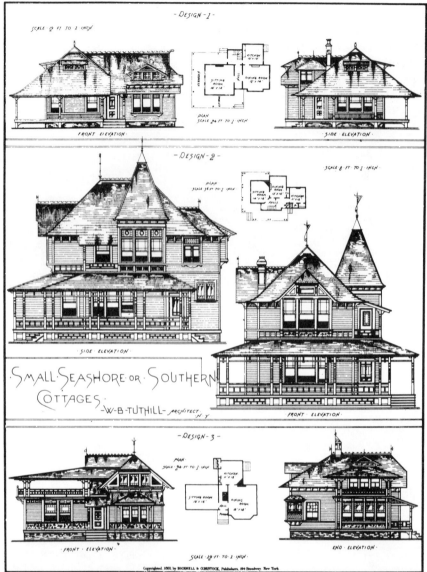

**Figure 8-3** Illustrations of William T. Comstock's "Modern Architectural Designs and Details."

reliable current figures for building the improvements that have been designed and can supervise the work. Spell out in writing what you want done and sign a reciprocal agreement that includes an estimate for the complete service. Some architects will give you plans, talk once or twice with the contractor, then go on to other work. You should have your architect take a more active part in the work. Set up times when the work ought to be inspected. Your contractor will get the necessary permits and notify the local building inspector when the place is ready to look over. But the architect takes orders from you, and it is up to you to see that the job is carried out as you specified. No matter how clear the drawings, a contractor may misinterpret them, and if the building continues long with this fault, there will be that much more *unbuilding* to do to get the feature right.

## Example: The Case of the Extra-Large Shower

The Brown family bought an old Victorian house in a picturesque village. It had only one bathroom upstairs. There were many possibilities for the house and the Browns wanted to make it liveable as quickly as possible, and then let refinements come into the house over a period of years. They decided that they would have a new bedroom made from the remodeled first floor parlor. A bathroom could be made from a large closet in the parlor, which happened to lie nearly below the bathroom upstairs. A friend of the Browns, an expert in Victorian architecture, told them they would have to compromise and could not have a bathtub with large legs in the old closet; they would have to settle for a stall shower built into one corner. The closet already had a series of cupboards and shelves just inside the door on the left. Pipes for the shower could go on the right, with additional cupboards to balance those on the left and which would provide access to the pipes, if necessary. The small bathroom had no window; a ventilation duct and fan had to be installed. There were interior walls available to take this up to the roof. On its way up it picked up another vent in the upstairs bathroom, which did have windows but needed mechanical ventilation on days when it was best to keep the windows closed. The emphasis of the architect's instruction was on the ductwork.

Everyone referred to the shower as "3 by 4"; the drawing was formalized and the shower seemed about square. The carpenter's helper roughed in the walls for the shower and had nailed a screen for the plaster base on the 2-by-4s when it was discovered that he had the shower coming four feet into the room instead of projecting three feet into the room and running 4 feet along the wall as intended. No one seemed to have noticed until the architect came by to see how things were moving along. The architect immediately felt uncomfortable in the closet-bathroom and soon found out why. The carpenter was taken to task, and knocked out the studding and rebuilt the shower walls. "We would have found that out sooner or later, but I'm glad I found it out before the plasterer came. That would have been a mess. With the shower into the room that way, you wouldn't have been able to open the door of the vanity opposite the shower and the symmetry of the shelves and closets would have been off, a constant reminder of the mistake."

In case you wonder what these improvements and remodeling will cost, Table 8-3 shows some recent figures. They are based on what a contractor would charge a homeowner in the metropolitan Baltimore–Washington, D.C. area in 1980. In your own country location, near some other metropolitan area, charges may be a little more, or a little less.

**Table 8-3**  Cost of Remodeling or Repairing Selected Home Components

| | |
|---|---|
| Remodel kitchen | $ 4,000– 6,000 |
| Remodel bath | $ 2,500– 4,500 |
| Add powder room | $ 1,500– 2,500 |
| Add full bath | $ 3,000– 3,500 |
| Increase electrical service to 200 amps | $ 400– 500 |
| Run separate electrical line for dryer | $ 75– 100 |
| Run separate line for air conditioner | $ 75– 125 |
| Install new warm air furnace | $ 800– 1,200 |
| Install central air conditioning, electric | $ 1,000– 1,500 |
| Install central air conditioning, gas | $ 1,500– 2,000 |
| Install humidifier | $ 180– 200 |
| Install electrostatic air cleaner | $ 400– 550 |
| Install new 40-gallon hot water heater | $ 200– 275 |
| Install new 30-gallon hot water heater | $ 175– 225 |
| Install attic ventilating fan | $ 150– 250 |
| Install storm windows, each | $ 30– 40 |
| Install replacement windows, each | $ 175– 250 |
| Install new gutters and downspouts, $2.50 per lineal foot | $ 300– 400 |
| Install new asphalt shingle roof | $ 1,000– 1,800 |
| Dig and install new well | $ 1,500– 2,500 |
| Install new septic system | $ 1,500– 2,500 |
| Build rear addition, approx. 300 sq. ft.–$35 to $45 per sq. ft. | $10,000–14,000 |
| Sand and finish floors, $.50 to $.70 per sq. ft. | $ 600– 1,200 |
| Install new drywall ceiling over plaster, per room | $ 150– 250 |
| Regrade around exterioi | $ 250– 500 |
| Install new sump pump | $ 250– 390 |
| Install French drain and sump pump | $ 1,500– 2,500 |
| Enclose porch | $ 2,500– 4,000 |
| Install new hot water boiler | $ 1,000– 1,800 |
| Install new copper horizontal water pipes in basement | $ 500– 900 |
| Insulate attic, $.50 per square foot | $ 350– 800 |
| Remove interior nonloadbearing wall | $ 300– 500 |
| Remove exterior wall and install sliding doors | $ 800– 1,200 |
| New single garage | $ 4,000– 5,000 |
| New double garage | $ 5,000– 8,000 |
| Masonry fireplace | $ 1,500– 2,500 |
| Pre-fab fireplace | $ 1,100– 1,500 |
| New kitchen floor—"no wax" $2 sq. ft. | $ 200– 500 |
| Basement apartment to meet code | $15,000–20,000 |
| Gut and renovate two-story townhouse, $20 to $25 per sq. ft. | $20,000–35,000 |

| | | |
|---|---|---|
| Replace disposal | $ 100– | 150 |
| Install new disposal-drop waste | $ 200– | 300 |
| Replace dishwasher | $ 300– | 500 |
| Replace refrigerator | $ 350– | 700 |
| Replace cooking equipment | $ 300– | 900 |
| Install countertop with stainless steel sink | $ 250– | 350 |
| Install bath vanity | $ 200– | 300 |
| Drop concrete floor—townhouse | $ 2,500– | 3,500 |
| Replace laundry tub—single fibreglas | $ 100– | 150 |
| Install plumbing for laundry—within 5 ft. of plumbing | $ 250– | 450 |
| Vent dryer—easy access | $ 25– | 50 |
| Pour concrete patio—$2 to $3 per sq. ft. | $ 300– | 800 |
| Install overhead garage door—single | $ 175– | 250 |
| Install overhead garage door—double | $ 350– | 500 |
| Install garage door opener | $ 250– | 300 |
| Replace flat roof—townhouse, salvage 4-ply built-up ($2 per sq. ft.) galvanized | $ 1,200– | 1,800 |
| Install storm door | $ 75– | 125 |
| Refine fireplace with terracotta | $ 1,000– | 1,400 |
| Repoint brick exterior $1 to $2 per sq. ft. | $ 300– | 500 |
| Install skylight | $ 500– | 800 |
| Install bars on windows $4 to $6 per sq. ft. (each) | $ 60– | 75 |
| Install wrought-iron door (each) | $ 150– | 200 |
| Install ceramic tile in tub area—mastic | $ 250– | 350 |
| —mud | $ 350– | 500 |
| Change sash cords in windows (per side) | $ 12 | |
| Install aluminum siding $1.50 to $2 per sq. ft. | $ 2,000– | 4,000 |
| Paint interior of house–small | $ 1,000— | 1,800 |
| –medium | $ 1,500– | 2,500 |
| –large | $ 2,000– | 4,000 |
| Replace slate roof, $3 per sq. ft. | $ 3,000– | 7,000 |
| cedar shake roof, $2 per sq. ft. | $ 2,000– | 6,000 |
| Install disappearing stairway to attic | $ 125– | 150 |
| Build redwood or pressure-treated deck (per sq. ft.) | $ 10– | 12 |
| Basement conversion—component items | $ 1,500– | 4,000 |

| Basement conversion—component items | |
|---|---|
| Kitchen | $3,000–5,000 |
| Bath | $2,000–3,500 |
| Electrical | $1,200–1,800 |
| Heating and air conditioning—separate | $1,500–2,500 |
| Heat copper baseboard | $ 800–1,500 |
| Paint | $ 400– 700 |
| Drywall | $1,500–2,500 |
| Carpentry | $1,500–2,500 |
| Drop Floor | $2,500–3,500 |

| | | |
|---|---|---|
| Build 30 ft. shell dormer—finished exterior | $ 4,000– | 5,000 |
| Run new water line to street | $ 800– | 1,500 |
| Install burglar alarm system if tied into central | $ 800– | 1,500 |
| charge per month | $ 18– | 25 |
| Replace front door | $ 200– | 500 |
| Build closet | $ 300– | 500 |

*Source:* Home Tech Systems, Bethesda, Maryland.

## REHABILITATING THE OLD COUNTRY HOUSE

Restoring an old farmhouse or colonial mansion can be one of the most rewarding tasks imaginable, if you have the patience for it and some of the skills. If you have to depend on outside experts to supply all the know-how, materials, and labor, you may get a very good restoration, but it will also cost you so much that profits, if any, will be slim unless you are willing to wait five to ten years to let the general rise in property values catch up with and surpass your dollar outlay.

Restoration probably works best when you do it for your own family house, and then live in it for a number of years. Then you get the shelter value of the upgraded house and you are not pressed to make an immediate profit. If the house is large enough, you can conveniently isolate some of the rooms under restoration and continue to live in the rest with a minimum of disturbance.

*Example: Case of the "Year of the Ladder"*
The Miller family bought an old barn in Suffolk County, Long Island. They had rented in the vicinity during past summers and liked the environment and the Atlantic beaches. They lived for nine months of the year in Brooklyn, where Bob Miller had a commercial art studio and Sue Miller was a book editor.

The barn had a fieldstone foundation, a rotted wooden floor, a large sliding entrance with a few windows in the foundation, and "old barn wood" all the way up to the leaking roof. The placement of the two hay mows, to the right and left, under which there were floors of wooden planks, suggested to the Millers that they really had a three-story house, living room on the main floor, bedrooms upstairs, and utilities, kitchen, and family room in the stone cellar.

The Millers had done a lot of hiking and backpacking with their two children, so camping out in the barn was not a problem. There was a makeshift toilet and kitchen that the previous owner had put in for summer rentals.

The barn had infinite potential, but little else save its location in a meadow that looked away to the sea on the one side and a woods on the other. The main house still belonged to the original owner and was a more-or-less Victorian frame house with a large front porch and shutters. The barn had no relationship in line or color to the house, but it was obviously the barn that belonged to that house, linked by a dirt road and hedges. The Millers had a friend who was an architect echo some of the Victorian lintels and shutters of the main house in the redone facade of the front of the barn. The rear faced south, so when they redid the roof, the Millers put solar-heat collecting panels, in addition to skylights, on both slopes of the roof. During their first year of ownership, they rebuilt the outer walls of the barn and the roof. The Millers watched the carpenters work during the summer, and sharpened their own skills enough to persuade themselves that they could finish much of the interior without professional help. This was a practical decision, because the Millers had borrowed as much as they could on their main house in Brooklyn to be able to afford a new kitchen and two new bathrooms and make the basic improvements. This done, they were out of money for the time being. They still hoped to improve the barn to a point where one of the local savings banks would give them a mortgage on the rehabilitated building based on the plans for finishing it. There was a tax credit, too, for investment in solar heating, and the Millers intended to rent the improved building for one of the best months next summer when they took a family vacation that they would spend with Sue's parents on a lake in Minnesota. The tenant was their architect friend who wanted to monitor the solarheating system and get the feel of the appliances he designed.

During the first winter of ownership, they roughed the walls for two bathrooms and a kitchen and covered them with sheetrock. A local plumber brought in the necessary pipes, and they experimented successfully with flooring and tiling.

In the spring, Bob Miller, badgered by Sue and the children about their upstairs bedrooms and bath, proclaimed them "on the balcony" as the family began to use the one bathroom roughed-in and two hay mows connected by a walkway and accessible by a ladder bolted into position. The upstairs would not have a staircase until next winter; it was not at the top of the priority list just yet. In the Miller family, and in the architect-tenant's family too, that year became known as the "year of the ladder."

The preceding case shows how two families made do during a difficult period of reconstruction. To an outsider it may have seemed like living in squalor, but they had a plan and fortunately they could stick to it. A lot of sweat goes into such a project, but the final home emerges as something individual, almost an instant heirloom. It does require some imagination and some sympathetic gestures toward the existing environment and architectural setting. The Millers showed good sense in their phases of remodeling, in their priorities, and in taking a large mortgage on their town house, which was in an established neighborhood of stable values. They justified increasing the value of the building in the country, which had negligible value to begin with except for its siting and land. Savings institutions are likely to lend little on mere land and a barn.

## TO RESTORE OR TO REMODEL?

*Restoring,* as a practical working term, means just that: It means considering the history of the building and taking it back to a period in time and "freezing it there." Items are reconstructed to re-create the building and its environment as of that period in time. This requires historical research through old photos and diagrams, and possibly with old architectural plans.

*Remodeling* is something else; it may mean keeping the facade and certain inside features but changing the rest of the structure substantially.

The Miller family remodeled with no attempt at historical restoration. They did respect the historical aspect of the old farm in echoing the style of the main house. But, essentially, the Millers remodeled an old barn, not a landmark house.

Some people like to *restore* a building in a historical district or of significant architectural charm. Other people prefer to save what is good and distinctive and *remodel* the rest, usually at considerably less cost than it takes to restore. For those country-property owners who are aggressively profit oriented, restoration, fun and esthetically rewarding as it can be, is not the quickest path to gains, and it may not in itself bring any financial rewards at all. You will inevitably pay extra to be authentic; your actual profits will depend on whether your restorations are what the next buyer will pay for.

*Example: The John Jay Restoration.*
John Jay, one of the founding fathers of the United States, was born in 1745 to a family of French Huguenots who exiled themselves to the United States. Following his education at Kings College (now known as Columbia University), Jay began his career as a lawyer. He was elected to the Continental Congress at the age of 29 and began a career of public service, which ended only when he retired. He served as president of the Continental Congress, was the first Chief Justice of the United States, was governor and Chief Justice of New York State, minister to Spain, and a principal author of New York State's first constitution. As his retirement approached, Jay planned renovations for a farm near Bedford, New York, that had been in his mother's family, the Van Courtlandts, since 1703. Earlier than that the land belonged to the Indian sachem, Katonah. Jay first built a house there in 1787. In preparation for his retirement, he renovated the house during the years 1799 to 1801 into a three-story frame mansion with mansard roof and a gracious front porch which led to lesser wings on each side. The house was white with dark shutters and combined a feeling of Hudson Valley country homes with a touch of New England homes of the Federal Period.

But that was only the beginning of the house and its subsequent remodeling. After he settled at this gracious homestead, John Jay continued his interest in improving his acres. He oversaw himself the various farm activities and arranged for the planting of many of the large maples, elms, and shrubs that continue to shade the grounds to this day. Descendants of Jay continued the farm and its agricultural, horticultural, and stock breeding experiments well into the 1940s. Five generations added to and subtracted from the basic residence. In the late nineteenth century, the house became more grand with Italianate portico, balcony, and dormers in the roof. One descendant added a west wing in 1924 to display the family portraits accumulated over the years.

When the historic homestead with its maintenance burden was donated to New York State in the 1940s, the question of restoration arose. Which house was the authentic Jay homestead? The dormers and Italianate ornaments were removed from the core house, but the portrait gallery was kept and the whole house still stands and is open to visitors the year round.

**Figure 8-4** Rundown Wisconsin farmhouse with renovation begun. *(Photo courtesy MTK.)*

## Example: Remodeling a Rundown Farmhouse

In Figures 8-4, 8-5, and 8-6 you can see the stages of remodeling of a Wisconsin farmhouse which had no distinctive architectural features and was heated by a fireplace and a wood stove in the summer kitchen. It was, however, nicely nestled into a hill on the shores of a lake. Buying it at the depth of the Depression years in the 1930s, the owners gradually, over a decade of progressive remodeling according to an architect's master plan, made of it a much larger home, in a Cape Cod style, with original foundations expanded by thick walls of native Lannon stone. A new kitchen was added, bedrooms were added and expanded on the upper

**Figure 8-5** Farmhouse remodeled to Cape Cod home on stone foundation. *(Photo courtesy C. Baerwald.)*

**Figure 8-6** Harmonizing two-story Cape Cod guest house and garage replaces barn with distinctive field and pointed stone foundation retained. *(Photo courtesy MTK.)*

floor. Central heating and a stone chimney were also added for winter comfort. The nondescript summer kitchen, located strategically to take advantage of cooling summer winds, was replaced by a screen porch which supports another bedroom. When the main house was finished, the adjacent barn/garage was gradually remodeled into an additional space for guests and a workshop.

## PITFALLS TO PROFITABLE RESTORATION AND REMODELING OF OLD HOUSES

Consider the following as a checklist of points to consider when you buy an old house or barn for the purpose of restoring or remodeling it.

The first thing you usually notice when you visit an old, restorable house is the *water damage*—or *watermarks*—the streaks that come from years of gradually leaking water. Evidence may lurk anywhere in the house. In the attic, discoloration of the insulation, the joists, and the under-roofing betray a leaking roof. Lower in the house, faulty gutters and downspouts can cause seepage into the eaves and walls, which causes stains on interior walls, wall paper to peel and bloat, paint to flake, woodwork to warp and show stains, and, finally, marks on the floors—or possibly warped and split floors. In the basement you may find rotted woodwork, lichens, a general scent of mildew and damp, and perhaps some remnant puddles where rain drops huddled in a low spot, at a loss as to where to run off because of the faulty pitch of the floor. The basement walls will show stains where water entered because of the wrong slope around the outside of the house, or as a result of dripping gutters, leaky eaves, or seepage from snow carelessly shoveled against the house or in such a place that it ran toward the house as it melted.

You can *count* on water running off and seeking its lowest level until it finally evaporates or disappears into the soil or sewer, or into sumps constructed to collect what cannot be prevented. All of these minor flaws can be corrected, but at a cost.

Another profit trap in an old house is likely to be the *plumbing*. Try the faucet in the highest sink in the house. Does it trickle fitfully, indicating poor pressure? Does it seem to bleed with a red-brown fluid? That means rust in galvanized pipes whose coating has been penetrated is feeding into the water system. Or the rust may be coming from the hot-water boiler and then circulating throughout the house. Check to see what *kind* of piping is in the house—galvanized steel, iron, lead, or possibly a mixture of these with some of the preferred copper. A good copper water and heating system should last the lifetime of the house, except for occasional repairs at joints. Or, if water with a heavy mineral content is allowed to circulate without softening, it is possible that mineral deposits will gradually fill the pipes and cause clogging even though the metal is sound. If you suspect a high mineral content, you can have a chemical analysis done of the water by the local water-softener service company who can then recommend appropriate chemical softening. This is a *must* if you want to keep an old plumbing and water supply system functioning as well as a new one.

If you intend to buy the house, consider the possibility of new plastic piping material for drainage pipe, now approved by most building codes in the United States. Consider this, too, for drainage systems from gutters and downspouts which carry water away from the house to a lower area in the lawn or into drywells where the accumulated water can gradually percolate into the subsoil. In this way you can build a kind of sponge into your lawn, which benefits the greenery, as well as disposing quickly of water from sudden storms.

If the house, as you enter it, reeks of methane gas, you had better check out the entire septic system; the traps may be faulty and gas has backed up from the septic or sewer system, or waste material is not getting through to the septic tank or sewer and is rotting in sinks, toilets, and waste pipes leading to the outside septic tank.

These telltale smells and discolorings signal trouble with the plumbing and you may find yourself planning for entirely new, modern piping and a new septic system. Try to find out about these flaws in your "charming old house" before you close on your contract, so that an adjustment can be made in the purchase price. If you tend to these details too late, you will be stuck with repair and replacement costs *after* purchasing what you thought were thoroughly functional systems.

*Example: The Well that Ran Dry*

The Wrangler family bought an old period house on a lake in Minnesota. It had been partly winterized by previous owners but still had the lines and the look of a summer house. The Wranglers didn't care; the house had a good location and they could remodel when and if they really wanted to. Meanwhile, there were three bedrooms and all the other family rooms they wanted while their children grew up and went to college. They were going to invest in their children's education first, then perhaps fix up the house. Ten or a dozen years hence, if they became empty-nesters and wanted smaller quarters, they would have the house in better shape and could expect to sell it for many times the amount they had paid for it.

It was more of a dream than a plan they later admitted. During the first year of occupancy the well, which had been giving good water for three-quarters of a century, ran dry for no discernible and repairable reason. The immediate need became a new well that cost $2,500. The Wranglers were inclined to believe that the previous owner had slipped something over on them, but they could prove nothing for the water flow had been tested and approved, but not guaranteed, by an inspecting engineer.

The second year, the septic system backed up and the verdict of the contractor who was called in was over-use of an old system. The previous owners were a family of three people; the Wranglers flooded the system with liquid wastes from a family of seven. The old system, said the contractor, was greased up and the leach bed was only half the size needed for the number of daily gallons of waste and the percolation factor of the soil. An entirely new system was recommended, with a cement tank replacing the badly rusted steel tank that had been installed only 10 years before; recommended also were cast iron pipes to replace the detached clay pipes that allowed roots to clog the drainage system as it led wastes from the tank to the leach bed. And an expanded leach bed was also suggested, since the old one was full of roots and kitchen grease and detergents that inhibited absorption of the effluent by the surrounding soil. The price tag for this extensive and necessary replacement was $3,500.

The Wranglers talked to their lawyer about suing the previous owner; the lawyer said they could file a nuisance suit which would cost money and probably would not be won unless the Wranglers could prove deliberate concealment of defects. As it happened, the engineer who inspected the property had characterized in writing the septic tank as "old, with clay pipes and galvanized steel tank with signs of rust, said to be installed 10 years ago; system functions, but eventually will have to be replaced with a larger one of contemporary materials."

Faced with this forecast by a man they hired themselves, the Wranglers could not expect to blame the previous owner who may or may not have feared the failures. The Wranglers simply had to accept that these failures are more likely to happen in a house that is three-quarters of a century old. Eventually the hole in their budget was filled, and they went on to renovate the kitchen, the roof, and the bathrooms. They were pleased, too, during the late 1960s and in the 1970s to see their picturesque dowager of a summer house increase 15 to 20 percent in value each year, according to a local realtor who offered to sell it for them at going market prices.

The house you like may have *termites,* a problem that seems worse in your imagination than in reality. They are pests, but they do not devour a house from one day to the next. If your country place is in the northern tier of the states, you may very well escape this problem because termites cannot endure winter cold. Further south, you would have to call in an exterminator and ask for recommendations as you remodel, so that you do not encourage termites to move in with the family and enjoy the new joists and woodwork. That is another reason why you should have an architect provide plans for any extensive remodeling you may want to do. An architect will automatically design foundations, siding, and floor joists to discourage an invasion. You can help prevent termite activity by seeing that there is a minimum of dirt, darkness, and dampness where the wood of the house approaches the ground. That is why contemporary houses in termite country are often built on concrete and have concrete or cement block basements or foundations. Of course, if the local exterminator confirms that the house already has termites, you will have to think of fumigation as well as other corrective measures. Do this before you start any renovating or improving lest the insects persist and put their choppers into your delectable new wood. Their life cycle requires soil and mud tunnels (for most species). By eliminating parts of this environment, you discourage them from using your wood as food.

*Roofs* in old houses are most likely to give trouble when it rains. The telltale stains of old leaks may not be there, yet the roof may betray you shortly after you move in. You ought to gather details from the previous owner, if possible, on when the roofing material was last changed—most materials last only about 20 years. Often the longer lasting roofs, such as those of slate, gravel or asphalt, or galvanized metal, may be essentially sound, although leaking at crucial joints which need to be capped or covered with new material. A roofing contractor can recommend the proper repair, but depend on an architect or engineer to tell you whether the roof should be repaired or *replaced.* Thousands of dollars may lie in the difference, and most contractors will play upon a common fear that repair is only a makeshift solution while a whole new roof seems nearly forever. The point is, it may not be necessary, and it is one of those components of a house that a future buyer will not accept as anything unusual. The buyer will not pay extra for it, yet will expect a leakless roof, whether new or 10 years old, and no matter what the material.

Water can damage *foundation walls* if it seeps down inside them and freezes. It can also cause cracking of retaining walls that may have been built to make garden levels on a hillside. Old houses often have retaining walls that create level terraces, confine dirt surrounding a foundation, or hold dirt brought in as a barrier against drainage from a higher elevation.

You cannot be sure why the wall is there; sometimes it could be there just for the appearance. But beware of letting it deteriorate, lest its unknown function be destroyed and you wake up one morning after a severe rainstorm to find the cellar flooded or the garden washed away. And once these outer defenses against water have been violated, the assault on the foundations of the house could well intensify.

The bane of residents in old houses is *falling plaster*. This, too, can be caused by excessive moisture, either because of leaks or lack of heating, or because there are too many variations of interior temperature. Houses left vacant for years can suffer from this problem and it is a costly one to solve. Usually, the old houses were constructed with wood lath, which shrinks and expands depending on moisture and can pull away from the joists. The staying power of wood lath depends on plaster passing through the spaces left between the laths and spreading around it a bit, thus forming a grip as it hardens. The plaster may not have made a satisfactory bond with the lath, as it does with contemporary plasterboard panels. Thus particularly on ceilings, with encouragement from vibrations, the brittleness of age, or excessive contraction and expansion due to temperature changes, the plaster lets go and requires replacement with rock lath or similar materials. Here a contractor is generally right in wanting to redo the entire plaster job. You can always get a second opinion, of course. If *any* plaster falls, examine all the rest for looseness, sags, water marks, and other symptoms that the life of your plaster ceiling has come to an end. That is why piecemeal patching will seldom do the job; the whole room probably needs repair and you can expect similar trouble in other rooms which have the same construction and abuse.

Another inadequacy of an old house is likely to be the *electrical wiring system,* which dates from an era when electricity was something new, ran no household machines, and possibly furnished one light in each major room. The house you like may have had subsequent periods of improvement and additional wiring, but no one ever provided it with a modern system of fuses or circuit breakers, several outlets at convenient locations in each room, and separate lines to major appliances, or for electric heating. Keep in mind that eventually solar energy will be translated into cheap electrical energy. That makes the all-electric house, carefully insulated, the probable house of the future, when there will be no natural gas and no heating oil left at economical prices. It is not too soon to wire the house of your choice accordingly.

This brings up a familiar subject, *conservation of energy,* which you, as a country-property owner, can carry out most efficiently by checking over the *insulation* of your house. It is the most economical and practical method for conserving energy and thus decreasing the operating expenses of the house. You probably checked out the heating bill when you thought of buying the house (you should have if you did not). When you want to sell the property, your improvement in the insulation should show in the fewer gallons of heating oil or square cubic feet of natural gas the house consumes. Most old houses are notoriously light on insulation. The fireplaces have poor dampers and always were inefficient—most of the heat went up the chimney. If you are going to use them, you may have to have them relined or at least cleaned so that the accumulated soot does not catch fire. Part of the insulating process is a filling of cracks and leaks. This may require repairing of doors, windows, walls, and roof. Double-glazed windows, now available in styles to suit the architecture of most houses, prevent heat loss as a result of convection currents brushing against the cold single pane of glass in winter. You have undoubtedly, particularly in the country, awakened in the morning to find that the moisture from your breath, coming in contact with the single pane of glass in most windows, has formed a fantastic frost on the inside. Later, this frost will melt and trickle down to the window sill, and possibly cause untimely peeling and cracking of the paint there. This demonstrates the damage that moisture can do to a paint job, and also the quantity of moisture that one can generate in just one night. There is the coldness of the pane of glass—in case you needed further proof of the value of double glazing, or at least the value of putting up the old-fashioned storm windows that came with the house.

The steps mentioned are improvements you want to make along with others. From a profit standpoint, you may not feel justified in making them simply for the sake of energy conservation. But if you are *adding* a room or extension, it would seem foolish not to have double-glazed windows and adequate insulation in it. Your architect will tell you that a good southern exposure can help warm the house in winter as the sun, low in the horizon, penetrates deep rooms with windows facing it during the middle of the day.

One of the drawbacks of old homes built of stone is that their interior walls customarily were in direct contact with the outer walls. Thus, there was no chance to put insulation materials between the conducting surfaces. The only way to overcome this difficulty is to create an insulating space by furring out the interior walls and installing a new interior wall. This reduces the dimensions of the room and gives you trouble with cornices and with the proportions of the windows and doorsills. You may want to accept a cold wall and keep the decor intact.

Figure 8-7 shows a rundown farmhouse before remodeling. Thick fieldstone walls dressed with painted cement were worth saving in this box-like farmhouse. Furred-out plasterboard and knotty pine panelling gave some interior insulation value without decreasing too much of the space in the small rooms. Figure 8-8 shows the same farmhouse after the

**Figure 8-7** Rundown Wisconsin farmhouse with summer kitchen before remodeling. *(Photo courtesy MTK.)*

remodeling was completed. A screen porch replaced the summer kitchen, which was originally sited to take advantage of prevailing summer breezes. The porch also supports a new bedroom addition designed with three window exposures.

Figure 8-9 will give you some idea of the amount of insulation thickness recommended for various geographic regions in the United States. The actual recommendations are by Owens-Corning Fiberglas Corporation, but they are similar to those recommended by the National Bureau of Standards. In Figure 8-10 the house is assumed to be located in Zone 1 and the insulation thicknesses are those recommended for that zone. The code letter **R** stands for a measure of thermal resistance and is interpreted as thickness of insulation in inches. As the **R** factor climbs, so does the need for thicker insulation.

As you go through the country dream house you want to buy, if it was built in the eighteenth or nineteenth century you may find that some of the

**Figure 8-8**  Farmhouse after architect remodeled upper story. *(Photo courtesy MTK.)*

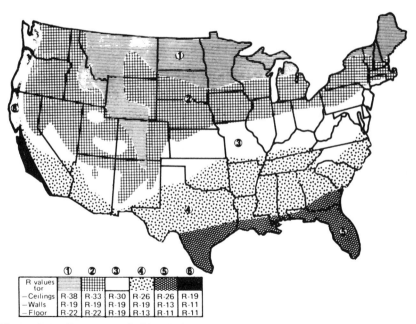

**Figure 8-9**  Recommended insulation levels in six US heating and cooling zones. *(Source: Professional Builder Magazine.)*

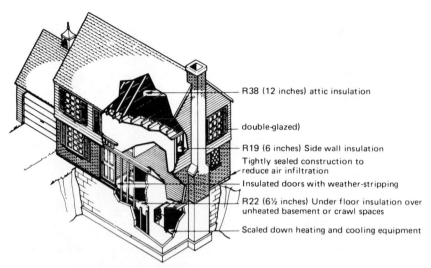

R38 (12 inches) attic insulation

double-glazed)

R19 (6 inches) Side wall insulation

Tightly sealed construction to reduce air infiltration

Insulated doors with weather-stripping

R22 (6½ inches) Under floor insulation over unheated basement or crawl spaces

Scaled down heating and cooling equipment

**Figure 8-10** Insulation recommended for a multistory house in heating/cooling zone 1. *(Source: Professional Builder Magazine.)*

old appliances and equipment still operate—after a fashion. Whether that old pump in the well pit will last the night is conjectural, but it still wheezes away and a fitful supply of water follows. You question the previous owner about it, and you are told it works better some days than others but it always gets *some* water up to the second floor, no matter what the day of the week, the weather, or the noise of its mood. You conclude that if you want more and more dependable water, a new pump will be needed. For the time being it will suffice. In order to keep up the value of the house, you had better put a high priority on a new or a rebuilt pump. Similar reasoning might be applied to old refrigerators, water heaters, oil burners, kitchen stoves, and all manner of equipment on a working farm. You may want to keep the most quaint appliances and implements for atmosphere. Enamelled cast iron bathtubs with claw feet are much prized. Old ice chests that required blocks of ice lend charm to a large Victorian kitchen and can be used for storage of canned goods. The point is, you do not have to throw away what is old and well made, you can recycle it to a new, creative use and have the job it was originally designed to do done by a contemporary improvement. A skillful designer can equip your nineteenth-century kitchen with a microwave oven that does not seem out of place at all. It just happens that money spent in a kitchen usually pays off when you sell a house. You could say the same about bathrooms, too. Chain-flush toilets with oak seats and a flush reservoir on the wall are coming back strong on the restoration market. You can get parts, too, from the same manufacturer. If one of these units still exists in a bathroom, improve it—but save the rig!

While on that subject, if by chance your country house still has an *outhouse,* treasure it and its lattice fencing. Grow clematis or morning glories on the trellis; keep garden tools in the *chic sales,* but *use* a modern all-weather toilet in your house. Other outbuildings worth preserving are woodsheds and summer kitchens, carriage horse barns, and the other characteristic outbuildings of a country place that was not a farm but needed these detached buildings for reasons of comfort and convenience. At worst, you can endure them as is, or as a potting shed against which you can lean a greenhouse. The possibilities are rich for a children's play-house, a kennel for dogs, perhaps a stable for a horse. Without heat and expensive alteration, but with a coat of paint and a repaired roof, these outbuildings add value to your old house because they help to create an environment from an older time. Though minor buildings, they complete the feeling of a small estate—"the way things were." With clever interior adaptation, with their exteriors kept painted and picturesque—perhaps with flower trellises against them (you can sometimes find out how they were landscaped from old pictures)—they recreate at almost no expense the authentic ambiance of an old house. The danger lies in overdoing their rehabilitation. For while they add atmosphere, a hard-headed buyer or appraiser, or a banker adding up value against which to give you a mort-gage, will not give you much additional value for calling a nicely painted shed a "guest house." Call it what you will, the hard-nosed appraiser may very well ignore the thing entirely and simply give the land a slightly higher value. A seller of the property, however, will certainly exploit the romance of these remnants of a bygone era.

The subject of windows and doors is related to insulation. No matter how well-insulated and vapor proof you make the walls with polyethylene sheets, if the house has poorly fitting windows, it will continue to leak its heat. You may find that you would have to insulate and make air-tight only part of the house, and that you can leave that old summer sleeping porch outside the insulated area. Or that the front porch, which was partly winterized but hopelessly hard to heat in the winter, is comfortable for about eight months of the year. Whatever heat it get might be suffi-cient for a winter garden where summer porch furniture can be stored. But for the sake of efficiency and energy conservation it would be best to leave it off the home-heating system.

Other windows and doors should have weather stripping of a kind recommended by a local heating contractor or architect. Most architects will now design windows and doors with specified weather-stripping fea-tures. Often they are prefabricated metal units that have easily inter-changeable screen- and storm-window inserts. If all your windows and doors are double glazed and weather stripped and your walls vapor proofed, you may begin to suffer a side effect of an air-tight shelter. The interior air may become stale, lose its pep (oxygen), and, at worst, poison you slightly with particulates and gases as various synthetic building materials gradually decompose. Self-cleaning ovens, gas stoves, working fireplaces, and habitual tobacco smokers in the family, will cause higher-than-normal carbon dioxide and carbon monoxide concentrations in the air. The answer is a ventilation system that brings new air into the house on winter days when doors and windows are kept closed, and a habit of opening strategic windows in more temperate weather so that the rooms can air out. It has been estimated that a model, energy-conserving house changes air only once in 10 hours, whereas the average leaky house usually changes all its air every two hours, even with all doors and windows closed. Take a lesson from the astronauts whose moon-walking suits and space capsules were impermeable to the outer atmosphere. They had to have an air supply and built-in handling of waste air. To a small extent, today's family in its energy-efficient, insulated house, complete with vapor films, will have to supply artificial ventilation when air exits and entrances are closed off to conserve heat.

## GUIDELINES FOR RESTORING OLD BUILDINGS

If the property you want to convert to a more profitable use is an old house or commercial building that has architectural value or an interesting history, pause to think for a moment before you launch into your conversion. Consider that you can *lower* the value of the property by excessive change. You may do more to the building than necessary and wind up with an expensive remodeling bill and less added to the building or property than you had imagined.

The federal government considered the mistreatment of old buildings important enough to ask the Office of Archeology and Historic Preservation of the National Park Service to prepare a set of guidelines that would help property owners and local officials carry out work on old structures effectively and with less expense.

Nine basic principles, briefly stated are:

1  Provide a compatible use for the building that will require minimum alteration to the structure and to its environment.

2  Preserve the distinguishing qualities or character of the property; keep removal or alteration of historic material or architectural features to a minimum.

3   Repair rather than replace architectural features whenever possible. If repairing, try to match material in composition, design, color, texture, and other visual qualities.

4   Replace missing architectural features with accurate duplications of originals.

5   Remember that alterations over the years may have developed significance in their own right and should be respected.

6   Treat distinctive stylistic features and examples of skilled craftswork with sensitivity.

7   Recognize buildings as products of their own time. Do not alter to create earlier styles.

8   Contemporary designs for new buildings in old neighborhoods or additions to existing buildings can enhance an old neighborhood, provided the designs are compatible in size, scale, color, material, and character to this neighborhood.

9   Make additions or alterations to a building so that if they are removed in the future, the essential form and integrity of the original building is retained.


## CHECKLIST FOR PROFITABLE UPGRADING OF USE

[ ]   Can the property be acquired at a price which has room for a profit on resale, or incresaed valuation when refinancing?

[ ]   Can the conversion or improvement be carried out at a cost that leaves room for a profit?

[ ]   Is the property located so that value and use trends justify the improvement or change in use?

[ ]   Is the political climate of the city or town such that municipal cooperation can be expected?

[ ]   Will the change in use justify adequate financing from the appropriate lender?

[ ]   Have you identified a market for the converted building at a price or rent which justifies acquisition and improvement?

Of course, you may want to convert a property for the sheer pleasure of living in it rather than reselling it to make a profit. Nonetheless, you can have it both ways—enjoying it and knowing that you have made a sound economic move in case you change your mind and want to sell later.

## UNCONVENTIONAL USES OF AN OLD BUILDING CAN INCREASE ITS VALUE

Some of the most rewarding adventures in real estate derive from the conversion of an old building in a country village or on a farm to a new use that increases its resale value. Here are some examples:

A barn or horse shed can be converted to a guest house or rental unit.

A country church can be converted to an office, theatre, community meeting place, a library, even a local city hall.

An abandoned railroad station can become a craft store or a cooperative or condominium retreat for several families.

A boat house or garage can be remodeled to include a guest apartment.

Various sheds or components can be moved to a main house to serve as guest wings or an extra family room, thus recycling valuable lumber although not always the building itself.

## GETTING ESTIMATES FOR IMPROVEMENTS TO OLD HOUSES

Period restorations are not *inexpensive*. You will have to decide how authentic you want to be. For personal pleasure, you may want to re-create board by board, glass pane by glass pane, the old house you have taken under your wing. You are likely to put into the restoration more tender loving care, costly materials, labor, and expenses for outside artisans than you would be able to justify on an income statement. It is not the way to maximize your dollar profits. But that is a decision you will have to make. If you plan to use the house for a decade or two, and possibly hope to have it become a family heirloom, by all means restore meticulously. If you plan to hold it for five years, restore only what will draw people to the house, such as a central staircase or the wide-board oak planking of the living room in a colonial house. Try to restrain yourself from making cheap modernizations on an old house. If you cannot justify the expense, leave well enough alone. Another buyer will undoubtedly fall in love with the house as you did and make additional restorations, and the house will gradually become itself again under the guidance of several owners, each of whom could make a profit on their investment.

## HOW LONG DO VARIOUS HOUSE COMPONENTS LAST?

As you manage your new or your old house and improve various parts of it, you may wonder how long some of the components can be expected to last. If you rent out a country property, you can take depreciation on a number of items. Table 8-4 lists some typical lifespans of components and materials, as worked out by Dean Crist of the Economics Department of the National Association of Home Builders. This list is useful for analyzing when you might have to replace a component. (In Table 8-3 you will find estimates of the average cost for some of the larger items on this list.) Note the remarks that Mr. Crist has made about many of the components and materials. It might be worth making a list of your own and checking off the items likely to require replacement or major repair during your expected ownership of the property. Give the items priority ranking and then prorate them per year on your tentative operating budget. Then be sure you make the improvement and, working with your accountant, set up a depreciation schedule for it. Remember, if you are in a fairly high tax bracket, say 50 percent, the government is subsidizing the remodeling of a rental property by that amount, in addition to all the interest you might pay on a loan to finance such remodeling or repairs.

**Table 8-4**  Life Expectancies of Various Parts of a House

| Item | Useful life | Remarks |
|---|---|---|
| *Footings and Foundations* | | |
| Footings | Life | First four items are likely to last |
| Foundation | Life | up to 250 years. There are homes |
| Concrete | Life | in the United States that are over |
| Waterproofing | | 300 years old. Structural defects |
| Bituminous coating | 5 years | that do develop are a result of |
| Parging with ionite | Life | poor soil conditions. |
| Termite proofing | 5 years | May be earlier in damp climates |
| Gravel outside | 30–40 years | Depends on usage |
| Cement block | Life | Less strong than concrete block |

**Table 8-4** Life Expectancies of Various Parts of a House (continued)

| Item | Useful life | Remarks |
|---|---|---|
| *Rough Structure* | | |
| Floor system (basement) | Life | |
| Framing exterior walls | Life | Usually plaster directly on masonry. Plaster is solid and will last forever. Provides tighter seal then drywall and better insulation. |
| Framing interior walls | Life | In older homes, usually plaster on wood lath. Lath strips lose resilience causing waves in ceilings and walls. |
| Concrete work | | |
| Slab | Life | (200 years) |
| Precast decks | 10–15 years | |
| Precast porches | 10–15 years | |
| Site-built porches and steps | 20 years | |
| *Sheet Metal* | | |
| Gutters, downspouts, and flashing | | |
| Aluminum | 20–30 years | Never requires painting but dents and pits. May need to be replaced sooner for appearance. |
| Copper | Life | Very durable and expensive. Requires regular cleaning and alignment. |
| Galvanized iron | 15–25 years | Rusts easily and must be kept painted every 3–4 years. |
| *Rough electrical* | | |
| Wiring | | |
| Copper | Life | |
| Aluminum | Life | |
| Romex | Life | |
| Circuit breaker | | |
| Breaker panel | 30–40 years | |
| Individual breaker | 25–30 years | |
| *Rough plumbing* | | |
| Pressure pipes | | |
| Copper | Life | Strongest and most common. Needs no maintenance. |
| Galvanized iron | 30–50 years | Rusts easily and is major expense in older homes. Most common until 1940. |
| Plastic | 30–40 years | |
| Waste pipe | | |
| Concrete | 20 years | |

**Table 8-4** Life Expectancies of Various Parts of a House (continued)

| Item | Useful life | Remarks |
|---|---|---|
| Vitreous china | 25–30 years | |
| Plastic | 50–70 years | Usage depends upon soil conditions. Acid soils can eat through plastic. |
| Cast iron | Life | |
| Lead | Life | A leak cannot be patched. If bathroom is remodeled, must be replaced. |
| *Heating and venting duct work* | | |
| Galvanized | 50–70 years | |
| Plastic | 40–60 years | Type used depends upon climate. |
| Fiberglas | 40–60 years | |
| Air conditioning rough-in | | Same as duct work |
| *Roof* | | |
| Asphalt shingles | 15–25 years | Most common. Deterioration subject to climate. Granules come off shingles. Check downspouts. |
| Wood shingles and shakes | 30–40 years | Expensive. Contracts and expands due to climate. |
| Tile | 30–50 years | Tendency to crack on sides |
| Slate | Life | High quality. Maintenance every 2–3 years as nails rust. |
| Metal | Life | Shorter life if allowed to rust |
| Built-up asphalt | 20–30 years | Maintenance required, especially after winter |
| Felt | 30–40 years | |
| Tar-gravel | 10–15 years | |
| Asbestos shingle | 30–40 years | Shingles get brittle when walked on. Maintenance every 1–3 years. |
| Composition shingles | 12–16 years | |
| Tin | Life | Will rust easily if not kept painted regularly. Found a lot in inner-city row houses. |
| 4 or 5 built-up ply | 15–25 years | Layers of tar paper on tar |
| *Masonry* | | |
| Chimney | Life | |
| Fireplace | 20–30 years | |
| Fire brick | Life | |
| Ash dump | Life | |
| Metal fireplace | Life | |
| Flue tile | Life | |
| Brick veneer | Life | Joints must be pointed every 5–6 years. |

**Table 8-4** Life Expectancies of Various Parts of a House (continued)

| Item | Useful life | Remarks |
|---|---|---|
| Brick | Life | |
| Stone | Life | Unless porous grade stone like limestone |
| Block wall | Life | |
| Masonry floors | Life | Must be kept waxed every 1–2 years. |
| Stucco | Life | Requires painting every 8-10 years. More susceptible to cracking than brick. Replacement is expensive. |
| | | Maintenance cycles for all types of masonry structures including those found in urban press subjected to dirt, soot, and chemicals. |
| | | Caulking  every 20 years |
| | | Pointing  every 35 years |
| | | Sandblasting  every 35 years |
| *Windows and doors* | | |
| Window glazing | 5–6 years | |
| Storm windows and gaskets | Life | Aluminum and wood |
| Screen doors | 5–8 years | |
| Storm doors | 10–15 years | |
| Interior doors (luan) | 10 years | |
| Sliding doors | 30–50 years | |
| Folding doors | 30–40 years | |
| Sliding screens | 30 years | |
| Garage doors | 20–25 years | Depends upon initial placement of springs, tracts, and rollers. |
| Steel casement windows | 40–50 years | Have leakage and condensation problems. Installed mostly in 1940s and 1950s. |
| Wood casement windows | 40–50 years | Older types very drafty |
| Jalousie | 30–40 years | Fair quality available in wood and aluminum. Used mostly for porches. |
| Wood double-hung windows | 40–50 years | |
| *Insulation* | | |
| Foundation | Life | |
| Roof, ceiling | Life | |
| Roof, electric vent | 10–15 years | |
| Walls | Life | |
| Floor Weatherstripping | Life | |
| Metal | 8–9 years | |
| Plastic gasket | 5–8 years | |

**Table 8-4**   Life Expectancies of Various Parts of a House (continued)

| Item | Useful life | Remarks |
|---|---|---|
| *Exterior trim* | | |
| Wood siding | Life | Must be kept painted regularly, every 5–7 years |
| Metal siding | Life | May rust due to climate |
| Aluminum siding | Life | Maintenance free if baked-on finish |
| Shutters | | |
| Wood | 20 years | |
| Metal | 20–30 years | |
| Plastic | Life | |
| Aluminum | Life | |
| Posts and columns | Life | |
| Gable vents | | |
| Wood | 10–14 years | |
| Aluminum | Life | |
| Gable vent screens | Same as gable vents | |
| Cornice and rake trim | Life | |
| Trellis | 20 years | Will rot in back even if painted because of moisture |
| *Exterior Paint* | | |
| Wood | 3–4 years | Climate a strong factor |
| Brick | 3–4 years | |
| Aluminum | 10–12 years | |
| Gutters, Downspouts, and Flashing | | |
| Aluminum | 10–12 years | |
| Copper | Life | No painting required |
| *Stairs* | | |
| Stringer | 50 years | |
| Risers | 50 years | |
| Treads | 50 years | |
| Baluster | 50 years | |
| Rails | 30–40 years | |
| Starting levels | 50 years | |
| Disappearing stairs | 30–40 years | |
| *Drywall and plaster* | | |
| Drywall | 40–50 years | Lifetime is adequately protected by exterior walls and roof. Cracks must be regularly spackled. |
| Plaster | Life | Thicker and more durable than drywall. Exterior must be properly maintained. |

**Table 8-4**  Life Expectancies of Various Parts of a House (continued)

| Item | Useful life | Remarks |
|---|---|---|
| Ceiling suspension | Life | |
| Acoustical ceiling | Life | |
| Luminous ceiling | 10–20 years | Discolors easily. |
| *Ceramic tile* | | |
| Tub alcove and shower stall | Life | Proper installment and |
| Bath wainscote | Life | maintenance required for long life. |
| Ceramic floor | Life | Cracks appear due to moisture and |
| Ceramic tile | Life | joints; must be grouted every 3–4 years. |
| *Finish carpentry* | | |
| Baseboard and shoe molding | 40–50 years | |
| Door and window trim | 40–50 years | |
| Wood paneling | 40–50 years | |
| Closet shelves | 40–50 years | |
| Fireplace mantel | 30–40 years | |
| *Flooring* | | |
| Oak floor | Life | In most older homes, 1st story |
| Pine floor | Life | floor is oak and 2nd and 3rd story |
| Slate flagstone floor | 40–50 years | floors are hard pine. |
| Resilient (vinyl) | 10–15 years | Because of scuffing may have to be replaced earlier. |
| Terrazzo | Life | |
| Carpeting | 5–8 years | Standard carpeting. |
| *Cabinets and vanities* | | |
| Kitchen cabinets | 18–30 years | |
| Bath vanities | 18–30 years | |
| Countertop | 18–30 years | |
| Medicine cabinets | 15–20 years | |
| Mirrors | 10–15 years | |
| Tub enclosures | 18–25 years | |
| Shower doors | 18–25 years | |
| Bookshelves | Life | Depends on wood used. |
| *Interior painting* | | |
| Wall paint | 3–5 years | |
| Trim and door | 3–5 years | |
| Wallpaper | 3–7 years | |
| *Electrical finish* | | |
| Electrical range and oven | 12–20 years | |
| Vent hood | 15–20 years | |
| Disposal | 5–12 years | |
| Exhaust fan | 8–10 years | |
| Water heater | 10–12 years | |

**Table 8-4**   Life Expectancies of Various Parts of a House (continued)

| Item | Useful life | Remarks |
|------|-------------|---------|
| Electric fixtures | 20–30 years | |
| Doorbell and chimes | 8–10 years | |
| Fluorescent bulbs | 3–5 years | |
| | | |
| *Plumbing finish* | | |
| Dishwasher | 5–15 years | |
| Gas water heater | 8–12 years | |
| Gas refrigerator | 15–25 years | |
| Toilet seats | 8–10 years | |
| Commode | 15–25 years | |
| Steel sinks | 15–20 years | |
| China sinks | 15–20 years | |
| Faucets | Life | Washers must be replaced frequently |
| Flush valves | 18–25 years | |
| Well and septic system | 15–30 years | Depends on soil and rock formations. |
| Hot water boilers | 30–50 years | Becomes increasingly inefficient with age and may have to be replaced before it actually breaks down. |
| | | |
| *Heating finish* | | |
| Wall heaters | 12–17 years | |
| Warm air furnaces | 25–30 years | Most common today |
| Radiant heating | | |
|    Ceiling | 20–30 years | |
|    Baseboard | 20–40 years | |
| Air conditioning unit | 8–18 years | |
| Air conditioning compressors | 10–18 years | Regular maintenance required |
| Humidifier | 7–8 years | |
| Electric air cleaners | 8–10 years | |
| | | |
| *Appliances* | | |
| Refrigerator | 15–25 years | |
| Washer | 8–12 years | |
| Dryer | 8–12 years | |
| Combination washer and dryer | 7–10 years | |
| Garage door opener | 8–10 years | |
| Disposal units | 8–12 years | |
| Dishwasher | 8–12 years | |
| Lawn mower | 7–10 years | Must be serviced regularly |
| Vacuum cleaner | 6–10 years | |
| Music system (intercom) | 30–40 years | |

**Table 8-4** Life Expectancies of Various Parts of a House (continued)

| Item | Useful life | Remarks |
|---|---|---|
| *Appointments* | | |
| Closet rods | Life | |
| Blinds | 10–15 years | |
| Drapes | 5–10 years | |
| Towel bars | 10–15 years | |
| Soap grab | 10–12 years | |
| | | |
| *Others* | | |
| Fences and screens | 20–30 years | |
| Splash blocks | 6–7 years | |
| Patios (concrete) | 15–50 years | |
| Gravel walks | 3–5 years | |
| Concrete walks | 10–25 years | |
| Sprinkler system | 15–25 years | |
| Asphalt driveway | 5–6 years | With patchwork may last 15–20 years |
| Tennis court | 20–40 years | |
| Swimming pool | | |
| Pool shell | 15–25 years | |
| Pool filter | 3–5 years | Must be cleaned yearly |
| Pool heater | 4–6 years | |

*Source:* Dean Crist, Economics Department, of the National Association of Home Builders.

## WHAT IT PAYS, AND WHAT IT DOES NOT PAY, TO REMODEL

For the country-property owner with profits as a major goal, you ought to hold firmly in mind some current rules of thumb about improvements. People will pay extra for some things, they expect others as a matter of course and do not expect to pay a premium.

A leading appraiser has estimated the percentage return on various remodeling projects as shown in Table 8-5.

These percentage figures apply to the cost of your improvement, whatever it may be in whatever part of the United States. Where contractor's labor and materials run higher than elsewhere, you will find that the amount a buyer is willing to pay for such an improvement will also run a bit higher. You see from the experiences of this appraiser that adding standard new equipment and new space is the best way to increase the value of your investment in your home on a dollar-for-dollar basis. Understand, of course, that once added to the house, the value moves up, year after year, by the same factor as does the entire house. For example, if the home you purchased for $87,000 gets a bathroom modernization costing a total of $8,750, on the basis of these percentages you could consider 50 percent of that immediately added to the value of the house.

$$
\begin{array}{r}
\$87,000 \\
4,375 \\
\hline
\$91,375
\end{array}
$$

But then at year's end if the houses in your neighborhood, according to a consensus of local realtors have been moving up an average of 11 percent a year in value, your move up would be based on the $91,375:

$$\$91,375 \times 11\% = \$10,051.25$$

Thus the value of the house and its new addition, after the end of the first year of ownership would be about $101,426. The profit hunter who fixes up a house for resale value should be prepared or ready to have time work for her or him. In an up market, house values compound at a remarkable rate. To ensure your own good profits, it is best to make the

**Table 8-5**  Return on Various Remodeling Projects

| When you add new space | You can expect this increase in value (based on improvement costs) |
| --- | --- |
| One bedroom added | 75–100% |
| New bath added | 70–100% |
| New kitchen added | 60–100% |
| Family or dining room added | 65–100% |
| *When you modernize an existing room* | |
| Basement converted to recreation room | 30% |
| Garage to family room | 30% |
| Attic to bedroom | 30–50% |
| Bathroom updated | 45–55% |
| Insulation | 100% |
| *When you pleasure yourself with luxurious improvements* | |
| Greenhouse | 20% or less |
| Fireplace | 25–40% |
| Decking or patio | 25% |
| Central air conditioning | 75–85% |

most meaningful additions early in your ownership. Then if your plans change, you can sell with a substantial and early profit. This might be the situation with an executive family which frequently moves from office to office, always to better neighborhoods and invariably at a profit.

*Example: The Peripatetic Executive Who Turned a Profit on Every Move but One*

Tom Olivero worked for one of the very largest manufacturing firms in the United States. He was a successful sales engineer and the company got into the habit of moving Tom and his family around to offices that needed a mature salesman to perk up the business. They had lived in several executive middle-to-upper-income suburbs in the East and the Midwest. It was their hobby to fix up each of the houses they inhabited, and they always made some money on the deal. About 10 years before his retirement Tom realized the company had kept him in a Chicago suburb for seven years. He checked, and as best he could measured his own career against that of older men on the sales force. Each, more or less, came to a point where they stayed in a community. Many were still living in those communities in their retirement. The Oliveros thought that now was the time to build a house in Evanston. They sold their present one at a good profit, and he and his wife Mary, with an architect, designed the house they had always dreamed of living in. They had many special features designed into the house, a greenhouse for Mary, a study where he could hole up on weekend afternoons to look at the football games on TV. There were intercoms between the rooms, a special mud room off the rear door where people could take off their galoshes and rubbers (a feature they always wished they had had when the children were young and tracking dirt into the kitchen). The architect kidded them, saying that they were building into that house all the features they had wanted but didn't have in their many previous homes.

Well, the moral of the story was that Tom's company, after that dream house was completed for about two years, asked him to move to New York headquarters, to develop the sales program for a new product. It was a definite promotion and a distinct challenge. Mary and Tom had been so used to moving that pulling up stakes once again didn't bother them, even if it meant leaving their dream house. But when they tried to put it on the market for what it cost them to build, they suddenly realized they had seriously overbuilt for their neighborhood. True, they had the best new house in that immediate vicinity, but also true, they had all the interesting and useful features most houses in that vicinity (or most contemporary houses, for that matter) did not have. Buyers were not going to put $125,000 into a house in a neighborhood where most houses ran $85,000. They might put in $100,000, and the Oliveros were lucky that a family with children fell in love with the mud hall and all the other special features and agreed to pay more because they felt it bought more. The buyers could make a sizable down payment and didn't have to worry about the appraisal coming in at a conventional figure. Still, the Oliveros consider their dream house "the one that lost them $25,000."

## REMODELING THAT TENDS TO INCREASE VALUE SIGNIFICANTLY

A consensus of appraisal people in real estate—realtors, appraisers, assessors, builders, and accountants, suggest that the following features will add significantly to the value of a contemporary house on today's market. This does not necessarily mean that tomorrow's market will support these improvements. The chances are, however, that it *will,* because the improvements have been mentioned in articles on the subject ever since World War II made better materials available for home building and technology gave the American kitchen the microwave oven.

**In the Kitchen**    Almost anything within reason will increase the value of the kitchen: easy-to-clean floors, a self-cleaning oven, handier cabinets, a microwave oven, efficient, well-lighted work centers, natural light, and views to let the cook in the family monitor and enjoy the children's play area. You should emphasize expanding and making the kitchen an interesting, productive work space. Many country homes, particularly farmhouses, had kitchens big enough by today's standards to be considered as family rooms. There was a big kitchen table and adjacent closets for outer clothes and equipment. The warmth of the food baking, and possibly new cookies to try out, made these old-fashioned family rooms pleasant and snug, and a good place for the children to do homework once the dishes were cleared away. In many country areas, where poorly insulated buildings were commonplace, the kitchen in the winter months was one of the few rooms that could be called warm. Today's kitchen, in a family that conserves energy, has again become the focal room and communication center.

If you need a new refrigerator, remember that it is a greedy consumer (along with your TV set) of energy. Put in the size you really need, and possibly consider, if you want a bit of both refrigeration and freezing, a double-door installation. You will probably open the refrigerator section more often than the freezer section, and you can set each section at energy-conserving levels. If you will need to freeze a lot of food for the family to save on food bills, you will definitely want to consider a larger, separate freezer unit, either in the basement or in an alcove of your large kitchen.

**In Bathrooms**    Keep things bright, but resist the flashiness you might expect to find in a city apartment but not in a home in the country. If you are living in a village, you might allow yourself a highly styled powder room for guests near the living room. Try for a large, simple family bathroom and a second bathroom in the children's area or off the kitchen, where children and gardeners can wash up after a stint in the garden without tracking dirt throughout the house. If your house is the kind that is set up for entertaining, you will need this powder room available for guests and committee meetings. Emphasize built-in counters with cupboards to hide the pipes. Of course, if you have gone in heavily for restoration, you will have to consider that sinks and tubs with legs were a Victorian fashion. Perhaps you can compromise and have one authentically old and one modern bathroom, but be sure both have adequate piping and ventilation, and discreet auxiliary heating if the old radiator cannot be trusted to keep the place warm in winter, or unless you are a polar bear. Most people like warm bathrooms. An electric heater in the ceiling with a fan or a radiant lamp can soothe worries about chills after stepping out of a hot shower or tub in a pristine state of vulnerability.

**Bedrooms**  You can go up to four of them and expect to get your money out of the additions. More than that and you are going beyond the needs of most families, even those who enjoy frequent guests. Of course, if your family is a big one and needs the extra rooms, build them, but have in mind, too, that one or two could later be consolidated into a family room.

**Family Rooms**  These are so important these days that you might consider sacrificing extra bedrooms or other excess room. Winterize that closed-in porch space and arrange to put in a fireplace and to have it air-conditioned—if not by central air conditioning, then by a room unit that can supply supplementary heat in winter and cool air in summer. Such units are on the market and may be connected to your existing heating system.

**Aluminum Siding**  Can add value to your house because it does not require painting. It is usually guaranteed to be colorfast without additional painting for up to 35 years. Since the energy crisis many home remodelers have switched to siding with a frameboard backing which offers maximum added insulation (up to about a 70 percent increase) in comparison with wooden siding with no insulating backup material.

**Air Conditioning**  This adds considerable value to a house, particularly in the South but even in the northern areas where the summer months can be hot and humid. This is a case of a new idea growing on the public. With more and more families having two breadwinners and with most people working in air-conditioned office buildings, families do not want to put up with uncomfortably hot or humid living conditions when they return home each night. They look for comfort and relaxation and do not want to waste time with temporary ways to "beat the heat."

**Garages**  A garage can pay its way in extra value, particularly if it has auxiliary heating and perhaps a tool- or workbench wall for home repairs. If you are putting up a detached building in cold or damp climates, you may consider an attic for extra storage (with a ready-made pull-down stair, not a hole that requires a ladder). If your country home is in a warm climate, you may only need a carport. With the energy shortage and the new focus on the efficiency of automobiles, protected shelter for your family cars has new value in the market place.

**Carpeting and Wallpaper**  Provided they are in good condition, these will hold their costs as added value to your house. Needless to say, there is a wide range of costs for both. You will not usually get your money back for anything heavily ornate or unusually luxurious or expensive. A good quality of paper, and carpeting that emphasizes endurance and longevity in traditional colors and styles, will serve you best when it comes time to resell your house.

## WHAT ABOUT SOLAR ENERGY AND OTHER FORMS OF NEW-TECHNOLOGY HEATING AND ELECTRICAL GENERATING SYSTEMS?

By and large, these new systems will hold their value, provided you can demonstrate they operate efficiently and dependably. With that general endorsement, it is only fair to point out that you can spend a lot on a solar-heating or a photovoltaic system. Even if it works well and you have the records to prove it, many home buyers are turned off by the experimental nature of the system. They fear it may fail after a year or two or more, and they cannot justify in their minds the added price tag you are asking for an experimental feature in your house. Prove that the system has been saving you an average of $1,500 a year in heating bills over a period of *ten* years, and you may have something that will certainly count as added value to the house. You will, in that period of time, have paid for the improvement yourself in savings alone.

Because of the gradual depletion of all economically feasible supplies of petroleum-based fuels during the next two or three decades, your house will have acquired value if:

1  It has been remodeled to make best use of passive solar heating.

2  It is well insulated.

3  It has the capability, with little additional expense, of being converted to one or more active systems of solar heat and power.

4 It has been so set up in its environment and its electrical supply that it can take economical advantage of lower-than-average electrical rates during off hours.

## Active and Passive Solar-Heating Systems

Most contemporary houses, and even primitive dwellings, incorporate some solar heating by simply facing windows toward the winter sun. The winter sun is lower and will come directly into a room as it shines through leafless trees at a lower angle than the summer sun. Country homes usually had large leaf-shedding trees around them to shade them from the summer sun and to inhibit as little as possible the inflow of winter sunlight. *Active systems* begin with solar collector panels on a house and grow to systems that include pumps, fans, and specially built storage units.

Indians who lived in pueblos in the Southwest utilized passive solar-heating principles with great sophistication. Studies of pueblo dwellings show that their walls were designed to expose more surface to solar radiation in winter than in summer, so that the net effect was a fairly well maintained temperature in the interior of the building, no matter what the season or whether it was day or night. The thickness of the walls and the dimensions of doorways promoted the storage of the sun's heat; the walls continued to radiate heat well into the night. The doors and windows were positioned so as to shade the interior from the high-sailing summer sun when its direct rays were not wanted during the day, and to encourage the lower-traveling winter sun to penetrate the interior when warmth was needed. Even the outdoor public plazas were designed so that the residential units did not shade the sun in winter, and by the way they were positioned in arcs on a hillside, protected the communal area from winter winds. Terraces outside the residential buildings provided horizontal areas for the preparation and drying of food and were seldom, if ever, in shadow.

In a different way, but using the same principles, the New England saltbox house exposed its high wall and most of its windows toward the south to capture the maximum amount of winter heat and to utilize the drying effect of the sun. The long slope of the roof ran toward the north or the prevailing winter winds, and had fewer windows. The interior of the house was oriented around a central chimney that served fireplaces and kitchen ovens, and also acted as a central structure of warm masonry. Parts of the house could be closed off effectively during winter months to save on fuel.

Early experimental solar houses at MIT in the 1930s and later at Princeton, as well as in isolated houses designed by architects and solar engineers, have demonstrated the feasibility and technological readiness for active solar heating. But is is only now that solar houses are being built and sold in competition with conventionally fueled structures. From less than a dozen such houses operating in the United States in 1972, there are now well over a thousand and they are coming on stream at a faster rate every year.

In Appendix B you will find a list of some books that go into the subject of solar heating and photovoltaic electrical generation in detail. It may be well here to review briefly the principles of solar energy because the concept is a dynamic and timely one for country-property owners. Any house with an efficient solar system in place will grow in value at a greater rate than the conventionally designed house, if other factors are equal.

As a collector, storer, and distributor of solar heat, the earth itself demonstrates the basic physics of solar-house heating. The sun heats exposed surfaces of the earth and the atmosphere acts as a protective cover that holds the heat near the earth's crust. Heat is stored both in land and water masses, and prevailing winds and water currents transport the stored heat to various parts of the globe.

In heating a country residence, a solar-heating system acts in much the same way, although on a much smaller scale. In passive heating systems this process takes place through the warming and cooling of building materials, and through the air currents present in any house. In active heating systems, this process is augmented and made more efficient by mechanical means. An absorbent material (such as the wall of a building or an absorber attached to a building) is exposed to the sun. In the case of an absorber, a cover of glass or plastic sheets is used to deter reradiation and cooling. Once trapped, the heat is removed from the absorbing device, either through air passages or pipes of liquid which distribute it throughout the building and then to storage where it can be held in a tank, or by rocks or similar material, for a number of days until its heating effect has gradually dissipated.

No matter how sophisticated the mechanical augmentation, the initial source of heat is by solar radiation, which arrives at the surface of a building in three ways—either as direct, diffuse, or reflected radiation. See Figure 8-11 for a simple diagram of how these methods of solar heat affect a building.

A solar house is built so that it emphasizes four basic objectives: (1) The collection of heat from the sun that falls upon the surfaces of the building, (2) storage of that heat so that it can be used during the night or on days when the sun is not shining, (3) distribution of the stored heat in a way that promotes comfort and efficiency of the system, and (4) retention of the heat within the building through insulation.

In colder climates, solar-heating systems that account for a major

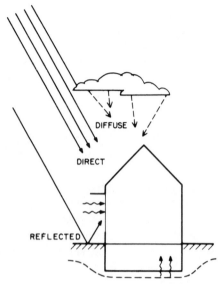

**Figure 8-11** How solar heat affects a conventional building.

portion of the heating of an individual house usually have separate "active" parts to achieve each of the objectives noted above. Pumps, fans, storage rocks or tanks of water, and ductwork are common "active" parts. They are necessary to maximize and magnify the sun's effects in cold climates. But there are simpler means for achieving all these functions by applications of passive design. In warmer climates, these features will perhaps prove sufficient to achieve sizable savings. You might keep them in mind when you remodel and improve your house. With no or little added cost you can often incorporate in your improvement—perhaps only with extra windows facing south—energy-savings principles that will reduce the cost of operating your house, make it more energy efficient, and thus enhance its value to a prospective buyer. Figure 8-12 will give you some idea of the savings you can effect.

In a northern climate, whether a building is solar heated or not, it should be designed to minimize the amount of heating energy required. This becomes of even greater importance with solar design so that the size and the cost of the collector and storage system can also be kept relatively small and less costly.

To use solar heat effectively once it is collected requires an efficient building enclosure with good insulation and other provisions against heat loss, such as double doors or "air locks" at entries or zoning the home's interior to reduce the amount of space that is fully heated. Your architect can incorporate these features in whatever building you construct and whatever additions you can make. Remember, too, that heating is just one aspect of the benefits. A truly solar house will be designed to prevent overheating in summer—perhaps it will even *cool* in summer, heat in winter, and *generate* electricity through photovoltaic cells.

Designers have been enjoying a field day in suggesting ways to apply

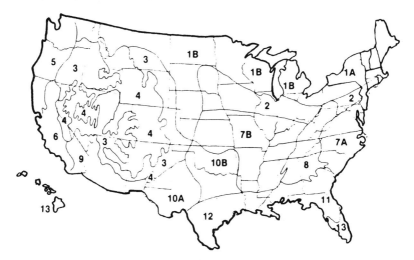

This map shows the 13 climatic regions of the country. The key below lists the minimum percentage of a home's energy needs that can be supplied by effective passive solar design in each region.

| Climatic region | % passive solar contribution to energy needs |
|---|---|
| 1A | 37% |
| 1B | 28% |
| 2 | 32% |
| 3 | 38% |
| 4 | 24% |
| 5 | 34% |
| 6 | 52% |
| 7A | 34% |
| 7B | 34% |
| 8 | 36% |
| 9 | 52% |
| 10A | 53% |
| 10B | 43% |
| 11 | 36% |
| 12 | 32% |
| 13 | 54% |

**Figure 8-12**   How much energy passive solar design can supply. *(Source: HUD's Regional Guidelines for Building Passive Energy Conserving Homes.)*

solar energy to new and remodeled homes. They usually feature solar-heat collectors or photovoltaic collectors and design of the wall of the house to suit various climates. Of course, many of these design adaptations have been used, in less sophisticated forms perhaps, by the primitive people who once inhabited a region.

In Figures 8-13, 8-14, 8-15, and 8-16 simple sketches of some of these variations show how the structure of a contemporary house or the addition to a house can suit a climate and use climatic conditions to advantage.

In the cool climate design, part of the structure is underground to take advantage of heat retained in the soil. The closeness to the soil encourages snow to accumulate and blanket the walls and roofs. Internal heat zoning and double entries that form air locks prevent escape of internal heat.

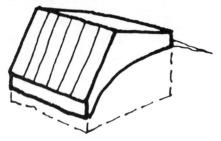

**Figure 8-13** Design for a cool climate that features maximum heat retention, maximum solar heat gain, and minimum wind resistance.

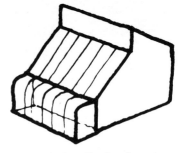

**Figure 8-14** Design for a temperate climate that features moderate heat retention, moderate solar heat gain, slight wind exposure (humidity control), and moderate internal air flow.

**Figure 8-15** Design for a hot dry climate that features minimum solar heat gain, moderate wind and dust resistance, and moderate internal air flow.

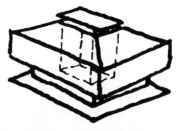

**Figure 8-16** Design for a hot wet climate that features maximum wind exposure and maximum internal air flow.

*Source: Donald Watson,* Designing and Building a Solar House, *Garden Way Publishing Company, Charlotte, Vermont.*

In temperate climates there is a danger of humidity accumulating within the building and in the building materials. Thus more of the building is exposed to the drying effects of the sun and wind. Greenhouses and other passive solar-heat features function efficiently in temperate climates. Roof ventilators and possibly a modest air-conditioning unit in the upper part of the house can provide the cooling needed for only a small portion of the summer.

In hot-dry climates, where night temperatures fall well below day averages, the design features natural cooling and heating. Interior courtyards help control sun and wind effects. Placing part of the house underground reduces the heat gain in the summer. Shaded windows and recessed doors give protection from glare and the intense direct sunlight, and against wind-blown dust and sand.

When wetness combines with heat, you will want a house cooled by available breezes. Flexible walls and windows with screens, ventilating louvers, and blinds will provide the necessary storm protection, insect control, privacy, and variable illumination. Courtyards and patios with roof vents can be used to stimulate air flow. In some places it may be a good idea to build the house on stilts, or on a hill, as if to hold it up to the wind and away from such insect threats as termites, which thrive in wet, warm soil.

### Active Solar Collectors Incorporated into the Design of Houses for Cool Climates

Solar heating makes the most economical sense in cooler climates where home heating costs vary with the coldness of the winter. Using the present state of the art, the most energy-efficient contemporary collectors may require a surface area as high as 40 percent of the building's heated floor space. This requires a design challenge because of its sheer bulk. Placement is crucial in maximizing the effect of the sun's rays. If the collectors are mounted on a nearby surface or on the ground, the design challenge is lifted from the house, but you begin to lose efficiency the greater the distance from the space to be heated.

# Chapter Nine

# Buying Country Property in a Development

There are three reasons why the "country house" of many Americans has transformed itself from a single-family house on an acre or more of land to a house on a lot in a development, to part of a mutlifamily condominium unit in a development, or perhaps to a one- or two-unit mobile home in a mobile-home park in the country.

The first of these reasons has to do with economics. Builders can achieve economies of scale; they can give you more shelter for your money if they can plan for many families at once, or, in the case of mobile homes, if they can run them off an assembly line. Whereas existing single-family homes now have a median price in the United States in excess of $60,000—$80,000 in the West, $50,000 in the North Central states, $52,000 in the South, and $58,000 in the Northeast, a single mobile-home unit may cost as little as $12,000 with perhaps $100 a month in lease and maintenance charges in a beautifully kept mobile-home park.

In the second place, the lots in many developments are supplied with utilities and sewers and again because of the economies of scale, cost less than the single lot in some remote country area where you will have to bring in utilities, create a water supply and sewerage system, *and maintain them.* In many of the condominium developments you do not buy *all* the land you use; you usually buy just the portion under the structure you occupy. Thus, you do not pay for land you do not personally use every day. You may contribute, however, through maintenance charges, to the upkeep of the common, public parts of your structure and to the land around it. But the developer, or the owners' association which eventually takes over in most cases from the developer, retains title to the land. As an owner you have a fractional and indirect interest in it. That does not prevent you from selling your own shelter independently, much as you would your own separate house in the city or a village. You may also, within the association's regulations, work in your yard, have a garden, and prune your own shrubs, but these tasks *outside* your own walls will normally be taken care of by the association. It is estimated that by the year 2000 half of the families of the United States will be living in condominiums, and will enjoy communal ownership of the surrounding land and private ownership of the "inside" of their own homes.

The third attraction of the condominium, the home on a lot in a development, or the mobile home in a park, is that many extra recreational facilities or amenities come with owning a minor, private part of the complex. You may get a golf course, a marina, swimming pool, shuttle service to the nearest public transportation, garden plots for private use, tennis and racquet-ball courts, country-club facilities with an auditorium and theatre, a dance floor, craft workrooms, a restaurant, a convenient shopping center for necessities, and catering facilities for parties larger than those you can accommodate in your own home. Poolside facilities may include a health club for keeping fit. And you can find all this in the midst of scenic countryside, with other people who have achieved approximately your own income level and financial status. Today, no matter *what* your inherited or achieved financial status, you can find a condominium in a development to suit your imagined sense of luxury.

Although condominium ownership is the wave of the future in country property for masses of people, rest assured that single-family country houses and farms, and investments in undeveloped acreage (land for potential development) will benefit financially from this demographic trend toward country living. You may be the kind of person or family who prefers buying right now in a development. Development living is particularly attractive to young couples, singles, and older couples. It is probably least attractive to families bringing up children, because they usually do not have their own schools or enough bedrooms and in the case of adult communities often do not encourage young folks under 18.

A drawback from the standpoint of an investor interested in profits is this: In the early years of any development your lot, condominium, or mobile home competes with new sales by the developer. You cannot expect, under these circumstances, your property to rise rapidly in resale value. Depending on the popularity of your particular development and the supply and demand situation, your investment will probably rise *slowly* in value. For the very economies of scale that bring in a finished home at a lower cost than comparable shelter in an independent single-family home also produce a certain sameness in structures. The five or ten models which you can choose from are then repeated over the land-scape. Until the development is finished, there is always a new "Deluxe" model available with a few individual touches that can be dictated by the buyer who purchases it *before* it is built. On the other hand, your "Deluxe" model has the advantage of having had a shake-down period under your ownership. Perhaps you have added some attractive individual features of your own. And anything that malfunctioned has probably been fixed or replaced. These investment advantages and disadvantages will vary with different developments, and you should protect your potential profit by identifying the pattern of these trends *before* you buy.

## BUYING A BUILDING LOT IN A DEVELOPMENT

In most developments your lot is clearly laid out for you; it has been surveyed, and in your contract of sale or your deed of purchase, you will find descriptive surveyor's figures on exactly where your property begins and ends on all sides. This is yet another advantage of buying into a development; identification of the property has been taken care of for you.

You still should have a real estate lawyer go over the description of the property. The lawyer should also investigate the legality of the deed or lease of the land and the financial strength of the sponsors and their obligations for completing the development. No matter how successful a developer may have been in the past, the current development could come a cropper. You and your lawyer should check to see whether a performance bond guarantees completion of all promised improvements.

*Example: And the Desert Flowered With Profits*
Bill Hansen and his wife Marjorie were leery about retiring to Arizona to a half-acre "ranchette." They had visited Phoenix and Tucson and liked the climate, but they had heard stories about lots sold in desert country for relatively little which turned out to be worth even less than that.

However, they did answer an ad in a retirement magazine and got a brochure of a development that was already built. The literature said that the recreational facilities were in place, that 30 of a proposed 150 units were already built in Section A of the Paradise Mesa, and that there were going to be about nine other sections, and room finally for 1,350 families. A representative of the sponsoring company in Des Moines, Iowa, invited them out for a week's stay—transportation not included, but free lodging in a nearby motel so they could enjoy all the recreational facilities and the climate, and could eat at the golf clubhouse dining room or at the coffee shop of the motel in which they were to stay. After sifting through several of these deals, they chose to visit Paradise Mesa and found that the desert, indeed, could bloom, provided it was understood by a horticulturist and landscape architect who knew what to plant and how it should be watered. The fertility and sun were there, but needed a hand to supply the water from deep beneath the surface of the dry ground. Bill and Marjorie already knew that the developer was reliable. They had even bothered to check out two references from a previously completed development, and on the golf course and at the swimming pool to ask tenants who had already moved in if they were satisfied. They met enough enthusiasm to overcome their reluctance. So they bought a lot and arranged for their house to be built on the basis of a furnished model they could inspect. Then they went back to Des Moines and waited. The only drawback was that the wait lasted longer than expected. But that gave them time to get the best price possible for their old home. They were pleasantly surprised, when they finally did move, to find that comparable lots and houses in the development were selling for 10 percent more than they paid for theirs.

## CHOOSING THE DEVELOPMENT WHICH SUITS YOU

Whether you are buying into a development primarily to have a weekend family home emphasizing recreational facilities and eventually a place for retirement, or to have a condominium in an adult community, or to reserve a place in a mobile-home park, there are many features which you *must* check out carefully. Fortunately there are today in the United States many very successful examples of all kinds of developments—even whole new towns, such as Columbia, Maryland, which have been developed. As you begin to focus on this type of purchase and its profit possibilities, be sure to visit those sites in the area of the country where you think you would like to settle. Perhaps you can rent a furnished unit in one of them for a month or a season. You will want to take into consideration the climate and geographic location of a development, just as you would any other parcel of country property on which you expect to live. In addition, you will want to investigate thoroughly, probably with the assistance of a real estate lawyer, the background of the sponsor and the way the development is structured and seems to be working out. Not all developments, of course, offer the same amenities; not all developments are well managed; not all developments have happy people living in them. Of the communal regulations you agree to follow in a development, you will soon realize you have bought into a community with a greater commitment to and reliance on your neighbors than if you were buying a lot and house in a country village or if you were buying a farm.

Thus you should consider the following checkpoints* when buying a lot and building in a planned community of any sort—even a mobile-home park . . .

---

* Adapted and expanded from a checklist courtesy of Davis R. Chant, Milford, Pennsylvania.

### Accessibility to Your Primary Residence, Family, or Old Friends

[ ] Does the development's location provide quick access to old familiar places? Are there expressways and toll roads? Is mass transportation available if you want to spare gasoline?

[ ] If you will be a commuter, do you have control over your driving hours so that you will not have to fight rush-hour traffic during your driving to and from your country development? Are new roads or highways planned out that way to relieve congestion?

[ ] What transportation facilities, such as shuttles or buses, does the development provide to meet public transportation or to take one to a nearby shopping mall?

[ ] Will the location of the development encourage visits from people you want to see more of, such as children, grandchildren, and old friends? Are some old friends or friends of relatives already owners in the development?

[ ] Are there libraries, churches, movie theatres, sports events of the kind you are used to attending in the vicinity of the development?

### Size of the Community

[ ] Most developed communities are planned with a minimum of 500 lots (and homes) up to several thousand—with the exception of mobile-home parks which may have as few as 25 or up to several hundred units. What are the ultimate plans of the developer for the community in which you think you would like to buy?

[ ] Has the developer had previous experience in building the size of community you are considering. Has the developer run such a community successfully?

[ ] Is this the size of community in which you would like to live? Would you prefer a smaller place? A larger one?

[ ] Does the community have its own water supply and waste disposal system? Security protection?

### Planned Amenities and Services—What Is Available Now? What Is the Cost?

[ ] What size lots are offered? Would it be better to buy more than one lot?

[ ] What recreational facilities (tennis and racquet-ball courts, bowling, swimming, health club, golf course, jogging paths, stables, bridle baths) are planned? Which are already constructed and usable? Has the developer been bonded to assure completion of the planned facilities?

[ ] What community services, such as a health-care station, party and banquet facilities, library, card rooms, shopping center for necessities, have been planned? Which are already functioning?

[ ] Once the development is completed, how will recreational facilities be handled? By the sponsor requiring a monthly fee? By an owners' association with a monthly fee? What is the fee likely to be?

[ ] When the development is completed, who will be responsible for maintaining roads? For collecting garbage? For landscaping and maintenance of landscaping?

[ ] What possible future assessments will be made on lot owners? On home owners?

[ ] What internal fire and security systems are there? Can authorized people enter the development at any point other than the designated gates?

## Physical Details of the Lot You Want to Buy

[ ] Are there steep hills or rough topography that will make drainage a problem? Will building be a problem?

[ ] What about the water supply? Is there a water-supply system or must you drill your own well? If you must drill, what has been the success of other owners in drilling? What has been the cost?

[ ] Is community sewage disposal provided? Must you pay for the laterals to hook up to the community system? Must you construct your own septic system? If you must construct a septic system, has the developer a certified percolation test to guide you?

[ ] Have you investigated the prospective lot for views in all seasons? What will full summer leafing do to your view? To the amount of light and heat you will receive?

[ ] If you are considering lake frontage, have you made a probe of the depth of the lake off your shore? Does the lake have water one can swim in without health hazards? Can you catch edible fish in it? What about the aquatic weeds? Are they under control?

[ ] Have you had a possible builder or two check out the lot to see if there are any special problems?

## Buying Details

[ ] Is there a lot-exchange privilege in case you wish to switch one lot for another after the initial purchase is made?

[ ] What are the terms on the purchase of a lot? What is the actual annual interest rate? Can you do better elsewhere?

[ ] Will the developer give you a discount price on the lot if you pay all cash?

[ ] When you build on the lot, will the developer supply suggested plans for a variety of houses? Can the developer recommend one or more builders?

[ ] In the case of a mobile-home site, what are the leasing details if the lot is not actually for sale? What will the lessor do to facilitate installation of the home when it arrives?

[ ] Does the developer, through a friendly bank, offer advantageous installment payments on the lot? When you build your house will the developer help you to arrange an advantageous mortgage on the house?

[ ] What are the real estate tax rates on lots? On lots plus homes of a given value?

[ ] Have you read carefully the property report on the development?

## Selling Details

[ ] What provision does the developer have for helping you resell your lot or your improved home and lot as a package?

[ ] What has been the recent resale experience in the development?

[ ] What has been the developer's experience in selling lots and homes? What has the developer been getting lately for homes like yours (or like the one you want to build)? Have you checked out these quotes with other owners?

[ ] If the developer has on-going plans for selling new sections of the development will the new lots and homes hinder the sale of yours at equivalent prices?

## Renting Possibilities

[ ]  Does the developer have a rental program in case you want to offer your home for rent during seasons of the year when you are not using it?

[ ]  What are the costs and rental income you can expect?

[ ]  Have you checked out the rental experience of other owners in the community? What rents have they been averaging?

## The Importance of Comparing

[ ]  Although you can make preliminary comparisons of various developments through their brochures and property reports, you *must* visit several suitable developments to sense the lay of the land, the types of houses that have already been built, and the various facilities already in use.

## BUYING LOTS FOR SPECULATION EARLY IN THE LIFE OF A DEVELOPMENT

Buying more lots than you need is always a teasing decision to make. For if you buy early in the life of a development, you will probably have the lowest prices offered in that development and you can dicker a bit with the sponsor over the price and the terms on several lots instead of just one lot. The sponsor wants to get the project off the ground so that further financing can be arranged. As the project begins to sell out you will find that prices are usually higher. The success of the project and the inflationary tendencies of the national economy tend to support a price increase every year or at periods coinciding with the project's growth toward maturity. The trouble is that you cannot always know the time schedule of the development. What the developers plan at the start is not always fulfilled on time.

In general, a development goes through three stages in its progress toward maturity: the startup and kickoff of sales, the moving-in period when first buyers begin to build, and the approaching sold-out period. You will usually find price rises occurring at the second and third stages. At that time you may want to unload your extra lots at a profit. In a very large development the selling-out of one section may signal the start of another section—with similar facilities offered at higher prices.

It is a common practice to buy more than one lot in a development where one has chosen to live. This gives you partial control over likely neighbors; it also gives you additional privacy, at least for the time being until the natural screen of the landscaping spreads up and out. You generate, in this way, a definite possibility for selling that extra lot later at a profit. The profit from this type of speculation depends heavily on the overall success of the development. But presumably you will be using at least one of the lots for building your own home or recreational retreat. You can thus monitor the on-going progress of the development and the pricing of lots similar to the ones you own. You can raise your resale price accordingly.

Sometimes this type of profitable speculation may extend to building another house or two on extra lots and selling them at a profit. You can probably get better prices for materials and labor if you have a larger job to offer the contractor. Actually, you will be ordering two or three times the labor and materials you would normally order. Or you may decide to build only your own house, live in it for a while, and then build the one or two extra houses based on what you have learned from your own house. Or, you might sell your own house and build one or two better ones, based on your experience and the improvements you would like to enjoy.

## BUILDING ON YOUR DEVELOPMENT LOT

When you buy a lot in a development you may also obligate yourself to follow certain building regulations designed to make the development fairly harmonious in style and to prevent one neighbor from encroaching on another. This may rub you a bit abrasively if your lot is a small one, perhaps only half an acre. Smaller lots give you closer neighbors, who may eliminate a lovely tree because they want their family room to have a particular view. And *your* family room may jut out in such a way that it could obscure your neighbor's view of the community's lake. A developer frequently tries to prevent these disputes by requiring a minimum lot size in relation to the area of the house planned and by regulating the positioning of the house on the lot in such a way as to minimize encroachments on neighbors.

One of the great advantages in building within a development, however, is the proven ability of the builders and the probable existence already in the development of the kind of house you want (and are allowed) to build. A typical development in the second stage of growth will have five or six basic house styles, possibly model homes, from which you can choose. Then, in agreement with the sponsor and the builder, you can modify the basic style to suit your individual needs. Thus you can *see* most of the features you want and order them accordingly. In developments where the developer also does the building, you are all the more likely to be able to inspect the siting and the features of the kind of house you want. This is particularly helpful in condominium complexes and multifamily units. On paper they seem one thing; on their sites and landscaped they seem something else—quiet, private, and thoroughly liveable.

## A Signed Agreement with the Builder You Choose

Whether you deal directly with a general contractor or builder or whether you work with the developer as builder, you should decide, one by one, the features going into your house. That means you need an architect's drawings of the house and you need builder's specifications. Get as many of these details as you can worked out verbally and then *put them on paper*.

A typical set of builder's specifications are given below. They will vary, of course, according to the type of home you are going to build and how the developer handles the building situation. When you say to the developer, "I want the Walden model built on my lot," you will probably get the Walden model, give or take a few variations. But you will not know what went into the Walden model or where it will sit in relation to lot lines unless you insist on architect's designs and building specifications. With the sophisticated copying devices now available, the office staff of the builder can certainly supply you with copies of the standard design as altered at your request and with specifications for your personal records. It is probably a good idea to have your real estate lawyer look over the specifications before you sign, or perhaps he can draw them up.

*Example: A Typical Set of Residential Building Specifications\**
The architectural plans and specifications are complementary and what is called for by one and not by the other shall be as binding on the general contractor and subcontractors as if called for by both, and any work not specifically mentioned but necessary to carry out the intent of the plans and specifications shall be performed as if set out here in full.

1. **Garage and Basement Floors.** Garage and basement floors shall be concrete, 4 inches thick, of same mixture as footings, troweled level and smooth. If top coat is required, mixture shall be one part cement and two parts sand. Main entrance porch shall be 4-inch concrete slab. Concrete mixture shall be 1-2-4: 1 part cement, 2 parts sand, 4 parts gravel.

---

\*Sample of builder's specifications. Courtesy of Robert J. Cooper and Emil J. Morey of Emil J. Morey Associates, Inc., Danbury, Connecticut.

2. **Footings** Footings shall be 8 inch by 20 inch poured concrete as one unit. They shall be 8 inches wider than the foundation walls. Concrete will be 1-2-4 mixture normally required by building inspector. Foundation wall shall be 10 inches of poured concrete. In areas of below-freezing temperature all footings shall be 42 inches below grade. If patio door and standard door is installed in walk-out basement, then the contractor shall install frost walls.

3. **Chimney** Chimney shall be constructed of concrete block, common-brick veneered above roof. The size of flues shall be as shown, all flues shall be properly lined with flue lining. Fireplace shall be built according to plan.

4. **Carpentry** The contractor shall and will provide all necessary labor and perform all carpenter work of every nature whatsoever to be done. He shall lay out all work and be responsible for all measurements and keep a competent foreman in charge. All work shall be done in a workmanlike manner; level, straight, plumb, and true, and strictly in accordance with the plans and specifications.

5. **Girders** Girders or supporting beams shall be as required by the size of the building, and shall be placed as shown on plans, all to be 6 inch by 8 inch. Lally columns are to be 4-inch steel lally columns.

6. **Joists** First floor joists to be 2 inch by 8 inch, placed 16 inches on center, grade #1 white fir. Ceiling joists to be 2 inch by 6 inch, placed 16 inches on center, grade #1 white fir. The rafters to be 2 inch by 6 inch, placed 16 inches on center, grade #1 white fir. Ridge rafters 2 inch by 8 inch, grade #1 white fir. Sills to be 2 by 6. All foundation sills to be treated with creosote.

7. **Studding and Partitions** Studdings shall be grade #1 western fir, size 2 by 4, spaced 16 inches on center. Single plate on bottom and double place on top of each wall or partition. Outside studdings shall be 2 by 4's, 16 inches on center. All windows and doors studs shall be doubled.

8. **Bridging** 5/4 by 3-inch wood bridging nailed to each joist.

9. **Rough Flooring** Subflooring shall be laid diagonal, with 1 inch by 8 inch North Carolina pine tongue and groove securely nailed, or ½-inch plyscore may be used. All joints shall be made on joists.

10. **Sheathing** Outside walls shall be covered with 1 inch by 8 inch tongue and groove sheathing or ½-inch plyscore securely nailed. Roof sheathing shall be of 1 inch by 8 inch tongue and groove sheathing or ½-inch plyscore.

11. **Siding** Siding shall be clapboard or shake shingles. Shakes shall have backer boards.

12. **Shingles** Roof shall be of 235-pound asphalt shingles laid on 15-pound felt paper. Where the pitch of the roof is less than 5 inches, then sealimatics shall be used.

13. **Insulation** Sidewalls and ceiling shall be insulated with single, thick-blanket wool insulation, with the exception of electric heat. Then, the standards set forth by the local utility company will be applicable.

14. **Outside Finish**   All lumber required for outside finish shall be white pine or cypress. Overhang soffits shall be ⅜-inch waterproof plywood. Louvers shall be aluminum screened.

15. **Windows and Door Frames**   All windows, except as noted otherwise, shall be double-hung, complete with weather stripping, two over two, or any special glass specified on plan.

16. **Interior Walls and Ceilings**   Interior walls and ceilings shall be ½-inch Sheetrock. All joints shall be taped with three coats of cement.

17. **Inside Finish**   Trim throughout shall be 2¼-inch pine clamshell molding. Baseboards 3½ inch with shoe molding. All trim shall be freshly cut and sanded at the mill.

18. **Doors**   All inside doors shall be 1-⅜-inch-thick mahogany, flush. Outside doors shall be 1-¾ inch-thick and weather stripped.

19. **Closets**   All closets shall have one shelf and one pole with pole brace where necessary.

20. **Hardware**   The contractor shall furnish all hardware, including finish and rough hardware. Finish hardware shall be Schlage or equivalent.

21. **Kitchen Cabinets**   Kitchen cabinets shall be supplied according to plan.

22. **Electrical Work**   Contractor shall provide all necessary labor and material and perform all electrical work of every nature whatsoever to be done. All work shall comply with local ordinances. All light outlets on plan shall be provided. All wiring shall be BX Cable. Service and meter box shall be installed, 220 volts to be connected to meter box. All plates shall be brass and chrome where needed. 8-inch fan shall be installed in kitchen. House shall be properly zoned, paying particular attention to oil burner, furnace, pumps, and electric kitchen stove, in such manner that said utilities shall be properly zoned apart from the other electric zones for the rest of the house. 100-amp service shall be supplied except when electric heat is used. Then the type of service shall be recommended by the local public utility company.

23. **Electrical Fixtures**   Electrical fixtures to the value of $250 shall be provided. This amount usually does not cover the cost. However, the $250 may be used toward the purchase of the fixture of your choice and installed by the contractor, wherever the plans call for light fixtures.

24. **Plumbing**   Contractor shall provide all labor and material and perform all plumbing work of every nature whatsoever in a first-class and workmanlike manner. Colored fixtures shall be provided in bathroom. 30-inch white sink shall be in kitchen. Soil pipe, standard C.I. to extend 10 feet outside foundation walls. Pipes and copper tubing shall be supplied. Also cleanouts wherever required for convenient access to the system. Water-supply mains ¾-inch copper tubing with ½-inch lines to hot water fixtures. Two outside sill cocks where directed by plan, together with interior shutoff. All of the above shall be properly installed according to local ordinance. Hot and cold water connections shall be made with bathtub, shower, lavatory, kitchen sink, and washing machine.

25. **Tile Work**   Contractor shall furnish and set all tile in a neat and workman-

like manner. The tile shall be of size and kind as follows: Bathroom shall have wainscot of tile about 4-feet high, and at tub, the tile shall be of shower height. Plain base and cap. Bathroom floor shall be linoleum. Tile accessories shall be furnished and installed, consisting of one soap and grab, one paper holder, one tumbler holder, one soap holder, two 24-inch towel bars and one double hook.

26. **Heating**  Contractor shall and will provide all necessary labor and material and perform all heating work of every nature whatsover to be done. System shall be one pipe circulating hot water. Such installation shall consist of the following: Tankless unit oil-burning boiler of ample capacity to heat the house to 70° in −10° weather, and to provide plenty of domestic hot water. Oil tank 275 gallons. Radiators shall be of baseboard type. All necessary valves, controls, circulator, thermostat, etc. shall be furnished. System shall be guaranteed for one year, including free service for one year, and greasing and adjustment. Oil burner shall be of ample size to develop the heating capacity of the boiler, and shall be installed according to the manufacturer's specifications.

27. **Copper Work and Flashing**  Contractor shall and will provide all necessary labor and material and perform all work of every nature whatsoever to be done, which includes gutters under all eaves with suitable conductors. Gutters shall be galvanized iron. Downspouts shall be 2 inch by 3 inch galvanized iron. Proper 16-oz. copper flashing shall be provided wherever necessary. Downspouts at grade. All work shall be done in a neat and workmanlike manner.

28. **Interior Painting**  All woodwork shall be carefully cleaned of finger marks, stains, and other defects before any oil, filling, paint, or varnish is applied, and all nail and brad holes shall be filled with colored putty to match. All interior woodwork and floors shall receive one coat of shellac and one coat of varnish.

29. **Decoration**  Decoration of inside walls shall include one coat of primer and one finish coat of paint.

30. **Exterior Painting**  All exterior woodwork shall have two coats of pure lead-and-oil paint. All sash and trim shall be neatly traced. All knots and other defective wood shall be shellacked, and all nail holes shall be puttied before last coat is applied.

31. **Garage**  Garage interior shall be finished with untaped Sheetrock walls.

32. **Cellar Walls**  10 inches of poured concrete.

33. **Septic Tank**  Size of fields and septic tank shall be determined by drainage conditions, with two septic tanks, if necessary, in compliance with FHA requirements.

34. **Driveway**  Driveway shall be 9 feet wide, with a suitable gravel base topped with 4 inches of hot colprovia rolled to 2 inches, or washed gravel, whichever is called for by the contract.

35. **Foundation Drainage**  Foundation drains shall be installed around perimeter of house footing, with floor drain in basement with 50-foot run off. When topo of land allows this, material used shall be in accordance with the recommendations of the local building inspector.

**Figure 9-1** Front and rear views of a country house. (*Source: Stuart Campbell, Building The House You Can Afford, Garden Way Publishing Co., Charlotte, Vermont.*)

## Architect's Drawings

Figures 9-1, 9-2, and 9-3 show architect's drawings for a three-bedroom country house. The lower bedroom can also be used as a family room. Such architect's plans are drawn to scale, usually one-quarter inch equal to one foot. An architect will know from experience what standard allowances and measures are required for a two-car garage, a kitchen with standard appliances, a bathroom with standard fixtures, windows of the desired type, door allowances, and all the interrelationships which a neophyte would overlook to his or her later regret. If you *have* ideas about disposition of rooms or unusual features, sketch the house on graph paper so that you maintain some idea of scale. Try the four "elevations" so that you see the house from all its exposures and approve of it. Then give the sketches to an architect for finishing. The architect will mark necessary measurements and specify choices and qualities of this or that material where there are several options open. Many of these details will also appear briefly in the building specification sheet. Your lawyer should look over such a form, perhaps draw it up.

Table 9-1 shows a form useful when you deal with either a general contractor or a subcontractor. It should identify in detail what that party should build, the time frame, and the cost.

Finally, in Table 9-2 there is a suggested checklist that you can use as a payment record, a timetable, and a permanent record of monies paid for a building, its remodeling, restoration, or any miscellaneous capital improvements. These factors could affect the capital-gains tax you may eventually pay. You will have, of course, a record of the price a later buyer pays. But the question will probably come up about the cost of the house to you. And, if the IRS happens to audit your return for the year you report the gain, it may very well want to see some proof of the expenses—such as cancelled checks. Keep all of them, and use this kind of schedule as an overall summary—even if you wait 20 years before selling the house. Who knows what the capital gains rate may be 20 years from now. Who knows whether the house you are building *now* will be your primary residence *then* and what the exemption might be if you move to a place of equal or greater value.

**Table 9-1**  Contractor's Agreement Form

### Subcontractors Contract

Subcontractor _____

Address _____

Builder _____

Date _____  Plan No. _____

W. Comp. Ins. Co. and Agent _____

Certificate No. _____  Expiration Date _____

Location of Work _____

Total Price per House _____  ($.....................) Dollars

Terms of Payment _____

Work to Be Performed and Materials To Be Supplied


FOR SUBCONTRACTOR _____
                          *Signature and Title*

FOR BUILDER _____
                          *Signature and Title*

**Table 9-2** Checklist for Construction Project—Building a House on a Country Lot

| Permit No. | | | |
|---|---|---|---|
| Street No. | Between | | |
| Bank or FHA NO. | Sub-Div. | Lot No. | |

Job Begin    Finish

| | Paid | Check No. | Date | | Paid | Check No. | Date |
|---|---|---|---|---|---|---|---|
| Attorney | | | | Lot | | | |
| Architect | | | | Linoleum | | | |
| Abstract | | | | Lumber, rough | | | |
| | | | | Lumber, rough | | | |
| Bricks | | | | Lumber, finish | | | |
| Bricks | | | | Lumber, finish | | | |
| Bricks, cleaning | | | | | | | |
| Bricks, laying | | | | Mirrors | | | |
| Blueprints | | | | Mortgage application | | | |
| Blocks | | | | | | | |
| | | | | Oil | | | |
| Cabinets, kitchen | | | | Oven, stove | | | |
| Caulking | | | | | | | |
| Carpenter, rough | | | | Plastering | | | |
| Carpenter, finish | | | | Permits | | | |
| Carpenters, finish | | | | Painting | | | |
| Cement | | | | Painting repair | | | |
| Cement | | | | Plumbing permits | | | |
| Clean house | | | | Plumbing, rough | | | |
| Commission | | | | Plumbing, finish | | | |
| | | | | | | | |
| Deed recording | | | | Roofing | | | |
| Dirt haul | | | | | | | |
| Doors, outside | | | | Sand and gravel | | | |
| Doors | | | | Siding | | | |
| Doors | | | | Stones | | | |
| Drywall | | | | Shades | | | |
| | | | | Steel I beam | | | |
| Excavator | | | | Steel column | | | |
| Electric, rough | | | | Septic tank | | | |
| Electric, finish | | | | Supplies | | | |
| Electric, temporary | | | | Survey | | | |
| Electric bills | | | | Storms, screens | | | |
| | | | | | | | |
| | | | | Tinning | | | |
| Floor | | | | Tile | | | |
| Floor laying | | | | Taxes, city | | | |
| Floor sanding | | | | Taxes, city | | | |
| Formica | | | | Taxes, county | | | |
| | | | | Taxes, county | | | |
| Glazing | | | | Tree removing | | | |
| Glazing repair | | | | Trusses | | | |
| Glass | | | | | | | |
| Gov. stamp | | | | Windows | | | |
| Grading | | | | Weather stripping | | | |
| Gas connection | | | | Wall poured | | | |
| Gas bills | | | | Well | | | |
| | | | | | | | |
| | | | | Miscellaneous | | | |
| Heating | | | | | | | |
| Hardware, rough | | | | Sold for | | | |
| Hardware, finish | | | | Extras | | | |
| | | | | | | | |
| | | | | Deposit | | | |
| Insulation | | | | | | | |
| Insurance | | | | | | | |
| Insurance claims | | | | | | | |

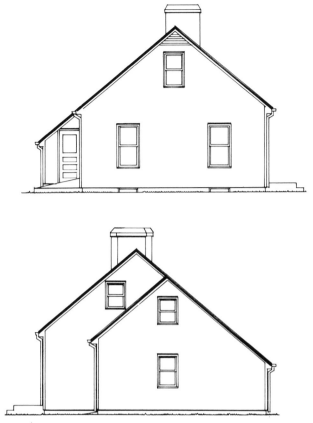

**Figure 9-2** Side views of a country house.

## CONDOMINIUMS—THE POPULAR SHELTER OF THE TWENTY-FIRST CENTURY

The number of condominium units built in the United States each year already exceeds the number of detached single-family homes, and because of rising costs of both land and construction material, it is expected by economists of the construction industry that multifamily units will continue their gains. Condominiums in the city, in the country, in adult communities, in recreational communities, in retirement communities will be the way the majority of people in the United States will shelter themselves in the twenty-first century.

Condominium living is particularly attractive today to young couples, to singles, and to older couples, all of whom have pressing economic reasons for wanting to minimize their investment in shelter yet wanting to *own* it in order to participate in the rising values of real estate. They want to get good, modern, even elegant, housing with minimum time and money spent in maintaining their properties.

Condominiums in the country have for years proven themselves popular as recreational resorts and adult retreats. They are a way to enjoy shelter and access to first-class sports and outdoor facilities which are too inconvenient or too expensive to use extensively in any other living or housing arrangement. The resort condominium can center around skiing,

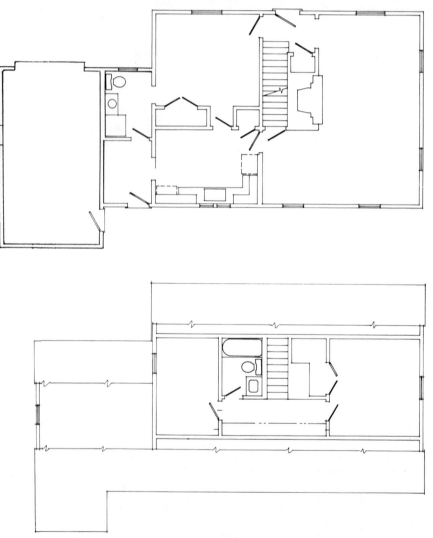

**Figure 9-3** Layout of rooms for a country house.

golf, or boating (by being on a lake or at the seashore). It can emphasize woods and trails, feature stables and horseback riding, have a health club for men and for women, swimming pools, tennis and other racquet-ball courts, jogging trails, and even a marina for yachting. In some cases, in the largest condominium developments, the recreational facilities are likely to include all of these and more. And, with the exception of a modest maintenance charge or recreational fee, you don't have to worry about enormous club dues or upkeep. Condominiums have been built successfully in the sunny deserts of California and Arizona, the mountains of Colorado, the valleys of middle California, the blissful seashores of Florida, the lush landscapes of Hawaii, the misty Atlantic shores near Boston, on the lakes of the Midwest, and on such islands as Martha's Vineyard and Nantucket. Say where you would like to live, relax, have a second, weekend home or a retirement location, and you can find a condominium development there today, already (or partly) built and available for purchase.

*Example: Innovative Conversion to Higher Use on Cape Cod Brings Profit and Stability to an Oceanfront Community*

Mary Grady, with her brothers and sisters, and cousins, had been taken to the Cape as a child every summer and had always hoped that she could continue to spend summers there. Her father had built a cottage colony a dune away from the large main house, and the colony, populated by friends and relatives of friends, brought in substantial rents over the years. In fact, as time passed, the youngsters of the renters married and it seemed that the summer colony was going to be a family colony. In the 1960s some of the experimentally inclined children even stayed over the winter.

But the years took their toll on the cottages. Upkeep and land values surged out of line with the rents which now seemed very modest. But the rents had for years supported the whole enterprise and allowed the senior Gradys to keep the entire place in good shape. Then, suddenly, Mike Grady, Senior, died and everyone wondered what would happen to "Gradyville," as the summer colony was called.

Young Mary persuaded her mother to let her try to sell the various cottages and their small plots of land as condominiums that the renters could take over and improve as they saw fit. This would solve the problem of liquidity in the Estate, and enable the entire Grady family to continue to enjoy the big house. It took only one summer to sell the colony; most renters bought the places they had been renting. If one or two did not, a neighbor or a neighbor's son or daughter would step in and ask for the cottage. Prices ranged from $19,900 to $27,000. In fact, the demand was so enthusiastic that Mary, putting her experience to work, is now selling cottage colonies for other owners on the Cape. She found this was not the only family that had built cottages and had a loyal group of tenants, but now needed to get out from under the maintenance and tax load, to realize some of the phenomenal gains in real estate values, and to put them into a more liquid investment. It is a form of diversifying one's assets.

## DIFFERENCE BETWEEN CONDOMINIUMS AND COOPERATIVES

Many people believe that condominium ownership and cooperative ownership are just about the same thing. They are not, and it is worthwhile to understand the difference. True, both types of ownership of real estate involve multifamily use of a common building or cluster of buildings. But the technical aspects of the ownership are quite different and could affect your profit as an investor.

Condominium ownership, which is relatively new in the United States but has been very common in Europe for decades, involves *individual* fee ownership, that is, outright ownership of space (a family unit) coupled with *common* ownership or right to use the community components of a building such as halls, lobby, elevators, stairs, and basement, plus land and facilities surrounding the building itself.

The developer of the condominium or the community of condominiums, generally establishes a *regime* under the specific statutes governing condominiums as set up by the state in which the condominium has been built. This statutory act is usually called simply a condominium act, but in some states it is still called a *horizontal property regime act*. Under such an act, unit owners can buy, sell, mortgage, and use their individual units as they see fit. Their actions are subject only to restrictions contained in the document establishing the regime and via the bylaws governing the specific condominium.

On the other hand a *cooperative* involves the ownership of stock in a nonprofit corporation which, in turn, owns the multiunit building. With the ownership of the stock, the cooperative owners get a *proprietary lease* granting sole use and occupancy of a specific space in the building. Use of the common elements of the building comes along with the lease; every stockholder gets the same common privileges, although the share of the building and the amount of stock owned may be twice or three times as much as a near neighbor. Few states give statutory authority specifically for cooperatives. Usually they are established under authority providing for nonprofit corporations. In some states the same effect is accomplished by authorizing a mutual-homes association. In general, cooperatives are much older than condominiums in their acceptance as shelter in the United States. Cooperatives have been popular in large cities as a way for tenants to take over older, luxury apartment buildings from landlords who are no longer interested in maintaining the buildings at their intended levels of elegance. New cooperatives are built with the same rationale in mind—the owners, because of their vested interest, will see to it that the building operates to their liking. Sometimes luxury buildings are put up as rental units and then converted to cooperatives later. In large cities such as Chicago and New York the cooperative concept has become so widespread that many buildings housing middle- and low-income families are working out tenant ownership plans along cooperative lines. Cooperatives, in general, are more conservative in their operation than condominiums; they have tended, until recently, to require an all-cash payment upon purchase. The cooperative stockholder can sell stock in the corporation, along with the proprietary lease, but in many cases the individual has no mortgageable interest in his or her apartment. There's usually one mortgage on the entire building, and it is the obligation of the corporation or the mutual-homes association. In the past 10 years, however, with the competition from condominiums and the participation in the movement by middle-class families, banks have found it advantageous to give families personal loans of up to about 75 percent of a cooperative's value. The proprietary lease is held as security for what amounts to a secured personal-installment loan, payable over 10 years at rates of interest somewhat higher than mortgage rates but lower than unsecured personal loans.

In the country, *condominium* ownership is by far the most popular. It is likely to become even more popular because it gives the owner almost as much freedom of action with a particular unit as individual home ownership. And it is admirably flexible when it comes to the operation of common areas and recreational facilities. The developer or sponsor *sometimes* retains ownership or operating rights to common areas and can thus afford to offer actual living units at more reasonable prices. On the other hand, there may come a time when the community of owners feels that it can operate the facilities more efficiently. It may then buy out the remnant interest of the original sponsor. Much of the bad press which condominiums received in their pioneering years was due to these mixed interests and occasional abuse by developers of their remaining concession, on which they made sizable profits. Ever-rising fees for the use of recreational facilities (which early owners did not realize they might have to pay) was a frequent way for developers to keep their oar in the golden flow. Full-disclosure laws passed in states where these complaints arose now eliminate most of these practices and misunderstandings.

*Example: Case of the Growing Popularity of Country Condominiums in the Boston Area*

In 1965 the first condominium in the Boston area was registered as a garden-type unit in Fairgreen, adjacent to a country club. There were great predictions about the future for condominiums but they did not take hold very quickly around Boston. Fourteen years later, a major bank surveyed the condominium market on the South Shore (near Boston) and found that 96 percent of the available condominiums in 18 developments had been sold. This included most of the inventory caught in the 1974–1975 recession.

Within the area studied, 1,874 units had been sold since 1972, the year of the first such development along the South Shore. Of these, 1,711 units had been sold to original buyers, and an estimated additional 300 units had been resold. In two developments which encountered financial difficulty during the recession, sales picked up and only about a dozen units remained unsold. In general, sales prices increased at a rate of 5 to 6 percent a year, less than conventional single-family homes, but good considering the area had been overbuilt at the time of the last recession. At one development, which a bank had to take over, prices were deliberately held below the market to stimulate sales. The strategy paid off. Resale experience, always a worry with new buyers, indicated about a 10 percent turnover; a seller could move a unit in an average of three months if the price were kept about $1,000 below that of new units with the most modern equipment. Such pricing inevitably brought the owner a profit provided he or she had been among the earliest owners. Two-bedroom units made up about 71 percent of the market; they ranged in space from 709 to 1,453 square feet and in price from $25,900 to $53,000. The next most popular were three-bedroom units, which made up 18 percent of the total units, ranged in size from 1,200 to 1,575 square feet, and were priced from $31,000 to $64,000. One bedroom condominiums accounted for 10 percent of the units. They ranged from 544 to 900 square feet and cost from $24,000 to $44,900.

Buyers were a mixed lot. The condominiums seemed to have attracted young married couples buying "starter" homes, retired people who wanted less maintenance worries and an easy mind as they traveled, and a growing number of singles interested in equity, appreciation, and tax advantages.

## THE REWARDS OF COMPARISON SHOPPING FOR CONDOMINIUMS

If you hear of an exceptionally well-designed condominium development in your vicinity, check it out whether the prices are right for you or not and even if you have no intention of buying in your present circumstances. Because condominiums, as shelter, are relatively new on the scene—they first made their appearance in the form of not especially attractive apartment towers or as sprawling two- and three-story blocks housing many families—you owe it to yourself to look over the many new design features which now make them much more gracious, private, and individual, particularly when they are built on country acres. The cluster concept is especially attractive, and Figure 9-4 shows a portion of the model-unit area at Heritage Hills of Westchester, an adult condominium complex near Somers, New York, that has won awards for its excellence in design. When the author last visited this development in mid-1979, there were about 750 units built and sold, with about 2,250 more planned on the extensive, wooded acreage. Already in operation were a nine-hole golf course, tennis courts, and a club house with indoor exercise facilities as well as an outdoor, heated swimming pool. The development had its own sewage disposal system and water supply, a shuttle transportation

**Figure 9-4**   Cluster concept as used at Heritage Hills.

service to local train and bus stations, and a 24-hour security patrol. The construction details of the units were particularly impressive and could serve as touchstones for similar developments.

Figure 9-5 shows various models and Table 9-3 lists their 1979 prices and maintenance costs. Each model comes with a workable wood-burning fireplace, and includes all kitchen appliances, air conditioning, and carpeting. Mortgages are available at 9.5 percent for up to 70 percent of the price and for a term of 25 to 30 years.

The rationale behind the overall design at Heritage Hills has been to preserve the natural beauty of the land and to avoid monotonous repetition of location patterns. The homes are constructed in small groups around courtyards that assure privacy. They are landscaped with the same kinds of trees, shrubs, and rock outcroppings that are characteristic of the 1,000-acre terrain on which the development is built. The one-, two-, and three-bedroom cluster homes emphasize one-level design and are situated on the lesser slopes of a gently rolling, wooded area. From adjacent, enclosed parking areas winding walkways lead into courtyards and to individual, private entrances. Some of the models have attached, enclosed garages; others have carports or garage-storage rooms in separate blocks adjacent to the parking areas. The number and type of buildings in each cluster varies to fit the land contours and to give each owner pleasing views.

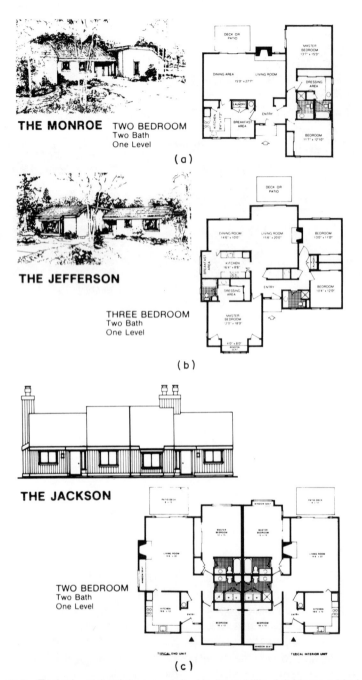

**Figure 9-5** Typical condominium models, Heritage Hills: (a) Monroe Model, (b) Jefferson Model, (c) Jackson Model, (d) Franklin Model, (e) Salem Model, (f) York Model, (g) Croton Model.

## THE FRANKLIN
ONE BEDROOM
One Bath
One Level

( d )

## THE SALEM

TWO BEDROOM
Two Bath
One Level

( e )

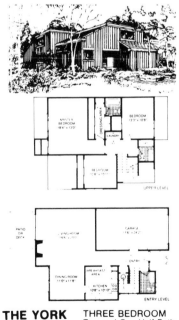

**THE YORK**   THREE BEDROOM
Two and One-Half Bath
Two Levels

( f )

**THE CROTON**   THREE BEDROOM
Two Bath
One Level

( g )

**Table 9-3** Price Ranges and Monthly Costs of Typical Condominium Models

| Model | Cluster houses | Prices | Total estimated monthly housing costs [a] |
|---|---|---|---|
| (D) Franklin | 1 bedroom, 1 bath | $ 64,000– 69,000 | $274.96 |
| (C) Jackson | 2 bedrooms, 2 baths | $ 80,000– 84,000 | $327.36 |
| (A) Monroe | 2 bedrooms, 2 baths | $ 94,000– 98,000 | $381.84 |
| (B) Jefferson | 3 bedrooms, 2 baths | $102,000– 107,000 | $449.59 |
| (B) Jefferson (2 car) | 3 bedrooms, 2 baths | $111,000– 114,000 | $469.86 |
| *Court Houses* (E) Salem | 2 bedrooms, 2 baths | $ 97,000– 102,000 | $408.18 |
| (F) York | 3 bedrooms, 2½ baths | $100,000– 104,000 | $427.25 |
| (G) Croton | 3 bedrooms, 2 baths | $108,000– 110,000 | $475.72 |
| (G) Croton (2 car) | 3 bedrooms, 2 baths | $110,000– 115,000 | $495.86 |

*Source:* Heritage Hills of Westchester

## WHAT TO LOOK FOR IN A CONDOMINIUM—DESIGN FEATURES AND FACILITIES

From your inspection of a leading condominium development such as Heritage Hills you will get an idea of some of the modern facilities and design features you should look for in any *well*-designed condominium. Features will vary, of course, with the geography, but you can use the following, taken from features at Heritage Hills, as a good checklist:

### Architecture

[ ] Private patios or sun decks

[ ] Wood-burning fireplace with built-in screen

[ ]  Convenient storage areas

[ ]  Partially enclosed carport or enclosed garage with storage areas

## Construction

[ ]  Custom features with special sound conditioning

[ ]  Double-pane glass windows and sliding doors

[ ]  All-electric heating and cooling

[ ]  Top-grade exterior siding

[ ]  Extra-heavy insulation in ceilings, walls, floors

[ ]  Abundant wall plugs and TV outlets and fuse-free circuit breakers

## Living Areas

[ ]  Wall-to-wall carpeting throughout in decorator colors

[ ]  Rooms individually air conditioned

[ ]  Rooms with individual heating controls

## Bathrooms

[ ]  Ceramic tile baths

[ ]  American Standard or equivalent quality in fixtures

[ ]  Custom bathroom cabinets

## Kitchens

[ ]  Color-coordinated Formica counter tops

[ ]  Vinyl flooring

[ ]  GE waste disposal

[ ]  GE automatic dishwasher

[ ]  GE full-size refrigerator/freezer

[ ]   GE electric range and oven

[ ]   Range hood with light and two-speed fan

[ ]   Custom cabinets

[ ]   Closeted laundry area with vinyl tile floor
     Optional GE washer and dryer

[ ]   Choice of decorator colors on all appliances with optional choice of
     deluxe models

To these features you ought to add passive solar-heating siting and components in a southern climate, and active solar-heating and cooling features in a northern climate. Since you will pay for your own heating and cooling, no matter what fuel you use, you will find that solar-home innovations in your condominium can save you operating expenses. And they will prove a strong, added attraction should you want to resell your unit.

## ADVANTAGES AND DISADVANTAGES OF CONDOMINIUM OWNERSHIP

The principal advantages of condominium ownership should already be evident to the reader: excellent design and use of proven materials and appliances, plus competent maintenance and repair people on the general premises. Also recreational facilities and scenic locations which are often too expensive for a single-family home may work out very well if shared by several families. Costs are prorated and paid for over many owners rather than by just one. The individual owner in a condominium can enjoy many economies of scale. For the majority of people, the closer sense of community in a country condominium provides a sense of companionship, mutual interests, and a feeling of security. In fact, many condominiums hire their own security force as part of "the family."

You can eventually overcome most disadvantages of condominium ownership. But the best way to buy into a condominium and accumulate capital gain profits, is to buy into one that minimizes the disadvantages. For example, condominium ownership does not give the owner the flexibility of a rental. You have to accept the responsibility of an owner and keep up the interior of your unit. In a recession, when real estate markets are relatively weak, it may be difficult to sell your unit at the price your paper-profit calculations would lead you to expect. Then, too, in a development that continues to expand over a period of years, your older unit may have to compete with new units sold by the sponsor. Also, over a period of years, assessments may be levied against owners for common-area improvements. It is simply a fact of the construction trade, too, that some condominiums lack privacy, have insufficient sound insulation, and otherwise fall short in their construction. With the exception of market disruptions which usually work out over a period of time, you can see that the best way to avoid the other disadvantages is to choose the right development in the right place. This can be done by checking out the experience of people who are already residents, and by checking out the conditions and morale in previous developments sponsored by the same builder or developer.

*Example: The Scharfmans Speculate in an Unbuilt Condominium*
Bob Scharfman had observed how condominium development proceeded in stages. When he was transferred from New York to the Houston headquarters of a major oil company, he and his family decided to live in a new, very attractive country development on the outskirts of the city. The commuting drive to town was not difficult or long, and a commercial bus and school buses passed right in front of the gates to the development, which had all the recreational amenities a growing family could want, in addition to tight security behind a wall along the highway and cyclone fencing along the limits of the property into pine woods.

The Scharfmans sensed that the development would sell well. It would house about 500 families, when all the units were completed, in elegant four-family homes on an acre of land. There were a variety of layouts, offering different numbers of bedrooms, stories, and window exposures.

Until their home in Scarsdale was sold and the children finished school, Bob lived in a rented apartment in downtown Houston. At the same time he and his wife, Betty, bought two of the condominiums in a unit that they personally wanted. One three-bedroom condominium cost $75,000, the other $67,500. They had to put down in escrow only 10 percent of the total, or $14,250.

Nine months later, when the condominiums were ready for occupancy, the prices had gone up 12 percent, so great was the demand. The Scharfmans decided to move into the $75,000 condominium, which was already worth $84,000, and sold the other one to a late arrival who was only too happy to pay $85,000 for it. This is how they wound up with their speculation:

| | |
|---|---|
| Paper profit on own condominium | $ 9,000 |
| Profit on sale of second condominium | 17,500 |
| | $26,500 |

Technically speaking, they made that profit on only $14,250 down. They could have sold their own condominium right then and there for $9,000 more than they paid for it but realized that they wouldn't be able to find as fine a place to live anywhere in Houston for that kind of money. And they knew, if the company were to transfer them again in the next five years or so, that the investment in the well-planned country condominium in a fast-growth area would pay off handsomely.

## CONDOMINIUMS ON LEASED LAND

It is common in Florida and in Hawaii to build condominiums on leased land. In Florida, the original leases are written for at least 98 years so that the residents are eligible for homestead exemption. Different kinds of leaseholds can be used. In Hawaii, the developer has to arrange for each owner to take a lease from the large landholder with whom the developer has a working relationship.

In Florida it would be more common for the developer to own the land and then lease it to individual condominium owners. The lease may or may not include an escalation clause, but it will set up a time frame and rights renewal. Increases in rent are sometimes tied to cost-of-living increases. You should have a real estate lawyer familiar with condominium laws, check out these details carefully. They are often a source of later dispute because of lack of initial understanding.

## MAINTENANCE FEES—WHAT THEY COVER

Maintenance fees differ with developments. Typically, however, they include water, sewer, garage, building insurance, lawn and pool care, and general maintenance of common areas. Some maintenance agreements include funds to paint building exteriors, replace damaged landscaping, roofs, elevators, and paths. In general, however, major or capital expenses are covered by an assessment voted by members of the owner's association.

When you or your lawyer investigate the maintenance fees, determine what other expenses are included in it and what you may have to pay extra for, such as gas, electricity, telephone, personal liability insurance, property taxes, fire insurance, recreation fees, mortgage interest and amortization, and other miscellaneous fees.

## WHAT ABOUT INCOME FROM RENTALS?

You will usually find in the condominium act the rules regarding rental of units. Renting is allowed unless specifically prohibited by the act. In many cases, tenants must be approved by the owners' association, and they must, of course, abide by the same rules and regulations accepted by the original owners. You should find out exactly what the rental experience has been for earlier owners and what provision the management has made to promote and manage rentals.

## WHAT ABOUT RESALES OF UNITS AT A PROFIT?

You will find regulations about resale also in the act. If not, you or your lawyer should examine the written policy, whatever it is, because it may be crucial to your future profitability. Some developments operate with such success that they cheerfully assign to their regular sales personnel the task of reselling. In such case, they will guide you in pricing and will probably take a commission on the sale. Other developers will not touch your resale, but may refer you to a good local realtor who could handle the matter.

Find out what the policy is in the development that looks most attractive to you. If there seem to be obstacles to reselling, find out why they exist. Most of the time a development salesperson will be only too glad to tell you about several successful resales. One of the best ways of overcoming objections to the current price is the fact that resales are bringing as much as or more than equivalent properties.

*Example: Robert and Rita Jackson Decide on a Condominium*
Frankly, Robert and Rita Jackson knew little about the real estate market when they married in Seattle, Washington. They both had good jobs; Robert was a lawyer and Rita was a mathematician. They sensed they would be better off buying a house as soon as they could rather than renting something and paying more for a house in a year or two. They asked their accountant whether it would be better for them—together they earned $32,000 a year—to rent or to buy a house. The accountant said that they could buy more living space in a condominium than in an existing single-family home and that condominiums generally appreciated in value at the same rate as single-family houses, once a development had matured and sold all of its existing properties.

A short checklist (see Table 9-4) was worked out for them so that they could make an informed decision based on the facts they found as they looked at some new condominiums (still building), some completed condominiums, and some possible rentals.

By working out the answers to the checklist in Table 9-4 you will learn the direct monthly costs of ownership. Any honest developer will

**Table 9-4** Checklist of Condominium Information

| Direct Monthly Costs | | Comparable Rental Costs | |
|---|---|---|---|
| Real estate taxes | | Estimated monthly rent | |
|   (monthly) | $_____ |   on a similar unit | $_____ |
| Monthly mortgage | | Fuel | _____ |
|   payment | _____ | Electricity | _____ |
| Common charges | | Water | _____ |
|   Fuel | _____ |     *Total Rental Cost* | $_____ |
|   Electricity | _____ | | |
|   Water | _____ | *Comparative Dollar* | |
|   Insurance | _____ | *Difference* | |
|   Maintenance (janitorial) | _____ | Net direct monthly costs | $_____ |
| Individual charges | | Less total rental costs | _____ |
|   Fuel | _____ |   *Comparative* | |
|   Electricity | _____ |   *difference* | $_____ |
|   Water | _____ | | |
|   Insurance | _____ | *Estimated appreciation of* | |
|     *Total monthly costs* | $_____ | *condo* | |
| | | Five years from purchase | $_____ |
|     Less monthly tax | | Ten years from purchase | $_____ |
|       benefit | _____ | *Estimated opportunity* | |
|     *Net direct monthly* | |   *costs* | $_____ |
|       *cost* | $_____ | Calculate as above for five- or ten-year period comparing with estimated appreciation | |

provide you with a list detailing your direct monthly costs. It is up to you to see that the list is complete and the estimates are realistic.

*Real estate taxes* depend on the local municipality's customs and may be assessed on the appraised value of the property or given as a percentage of the purchase price. The developer may quote you current taxes on a pro rata per unit basis. These taxes may rise based on the purchase price you pay for your fraction of the whole.

*Use of fuel, electricity, and water* generates monthly charges for your unit as well as for common areas that are jointly owned by all. See to it that you get estimates for both portions and that both are metered separately.

*Maintenance and janitor costs* have often been understated by developers. Sometimes these costs are reduced by subsidy. As a potential buyer you will have to cross-examine the developer very aggressively on what these costs do and don't cover, and what future needs and inflation will do to them. Remember, your part of the building will need paint from time to time, and also window and roof repairs.

Most prices for *insurance* will cover premiums for common areas and your building as a whole but *not,* in many cases, for damage to your own particular unit. You may want better coverage for your own unit and you should add this cost to your estimate for insurance.

Your *mortgage amount* is the result you get from subtracting your down payment from the purchase price. Your monthly payment then depends on how long the mortgage is and at what rate of interest the bank carries it. Most developers will have an amortization table supplied by a local bank; be sure that this is the best rate you can get in that locality.

After you have listed these costs, you are ready to figure out how you can reduce them through tax deductions. In general, the more money you earn, the more a condominium investment will save you since real estate taxes and the interest portion of your mortgage payment are tax deductible. For example, if your condominium costs $2,000 a year in interest and $500 in real estate taxes, you have then a $2,500 deductible expense. If you are in a 20 percent tax bracket, your savings will be $400 a year, or $42 a month; if you are in a 40 percent bracket, you will save $1,000 a year, or $82 a month.

Subtracting your tax benefits from total direct costs, you will arrive at a net monthly cost. Compare this with the *rent* you would be paying for that same unit or a similar one. This comparison tells you how much more you pay to buy (rather than rent) the same standard of living. Any cost of ownership in excess of rent for the same shelter is money you could either spend elsewhere or put in the bank to earn interest. As you determine rent for the condominium, do not be misled by overly optimistic promises of the salesperson. Ask previous or present tenants in the development what the going rental rate is.

The difference between ownership costs and rental costs (usually lower) is an amount which economists call an *opportunity cost*. You have to justify this in one way or another, and the most popular way is to point out the expected appreciation in value of the condominium. One further word of caution—your condominium will not begin to increase in value until all similar units in the development are sold. Until then, you will be competing with your developer who is in a better position than you to offer mortgage help and special discounts. If your opportunity cost is considerably larger than realistic appreciation, you are probably better off renting that condominium rather than buying it. You can get a better return for your opportunity money (and greater liquidity) at your local savings bank's on six-month certificates tied to Treasury-bill interest rates.

## WHAT THE DEVELOPER MUST DISCLOSE TO THE PURCHASER BEFORE THE SALE

Although state requirements regarding disclosure in condominium sales vary, you should use the following as a checklist of the documents you and your lawyer should examine. If they cover the ground intended, you should at least know where you stand on the issues of condominium ownership rights and responsibilities.

[ ]   Declaration of condominium, condominium act, or horizontal property regime act—the statutory authority for establishing the condominium

[ ]   Copy of articles of incorporation of association

[ ]   Copy of bylaws of the association

[ ]   Copy of underlying ground lease or deed of ownership

[ ]   Copy of management agreement

[ ]   Copy of recreation lease

[ ]   Copy of projected operating budget

[ ]   Letter concerning easements

[ ]   Floor plan of the apartments

[ ]   Plan of recreation facilities

[ ]   Site and parking plan

At times, these documents may overlap, or be called something else, or be consolidated in a document of a similar title. Often they are included in a property report that federal law requires be given to prospective buyers by a developer engaged in interstate business. It is imperative that you and your lawyer examine these documents, and that their ramifications are explained to you.

Note how often a real estate lawyer can guide you. Through a bank or other business connection—preferably not through a recommendation by the developer, select a real estate lawyer who will represent *your consumer interest* and who has had experience in the geographic area in which your development is located. One regional guide to condominiums recommends three basic rules for buying a condominium: (1) Select a reputable, experienced builder-developer, (2) hire a local attorney who knows real estate laws thoroughly, and (3) follow your attorney's advice.

You may think your relatively small, conservative purchase in a development is not worth all the trouble of hiring an attorney, particularly when the developer has all the papers in order and everything seems spelled out clearly. *That's just why* you need a lawyer; a great deal is usually spelled out as required by law, but only a real estate lawyer can interpret its meaning to you in terms of what you can and cannot do, and what you can and cannot expect in the way of profit. Although your purchase may be relatively small in a bigger scheme, the entire development may be worth many millions and have many escape clauses for the developer written into the various agreements facilitating the buying of the land, the financing of the development and building, the sales projections, and the advertising and sale of the individual parcels. All your pleasures and financial benefits hang on the smooth fulfillment of the dreams you see pictured on paper and partly started around the visitor's reception center. Your lawyer can tell you what escape clause, if any, you can use when promises are not fulfilled. Most of the time promises are fulfilled, and that is why condominium living has become as popular as it is and why so many people in the United States will be living in country condominiums in the years to come.

## PURPOSE OF THE CONDOMINIUM OWNERS' ASSOCIATION

The association of condominium owners serves as the voice of the various owners. The association, to which an owner automatically belongs, elects representatives and officers, organizes committees to work with management, and sometimes itself assumes management control. It approves subsequent purchasers, negotiates bids for changes and improvements, and, in general, governs the condominium. The power of the association will vary with the degree to which the original developer relinquishes control. Developers frequently want to retain control of recreation facilities in order to earn a continuing income from the project after it has matured and all units are sold. Sometimes, for the same reason, the developer retains ownerhsip of all or part of the land and leases it to the owners' association.

## ARE THERE UNRECOGNIZED ADVANTAGES IN USED CONDOMINIUMS?

Once in a while, in an older condominium complex a resale that can be classified as a bargain becomes available. This is so because all sales emphasis is on newly constructed units. They are the ones you hear about and see advertised. Yet now that the concept has gained wider acceptance, the older units bear watching for relative price advantages. The owner's offer to sell may seem rather feeble in relation to the promotional efforts of the developer for the new units. So you may have to be more aggressive in seeking out the bargain that comes to market. Ask local realtors for help, and be sure to ask the sales representative of a development you like about resales in older sections.

There are a number of reasons why older condominiums that have had one or two owners already may be a good buy for you—if everything else proves out.

**1** The older unit may enjoy a location more convenient to recreation facilities, transportation, and shopping. The developer wanted them to sell out quickly, so they often have the most convenient location.

**2** You may get more square feet of shelter for your money because building costs undoubtedly have risen since the older condominium was constructed.

**3** You may be able to pick up the remains of an original mortgage if you have sufficient money for a larger-than-usual down-payment. That may give you a rate of interest substantially below the current market rate.

**4** Operating expenses in the older condominium have balanced out. Unwanted services have probably been eliminated; needed services have been added. You will have a better idea of actual monthly maintenance fees and recreational fees.

**5** Building and facilities will have passed through their shakedown period, and adjustments will have been made for possible minor construction and architectural errors.

**6** Malcontents—those people who made a mistake in choosing condominium living—will have left. In fact you might uncover a very favorable asking price from a family that can't wait to leave its mistake.

**7** A good record for resales probably has been established and thus the marketability of the older condominium units has become more steady and assured.

No matter how attractive the newest units look, remember to ask to see some of the old ones as well. They may tell a tale of endurance under extensive use; in a way, they give you a peek at the future and suggest what you can expect when your own, spankingly new unit (if that is what you finally select) wears a bit.

*Example: Happiness as a Florida Condominium*
Harold and Sally Sussman, who had lived and worked in Pittsburgh for years, wanted to get their share of the Florida sun during the winter and maybe even move down there entirely when they decide to retire. Five years ago they bought a condominium. It was in one of the early developments that was well financed, prospered, and then paused during, but survived, the 1974-1975 recession. Harold and Sally bought their unit when prices were low and the pause was on. Their one-story, two-bedroom place in the sun, built on a concrete slab with a neighboring twin, cost only $19,900. Mortgage, maintenance, utility and property tax bills totaled about $285 per month. The Shorecrest Community had a golf course, health club, tennis and racquet-ball courts, a theater with an auditorium that often featured celebrity entertainers, fully equipped craft centers, and "much more" as the advertising promised and the development's management delivered.

Both of the Sussmans were in radio. Harold managed advertising promotion for one Pittsburgh station, Sally ran the news copy desk for another. They both quickly volunteered for work on the Shorecrest committee which coordinated community entertainments. They expected, for the time being, to spend only a few weeks each year actually living in their new condominium. As soon as they bought it, they took a month's vacation to buy and place inexpensive but attractive furniture in the rooms, to paint, and to do a bit of wallpapering. They had the water and electrical systems checked out thoroughly by a Florida architect-engineer who specialized in home inspections and charged them only $50 for a thorough visit. The engineer was familiar with that particular development and assured the Sussmans that it was well built and that all systems were holding up under moderate use. It was suggested that the Sussmans enclose their corner patio with jalousie blinds and use it as a more private porch. It already had a substantial roof overhang to shade it from the sun. This the Sussmans did.

For the first six months the management of the development supplied older couples who wanted to rent. One couple was "trying out the development" and later bought a unit themselves. The other people were snowbirds, who liked to migrate to different places each spring for two or three months at a time.

Then old friends from Pittsburgh wanted to come down, and before long Harold and Sally had regular and repeating tenants for all of the year they weren't there. Rent came in on the average of $350 per month. And to the Sussman's delight the prices of comparable units had risen to $28,000 after five years. That was an $8,000 gain on the original price of about $20,000, or 40 percent in the five-year period (including a recession). This came to about 8 percent a year in paper gains, as well as sufficient income to cover the mortgage interest, amortization, and all maintenance costs. They regard their Florida condominium as a small but steady money machine. The Sussmans are investigating radio stations in the West Palm Beach and Orlando areas to see if they can find similar jobs in Florida and live there the year-round. They are thinking of continuing the original money-making condominium as a rental and buying a new one in a new section. They expect to decorate it in a more luxurious style to suit themselves. And they expect it to bring in more rent when they are not in residence.

## THE UNDISCOVERED PROFIT POSSIBILITIES OF MOBILE HOMES IN THE COUNTRY

Until the last five years or so, mobile homes were scorned as a family shelter. Families who prayed, played, and stayed together bought recreational vehicles, vans, and campers, but homes on wheels in trailer parks were for some subspecies of humanity—migrant workers and wanderers not interested in putting down roots. Most communities zoned against trailer parks, with their rows of ever-longer trailers, even though trailers were becoming ever more sleek and more luxurious housing.

As the metamorphosis continued, the upgraded trailers became "mobile-home units" and settled into more spacious and landscaped mobile-home parks. For they met a desperate economic need for well-built, inexpensive, compact housing. Today, most of these units are meant to take only one trip—to a permanent foundation in an attractive country setting with many recreational amenities such as tennis courts, swimming pools, convenient shopping facilities, permanent sewer and water hookups and, of course, electricity. Sometimes families, delighted with the ease of installation and the ingenuity of the prefabricating process buy two units, or "double widths," and install them as one house. A family now can easily spend over $100,000 on two or more units placed on multiple park lots.

One of the great attractions of mobile homes is their price. You can still get two-bedroom models for as little as $15,000 delivered and installed. To this cost you will have to add maintenance expenses and rental payments for the lot in the park plus (or including) utility fees. In reality, the mobile home is the prototype for a new wave of manufactured housing modules. Even the industry's trade association, the Mobile Home Manufacturers' Association, has changed its name to the Manufactured Housing Institute.

A marketing consultant for the industry estimates that manufactured homes already account for almost 95 percent of the new single-family homes selling for under $20,000, as well as 70 percent of those in the under-$30,000 market. The same consultant predicts that manufactured homes will represent 33 percent of all housing starts in 1985—more than twice the 16 percent of 1975.

The industry already has weathered one boom-and-bust period. In 1978 the manufacturers of these units shipped over 400,000 homes, a vigorous rebound from the 225,000 units shipped in 1975. During previous boom years in 1972 and 1973 the industry averaged 375,000 homes a year. Woodall's Park Development Service estimates consumer demand at about 450,000 spaces per year. Some families, of course, rent or buy double units.

With the recent inflation, there has been a strong rise in demand for mobile homes because a family of two or three people can still live comfortably, if a bit closely packed, in a manufactured home costing from $15,000 to $20,000. Interest rates for financing still run higher than for conventional houses and are for much shorter terms. Banks are not yet accustomed to thinking of these manufactured homes as permanent. Bankers talk of *loans* rather than of *mortgages,* and the loans customarily are of the personal-installment type that run for from three to five years. There is still the stigma of the house on wheels or the trailer as the parent of the manufactured home, but it is dissolving fast in the face of economic reality.

A typical park will work with one or two manufacturers and thus can standardize foundations and hookups. The park management can also facilitate financing, and will rent a unit if a family sets it up as a second home or encampment in a country recreational area and wants to get an income from it. Zoning laws in many cities and their suburbs, although relaxing in some places, still tend to force mobile-home parks to locations in the country where everyone can enjoy more breathing space and less opposition from neighbors with conventional housing.

In many states there are no property taxes on mobile homes, although there are sometimes personal taxes on them and the trend is moving toward conventional real estate taxes. There is, of course, a real estate tax on the mobile-home *park,* and the tenant pays part of this in the ground rent. It is probable, as local governments become more accustomed to the stability and good design of many mobile homes, that they will be received more hospitably as another kind of development which can house a segment of the population and furnish tax revenue. Already the local police and fire-fighting forces provide the same services for mobile-home owners as they do for condominium owners or for owners of detached single family homes. Investors in mobile homes in the country can deduct from taxes the interest they pay on financing. If the mobile home is used as income property, some of the ground lease and upkeep expenses and also depreciation can be deducted.

In the resale market, mobile homes—unlike automobiles—*appreciate* in value and can be sold *in place.* As banks get used to this, buyers will be able to get long-term mortgages more easily and be able to transfer them. At present, many mobile homes are sold on an installment contract by the manufacturer, who may then sell the receivables to a finance company. Mobile homes sometimes *are* repossessed and hauled away, but this is likely to stop entirely as the concept, like the unit itself, settles into acceptance as a standard country property.

## GROWING ACCEPTANCE BY HUD OF INSURED MORTGAGES ON MOBILE HOMES

One sign of the growing acceptance of mobile homes as a low-priced, permanent housing alternative is the expansion by the U.S. Department of Housing and Urban Development (HUD) of the number of government-insured mortgages it makes available annually for manufactured housing units. It recently doubled the number from 25,000 to 50,000. The Federal Home Loan Bank Board has also acted to make applications for mortgage funds through federally regulated savings institutions more competitive with conventional housing loans. HUD has also put into effect a National Standard for Mobile Homes. This requires an official inspection and certification of each unit before it is delivered and installed on its site. The code is carried out by a network of state and private engineering and inspection agencies—really a built-in inspection system which protects the buyer. It covers fire safety, basic construction, plumbing, fuel-burning systems, and transportation chassis.

As part of the code, there is a recall system, similar to the recall of cars discovered to have flaws or defects. Mobile-home owners are informed of the problem and told what to do about it.

## ADVANTAGES OF MOBILE HOMES OVER SITE-BUILT HOMES

The primary advantage of manufactured housing installed on a leased (or owned) lot is price. The second is design technology. The mobile-home market opens up to people of limited means a modern, well-designed pre-inspected shelter. Figure 9-6 shows a recent award-winning model of a contemporary or mobile manufactured home. Table 9-5 gives some price comparisons between mobile homes and small site-built homes in years gone by. Both price series run higher now.

**Figure 9-6** A contemporary mobile home in an attractive, planned community.

**Table 9-5**  Price Comparison of Mobile Homes and Site-Built Homes

| Mobile homes | 1970 | 1971 | 1972 | 1973 | 1974 |
|---|---|---|---|---|---|
| Average retail price | $ 6,110.00 | $ 6,640.00 | $ 6,950.00 | $ 7,770.00 | $ 9,760.00 |
| Price per square foot | $     8.35 | $     9.07 | $     8.73 | $     8.84 | $    10.63 |
| Square footage | 732 | 780 | 780 | 882 | 910 |
| *Site-built homes* | | | | | |
| Median sales price | $23,400.00 | $25,200.00 | $27,600.00 | $32,500.00 | $35,900.00 |
| Price per square foot | $    13.95 | $    14.55 | $    15.35 | $    17.10 | $    21.00 |
| Median square footage | 1,400 | 1,415 | 1,460 | 1,540 | 1,550 |

Source:  Manufactured Housing Institute.

With preconceptions fading from the minds of bankers and those who pass zoning laws in suburban and country areas, the mobile home and mobile-home park offer what amounts to very low-priced condominium ownership in a development. In fact, some of the owners of highly styled mobile-home parks are organizing their sold-out parks into a development of condominiums, with the various owners, in association, buying the land and governing themselves. The park owner, profits in pocket, then goes on to develop other country parks on a larger scale. This has happened frequently in Florida, where these kinds of communities have mushroomed, have been closely regulated by the state, and have won greater acceptance than in other parts of the country.

*Example: Case of the Retired Widow and Her Mobile Gold Mine*
Marilyn and Bob Byrd were from well-to-do families in Ohio. Bob was a lawyer with a leisurely style and whose innovative ideas usually set his conservative client's teeth on edge. He did, however, play a good game of golf, and so made his way in the world, raised two children, and decided, when he and Marilyn were 55, to relax more and enjoy life. The Byrds could still manage to maintain their winterized summer house on an exclusive lake in Michigan, but did not want to stay there during the icy months when no golf links were open for play. They sold their family home in Cleveland, took their $100,000 one-time capital-gains exemption, and invested the proceeds. They bought a luxurious trailer—a land cruiser, really—and said they were "going to follow the sun" during the winter months. They did—as far as a pleasant oceanside community on the west coast of Florida where they parked for the first winter. There was a good golf course nearby, ocean bathing and fishing, and a lot of midwesterners to talk to, to bowl with, and with whom to enjoy fishing cruises. The Byrds soon put a permanent foundation under their trailer and added to it; there was room on the generous double lot they rented. Marilyn planted a garden; Bob paved a patio and closed in a porch with blinds and screens. The 50 other owners in the park, none as well-off as Bob and Marilyn, nevertheless followed their lead because it was not an expensive one. They all seemed to get on well together. As rents began to climb, Bob proposed

that the tenants get together and buy the land they had been renting. He worked with a local real estate lawyer and through family connections to get a local banker to draw up a workable plan. They put through the purchase when the owner, during the 1974–1975 recession, was caught a bit short financially in the midst of developing another park nearby. The Byrds and their neighbors got the land for a good price and set up an owner's association. They ran their 50-unit development like a small community of condominiums. Bob died shortly after the change, but left Marilyn well-off and proud of their accomplishments. Bob is still known as "the father" of The Anchorage and Marilyn points out that the new prestige of mobile homes and their parks have added substantially to the value of each unit. The Byrds bought their luxury trailer in 1965 for $10,000. They added about $6,000 worth of improvements to it and bought their double lot for $10,000. Today Marilyn's yard and home are worth $85,000 on a total investment of $26,000 plus some trendy thinking and a leisurely country attitude toward life. Marilyn still "goes home" for the summer months to that lake in Michigan, and she sometimes travels during the winter with friends from The Anchorage. She encourages the kids and grandchildren to enjoy The Anchorage for a month or two. The owners, when they took over, saw to it that there were no rules against children.

Of course you don't have to be so easy-going about your good fortune with country property. You can exploit the profitability and move on to something more ambitious. Or you can just eventually relax, enjoy, and share your good fortune with others.

# Selected Charts and Figures of Use to Country Property Buyers and Owners

## Table A-1

### FARM REAL ESTATE: INDEXES OF AVERAGE VALUE PER ACRE (1967=100)

| State | 1969 | 1972 | 1973 | 1974 | 1975 | 1976 | 1977 | 1978 | 1979 |
|---|---|---|---|---|---|---|---|---|---|
| **Northeast** | | | | | | | | | |
| Maine ......... | 120 | | | | | | | | |
| New Hampshire .. | 125 | | | | | | | | |
| Vermont ....... | 133 | | | | | | | | |
| Massachusetts ... | 117 | 174 | 198 | 231 | 257 | 278 | 301 | 332 | 365 |
| Rhode Island .... | 120 | | | | | | | | |
| Connecticut ..... | 121 | | | | | | | | |
| | | | | | | | | | |
| New York ...... | 114 | 155 | 176 | 233 | 275 | 296 | 313 | 318 | 347 |
| New Jersey ..... | 130 | 180 | 211 | 278 | 340 | 377 | 377 | 387 | 418 |
| Pennsylvania .... | 123 | 167 | 201 | 262 | 315 | 350 | 422 | 471 | 537 |
| Delaware ....... | 107 | 134 | 155 | 199 | 242 | 288 | 334 | 374 | 430 |
| Maryland ....... | 125 | 162 | 191 | 227 | 248 | 299 | 316 | 368 | 420 |
| | | | | | | | | | |
| **Lake States** | | | | | | | | | |
| Michigan ....... | 110 | 127 | 150 | 174 | 184 | 201 | 256 | 287 | 319 |
| Wisconsin ...... | 114 | 148 | 179 | 214 | 240 | 271 | 322 | 381 | 446 |
| Minnesota ...... | 112 | 127 | 144 | 186 | 242 | 294 | 369 | 413 | 483 |
| | | | | | | | | | |
| **Corn Belt** | | | | | | | | | |
| Ohio ......... | 110 | 127 | 147 | 184 | 208 | 252 | 331 | 373 | 448 |
| Indiana ........ | 106 | 113 | 131 | 161 | 200 | 244 | 321 | 361 | 415 |
| Illinois ........ | 109 | 116 | 129 | 173 | 209 | 260 | 353 | 390 | 441 |
| Iowa .......... | 111 | 122 | 141 | 189 | 234 | 294 | 397 | 413 | 475 |
| Missouri........ | 119 | 143 | 160 | 207 | 214 | 241 | 284 | 325 | 364 |
| | | | | | | | | | |
| **Northern Plains** | | | | | | | | | |
| North Dakota ... | 117 | 127 | 142 | 193 | 265 | 310 | 349 | 369 | 413 |
| South Dakota ... | 108 | 118 | 130 | 172 | 214 | 241 | 287 | 336 | 380 |
| Nebraska ....... | 113 | 127 | 145 | 183 | 215 | 271 | 307 | 295 | 360 |
| Kansas ......... | 110 | 118 | 137 | 178 | 211 | 235 | 267 | 270 | 310 |
| | | | | | | | | | |
| **Appalachian** | | | | | | | | | |
| Virginia ........ | 110 | 149 | 171 | 223 | 250 | 278 | 302 | 327 | 386 |
| West Virginia .... | 124 | 177 | 211 | 275 | 317 | 398 | 417 | 426 | 498 |
| North Carolina .. | 116 | 138 | 164 | 200 | 216 | 232 | 246 | 253 | 299 |
| Kentucky ...... | 111 | 137 | 153 | 182 | 203 | 239 | 281 | 317 | 374 |
| Tennessee ...... | 117 | 142 | 167 | 206 | 236 | 251 | 275 | 307 | 338 |
| | | | | | | | | | |
| **Southeast** | | | | | | | | | |
| South Carolina .. | 125 | 162 | 179 | 238 | 273 | 284 | 311 | 319 | 373 |
| Georgia ........ | 126 | 175 | 201 | 264 | 298 | 299 | 322 | 357 | 386 |
| Florida[2] ....... | 109 | 136 | 155 | 200 | 224 | 237 | 253 | 273 | 303 |
| Alabama ....... | 117 | 146 | 167 | 211 | 233 | 258 | 275 | 288 | 328 |
| | | | | | | | | | |
| **Delta States** | | | | | | | | | |
| Mississippi ...... | 118 | 129 | 144 | 182 | 204 | 205 | 217 | 249 | 279 |
| Arkansas ....... | 123 | 143 | 159 | 186 | 191 | 213 | 238 | 261 | 316 |
| Louisiana....... | 110 | 139 | 148 | 174 | 191 | 201 | 218 | 251 | 286 |
| | | | | | | | | | |
| **Southern Plains** | | | | | | | | | |
| Oklahoma ...... | 108 | 131 | 150 | 183 | 212 | 234 | 258 | 284 | 312 |
| Texas.......... | 114 | 138 | 156 | 191 | 193 | 213 | 228 | 252 | 282 |
| | | | | | | | | | |
| **Mountain** | | | | | | | | | |
| Montana ....... | 111 | 142 | 159 | 203 | 237 | 278 | 321 | 355 | 394 |
| Idaho.......... | 116 | 141 | 159 | 203 | 243 | 264 | 296 | 320 | 349 |
| Wyoming ....... | 102 | 134 | 153 | 191 | 218 | 254 | 273 | 285 | 322 |
| Colorado ....... | 105 | 128 | 152 | 194 | 209 | 244 | 285 | 305 | 369 |
| | | | | | | | | | |
| New Mexico .... | 112 | 136 | 151 | 186 | 197 | 206 | 227 | 236 | 253 |
| Arizona ........ | 115 | 159 | 170 | 208 | 211 | 217 | 227 | 237 | 254 |
| Utah .......... | 122 | 173 | 186 | 216 | 232 | 261 | 289 | 305 | 326 |
| Nevada ........ | 132 | 213 | 251 | 299 | 299 | 307 | 307 | 341 | 365 |
| | | | | | | | | | |
| **Pacific** | | | | | | | | | |
| Washington ..... | 121 | 130 | 145 | 160 | 178 | 213 | 249 | 268 | 297 |
| Oregon ........ | 120 | 170 | 187 | 213 | 228 | 242 | 254 | 277 | 302 |
| California ...... | 109 | 112 | 114 | 122 | 133 | 136 | 137 | 155 | 191 |
| | | | | | | | | | |
| 48 States ..... | 113 | 132 | 150 | 187 | 213 | 242 | 283 | 308 | 351 |

## Table A-2

### FARM REAL ESTATE: INDEXES OF AVERAGE PER ACRE OF GRAZING LAND (1967=100)

| Year | Mont. | Idaho | Wyo. | Colo. | New Mex. | Ariz. | Utah | Nev. | Wash. | Oreg. | Calif. | 11 Western States | Nebr.[2] | Texas[2] |
|------|-------|-------|------|-------|----------|-------|------|------|-------|-------|--------|-------------------|----------|----------|
| 1950 | 30 | 29 | 34 | 43 | 43 | 23 | 48 | 39 | 33 | 24 | 35 | 34 | | |
| 1951 | 37 | 34 | 41 | 47 | 49 | 26 | 54 | 44 | 38 | 28 | 42 | 39 | | |
| 1952 | 41 | 37 | 45 | 54 | 56 | 30 | 63 | 50 | 42 | 31 | 47 | 45 | | |
| 1953 | 42 | 37 | 45 | 53 | 55 | 33 | 63 | 49 | 46 | 30 | 46 | 45 | | |
| 1954 | 40 | 36 | 43 | 52 | 53 | 33 | 62 | 54 | 45 | 30 | 46 | 44 | | |
| 1955 | 42 | 38 | 42 | 52 | 54 | 32 | 61 | 56 | 47 | 32 | 47 | 45 | | |
| 1956 | 46 | 40 | 44 | 51 | 54 | 34 | 63 | 58 | 48 | 33 | 50 | 47 | | |
| 1957 | 50 | 45 | 47 | 56 | 52 | 38 | 67 | 60 | 50 | 34 | 54 | 50 | | |
| 1958 | 55 | 52 | 52 | 60 | 55 | 41 | 70 | 63 | 52 | 37 | 58 | 54 | | |
| 1959 | 62 | 54 | 58 | 63 | 56 | 42 | 75 | 65 | 54 | 40 | 63 | 58 | | |
| 1960 | 67 | 55 | 59 | 67 | 59 | 44 | 77 | 67 | 56 | 41 | 67 | 61 | 67 | 61 |
| 1961 | 69 | 57 | 70 | 72 | 61 | 50 | 80 | 70 | 64 | 51 | 72 | 66 | 67 | 62 |
| 1962 | 74 | 54 | 77 | 79 | 67 | 58 | 83 | 73 | 63 | 55 | 75 | 70 | 77 | 66 |
| 1963 | 76 | 59 | 81 | 83 | 72 | 64 | 84 | 75 | 73 | 66 | 81 | 76 | 75 | 70 |
| 1964 | 83 | 71 | 74 | 92 | 80 | 73 | 85 | 78 | 81 | 72 | 86 | 81 | 85 | 83 |
| 1965 | 89 | 89 | 89 | 94 | 86 | 81 | 86 | 82 | 84 | 86 | 87 | 86 | 88 | 86 |
| 1966 | 97 | 92 | 89 | 101 | 94 | 91 | 94 | 90 | 87 | 90 | 91 | 92 | 94 | 96 |
| 1967 | 100 | 100 | 100 | 100 | 100 | 100 | 100 | 100 | 100 | 100 | 100 | 100 | 100 | 100 |
| 1968 | 105 | 124 | 103 | 104 | 107 | 108 | 110 | 115 | 120 | 112 | 105 | 108 | 109 | 111 |
| 1969 | 112 | 137 | 103 | 106 | 114 | 119 | 128 | 136 | 130 | 129 | 114 | 117 | 113 | 117 |
| 1970 | 126 | 146 | 118 | 109 | 123 | 135 | 147 | 163 | 138 | 148 | 115 | 126 | 114 | 125 |
| 1971 | 137 | 159 | 118 | 122 | 132 | 150 | 168 | 194 | 143 | 171 | 115 | 134 | 117 | 132 |
| 1972 | 157 | 178 | 135 | 143 | 142 | 175 | 192 | 231 | 151 | 197 | 119 | 148 | 125 | 146 |
| 1973 | 171 | 197 | 159 | 173 | 159 | 190 | 209 | 276 | 180 | 223 | 126 | 164 | 147 | 171 |
| 1974 | 215 | 254 | 197 | 226 | 199 | 231 | 245 | 328 | 197 | 253 | 132 | 190 | 178 | 208 |
| 1975 | 256 | 294 | 226 | 232 | 208 | 231 | 258 | 328 | 215 | 270 | 140 | 203 | 207 | 212 |
| 1976 | 301 | 302 | 271 | 280 | 215 | 238 | 284 | 336 | 264 | 275 | 140 | 217 | 256 | 234 |
| 1977 | 343 | 341 | 288 | 331 | 237 | 244 | 316 | 336 | 299 | 288 | 138 | 231 | 290 | 251 |
| 1978 | 384 | 376 | 294 | 348 | 245 | 257 | 335 | 373 | 320 | 314 | 153 | 249 | 271 | 279 |
| 1979 | 422 | 414 | 332 | 432 | ³265 | ³278 | ³362 | ³403 | 358 | 342 | 190 | 281 | 333 | 312 |

[1] March 1 values for 1950-1975 and February 1 values for 1976-1979. Includes improvements. [2] Data not available for Nebraska and Texas prior to 1960. [3] The average rate of change for these 4 southwestern mountain States was used to calculate the individual State indexes.

## Table A-3

### VALUE PER ACRE OF IRRIGATED LAND (1967=100)

| Year | Mont. | Idaho | Wyo. | Colo. | New Mex. | Ariz. | Utah | Nev. | Wash. | Oreg. | Calif. | 11 Western States | Nebr.[2] | Texas[2] |
|------|-------|-------|------|-------|----------|-------|------|------|-------|-------|--------|-------------------|----------|----------|
| 1950 | 45 | 55 | 46 | 47 | 51 | 51 | 58 | 41 | 52 | 44 | 42 | 46 | | |
| 1951 | 54 | 63 | 51 | 56 | 61 | 58 | 67 | 49 | 60 | 47 | 47 | 53 | | |
| 1952 | 62 | 68 | 53 | 60 | 65 | 64 | 72 | 55 | 67 | 51 | 54 | 59 | | |
| 1953 | 61 | 71 | 53 | 57 | 64 | 67 | 73 | 58 | 70 | 54 | 55 | 60 | | |
| 1954 | 60 | 70 | 51 | 57 | 67 | 66 | 71 | 58 | 69 | 53 | 54 | 59 | | |
| 1955 | 58 | 73 | 53 | 59 | 66 | 71 | 75 | 56 | 71 | 54 | 57 | 62 | | |
| 1956 | 60 | 77 | 55 | 60 | 70 | 73 | 77 | 58 | 73 | 55 | 62 | 65 | | |
| 1957 | 63 | 76 | 55 | 60 | 70 | 79 | 79 | 60 | 77 | 57 | 67 | 68 | | |
| 1958 | 64 | 78 | 60 | 63 | 70 | 84 | 81 | 60 | 78 | 58 | 72 | 72 | | |
| 1959 | 67 | 84 | 64 | 65 | 73 | 91 | 84 | 64 | 79 | 59 | 79 | 77 | | |
| 1960 | 70 | 88 | 68 | 67 | 77 | 97 | 87 | 66 | 81 | 60 | 84 | 81 | 66 | 91 |
| 1961 | 70 | 87 | 70 | 63 | 71 | 97 | 87 | 69 | 81 | 71 | 89 | 84 | 67 | 92 |
| 1962 | 82 | 90 | 73 | 73 | 81 | 98 | 89 | 72 | 82 | 70 | 92 | 87 | 71 | 94 |
| 1963 | 86 | 92 | 74 | 76 | 86 | 98 | 90 | 75 | 84 | 76 | 95 | 90 | 73 | 97 |
| 1964 | 85 | 92 | 74 | 82 | 98 | 98 | 92 | 79 | 86 | 80 | 97 | 92 | 79 | 99 |
| 1965 | 91 | 93 | 85 | 78 | 98 | 99 | 94 | 85 | 89 | 90 | 99 | 95 | 84 | 101 |
| 1966 | 97 | 97 | 83 | 90 | 101 | 100 | 97 | 92 | 95 | 93 | 100 | 97 | 93 | 100 |
| 1967 | 100 | 100 | 100 | 100 | 100 | 100 | 100 | 100 | 100 | 100 | 100 | 100 | 100 | 100 |
| 1968 | 110 | 104 | 98 | 95 | 101 | 101 | 105 | 106 | 106 | 101 | 104 | 103 | 110 | 101 |
| 1969 | 108 | 108 | 96 | 103 | 106 | 101 | 110 | 111 | 110 | 106 | 100 | 103 | 117 | 98 |
| 1970 | 119 | 108 | 111 | 100 | 110 | 102 | 117 | 114 | 112 | 119 | 100 | 105 | 122 | 96 |
| 1971 | 129 | 112 | 125 | 110 | 110 | 102 | 124 | 116 | 113 | 123 | 99 | 107 | 123 | 96 |
| 1972 | 134 | 121 | 130 | 122 | 113 | 103 | 131 | 118 | 115 | 129 | 100 | 110 | 132 | 96 |
| 1973 | 156 | 140 | 135 | 141 | 120 | 104 | 136 | 122 | 125 | 129 | 98 | 114 | 146 | 101 |
| 1974 | 195 | 173 | 170 | 175 | 140 | 129 | 158 | 145 | 136 | 153 | 112 | 134 | 192 | 124 |
| 1975 | 241 | 225 | 186 | 197 | 164 | 142 | 175 | 148 | 145 | 172 | 127 | 154 | 238 | 127 |
| 1976 | 284 | 245 | 195 | 225 | 174 | 147 | 209 | 154 | 168 | 198 | 132 | 167 | 293 | 148 |
| 1977 | 298 | 272 | 223 | 260 | 199 | 175 | 228 | 154 | 200 | 204 | 137 | 181 | 345 | 158 |
| 1978 | 338 | 293 | 255 | 288 | 201 | 175 | 238 | 175 | 208 | 222 | 158 | 200 | 324 | 169 |
| 1979 | 389 | 314 | 293 | 325 | ³209 | ³182 | ³248 | ³182 | 226 | 244 | 190 | 226 | 395 | 188 |

[1] March 1 values for 1950-1975 and February 1 values for 1976-1979. Includes improvements. [2] Data not available for Nebraska, and Texas prior to 1960. [3] The average rate of change for these 4 southwestern mountain States was used to calculate the individual State indexes.

## Table A-4

**FARM REAL ESTATE: INDEXES OF AVERAGE VALUE PER ACRE OF DRY CROPLAND (1967=100)**

| Year | Mont. | Idaho | Wyo. | Colo. | New Mex. | Ariz. | Utah | Nev. | Wash. | Oreg. | Calif. | 11 Western States | Nebr.[2] | Texas[2] |
|------|-------|-------|------|-------|----------|-------|------|------|-------|-------|--------|-------------------|----------|----------|
| 1950 ..... | 39 | 46 | 47 | 54 | 33 | 30 | 42 | 41 | 51 | 43 | 26 | 41 | | |
| 1951 ..... | 47 | 54 | 57 | 65 | 38 | 34 | 46 | 50 | 60 | 50 | 31 | 48 | | |
| 1952 ..... | 52 | 58 | 59 | 70 | 42 | 39 | 51 | 58 | 63 | 50 | 31 | 51 | | |
| 1953 ..... | 54 | 59 | 59 | 69 | 43 | 40 | 54 | 61 | 66 | 55 | 37 | 54 | | |
| 1954 ..... | 54 | 58 | 56 | 68 | 44 | 40 | 55 | 59 | 65 | 53 | 35 | 53 | | |
| 1955 ..... | 57 | 61 | 58 | 64 | 43 | 41 | 53 | 60 | 68 | 55 | 37 | 54 | | |
| 1956 ..... | 61 | 64 | 58 | 66 | 44 | 42 | 52 | 61 | 71 | 59 | 40 | 58 | | |
| 1957 ..... | 64 | 67 | 62 | 64 | 45 | 44 | 55 | 63 | 73 | 62 | 42 | 60 | | |
| 1958 ..... | 68 | 69 | 64 | 68 | 46 | 46 | 57 | 65 | 77 | 63 | 47 | 63 | | |
| 1959 ..... | 74 | 74 | 70 | 73 | 50 | 51 | 62 | 70 | 78 | 65 | 51 | 67 | | |
| 1960 ..... | 77 | 75 | 72 | 76 | 54 | 57 | 65 | 73 | 81 | 65 | 55 | 70 | 71 | 70 |
| 1961 ..... | 77 | 73 | 73 | 76 | 56 | 62 | 75 | 75 | 84 | 77 | 58 | 72 | 71 | 74 |
| 1962 ..... | 81 | 83 | 86 | 84 | 75 | 64 | 72 | 75 | 81 | 79 | 64 | 76 | 75 | 78 |
| 1963 ..... | 83 | 83 | 86 | 93 | 80 | 69 | 77 | 82 | 86 | 86 | 70 | 81 | 75 | 84 |
| 1964 ..... | 86 | 80 | 89 | 92 | 88 | 75 | 74 | 88 | 89 | 90 | 76 | 85 | 80 | 89 |
| 1965 ..... | 89 | 90 | 88 | 92 | 89 | 82 | 83 | 91 | 89 | 102 | 82 | 89 | 85 | 90 |
| 1966 ..... | 96 | 96 | 94 | 101 | 95 | 89 | 90 | 96 | 97 | 104 | 91 | 96 | 91 | 98 |
| 1967 ..... | 100 | 100 | 100 | 100 | 100 | 100 | 100 | 100 | 100 | 100 | 100 | 100 | 100 | 100 |
| 1968 ..... | 110 | 101 | 102 | 101 | 97 | 110 | 111 | 109 | 115 | 104 | 111 | 109 | 108 | 106 |
| 1969 ..... | 111 | 108 | 105 | 105 | 102 | 118 | 127 | 118 | 122 | 116 | 117 | 115 | 112 | 112 |
| 1970 ..... | 125 | 113 | 105 | 103 | 105 | 103 | 140 | 124 | 120 | 135 | 115 | 119 | 114 | 115 |
| 1971 ..... | 121 | 124 | 113 | 104 | 108 | 138 | 160 | 133 | 116 | 144 | 116 | 120 | 116 | 118 |
| 1972 ..... | 121 | 139 | 130 | 111 | 109 | 149 | 181 | 145 | 122 | 159 | 120 | 126 | 127 | 136 |
| 1973 ..... | 143 | 155 | 138 | 132 | 113 | 156 | 194 | 152 | 130 | 175 | 113 | 135 | 144 | 141 |
| 1974 ..... | 187 | 204 | 172 | 164 | 132 | 188 | 218 | 188 | 148 | 196 | 116 | 158 | 184 | 178 |
| 1975 ..... | 204 | 215 | 219 | 186 | 138 | 175 | 250 | 194 | 172 | 205 | 122 | 173 | 214 | 175 |
| 1976 ..... | 240 | 256 | 224 | 208 | 159 | 181 | 286 | 218 | 205 | 224 | 131 | 197 | 273 | 189 |
| 1977 ..... | 292 | 293 | 251 | 241 | 176 | 181 | 321 | 254 | 245 | 242 | 127 | 223 | 306 | 203 |
| 1978 ..... | 313 | 310 | 274 | 252 | 190 | 186 | 329 | 264 | 270 | 264 | 151 | 244 | 300 | 223 |
| 1979 ..... | 360 | 338 | 312 | 292 | [3]211 | NA | [3]365 | [3]293 | 300 | 293 | 181 | 278 | 366 | 252 |

[1] March 1 values for 1950-1975 and February 1 values for 1976-1979. Includes improvements. [2] Data not available for Nebraska and Texas prior to 1960. [3] The average rate of change for these 4 southwestern mountain States was used to calculate the individual State indexes.

## Table A-5

**FARM REAL ESTATE VALUES: AVERAGE VALUE PER ACRE OF LAND AND BUILDINGS AND PERCENT CHANGE FROM THE PREVIOUS YEAR**

| State | March 1, 1973 | | March 1, 1975 | | Feb. 1, 1977 | | Feb. 1, 1978 | | Feb. 1, 1979[1] | |
|---|---|---|---|---|---|---|---|---|---|---|
| | Value | % chg. | Value | % chg. | Value | % chg. | Value | % chg. | Value | % chg. |
| **Northeast** | | | | | | | | | | |
| Maine[2] | $ 253 | 17 | $ 341 | 13 | $ 400 | | $ 441 | | $ 485 | |
| New Hampshire[2] | 404 | 19 | 564 | 14 | 661 | | 729 | | 802 | |
| Vermont[2] | 346 | 16 | 462 | 13 | 541 | | 597 | | 657 | |
| Massachusetts[2] | 766 | 11 | 961 | 10 | 1,126 | 8% | 1,242 | 10% | 1,366 | 10% |
| Rhode Island[2] | 1,124 | 16 | 1,500 | 12 | 1,758 | | 1,939 | | 2,133 | |
| Connecticut[2] | 1,229 | 11 | 1,525 | 9 | 1,779 | | 1,962 | | 2,158 | |
| New York | 356 | 10 | 510 | 15 | 580 | 6 | 589 | 2 | 642 | 9 |
| New Jersey | 1,337 | 9 | 1,807 | 14 | 2,004 | 0 | 2,057 | 3 | 2,222 | 8 |
| Pennsylvania | 491 | 17 | 734 | 18 | 978 | 20 | 1,092 | 12 | 1,245 | 14 |
| Delaware | 645 | 14 | 971 | 20 | 1,340 | 16 | 1,500 | 12 | 1,725 | 15 |
| Maryland | 843 | 15 | 1,060 | 8 | 1,355 | 6 | 1,578 | 16 | 1,799 | 14 |
| **Lake States** | | | | | | | | | | |
| Michigan | 444 | 20 | 553 | 6 | 767 | 27 | 860 | 12 | 955 | 11 |
| Wisconsin | 328 | 20 | 434 | 12 | 583 | 19 | 690 | 18 | 807 | 17 |
| Minnesota | 269 | 12 | 429 | 27 | 652 | 25 | 730 | 12 | 854 | 17 |
| **Corn Belt** | | | | | | | | | | |
| Ohio | 505 | 15 | 706 | 13 | 1,121 | 31 | 1,263 | 13 | 1,516 | 20 |
| Indiana | 494 | 14 | 720 | 22 | 1,159 | 32 | 1,303 | 12 | 1,498 | 15 |
| Illinois | 567 | 9 | 846 | 18 | 1,431 | 36 | 1,581 | 10 | 1,786 | 13 |
| Iowa | 466 | 13 | 719 | 20 | 1,219 | 35 | 1,268 | 4 | 1,458 | 15 |
| Missouri | 294 | 13 | 396 | 3 | 526 | 18 | 602 | 14 | 674 | 12 |
| **Northern Plains** | | | | | | | | | | |
| North Dakota | 108 | 10 | 195 | 35 | 258 | 13 | 273 | 6 | 306 | 12 |
| South Dakota | 94 | 8 | 145 | 22 | 194 | 19 | 227 | 17 | 257 | 13 |
| Nebraska | 193 | 14 | 282 | 17 | 401 | 13 | 385 | -4 | 470 | 22 |
| Kansas | 199 | 14 | 296 | 17 | 376 | 14 | 380 | 1 | 437 | 15 |
| **Appalachian** | | | | | | | | | | |
| Virginia | 391 | 13 | 558 | 11 | 676 | 9 | 732 | 8 | 864 | 18 |
| West Virginia | 204 | 18 | 300 | 15 | 394 | 5 | 403 | 2 | 472 | 17 |
| North Carolina | 461 | 16 | 590 | 7 | 675 | 6 | 694 | 3 | 819 | 18 |
| Kentucky | 327 | 11 | 427 | 11 | 595 | 18 | 671 | 13 | 792 | 18 |
| Tennessee | 346 | 15 | 467 | 13 | 545 | 10 | 608 | 12 | 669 | 10 |
| **Southeast** | | | | | | | | | | |
| South Carolina | 336 | 7 | 467 | 12 | 529 | 9 | 543 | 3 | 635 | 17 |
| Georgia | 329 | 13 | 474 | 12 | 509 | 7 | 564 | 11 | 609 | 8 |
| Florida[3] | 464 | 15 | 685 | 13 | 777 | 7 | 838 | 8 | 930 | 11 |
| Alabama | 267 | 13 | 364 | 10 | 432 | 7 | 452 | 5 | 515 | 14 |
| **Delta States** | | | | | | | | | | |
| Mississippi | 270 | 12 | 379 | 11 | 404 | 6 | 464 | 15 | 520 | 12 |
| Arkansas | 337 | 14 | 419 | 3 | 521 | 12 | 571 | 10 | 691 | 21 |
| Louisiana | 403 | 6 | 512 | 9 | 581 | 8 | 669 | 15 | 763 | 14 |
| **Southern Plains** | | | | | | | | | | |
| Oklahoma | 219 | 13 | 302 | 15 | 365 | 10 | 402 | 10 | 442 | 10 |
| Texas | 196 | 13 | 243 | 1 | 286 | 7 | 316 | 11 | 354 | 12 |
| **Mountain** | | | | | | | | | | |
| Montana | 76 | 12 | 112 | 17 | 152 | 15 | 168 | 11 | 186 | 11 |
| Idaho | 229 | 12 | 339 | 18 | 412 | 12 | 445 | 8 | 485 | 9 |
| Wyoming | 55 | 15 | 80 | 14 | 101 | 7 | 105 | 4 | 119 | 13 |
| Colorado | 137 | 18 | 188 | 7 | 256 | 17 | 274 | 7 | 332 | 21 |
| New Mexico | 56 | 14 | 78 | 7 | 89 | 10 | 93 | 4 | 100 | |
| Arizona | 91 | 6 | 111 | 1 | 120 | 5 | 125 | 4 | 134 | [4]7 |
| Utah | 141 | 10 | 188 | 10 | 235 | 11 | 248 | 6 | 265 | |
| Nevada | 74 | 12 | 85 | 0 | 87 | 0 | 97 | 11 | 104 | |
| **Pacific** | | | | | | | | | | |
| Washington | 273 | 15 | 350 | 14 | 491 | 17 | 528 | 8 | 586 | 11 |
| Oregon | 205 | 10 | 250 | 7 | 278 | 5 | 303 | 9 | 330 | 9 |
| California | 509 | 3 | 653 | 15 | 673 | 1 | 761 | 13 | 936 | 23 |
| 48 States | 246 | 12 | 339 | 13 | 448 | 16 | 488 | 9 | 559 | 15 |

[1] Preliminary. [2] Average rate of change for the 6 New England States was used to project the dollar values for 1976 to 1979. [3] Values are based upon an index estimated from the average of the percentage change in Georgia and Alabama index values. [4] The average rate of change for irrigated and dry cropland and pasture land for the 4 Southwestern mountain States was used to project the dollar value.

## Table A-6

### FARMS RENTED FOR CASH: GROSS CASH RENT PER ACRE AND RATIO OF RENT-TO-VALUE

| State | Rent per acre | | | | Ratio of rent-to-value | | | |
|---|---|---|---|---|---|---|---|---|
| | 1976 | 1977 | 1978 | 1979 | 1976 | 1977 | 1978 | 1979 |
| | · · · Dollars · · · | | | | · · · Percent · · · | | | |
| **Northeast** | | | | | | | | |
| Pennsylvania[3] | 23.50 | 25.70 | 27.80 | 29.40 | 2.7 | 2.7 | 2.6 | 2.3 |
| Delaware | 32.60 | 36.20 | 41.40 | 41.70 | 3.4 | 3.4 | 3.1 | 2.9 |
| Maryland[3] | 23.60 | 26.80 | 27.10 | 37.10 | 2.0 | 2.4 | 1.9 | 2.8 |
| **Lake States** | | | | | | | | |
| Michigan[4] | 30.80 | 35.80 | 37.40 | 40.00 | 5.2 | 5.0 | 4.7 | 4.5 |
| Wisconsin | 30.20 | 36.50 | 39.60 | 42.00 | 6.7 | 6.7 | 6.3 | 5.6 |
| Minnesota[5] | 42.70 | 47.30 | 48.50 | 52.50 | 7.1 | 6.2 | 5.6 | 5.3 |
| **Corn Belt** | | | | | | | | |
| Ohio | 45.60 | 53.00 | 59.60 | 69.00 | 4.5 | 4.7 | 4.6 | 4.1 |
| Indiana | 65.10 | 78.00 | 80.10 | 85.00 | 6.8 | 5.9 | 5.6 | 5.2 |
| Illinois | 68.00 | 81.00 | 85.00 | 92.00 | 5.5 | 4.9 | 4.4 | 4.3 |
| Iowa | 68.60 | 78.00 | 82.00 | 89.00 | 6.2 | 5.6 | 5.3 | 5.0 |
| Missouri[6] | 31.00 | 36.30 | 40.00 | 44.30 | 6.2 | 6.4 | 6.3 | 5.9 |
| **Northern Plains** | | | | | | | | |
| North Dakota | 19.90 | 20.10 | 19.70 | 22.40 | 7.3 | 6.7 | 6.5 | 6.2 |
| South Dakota[7] | 13.90 | 15.60 | 16.50 | 17.80 | 6.6 | 6.4 | 6.1 | 5.9 |
| **Appalachian** | | | | | | | | |
| Virginia | 21.20 | 31.40 | 28.70 | 28.50 | 3.7 | 5.2 | 4.2 | 3.8 |
| North Carolina | 26.70 | 31.70 | 28.50 | 34.40 | 4.3 | 4.7 | 4.1 | 4.5 |
| Kentucky[8] | 30.00 | 39.30 | 38.00 | 40.10 | 5.5 | 6.3 | 5.4 | 4.7 |
| Tennessee | 29.00 | 32.50 | 36.60 | 37.00 | 5.6 | 5.7 | 5.5 | 4.9 |
| **Southeast** | | | | | | | | |
| South Carolina | 18.30 | 20.30 | 21.20 | 23.70 | 4.2 | 4.0 | 3.9 | 3.9 |
| Georgia | 25.00 | 28.30 | 29.20 | 29.40 | 4.7 | 5.1 | 5.0 | 4.7 |
| Florida[9] | 13.50 | 15.70 | 18.40 | 20.30 | 2.3 | 2.3 | 2.7 | 2.3 |
| Alabama | 19.30 | 22.60 | 23.50 | 25.60 | 5.3 | 5.4 | 5.4 | 5.2 |
| **Delta** | | | | | | | | |
| Mississippi | 24.30 | 26.70 | 28.00 | 30.50 | 5.9 | 6.2 | 5.5 | 5.3 |
| Arkansas | 23.30 | 29.00 | 30.80 | 32.90 | 5.5 | 6.0 | 5.3 | 4.7 |
| **Southern Plains** | | | | | | | | |
| Oklahoma[10] | 16.00 | 17.10 | 16.50 | 19.50 | 4.0 | 4.0 | 3.7 | 3.8 |

[1] Revised. Based on data obtained from crop reporters, ESCS, USDA. Selection of States is based upon adequacy of data. [2] Figures omit crop district (CD) No. 3. [3] Figures omit crop district (CD) 1 in 1976-78. [4] Figures omit crop district (CD) 1, 2, 3 and 4. [5] Figures omit crop district (CD) 2 and 3. [6] Figures omit crop district (CD) 8. [7] Figures omit crop district (CD) 7. [8] Figures omit crop district (CD) 4. [9] Figures omit crop district (CD) 8. [10] Figures omit crop district (CD) 9.

## Table A-7

### CROPLAND RENTED FOR CASH: GROSS CASH RENT PER ACRE AND RATIO OF RENT-TO-VALUE

| State | 1976 | 1977 | 1978 | 1979 | 1976 | 1977 | 1978 | 1979 |
|---|---|---|---|---|---|---|---|---|
| | · · · Dollars · · · | | | | · · · Percent · · · | | | |
| **Northeast** | | | | | | | | |
| New Hampshire | 23.20 | 23.00 | 26.00 | 26.80 | 4.1 | 3.5 | 3.3 | 2.9 |
| Vermont | 19.70 | 20.70 | 21.10 | 22.40 | 4.7 | 4.3 | 4.2 | 3.6 |
| Massachusetts | 25.30 | 29.00 | 29.00 | 30.40 | 2.8 | 2.7 | 2.4 | 2.3 |
| Connecticut | 24.40 | 26.00 | 28.60 | 31.90 | 1.8 | 1.8 | 1.8 | 1.9 |
| New York[2] | 24.90 | 27.50 | 28.40 | 29.20 | 6.6 | 6.9 | 6.8 | 6.9 |
| Pennsylvania[3] | 24.90 | 27.80 | 30.70 | 32.60 | 2.6 | 2.6 | 2.4 | 2.2 |
| Delaware | 33.60 | 38.00 | 42.50 | 45.60 | 2.8 | 3.3 | 3.1 | 3.0 |
| Maryland[4] | 25.00 | 30.20 | 30.30 | 40.80 | 2.2 | 2.5 | 2.1 | 2.9 |
| **Lake States** | | | | | | | | |
| Michigan[5] | 32.50 | 39.50 | 37.70 | 41.60 | 5.3 | 5.3 | 4.7 | 4.6 |
| Wisconsin | 37.90 | 42.60 | 46.20 | 48.00 | 7.1 | 6.7 | 6.4 | 5.6 |
| Minnesota[6] | 46.60 | 51.40 | 54.00 | 58.30 | 7.0 | 6.2 | 5.7 | 5.3 |
| **Corn Belt** | | | | | | | | |
| Ohio | 50.80 | 59.80 | 68.00 | 76.80 | 5.2 | 4.8 | 4.6 | 4.2 |
| Indiana | 72.00 | 87.00 | 86.00 | 91.70 | 6.7 | 6.0 | 5.6 | 5.3 |
| Illinois | 75.80 | 89.00 | 93.00 | 99.00 | 5.7 | 5.0 | 4.5 | 4.3 |
| Iowa | 76.90 | 90.00 | 92.00 | 98.50 | 6.3 | 5.7 | 5.4 | 5.1 |
| Missouri[7] | 40.80 | 46.50 | 50.90 | 57.80 | 6.8 | 6.8 | 6.7 | 6.5 |
| **Northern Plains** | | | | | | | | |
| North Dakota | 25.00 | 25.20 | 24.70 | 27.80 | 7.7 | 7.0 | 6.6 | 6.4 |
| South Dakota[8] | 20.50 | 23.00 | 23.40 | 25.50 | 7.1 | 6.8 | 6.4 | 6.1 |
| Nebraska (Nonirrigated) | 31.10 | 35.10 | 36.30 | 41.00 | 6.3 | 6.4 | 6.4 | 6.1 |
| (Irrigated) | 79.40 | 88.30 | 87.80 | 91.60 | 7.5 | 7.4 | 7.5 | 7.0 |
| Kansas (Nonirrigated) | 23.30 | 24.80 | 25.40 | 27.90 | 6.2 | 6.0 | 5.5 | 5.4 |
| (Irrigated) | 59.10 | 57.50 | 51.70 | 58.80 | 8.3 | 7.4 | 7.4 | 7.3 |
| (All cropland) | 25.80 | 27.00 | 27.20 | 30.00 | 6.4 | 6.2 | 5.7 | 5.6 |
| **Appalachian** | | | | | | | | |
| Virginia | 31.40 | 36.90 | 36.00 | 34.30 | 4.3 | 4.8 | 4.4 | 3.8 |
| North Carolina | 28.60 | 36.40 | 34.50 | 37.10 | 4.0 | 4.5 | 4.3 | 4.1 |
| Kentucky[9] | 40.60 | 49.50 | 50.00 | 51.90 | 6.8 | 7.0 | 6.0 | 5.0 |
| Tennessee | 37.80 | 41.10 | 43.10 | 47.10 | 6.4 | 6.0 | 5.9 | 5.5 |
| **Southeast** | | | | | | | | |
| South Carolina | 20.70 | 22.70 | 23.60 | 27.60 | 4.0 | 4.0 | 3.9 | 4.0 |
| Georgia | 30.60 | 32.90 | 30.60 | 36.10 | 5.4 | 5.3 | 4.7 | 4.7 |
| Alabama | 23.80 | 27.20 | 28.80 | 31.60 | 5.6 | 5.6 | 5.9 | 5.4 |
| **Delta** | | | | | | | | |
| Mississippi | 32.90 | 33.80 | 35.10 | 38.60 | 7.0 | 6.5 | 5.8 | 5.7 |
| Arkansas | 35.30 | 34.00 | 39.70 | 42.20 | 6.9 | 6.1 | 6.1 | 5.2 |
| **Southern Plains** | | | | | | | | |
| Oklahoma[10] | 22.90 | 25.70 | 24.60 | 28.00 | 4.7 | 4.8 | 4.4 | 4.3 |
| Texas (Nonirrigated)[11] | 16.00 | 17.00 | 17.80 | 18.30 | 4.3 | 4.1 | 3.8 | 3.6 |

[1] Revised. Based on data obtained from crop reporters. Selection of States is based upon adequacy of data. [2] Figures omit crop district (CD) No. 3, 8, and 9. [3] Figures omit crop district (CD) No. 3. [4] Figures omit crop district (CD) No. 1. [5] Figures omit crop district (CD) No. 1, 2, 3, and 4. [6] Figures omit crop district (CD) No. 2 and 3. [7] Figures omit crop district (CD) No. 8. [8] Figures omit crop district (CD) No. 7. [9] Figures omit crop district (CD) No. 4. [10] Figures omit crop district (CD) No. 9. [11] Figures omit crop district (CD) No. 60.

## Table A-8

### PASTURE RENTED FOR CASH: GROSS CASH RENT PER ACRE
### AND RATIO OF RENT-TO-VALUE

| State | Rent per acre | | | | Ratio of rent-to-value | | | |
|---|---|---|---|---|---|---|---|---|
| | 1976 | 1977 | 1978 | 1979 | 1976 | 1977 | 1978 | 1979 |
| | ...Dollars... | | | | ...Percent... | | | |
| **Northeast** | | | | | | | | |
| Maine[2] | 10.60 | 10.40 | 10.80 | 12.20 | 5.5 | 4.4 | 3.9 | 4.1 |
| Connecticut | 13.10 | 14.00 | 15.30 | 17.40 | 2.4 | 1.5 | 1.7 | 1.6 |
| New York[3] | 9.80 | 11.00 | 11.00 | 13.50 | 6.9 | 7.6 | 6.4 | 7.2 |
| Pennsylvania[4] | 11.50 | 12.50 | 13.50 | 14.10 | 2.5 | 2.1 | 2.2 | 1.8 |
| **Lake States** | | | | | | | | |
| Wisconsin | 15.80 | 17.20 | 18.40 | 20.20 | 6.8 | 6.1 | 5.6 | 5.0 |
| Minnesota[5] | 15.70 | 19.00 | 17.50 | 21.10 | 6.4 | 6.1 | 5.3 | 4.9 |
| **Corn Belt** | | | | | | | | |
| Ohio | 16.00 | 20.30 | 18.20 | 24.90 | 3.8 | 3.9 | 3.0 | 3.1 |
| Illinois | 23.20 | 27.80 | 29.10 | 30.20 | 4.6 | 4.0 | 3.5 | 3.2 |
| Iowa | 30.00 | 33.90 | 30.10 | 35.00 | 6.0 | 5.1 | 4.6 | 4.6 |
| Missouri[6] | 18.40 | 21.40 | 21.90 | 22.60 | 5.1 | 5.4 | 5.1 | 4.5 |
| **Northern Plains** | | | | | | | | |
| North Dakota | 7.20 | 7.60 | 7.40 | 7.80 | 5.5 | 5.0 | 4.8 | 4.4 |
| South Dakota[7] | 6.70 | 7.80 | 7.90 | 9.20 | 5.4 | 5.5 | 5.2 | 5.4 |
| Nebraska | 8.00 | 8.70 | 9.10 | 10.20 | 5.2 | 4.9 | 5.3 | 5.0 |
| Kansas | 8.60 | 9.10 | 9.60 | 11.60 | 3.7 | 3.5 | 3.6 | 3.8 |
| **Appalachian** | | | | | | | | |
| Virginia[8] | 14.70 | 17.60 | 15.80 | 18.40 | 3.4 | 3.4 | 2.9 | 3.1 |
| Kentucky[9] | 15.90 | 19.00 | 17.30 | 22.50 | 3.8 | 4.1 | 3.5 | 3.6 |
| Tennessee | 15.70 | 17.40 | 20.00 | 20.30 | 3.2 | 3.4 | 3.5 | 3.3 |
| **Southeast** | | | | | | | | |
| South Carolina | 12.90 | 12.90 | 13.40 | 15.40 | 3.3 | 3.2 | 2.7 | 3.0 |
| Georgia | 16.00 | 16.50 | 17.80 | 19.00 | 3.3 | 3.4 | 3.3 | 3.2 |
| Alabama | 10.90 | 11.80 | 12.10 | 13.60 | 3.6 | 3.4 | 3.4 | 3.3 |
| **Delta** | | | | | | | | |
| Arkansas | 10.80 | 12.10 | 12.80 | 15.30 | 3.9 | 4.1 | 3.7 | 3.6 |
| **Southern Plains** | | | | | | | | |
| Oklahoma[10] | 7.80 | 8.30 | 8.40 | 9.80 | 3.0 | 2.9 | 2.6 | 2.7 |
| Texas[11] | 5.30 | 5.40 | 5.40 | 6.00 | 2.1 | 2.0 | 1.8 | 1.8 |

[1] Revised. Based on data obtained from crop reporters, Economics, Statistics, and Cooperatives Service, USDA. Selection of States is based upon adequacy of data. [2] Figures omit crop district (CD) No. 1. [3] Figures omit crop district (CD) No. 3, 8, and 9. [4] Figures omit crop district (CD) No. 3 and 6. [5] Figures omit crop district (CD) No. 2 and 3. [6] Figures omit crop district (CD) No. 8 and 9. [7] Figures omit crop district (CD) No. 7. [8] Figures omit crop district (CD) No. 6. [9] Figures omit crop district (CD) No. 4. [10] Figures omit crop district (CD) No. 9. [11] Figures omit crop district (CD) No. 60, 82, and 97.

## Table A-9

### AVERAGE MONTHLY RATE PER HEAD FOR PASTURING CATTLE
### ON PRIVATELY OWNED LAND

| States | Monthly rate per head | | | | | | |
|---|---|---|---|---|---|---|---|
| | 1973 | 1974 | 1975 | 1976 | 1977 | 1978 | 1979 |
| | ...Dollars... | | | | | | |
| Montana | 4.80 | 6.60 | 7.00 | 7.40 | [2]7.30 | 7.40 | 8.40 |
| Idaho | 4.40 | 5.40 | 5.60 | 6.10 | 6.20 | 6.60 | 7.70 |
| Wyoming | 5.00 | 5.80 | 6.30 | 7.10 | 7.70 | 7.50 | 7.80 |
| Colorado | 5.10 | 5.50 | 5.80 | 6.30 | 6.60 | 6.80 | 7.60 |
| New Mexico | 4.10 | 4.40 | 4.90 | 5.20 | [3]5.80 | 5.20 | 6.70 |
| Utah | 4.80 | 5.00 | 5.50 | 6.00 | 6.90 | 6.40 | 7.50 |
| Washington | 4.40 | 5.30 | 5.30 | 5.80 | 5.80 | 5.60 | 5.60 |
| Oregon | 4.20 | 5.10 | 5.10 | 5.20 | 5.30 | 5.30 | 5.80 |
| California | 4.70 | 5.20 | 5.70 | 7.00 | 8.50 | 7.70 | 8.10 |
| 9 State Ave. | 4.70 | 5.40 | 5.80 | 6.50 | 7.20 | 6.90 | 7.50 |
| 11 State Ave | 4.60 | 5.30 | 5.70 | | | | |

[1] Based on data obtained from crop reporters, Economics, Statistics, and Cooperatives Service, USDA. Selection of States is based upon adequacy of data. [2] Figure omits crop District (CD) No. 8. [3] Figure omits CD No. 7. [4] The 11 State average, including Nevada and Arizona, is shown for 1973-75 for comparison with the 9-State average.

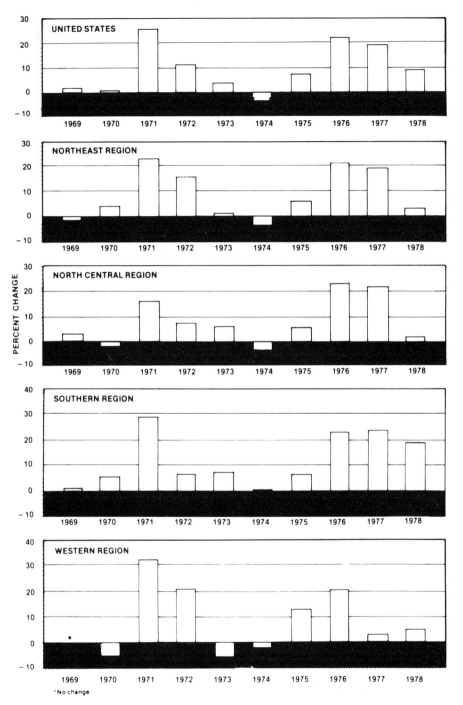

**Figure A-1** Percent change in existing home sales for the United States and each region, 1969-1978.

MEDIAN
PRICE

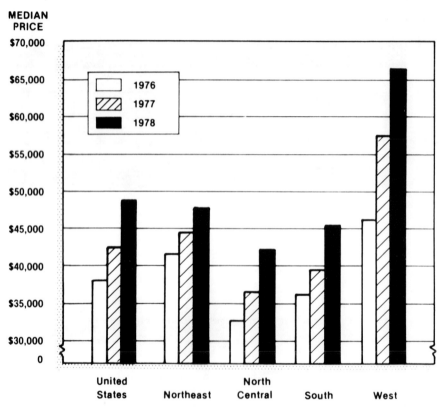

**Figure A-2** Median sales prices of existing single-family homes for the United States and each region, 1976, 1977, and 1978.

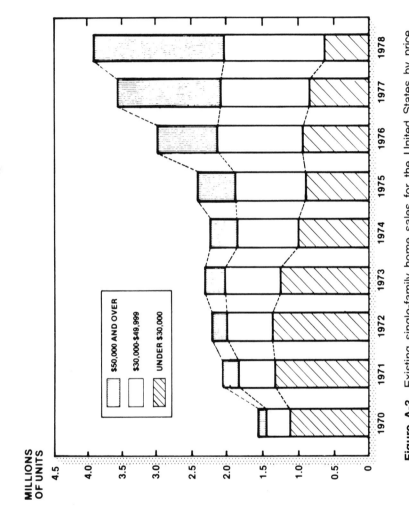

**Figure A-3** Existing single-family home sales for the United States by price class.

## Table A-10

### DOLLAR VOLUME OF EXISTING SINGLE-FAMILY HOME SALES FOR THE UNITED STATES MONTHLY, 1968-1978
*(Not Seasonally Adjusted in Billions of Dollars)*

| Month | 1968 | 1969 | 1970 | 1971 | 1972 | 1973 | 1974 | 1975 | 1976 | 1977 | 1978 |
|---|---|---|---|---|---|---|---|---|---|---|---|
| Jan | $ 2.1 | $ 2.6 | $ 2.6 | $ 3.3 | $ 4.1 | $ 5.3 | $ 5.6 | $ 5.1 | $ 7.2 | $ 9.1 | $ 12.1 |
| Feb | 2.5 | 2.8 | 2.7 | 3.7 | 4.7 | 5.9 | 6.2 | 6.2 | 8.4 | 10.5 | 13.3 |
| Mar | 2.9 | 3.3 | 3.1 | 4.9 | 5.9 | 7.2 | 7.7 | 7.6 | 11.1 | 14.7 | 18.3 |
| Apr | 3.0 | 3.5 | 3.5 | 5.1 | 5.5 | 6.9 | 8.1 | 8.6 | 11.1 | 14.4 | 18.1 |
| May | 3.3 | 3.7 | 3.6 | 5.2 | 6.2 | 7.5 | 8.4 | 9.0 | 11.1 | 15.5 | 20.7 |
| Jun | 3.3 | 3.8 | 4.2 | 5.5 | 6.7 | 7.8 | 7.8 | 9.5 | 13.0 | 16.5 | 21.0 |
| Jul | 3.6 | 3.8 | 4.2 | 5.5 | 6.3 | 7.7 | 8.4 | 9.2 | 12.1 | 15.6 | 19.8 |
| Aug | 3.5 | 3.6 | 4.2 | 5.4 | 6.8 | 7.5 | 8.0 | 9.4 | 12.6 | 17.6 | 22.7 |
| Sep | 3.1 | 3.3 | 3.8 | 4.7 | 5.8 | 5.7 | 6.1 | 8.7 | 11.4 | 15.3 | 19.0 |
| Oct | 3.2 | 3.2 | 3.5 | 4.3 | 5.5 | 5.9 | 5.8 | 8.5 | 10.4 | 14.2 | 19.2 |
| Nov | 2.6 | 2.5 | 3.1 | 4.2 | 4.9 | 5.2 | 5.0 | 7.1 | 9.7 | 13.7 | 17.4 |
| Dec | 2.2 | 2.2 | 2.7 | 3.5 | 4.0 | 4.0 | 4.2 | 6.7 | 8.7 | 11.4 | 13.7 |
| Annual | $35.0 | $37.8 | $41.4 | $56.5 | $67.8 | $76.8 | $81.3 | $95.6 | $126.7 | $171.1 | $216.7 |

Components may not agree with totals due to rounding.

## Table A-11

### SALES OF EXISTING SINGLE-FAMILY HOMES FOR THE UNITED STATES BY PRICE CLASS, 1968-1978
*(Percentage Distribution)*

| Price Class | 1968 | 1969 | 1970 | 1971 | 1972 | 1973 |
|---|---|---|---|---|---|---|
| $19,999 or under | 49.9 | 43.6 | 38.6 | 31.2 | 26.5 | 21.5 |
| $20,000-$29,999 | 32.1 | 32.8 | 34.2 | 35.8 | 34.4 | 32.0 |
| $30,000-$39,999 | 11.4 | 14.1 | 15.9 | 18.4 | 20.5 | 22.1 |
| $40,000-$49,999 | 3.9 | 5.4 | 6.3 | 8.1 | 9.6 | 11.7 |
| $50,000-$59,999 | | | | | | |
| $60,000-$69,999 | | | | | | |
| $70,000-$79,999 | | | | | | |
| $80,000-$89,999 | | | | | | |
| $90,000-$99,999 | | | | | | |
| $100,000-$119,999 | 2.7 | 4.1 | 5.0 | 6.5 | 9.0 | 12.7 |
| $120,000-$159,999 | | | | | | |
| $160,000-$199,999 | | | | | | |
| $200,000-$249,999 | | | | | | |
| $250,000 and over | | | | | | |
| Total | 100.0 | 100.0 | 100.0 | 100.0 | 100.0 | 100.0 |
| Median Price | $20,100 | $21,800 | $23,000 | $24,800 | $26,700 | $28,900 |

| Price Class | 1974 | 1975 | 1976 | 1977 | 1978 | |
|---|---|---|---|---|---|---|
| $19,999 or under | 17.1 | 13.3 | 10.6 | 7.5 | 5.4 | |
| $20,000-$29,999 | 28.0 | 23.9 | 21.0 | 17.2 | 12.5 | |
| $30,000-$39,999 | 23.9 | 24.1 | 22.6 | 20.4 | 17.4 | |
| $40,000-$49,999 | 14.1 | 16.3 | 17.6 | 17.3 | 16.8 | |
| $50,000-$59,999 | | 9.4 | 11.2 | 12.9 | 14.0 | |
| $60,000-$69,999 | | 5.5 | 6.7 | 9.0 | 11.3 | |
| $70,000-$79,999 | | 3.0 | 3.9 | 5.5 | 7.3 | |
| $80,000-$89,999 | | 1.7 | 2.3 | 3.6 | 4.8 | |
| $90,000-$99,999 | 16.9 | | | | 3.2 | |
| $100,000-$119,999 | | | | | 2.8 | |
| $120,000-$159,999 | | 2.8 | 4.1 | 6.6 | 2.8 | 10.5 |
| $160,000-$199,999 | | | | | 1.0 | |
| $200,000-$249,999 | | | | | 0.4 | |
| $250,000 and over | | | | | 0.3 | |
| Total | 100.0 | 100.0 | 100.0 | 100.0 | 100.0 | |
| Median Price | $32,000 | $35,300 | $38,100 | $42,900 | $48,700 | |

## Table A-12

### MEDIAN SALES PRICE OF EXISTING SINGLE-FAMILY HOMES
### FOR THE UNITED STATES, MONTHLY, 1968-1978
*(Not Seasonally Adjusted)*

| Month | 1968 | 1969 | 1970 | 1971 | 1972 | 1973 | 1974 | 1975 | 1976 | 1977 | 1978 |
|---|---|---|---|---|---|---|---|---|---|---|---|
| Jan | $19,700 | $21,100 | $22,200 | $23,700 | $25,300 | $27,400 | $30,600 | $33,200 | $36,300 | $39,600 | $45,500 |
| Feb | 19,900 | 21,000 | 22,500 | 24,200 | 25,400 | 28,000 | 30,600 | 33,900 | 36,200 | 40,700 | 46,300 |
| Mar | 19,700 | 21,200 | 22,800 | 24,300 | 25,900 | 28,400 | 31,400 | 34,200 | 37,200 | 41,000 | 46,500 |
| Apr | 20,000 | 21,500 | 22,900 | 24,600 | 26,300 | 28,500 | 31,700 | 34,900 | 37,700 | 42,000 | 48,200 |
| May | 20,100 | 21,600 | 23,100 | 25,100 | 26,900 | 28,800 | 32,100 | 35,200 | 37,600 | 42,200 | 47,800 |
| Jun | 20,700 | 22,200 | 23,300 | 25,100 | 27,300 | 29,200 | 32,900 | 36,200 | 38,600 | 43,400 | 48,400 |
| Jul | 20,800 | 23,000 | 23,700 | 25,400 | 27,500 | 29,900 | 33,000 | 35,900 | 38,900 | 43,700 | 49,400 |
| Aug | 20,600 | 22,600 | 23,500 | 25,300 | 27,400 | 29,900 | 32,900 | 36,800 | 39,400 | 43,900 | 50,300 |
| Sep | 20,500 | 21,700 | 23,100 | 24,800 | 27,000 | 29,100 | 32,400 | 35,800 | 38,700 | 43,800 | 50,200 |
| Oct | 20,100 | 21,900 | 22,700 | 24,800 | 26,900 | 28,900 | 31,900 | 35,400 | 38,500 | 44,000 | 50,100 |
| Nov | 20,500 | 22,100 | 23,200 | 25,100 | 27,000 | 29,700 | 32,100 | 35,700 | 38,800 | 44,500 | 50,700 |
| Dec | 20,900 | 22,000 | 22,800 | 24,900 | 27,100 | 29,500 | 32,700 | 35,800 | 39,000 | 44,200 | 50,900 |
| Annual | $20,100 | $21,800 | $23,000 | $24,800 | $26,700 | $28,900 | $32,000 | $35,300 | $38,100 | $42,900 | $48,700 |

## Table A-13

### AVERAGE (MEAN) SALES PRICE OF EXISTING SINGLE-FAMILY HOMES
### FOR THE UNITED STATES, MONTHLY, 1968-1978
*(Not Seasonally Adjusted)*

| Month | 1968 | 1969 | 1970 | 1971 | 1972 | 1973 | 1974 | 1975 | 1976 | 1977 | 1978 |
|---|---|---|---|---|---|---|---|---|---|---|---|
| Jan | $21,800 | $23,200 | $24,600 | $26,100 | $28,000 | $30,900 | $34,400 | $36,900 | $40,200 | $44,000 | $50,300 |
| Feb | 22,100 | 23,300 | 24,800 | 26,600 | 28,000 | 31,600 | 34,500 | 37,600 | 40,100 | 45,100 | 51,300 |
| Mar | 22,000 | 23,400 | 25,100 | 26,600 | 28,600 | 32,200 | 35,200 | 38,000 | 41,200 | 45,500 | 51,100 |
| Apr | 22,300 | 23,800 | 25,200 | 27,300 | 29,000 | 32,500 | 35,600 | 38,800 | 41,700 | 46,500 | 53,600 |
| May | 22,400 | 24,000 | 25,300 | 27,800 | 29,600 | 32,800 | 35,800 | 39,000 | 42,900 | 46,800 | 54,800 |
| Jun | 22,900 | 24,400 | 25,700 | 27,700 | 29,900 | 33,400 | 36,600 | 40,000 | 41,900 | 47,700 | 55,100 |
| Jul | 23,000 | 24,800 | 26,100 | 28,000 | 30,200 | 34,000 | 36,800 | 39,600 | 43,200 | 48,000 | 56,500 |
| Aug | 22,800 | 24,700 | 25,900 | 28,000 | 30,200 | 33,800 | 37,700 | 40,600 | 43,400 | 48,100 | 57,500 |
| Sep | 22,600 | 23,900 | 25,400 | 27,600 | 29,700 | 33,200 | 36,100 | 39,400 | 42,700 | 47,900 | 57,700 |
| Oct | 22,400 | 24,100 | 25,000 | 27,400 | 29,600 | 32,800 | 35,400 | 38,900 | 42,400 | 48,200 | 57,300 |
| Nov | 22,600 | 24,500 | 25,700 | 27,900 | 29,700 | 33,500 | 35,900 | 39,300 | 42,900 | 48,500 | 57,400 |
| Dec | 23,100 | 24,300 | 25,300 | 27,600 | 29,700 | 33,300 | 36,100 | 39,400 | 43,300 | 48,300 | 58,100 |
| Annual | $22,300 | $23,700 | $25,700 | $28,000 | $30,100 | $32,900 | $35,800 | $39,000 | $42,200 | $47,900 | $55,500 |

## Table A-14

**SALES PRICE OF EXISTING SINGLE-FAMILY HOMES
FOR THE UNITED STATES AND EACH REGION, 1968-1978**
*(Not Seasonally Adjusted)*

| Year | United States Median | Average (Mean) | Northeast Median | Average (Mean) | North Central Median | Average (Mean) | South Median | Average (Mean) | West Median | Average (Mean) |
|------|--------|--------|--------|--------|--------|--------|--------|--------|--------|--------|
| 1968 | $20,100 | $22,300 | $21,400 | $24,200 | $18,200 | $19,900 | $19,000 | $22,000 | $22,900 | $25,200 |
| 1969 | 21,800 | 23,700 | 23,700 | 26,600 | 19,000 | 21,100 | 20,300 | 23,500 | 23,900 | 26,700 |
| 1970 | 23,000 | 25,700 | 25,200 | 28,400 | 20,100 | 22,600 | 22,200 | 25,300 | 24,300 | 27,400 |
| 1971 | 24,800 | 28,000 | 27,100 | 30,600 | 22,100 | 24,300 | 24,300 | 27,800 | 26,500 | 29,700 |
| 1972 | 26,700 | 30,100 | 29,800 | 33,600 | 23,900 | 25,700 | 26,400 | 30,100 | 28,400 | 32,300 |
| 1973 | 28,900 | 32,900 | 32,800 | 36,800 | 25,300 | 28,100 | 29,000 | 33,200 | 31,000 | 35,400 |
| 1974 | 32,000 | 35,800 | 35,800 | 39,700 | 27,700 | 30,600 | 32,300 | 36,200 | 34,800 | 39,000 |
| 1975 | 35,300 | 39,000 | 39,300 | 43,600 | 30,100 | 33,100 | 34,800 | 38,800 | 39,600 | 44,100 |
| 1976 | 38,100 | 42,200 | 41,800 | 45,900 | 32,900 | 35,900 | 36,500 | 40,900 | 46,100 | 50,300 |
| 1977 | 42,900 | 47,900 | 44,400 | 49,100 | 36,700 | 40,200 | 39,800 | 45,000 | 57,300 | 63,200 |
| 1978 | 48,700 | 55,500 | 47,900 | 55,200 | 42,200 | 45,700 | 45,100 | 51,300 | 66,700 | 75,500 |

## Table A-15

**SALES OF EXISTING SINGLE-FAMILY HOMES FOR THE
UNITED STATES BY NUMBER OF BEDROOMS
FOR SELECTED YEARS**
*(Percentage Distribution)*

| Number of Bedrooms | 1968 | 1970 | 1972 | 1974 | 1976 | 1978 |
|------|------|------|------|------|------|------|
| Two Bedrooms or less | 21.1 | 20.8 | 19.0 | 18.5 | 18.1 | 18.7 |
| Three Bedrooms | 56.5 | 55.0 | 54.9 | 55.4 | 55.5 | 55.8 |
| Four Bedrooms or more | 22.4 | 24.2 | 26.1 | 26.1 | 26.4 | 25.5 |
| Total | 100.0 | 100.0 | 100.0 | 100.0 | 100.0 | 100.0 |

## Table A-16

**SALES OF EXISTING SINGLE-FAMILY HOMES
FOR THE UNITED STATES AND EACH REGION
BY NUMBER OF BEDROOMS, 1978**
*(Percentage Distribution)*

| Number of Bedrooms | United States | Northeast | North Central | South | West |
|------|------|------|------|------|------|
| Two Bedrooms or less | 18.7 | 11.4 | 22.1 | 16.7 | 20.0 |
| Three Bedrooms | 55.8 | 51.3 | 57.7 | 57.3 | 53.0 |
| Four Bedrooms or more | 25.5 | 37.3 | 20.2 | 26.0 | 27.0 |
| Total | 100.0 | 100.0 | 100.0 | 100.0 | 100.0 |

## Table A-17

### RESIDENT POPULATION–STATES: 1960 TO 1978

Estimates as of **July 1**. Includes Armed Forces stationed in area. See p. 2 for basis of estimates. For explanation of methodology, see source. For enumerated population, 1920 to 1970, see table 10. Minus sign (−) denotes decrease. For explanation of average annual percent change, see Guide to Tabular Presentation]

| DIVISION AND STATE | 1960 (1,000) | 1965 (1,000) | 1970 (1,000) | 1975 (1,000) | 1976 (1,000) | 1977 (1,000) | 1978 POPULATION, prel. Rank order | Total (1,000) | Per sq. mi. of land area¹ | AVG ANNUAL PCT CHANGE 1950–1960 | 1960–1970 | 1970–1978 |
|---|---|---|---|---|---|---|---|---|---|---|---|---|
| U.S. | ²179,979 | ²193,526 | ²203,806 | 213,032 | ²214,680 | 216,383 | (X) | 218,059 | 61.7 | 1.7 | 1.3 | .8 |
| N.E. | 10,532 | 11,329 | 11,883 | 12,187 | 12,205 | 12,238 | (X) | 12,256 | 194.7 | 1.2 | 1.2 | .4 |
| Maine | 975 | 997 | 997 | 1,058 | 1,071 | 1,084 | 38 | 1,091 | 35.3 | .6 | .2 | 1.1 |
| N.H. | 609 | 676 | 742 | 812 | 827 | 850 | 42 | 871 | 96.5 | 1.4 | 2.0 | 2.0 |
| Vt. | 389 | 404 | 446 | 472 | 477 | 482 | 48 | 487 | 52.6 | .3 | 1.4 | 1.1 |
| Mass. | 5,160 | 5,502 | 5,706 | 5,814 | 5,791 | 5,777 | 10 | 5,774 | 737.8 | 1.0 | 1.0 | .1 |
| R.I. | 855 | 893 | 951 | 931 | 936 | 937 | 39 | 935 | 891.3 | .8 | 1.1 | −.2 |
| Conn. | 2,544 | 2,857 | 3,041 | 3,100 | 3,102 | 3,107 | 24 | 3,099 | 637.4 | 2.4 | 1.8 | .2 |
| M.A. | 34,270 | 36,122 | 37,274 | 37,269 | 37,195 | 37,066 | (X) | 36,825 | 367.1 | 1.3 | .8 | −.2 |
| N.Y. | 16,838 | 17,734 | 18,268 | 18,076 | 18,053 | 17,932 | 2 | 17,748 | 371.1 | 1.3 | .8 | −.4 |
| N.J. | 6,103 | 6,767 | 7,193 | 7,333 | 7,339 | 7,338 | 9 | 7,327 | 974.2 | 2.3 | 1.7 | .2 |
| Pa. | 11,329 | 11,620 | 11,813 | 11,860 | 11,802 | 11,796 | 4 | 11,750 | 261.3 | .8 | .4 | −.1 |
| E.N.C. | 36,291 | 38,406 | 40,313 | 40,945 | 40,918 | 41,066 | (X) | 41,233 | 168.9 | 1.7 | 1.1 | .3 |
| Ohio | 9,734 | 10,201 | 10,664 | 10,735 | 10,690 | 10,696 | 6 | 10,749 | 262.3 | 2.0 | .9 | .1 |
| Ind. | 4,674 | 4,922 | 5,202 | 5,313 | 5,313 | 5,350 | 12 | 5,374 | 148.9 | 1.7 | 1.1 | .4 |
| Ill. | 10,086 | 10,693 | 11,128 | 11,197 | 11,193 | 11,228 | 5 | 11,243 | 201.7 | 1.4 | 1.0 | .1 |
| Mich. | 7,834 | 8,357 | 8,890 | 9,111 | 9,113 | 9,148 | 7 | 9,189 | 161.7 | 2.0 | 1.3 | .4 |
| Wis. | 3,962 | 4,232 | 4,429 | 4,589 | 4,610 | 4,644 | 16 | 4,679 | 85.9 | 1.4 | 1.1 | .7 |
| W.N.C. | 15,424 | 15,819 | 16,360 | 16,690 | 16,797 | 16,903 | (X) | 17,018 | 33.5 | .9 | .6 | .5 |
| Minn. | 3,425 | 3,592 | 3,815 | 3,921 | 3,954 | 3,975 | 19 | 4,008 | 50.5 | 1.3 | 1.1 | .6 |
| Iowa | 2,756 | 2,742 | 2,832 | 2,861 | 2,874 | 2,888 | 26 | 2,896 | 51.8 | .5 | .3 | .3 |
| Mo. | 4,326 | 4,467 | 4,688 | 4,767 | 4,787 | 4,822 | 15 | 4,860 | 70.4 | .9 | .8 | .5 |
| N. Dak. | 634 | 649 | 620 | 637 | 645 | 650 | 46 | 652 | 9.4 | .2 | −.2 | .6 |
| S. Dak. | 683 | 692 | 668 | 681 | 686 | 688 | 44 | 690 | 9.1 | .4 | −.2 | .4 |
| Nebr. | 1,417 | 1,471 | 1,488 | 1,544 | 1,552 | 1,555 | 35 | 1,565 | 20.5 | .7 | .5 | .6 |
| Kans. | 2,183 | 2,206 | 2,249 | 2,280 | 2,299 | 2,320 | 32 | 2,348 | 28.7 | 1.3 | .3 | .5 |
| S.A. | 26,091 | 28,743 | 30,805 | 33,658 | 33,934 | 34,251 | (X) | 34,579 | 129.5 | 2.1 | 1.7 | 1.4 |
| Del. | 449 | 507 | 551 | 579 | 582 | 582 | 47 | 583 | 294.1 | 3.4 | 2.1 | .7 |
| Md. | 3,113 | 3,600 | 3,938 | 4,122 | 4,125 | 4,137 | 18 | 4,143 | 418.9 | 2.8 | 2.4 | .6 |
| D.C. | 765 | 797 | 756 | 712 | 700 | 685 | (X) | 674 | (³) | −.5 | −.1 | −1.4 |
| Va. | 3,986 | 4,411 | 4,659 | 4,981 | 5,052 | 5,095 | 13 | 5,148 | 129.4 | 1.9 | 1.6 | 1.2 |
| W. Va. | 1,853 | 1,786 | 1,751 | 1,799 | 1,832 | 1,853 | 34 | 1,860 | 77.3 | −.8 | −.6 | .8 |
| N.C. | 4,573 | 4,863 | 5,098 | 5,441 | 5,462 | 5,515 | 11 | 5,577 | 114.3 | 1.2 | 1.1 | 1.1 |
| S.C. | 2,392 | 2,494 | 2,597 | 2,816 | 2,844 | 2,878 | 25 | 2,918 | 96.5 | 1.2 | .8 | 1.5 |
| Ga. | 3,956 | 4,332 | 4,607 | 4,931 | 4,984 | 5,041 | 14 | 5,084 | 87.5 | 1.4 | 1.5 | 1.2 |
| Fla. | 5,004 | 5,848 | 6,848 | 8,277 | 8,353 | 8,466 | 8 | 8,594 | 158.9 | 5.9 | 3.2 | 2.8 |
| E.S.C. | 12,073 | 12,627 | 12,839 | 13,515 | 13,689 | 13,836 | (X) | 14,001 | 78.2 | .5 | .6 | 1.1 |
| Ky. | 3,041 | 3,140 | 3,231 | 3,387 | 3,436 | 3,468 | 23 | 3,498 | 88.2 | .4 | .6 | 1.0 |
| Tenn. | 3,575 | 3,798 | 3,937 | 4,173 | 4,234 | 4,292 | 17 | 4,357 | 105.4 | .7 | 1.0 | 1.3 |
| Ala. | 3,274 | 3,443 | 3,451 | 3,615 | 3,653 | 3,691 | 22 | 3,742 | 73.8 | .5 | .5 | 1.0 |
| Miss. | 2,182 | 2,246 | 2,220 | 2,341 | 2,365 | 2,385 | 30 | 2,404 | 50.8 | (Z) | .2 | 1.0 |
| W.S.C. | 17,010 | 18,209 | 19,388 | 20,867 | 21,361 | 21,705 | (X) | 22,046 | 51.5 | 1.5 | 1.3 | 1.6 |
| Ark. | 1,789 | 1,894 | 1,932 | 2,110 | 2,117 | 2,152 | 33 | 2,186 | 42.1 | −.6 | .8 | 1.5 |
| La. | 3,260 | 3,496 | 3,652 | 3,806 | 3,875 | 3,930 | 20 | 3,966 | 88.3 | 1.9 | 1.1 | 1.0 |
| Okla. | 2,336 | 2,440 | 2,567 | 2,715 | 2,770 | 2,817 | 27 | 2,880 | 41.9 | .5 | .9 | 1.4 |
| Tex. | 9,624 | 10,378 | 11,236 | 12,237 | 12,599 | 12,806 | 3 | 13,014 | 49.6 | 2.2 | 1.6 | 1.8 |
| Mt. | 6,916 | 7,740 | 8,348 | 9,625 | 9,820 | 10,060 | (X) | 10,289 | 12.0 | 3.1 | 1.9 | 2.6 |
| Mont. | 679 | 706 | 698 | 746 | 755 | 766 | 43 | 785 | 5.4 | 1.4 | .3 | 1.5 |
| Idaho | 671 | 686 | 718 | 813 | 833 | 856 | 41 | 878 | 10.6 | 1.3 | .7 | 2.5 |
| Wyo. | 331 | 332 | 334 | 376 | 391 | 406 | 49 | 424 | 4.4 | 1.3 | (Z) | 3.0 |
| Colo. | 1,769 | 1,985 | 2,223 | 2,541 | 2,575 | 2,625 | 28 | 2,670 | 25.7 | 2.9 | 2.3 | 2.3 |
| N. Mex. | 954 | 1,012 | 1,023 | 1,144 | 1,172 | 1,196 | 37 | 1,212 | 10.0 | 3.3 | .7 | 2.1 |
| Ariz. | 1,321 | 1,584 | 1,792 | 2,212 | 2,249 | 2,305 | 31 | 2,354 | 20.8 | 5.7 | 3.1 | 3.4 |
| Utah | 900 | 991 | 1,066 | 1,203 | 1,232 | 1,270 | 36 | 1,307 | 15.9 | 2.6 | 1.7 | 2.5 |
| Nev. | 291 | 444 | 493 | 590 | 613 | 637 | 45 | 660 | 6.0 | 6.0 | 5.4 | 3.6 |
| Pac. | 21,368 | 24,254 | 26,600 | 28,274 | 28,750 | 29,251 | (X) | 29,811 | 33.4 | 3.4 | 2.2 | 1.4 |
| Wash. | 2,855 | 2,967 | 3,413 | 3,559 | 3,611 | 3,681 | 21 | 3,774 | 56.7 | 1.8 | 1.8 | 1.3 |
| Oreg. | 1,772 | 1,937 | 2,101 | 2,284 | 2,326 | 2,385 | 29 | 2,444 | 25.4 | 1.5 | 1.7 | 1.9 |
| Calif. | 15,870 | 18,585 | 20,007 | 21,198 | 21,522 | 21,887 | 1 | 22,294 | 142.6 | 4.0 | 2.3 | 1.4 |
| Alaska | 229 | 271 | 304 | 365 | 408 | 413 | 50 | 403 | .7 | 5.4 | 2.9 | 3.5 |
| Hawaii | 642 | 704 | 774 | 868 | 884 | 891 | 40 | 897 | 139.6 | 2.6 | 1.9 | 1.8 |

X  Not applicable.   Z  Less than .05 percent.   ¹ For area figures used to derive these data, see table 344.   ² U.S. total revised. State data revisions not available; therefore, detail will not add to total.   ³ 11,049.2.

Source: U.S. Bureau of the Census, *Current Population Reports*, series P-25, Nos. 460, 727, and 799.

## Table A-18

COMPONENTS OF POPULATION CHANGE—STATES: 1960-1970 AND 1970-1977

[In thousands, except percent. Total resident population. For explanation of methodology, see source. Minus sign (−) denotes decrease or net outmigration. See also *Historical Statistics, Colonial Times to 1970,* series C 25–75]

| STATE | APRIL 1, 1960, TO APRIL 1, 1970 | | | | | APRIL 1, 1970, TO JULY 1, 1977 | | | | |
| | Net change | | Births | Deaths | Net total migra-tion[2] | Net change | | Births | Deaths | Net total migra-tion[2] |
| | Num-ber | Per-cent[1] | | | | Num-ber | Per-cent[1] | | | |
| United States | 23,912 | 13.3 | 39,033 | 18,192 | 3,070 | 13,081 | 6.4 | 23,874 | 13,978 | 3,185 |
| New England | 1,338 | 12.7 | 2,169 | 1,147 | 316 | 391 | 3.3 | 1,180 | 824 | 35 |
| Maine | 24 | 2.5 | 203 | 109 | −69 | 91 | 9.1 | 117 | 78 | 51 |
| New Hampshire | 131 | 21.5 | 133 | 71 | 69 | 112 | 15.2 | 87 | 54 | 79 |
| Vermont | 55 | 14.1 | 85 | 45 | 15 | 37 | 8.4 | 52 | 31 | 17 |
| Massachusetts | 541 | 10.5 | 1,040 | 574 | 74 | 88 | 1.5 | 546 | 404 | −54 |
| Rhode Island | 90 | 10.5 | 171 | 93 | 13 | −12 | −1.3 | 91 | 67 | −36 |
| Connecticut | 497 | 19.6 | 537 | 255 | 214 | 75 | 2.5 | 287 | 190 | −23 |
| Middle Atlantic | 3,034 | 8.9 | 6,725 | 3,749 | 59 | −147 | −.4 | 3,734 | 2,679 | −1,202 |
| New York | 1,458 | 8.7 | 3,361 | 1,852 | −51 | −309 | −1.7 | 1,816 | 1,293 | −863 |
| New Jersey | 1,101 | 18.2 | 1,259 | 645 | 488 | 166 | 2.3 | 721 | 487 | −67 |
| Pennsylvania | 475 | 4.2 | 2,105 | 1,252 | −378 | −4 | − | 1,167 | 900 | −272 |
| East North Central | 4,028 | 11.1 | 7,832 | 3,652 | −153 | 803 | 2.0 | 4,687 | 2,698 | −1,186 |
| Ohio | 946 | 9.7 | 2,047 | 975 | −126 | 39 | .4 | 1,223 | 716 | −468 |
| Indiana | 531 | 11.4 | 1,023 | 475 | −16 | 155 | 3.0 | 630 | 350 | −126 |
| Illinois | 1,033 | 10.2 | 2,153 | 1,077 | −43 | 117 | 1.1 | 1,294 | 780 | −397 |
| Michigan | 1,052 | 13.4 | 1,754 | 729 | 27 | 266 | 3.0 | 1,052 | 556 | −229 |
| Wisconsin | 466 | 11.8 | 856 | 395 | 4 | 226 | 5.1 | 487 | 295 | 34 |
| West North Central | 930 | 6.0 | 3,133 | 1,604 | −599 | 576 | 3.5 | 1,836 | 1,176 | −85 |
| Minnesota | 391 | 11.5 | 744 | 327 | −25 | 174 | 4.6 | 423 | 213 | −6 |
| Iowa | 68 | 2.4 | 541 | 291 | −183 | 62 | 2.2 | 307 | 209 | −36 |
| Missouri | 358 | 8.3 | 857 | 502 | 2 | 145 | 3.1 | 524 | 367 | −12 |
| North Dakota | −15 | −2.3 | 135 | 55 | −94 | 32 | 5.3 | 76 | 41 | −2 |
| South Dakota | −14 | −2.1 | 146 | 65 | −94 | 21 | 3.2 | 82 | 48 | −13 |
| Nebraska | 72 | 5.1 | 291 | 146 | −73 | 70 | 4.7 | 175 | 108 | 3 |
| Kansas | 70 | 3.2 | 419 | 218 | −130 | 71 | 3.1 | 250 | 160 | −19 |
| South Atlantic | 4,700 | 18.1 | 5,965 | 2,598 | 1,332 | 3,573 | 11.6 | 3,723 | 2,194 | 2,043 |
| Delaware | 102 | 22.8 | 109 | 45 | 38 | 34 | 6.2 | 64 | 35 | 5 |
| Maryland | 822 | 26.5 | 740 | 303 | 385 | 213 | 5.4 | 411 | 237 | 40 |
| District of Columbia | −7 | −1.0 | 182 | 89 | −100 | −72 | −9.5 | 83 | 57 | −97 |
| Virginia | 682 | 17.2 | 909 | 369 | 141 | 443 | 9.5 | 543 | 291 | 191 |
| West Virginia | −116 | −6.2 | 339 | 190 | −265 | 109 | 6.3 | 210 | 143 | 43 |
| North Carolina | 526 | 11.5 | 1,032 | 412 | −94 | 430 | 8.5 | 633 | 335 | 132 |
| South Carolina | 208 | 8.7 | 573 | 216 | −149 | 287 | 11.1 | 359 | 173 | 100 |
| Georgia | 646 | 16.4 | 975 | 379 | 51 | 453 | 9.9 | 624 | 307 | 136 |
| Florida | 1,838 | 37.1 | 1,107 | 596 | 1,326 | 1,675 | 24.7 | 798 | 615 | 1,492 |
| East South Central | 754 | 6.3 | 2,665 | 1,213 | −698 | 1,028 | 8.0 | 1,661 | 942 | 310 |
| Kentucky | 181 | 6.0 | 647 | 313 | −153 | 247 | 7.7 | 408 | 212 | 81 |
| Tennessee | 357 | 10.0 | 755 | 353 | −45 | 366 | 9.3 | 478 | 282 | 170 |
| Alabama | 177 | 5.4 | 729 | 319 | −233 | 246 | 7.2 | 445 | 249 | 50 |
| Mississippi | 39 | 1.8 | 534 | 228 | −267 | 169 | 7.6 | 330 | 169 | 8 |
| West South Central | 2,371 | 14.0 | 4,012 | 1,599 | −42 | 2,379 | 12.3 | 2,655 | 1,314 | 1,037 |
| Arkansas | 137 | 7.7 | 401 | 193 | −71 | 229 | 11.9 | 250 | 156 | 135 |
| Louisiana | 386 | 11.9 | 832 | 316 | −130 | 285 | 7.8 | 505 | 247 | 26 |
| Oklahoma | 231 | 9.9 | 461 | 244 | 13 | 258 | 10.1 | 314 | 195 | 139 |
| Texas | 1,617 | 16.9 | 2,318 | 847 | 146 | 1,607 | 14.4 | 1,586 | 716 | 737 |
| Mountain | 1,429 | 20.8 | 1,724 | 602 | 307 | 1,770 | 21.4 | 1,265 | 509 | 1,015 |
| Montana | 20 | 2.9 | 144 | 66 | −58 | 71 | 10.3 | 88 | 49 | 32 |
| Idaho | 46 | 6.9 | 146 | 58 | −42 | 143 | 20.0 | 113 | 47 | 77 |
| Wyoming | 2 | .7 | 70 | 28 | −39 | 74 | 22.1 | 48 | 22 | 48 |
| Colorado | 453 | 25.8 | 401 | 163 | 215 | 415 | 18.8 | 290 | 130 | 255 |
| New Mexico | 65 | 6.8 | 263 | 68 | −130 | 179 | 17.6 | 157 | 58 | 80 |
| Arizona | 470 | 36.1 | 365 | 122 | 228 | 529 | 29.8 | 282 | 120 | 367 |
| Utah | 169 | 18.9 | 245 | 65 | −11 | 211 | 19.9 | 219 | 54 | 45 |
| Nevada | 203 | 71.3 | 91 | 31 | 144 | 148 | 30.3 | 67 | 31 | 112 |
| Pacific | 5,328 | 25.1 | 4,808 | 2,028 | 2,547 | 2,708 | 10.2 | 3,132 | 1,643 | 1,219 |
| Washington | 556 | 19.5 | 591 | 284 | 249 | 268 | 7.8 | 379 | 218 | 107 |
| Oregon | 323 | 18.2 | 346 | 182 | 159 | 293 | 14.0 | 242 | 147 | 199 |
| California | 4,236 | 27.0 | 3,634 | 1,511 | 2,113 | 1,916 | 9.6 | 2,343 | 1,236 | 809 |
| Alaska | 76 | 33.6 | 73 | 13 | 16 | 110 | 36.3 | 53 | 11 | 68 |
| Hawaii | 137 | 21.7 | 164 | 37 | 11 | 121 | 15.8 | 115 | 31 | 37 |

−  Represents zero or rounds to zero.
[1] 1960 to 1970 based on 1960 population; 1970 to 1977 based on 1970 population.
[2] Comprises both net immigration from abroad and net interdivisional or interstate migration according to the area shown. Includes movements of persons in the Armed Forces.

Source: U.S. Bureau of the Census, *Current Population Reports,* series P-25, Nos. 460 and 799.

# A Selective, Annotated Bibliography

Adams, Anthony: *Your Energy Efficient House,* Garden Way Publishing, Charlotte, Vt., 1975.

Shows basic ways to use natural heating and cooling forces in your house as well as with landscaping. A book full of ideas for the person who is remodeling and wants to make country buildings less costly to heat or cool.

Bruns, R. M. (ed.): *How to Buy and Fix up an Old House,* Home-Tech Publications, Bethesda, Md., 1978.

Takes the step-by-step approach to finding and buying an old house, financing the purchase, and then planning, estimating and contracting for the renovation.

Butcher, Lee: *The Condominium Book,* Dow Jones Books, Princeton, N. J., 1975.

This is the comprehensive buyer's guide to getting the most for your money from condominiums, the "shelter of the future" for most U.S. families.

Campbell, Stuart: *Let it Rot,* Garden Way Publishing, Charlotte, Vt., 1975.

Campbell's book covers all dimensions of scientific composting, which becomes, in his words, a fascinating diversion. It guides the reader through all phases for transmuting most kitchen waste into stable humus.

Campbell, Stuart: *Building the House You Can Afford,* Garden Way Publishing, Charlotte, Vt., 1979.

Sorts out for a person building a home what can be done with sweat input and what should be done by a contractor. Promises to save at least 20 percent on building costs without sacrificing quality.

Clegg, Peter, and Ralph Wolfe: *Home Energy for the Eighties,* Garden Way Publishing, Charlotte, Vt., 1979.

A comprehensive sourcebook of alternate energy systems. Solar energy, water power, wind power, and wood heating are covered. Conservation techniques—the best energy investment of all—are applied to the rural and urban home. Includes catalog sections that describe current products and information sources with each chapter.

Cobb, Betsy, and Hubbard Cobb: *City People's Guide to Country Living,* Macmillan, New York, 1973.

For city people who may feel bewildered by the lifestyles of their country cousins. Probably the best book on how to cope, day to day, in the country.

Creedy, Judith, and Norbert F. Wall: *Real Estate Investment by Objective,* McGraw-Hill, New York, 1979.

Shows how to select the type of property—housing, retail, industrial, land, or special-purpose real estate—that will best meet your personal investment objectives. Explains and clarifies the four basic investment objectives: income, turnover, tax shelter, and long-term gain. Although it touches only now and then on country property, its step-by-step logical approach to sorting out motives and objectives applies directly to making profits from country real estate.

Gladstone, Bernard: *Complete Manual of Home Repair,* Times Books, New York, N.Y., 1978.

A complete guide to all types of home repair and home maintenance in one volume. Written from a practical background in maintenance and repair in a language as simple and nontechnical as possible. Photographs and drawings illustrate the various subjects and clarify the directions. Fine for the do-it-yourselfer and a protective guide for those who are shopping for outsiders to do the job.

Halsted, Byron D. (ed.): *Barns, Sheds, and Outbuildings,* Stephen Green Press, Brattleboro, Vt., 1881, 1977.

The most useful in a series of books from this press, which are essentially reprints of nineteenth century how-to-do-it books. Has 257 quaint illustrations which tell a story of progress and which is still of practical use today.

Hayes, Jack (ed.): *Living on a Few Acres,* U.S. Department of Agriculture, Washington, D.C., 1979.

Annual book of useful and carefully edited essays which might, in sum, be considered a handbook for the small farmer. Suggest many government sources of help in obtaining free or nearly free information. Ask your representative for a free copy of the current edition, or write the U.S. Government Printing Office.

Kinney, Jean, and Cle Kinney: *42 Creative Homes That Started as Bargain Buildings,* Funk & Wagnalls, New York, 1974.

Has hundreds of photos, plans, and diagrams showing actual conversions of windmills, lighthouses, jails, churches, service stations, and about every other kind of building that can stir up the imagination of creative renovators.

Maslow, Abraham H.: *Motivation and Personality,* Harper & Row, New York, N.Y., 1970. Paperback.

Revised edition of a basic exploration of human psychology. It builds upon the classical psychologies and enlarges the conception of the human personality by reaching into the higher levels of human nature and stressing its holistic aspects.

Mead, Gretchen, and Nancy Thurber: *Keeping the Harvest,* Garden Way Publishing, Charlotte, Vt., 1976.

A very practical handbook, written by practitioners, of home storage of vegetables and fruits. Contains over 100 new step-by-step photographs of the authors at work, canning, blanching, freezing, drying, salting, pickling, and making jams and juices.

Moral, Herbert R.: *Buying Country Property,* Garden Way Publishing, Charlotte, Vt., 1977.

A short, pioneering work in this field with pithy advice on buying, maintaining, and enjoying country property.

Osgood, William E.: *How to Earn a Living in the Country (Without Farming),* Garden Way Publishing, Charlotte, Vt., 1974.

Contains many case histories of people who have tried farming. Stresses economy, frugality, and hard work.

Philbrick, Helen and John Philbrick: *The Bug Book,* Garden Way Publishing, Charlotte, Vt., 1974.

Identifies more than 100 bugs you are likely to do battle with on your country property. Tells how to deal with your enemies, ways of respecting your friends.

Porter, Sylvia: *Sylvia Porter's Money Book for the 80's,* Doubleday & Company, Inc., Garden City, N.Y., 1979.

Her chapter entitled, "A Roof Over Your Head" in this classic and pioneering book is invaluable for anyone who wants to buy a home in the country or elsewhere. Her column in newspapers and articles in magazines often contains useful advice for homeowners and potential buyers of homes.

Reynolds, Henry, (ed.): *Home-Tech Restoration and Renovation Cost Estimator,* Home-Tech, Bethesda, Md., 1979.

An annual publication which allows you to estimate common costs for restoring and renovating your home. With the manual you will receive an individualized cost modification index to allow for local variations in cost of materials and labor.

Scher, Les: *Finding and Buying Your Place in the Country,* Collier, New York, 1974.

Reviews the process of locating and buying a residence or land in the country. The author is an attorney and consumer advocate and writes from those points of view. Extremely valuable for the buyer who wants to know the legal implications of land purchase. Also includes useful lists of government sources of information.

Schwenke, Karl: *Successful Small-Scale Farming,* Garden Way Publishing, Charlotte, Vt., 1979.

Must reading for anyone who aspires to count dreams of country living on a working farm. Gives necessary down-to-earth advice to dreamers and should spur on those willing to give sweat equity to their own acres.

Shafer, Ronald G., and Michael Sumichrast: *The Complete Book of Home Buying,* Dow Jones Books, Princeton, N.J., 1979.

This book is a slapdash collection of valuable pointers and examples of how to buy a house primarily in the city and the suburbs, but the advice on financing and taking advantage of tax changes, remodeling, and repairing can apply to a country house as well.

Watkins, A.M.: *Buying Land,* Quadrangle, New York, 1975.

The best book to use when you want to buy undeveloped land. Guides you through the financial and bureaucratic maze to possible profits through selection of the right parcel of land and moving it up to its highest and best use.

Watson, Donald: *Designing and Building a Solar House,* Garden Way Publishing, Charlotte, Vt., 1977.

A basic book for understanding how solar energy can heat a house and its water supply. Also has interesting historical review of how other, earlier cultures have used the sun as an energy source in housing.

# Sources of Additional Information

In the case of government agencies, check your nearest metropolitan U.S. Government listings to see which agencies have regional offices near you. Call or write them for information.

*Amrex,* the American Real Estate Exchange, matches buyers and sellers through national WATS lines and a computer-information system. Headquarters, 150 Chestnut at Montgomery Street, San Francisco, California 94111, has a trading floor. Also publishes for members a *Real Estate Market Newsletter.* Particularly good source of information for investors who want to invest $1 million or more in land, ranches, farms.

*Changing Times,* published monthly. Sidney Sulkin Editor, The Kiplinger Washington Editors, Inc., Editor Park, Maryland 20782. Subscriptions $12 a year. Lively listings of published material of help to the home owner. Articles of consumer interest. Mostly about managing personal money for greater value.

*Country Business Services,* 225 Main Street, Brattleboro, Vermont 05301. Conducts seminars for people interested in going into business in the country. Affiliated with *Country Business Broker,* which specializes in the buying and selling of viable businesses in the country.

*Country Journal,* a monthly magazine with articles keyed to people who live in the country or on small farms. Has a literary flair with appeal in its essaylike articles and illustrations to leisurely reading. Subscriptions $13.50 a year. P. O. Box 2405, Boulder, Colorado 80322.

*Country Living*, a bi-monthly magazine published by Good Housekeeping, Rachel Newman, Editor, 959 Eighth Avenue, New York, New York 10019. $1.95 per issue. Ideas in pictures and editorial matter for country-home owners and gardeners.

*Country Property News*, a monthly newsletter. A.M. Koch and J.H. Koch, Editors, 1020 Park Avenue, New York, New York 10028. Subscriptions $22 a year. Regular reports on opportunities for profit in rural land, farms, single- and multifamily homes in the country. Includes updating on maintaining, improving, insuring, buying, financing, and selling, as well as new ideas in development.

*Doane Appraisal Newsletter*, published periodically by The Doane Appraisal Service, 8900 Manchester Road, St. Louis, Missouri 63144. Ask for this newsletter. It carries current prices achieved on recent farm sales and other cost factors in owning and managing land and farms. Doane Agricultural Service, Inc., the parent company, also manages farms for owners and appraises rural, urban, commercial, and industrial properties.

*Federal Housing Administration*, a department of U.S. Department of Housing and Urban Development, Washington, D.C. 20410. Offers many financing plans which can be identified through asking a regional FHA office or by writing to Washington headquarters.

*Garden Way Publishing*, Charlotte, Vermont, 05445. A publishing house that specializes in all manner of quality paperback originals of use to the country property owner and potential buyer. A number of outstanding titles are listed in Appendix B. Write for a free catalog of current books in print.

*Housesmiths Newsletter*, a quarterly. James Brooks, Editor. Subscriptions $6 a year. Write Dovetail Press, Ltd., Box 1496, Boulder, Colorado 80306. For people who want to build their own houses and particularly those that want to use timber-frame construction techniques.

*Investing in Real Estate*, a monthly investment service for clients of The Data Realty Companies, 358 Chestnut Hill Avenue, Boston, Massachusetts 02146. This letter is particularly good at suggesting ways to finance all kinds of property. Also explains methods of swapping, and tax-free exchanges, real estate terminology and concepts.

*Manufactured Housing Institute*, 1745 Jefferson Davis Highway, Arlington, Virginia 22202. A nonprofit trade association promoting the quality of mobile homes and their sale to consumers.

*Money*, Monthly. William S. Rukeyser, Editor, 541 North Fairbanks Court, Chicago, Illinois 60611. Subscriptions $17.95 a year. Magazine for consumers and investors who want to learn how to manage their money better. Frequently furnishes information on financing houses.

*National Association of Home Manufacturers,* 6521 Arlington Boulevard, Falls Church, Virginia 22042. A non-profit trade association promoting the efficient manufacture of homes and their marketing to consumers. Publishes a good introduction with illustrations of various kinds of homes available today . . . *Guide to Manufactured Homes.*

*Old-House Journal,* Clem Labine, Editor. Monthly newsletter. Free copy available on request. 69A Seventh Avenue, Brooklyn, New York 11217. Also publishes informative brochures such as "Guidelines for Restoring Old Buildings," "Inspection Checklist for Vintage Houses," "How to Date an Old House," "Field Guide to Old-House Styles." Annual catalog and buyer's guide to companies and products and services for owners of houses built before 1920.

*Preservation,* a quarterly publication of the National Trust for Historic Preservation. Available to members. See *Preservation News* for membership details.

*Preservation News,* monthly newspaper. Write to 740 Jackson Place, N.W., Washington, D.C. 20006. Published by the National Trust for Historic Preservation, this monthly newspaper keeps its readers informed about national and international preservation activities. Some of these activities are in the country. Subscriptions are not available separate from membership which costs $10 annually.

*Preview's Guide to the World's Fine Real Estate,* Ann Wilder, Editor, Previews, Inc., Greenwich Office Park, Greenwich, Connecticut 06830. Annual catalog by realtor who specializes in luxury real estate, much of it in the country around the world. Frequently contains editorial material of interest to investors in country property. $9 a copy.

*Real Estate Investing Letter,* publishes monthly by HBJ Newsletters, Inc., 757 Third Avenue, New York, N.Y. 10017, $39 per year.

*Real Estate Review,* a quarterly of opinions and research on real estate published by Warren, Gorham & Lamont, Incorporated, 210 South Street, Boston, Massachusetts 02111. $28 a year.

*Statistical Abstract of the United States,* published by the U.S. Bureau of the Census, U.S. Department of Commerce, 100th Edition, Washington, D.C. 1979. Among other things, it documents population trends and characteristics of people who live in various sections of the U.S.

U.S. Department of Housing and Urban Development (HUD), 451 Seventh Street, S.W., Washington, D.C. 20410, issues many pamphlets (see titles below), usually free, which can be obtained at regional offices or directly from Washington headquarters. Of special interest are two of these which outline financing possibilities through HUD and its department, the Federal Housing Administration (FHA). Ask for "More than Shelter" and "Programs of HUD."

U.S. Department of Agriculture, Washington, D.C. 20250, has an avalanche of pamphlets on how to farm better on a small or large scale. Write for a list of titles available for purchase from the Superintendent of Documents, U.S. Government Printing Office, Washington, D.C. 20402.

Veterans Administration, Washington, D.C. 20420, issues many pamphlets on real estate acquisition by veterans. You can obtain them by applying at your Veterans Administration Regional Office or at Washington, D.C. headquarters.

## CONSUMER LITERATURE ON HOME PURCHASING, MAINTENANCE, PROTECTION, AND OTHER TOPICS

**Appraisals**

| | |
|---|---|
| Questions and Answers on FHA Home Property Appraisals | HUD-38-F |

**Condominiums**

| | |
|---|---|
| Financing Condominium Housing | HUD-77-F |
| HUD/FHA Non-Assisted Program for Condominium Housing | HUD-227-F |
| Questions About Condominiums | HUD-365-F |
| HUD/FHA Comparison of Condominium and Cooperative Housing | HUD-321-F |

**Cooperatives**

| | |
|---|---|
| Let's Consider Cooperatives | HUD-17-F |
| HUD/FHA Program for Unsubsidized Cooperative Housing | HUD-256-F |

**Home Mortgage Insurance**

| | |
|---|---|
| Home Mortgage Insurance | HUD-43-F |
| Programs for Home Mortgage Insurance | HUD-97-F |

**Home Ownership**

| | |
|---|---|
| The Home Buying Serviceman | HUD-121-F |
| HUD's Home Ownership Subsidy Program | HUD-419-HPMC |

**Miscellaneous**

| | |
|---|---|
| Protecting Your Home Against Theft | HUD-315-F |
| Termites | HUD-323-F |
| Be an Energy Miser in Your Home | HUD-324-PA |

**Mobile Homes**

| | |
|---|---|
| Buying and Financing a Mobile Home | HUD-243-F |
| Mobile Home Financing Through HUD | HUD-265-F |

**General Interest**

| | |
|---|---|
| Wise Home Buying | HUD-267-F |
| Should You Buy or Rent a Home | HUD-328-F |
| Protecting Your Housing Investment | HUD-346-PA |
| Home Owners Glossary of Building Terms | HUD-369-F |
| Home Buyers Vocabulary | HUD-383-HM |
| Your Housing Rights | HUD-177-EO |

# Index

# Index

63191

J. M. HODGES LEARNING CENTER
WHARTON COUNTY JUNIOR COLLEGE
WHARTON, TEXAS 77488

**DATE DUE**